W

Himalayan Dialogue

The Tibetan village of Tshap in the Gyasumdo region of Nepal

Himalayan Dialogue

TIBETAN LAMAS AND

GURUNG SHAMANS

IN NEPAL

Stan Royal Mumford

THE UNIVERSITY OF WISCONSIN PRESS

The University of Wisconsin Press
114 North Murray Street
Madison, Wisconsin 53715

3 Henrietta Street
London WC2E 8LU, England

5   4   3   2   1

Printed in the United States of America

Library of Congress Cataloging-in-Publication Data
Mumford, Stan.
    Himalayan dialogue: Tibetan lamas and Gurung shamans in Nepal/
Stan Royal Mumford.
    298 pp.   cm.
    Bibliography: pp. 265–274.
    Includes index.
    1. Gyasumdo (Nepal)—Religious life and customs. 2. Rites and
ceremonies—Nepal—Gyasumdo. 3. Rñin-ma-pa (Sect)—Nepal—Gyasumdo—
Customs and practices. 4. Tibetans—Nepal—Gyasumdo—Religion.
5. Gurung (Nepalese people)—Nepal—Gyasumdo—Religion.
6. Shamanism—Nepal—Gyasumdo. I. Title.
BL2034.3.G93M85   1989
306.6'943923'095496—DC20   88-40440
ISBN 0-299-11980-7   CIP
ISBN 0-299-11984-X (pbk.)

Contents

IV. Historical Consciousness

Illustrations

A THOROUGH ETHNOGRAPHY of Tibetan village Lamaism has been possible on the Nepal side of the Himalayas, just below the Tibetan border, which could not have been done in Tibet itself. It has been five years since my research was completed, toward the end of 1983. I have often wondered: would there be much left of this complex ritual tradition in rural Tibet itself, since the destruction of the monastic way of life that occurred after Tibet was incorporated into China?

Just prior to the publication of this book I had a chance to find out. During the summer of 1988 Tibet was again opening up. Foreigners from all over the world were pouring into Lhasa, and individual travelers were gaining access to rural areas. I interviewed Tibetan villagers in the Lhasa area, in Samye and Gyantse, then in the remote rural towns of Shegar and Tingri, and further, in villages lying between these towns and Rongbuk monastery behind Mount Everest.

My study of Tibetan rites in Nepal had provided me with a rural vocabulary and a degree of folk knowledge that brought immediate rapport with these villagers inside Tibet. I found that even though the number of lamas, monks, and nuns has been greatly reduced, virtually all of the Lamaist rites that are portrayed in this book are still being practiced in contemporary Tibet. Not only the elderly, but even the young, most of them not yet incorporated into the new educational system, are still embedded in Lamaist traditions of fertility rites, guardian deities, demon exorcism, calling the soul, and the Tibetan death rite.

It is my hope that, while this book will contribute to Tibetan and Nepalese studies, it will also find its way into the backpacks of serious trekkers on both sides of the Himalayas, many having expressed deep interest in such an ethnography. For it is those who have direct experience of this fascinating cultural region who will be most keen to know that the traditions portrayed in these pages are still going on.

Acknowledgments

THIS STUDY would not have been possible without my wife Maria, who was my research companion for two and a half years in the Himalayas. Her friendship and gifts of healing and teaching won the hearts of the Tibetan people with whom we lived. Our many friend-informants in Tshap village as well as in the Gurung villages nearby can never be forgotten, but I must give special credit to the extraordinary Lama Dorje, whose real name I cannot reveal. His articulate Tibetan voice is as clear as ever on the many taped commentaries that he did for me. I am also indebted to our Tibetan friend Kalden Dingtsa and his family of monks and nuns, who translated texts for me in Kathmandu, and Prayag Raj Sharma of Tribhuvan University in Kathmandu, who paved the way for the government permission I received to do the research for so long a period.

Among Princeton faculty, Hildred Geertz has been our constant friend and guide, her letters reaching us in our remote village during the entire stay. James Fernandez's ideas and metaphors influenced me far more than he may realize. Gananath Obeyesekere has been my advisor, critic, and mediator in transforming this experience into written form. He recognized immediately the significance of what I had discovered and engaged in long dialogue over the theoretical issues and provocative ideas, going over the manuscript with me many times.

Finally, I would like to thank the various scholars and friends who have made helpful remarks and suggestions on the papers that I have presented on this material at conferences over the past three years.

Note on Transliteration

Italics will be used for all properly transliterated Tibetan terms, using the Jäschke dictionary standard. Phonetic spelling will be employed for personal names, which are fictitious. Phonetic spelling will also be used for terms such as *lama, dharma, torma,* etc., which have become highly familiar in English, and for certain terms that are introduced and repeated in the course of the work such as Drogpa, Gompa and Srungma, which will be capitalized. The letter T. may appear when a Tibetan term is being given alongside the equivalent in Sanskrit (Skt.), Nepali (N.) or Gurung (G.). Gurung terms are used less frequently and will appear as phonetic transliterations.

Part I

_____

Lamas and Shamans

Introduction

DURING THE YEARS 1981–83 I was living in the Nepal Himalayas to make an anthropological study of a Tibetan community. The research goal was to understand Tibetan Buddhist culture in the light of the historic encounter with its non-Buddhist shamanic rivals. I hoped that such a study could be made in depth in the mountain valleys of Nepal where Tibetan communities have been established through migrations from the north over the last few centuries. Tibetan Lamaism, as one of the world's great ritual traditions, could then be understood as a process that emerges through dialogue with the more ancient folk layer that it confronts, rather than as a completed cultural entity represented in the texts.

The problem was to find a Tibetan community that retained a genuine Tibetan dialect, but that had been settled in Nepal long enough to have developed a rich local tradition. Ideally, it would be a culture of village Lamaism as it might have been practiced in rural Tibet within the last century. A good area would have been the Nupri region near the Tibetan border in the Gorkha District, but I found that Nupri was forbidden to foreign researchers. The Nepalese minister of frontier regions pointed out to me that in Gyasumdo, located in the eastern part of Manang District, there are Tibetan villages that had been established more than a hundred years ago as a spill-over migration from the Nupri region and had the same Kyirong Tibetan dialect and traditions.

To reach Gyasumdo, I had to trek five days on the trail leading north from the town of Dumre that lies just east of Pokhara. Between seven and nine thousand feet in altitude I found five Tibetan villages along the Marsyandi River. They were surrounded by Gurung villages on the hillside above, which were vital strongholds of Gurung shamanism. Among the Tibetan villages there were four main Tibetan Buddhist temple centers, called Gompas. Two were headed by married lamas and two by celibate (*dge-slong*) lamas. Some of these lamas and their monk assistants had taken their training in monasteries in Tibet itself, others on the Nepal side of the border, in Nupri or in Thak Khola.

One of the Tibetan villages, called Tshap, was located in a beautiful valley nestled between the giant peaks of Manaslu to the east and Annapurna II to the west. In Tshap I had no introduction to anyone, but because the villagers could understand the Lhasa Tibetan that I had been studying in Kathmandu, and because I managed to plunge immediately into ritual participation in the Nyungne (*smyung-gnas*) fast that was then being held, I was quickly accepted, despite the fact that their dialect was so difficult that it would be months before I would be able to converse adequately with them. When my wife joined me a month later and helped by sharing our medicine and teaching in the local government school, the remaining reserve and suspicion fell away, so that we were able to remain in the village for a fruitful period lasting two and a half years.

Tshap village, with a population of about two hundred, was ideal since it was the strongest center of the Nyingma sect of Tibetan Lamaism that had been developing in Gyasumdo, and it was also located near the Gurung villages that were centers of shamanism. The Gompa at Tshap village was headed by Lama "Dorje" (a fictitious name), who had done his training in Nupri and Shyang. With him was another monk of lama rank, along with three lama students and five nuns, all living in the Gompa compound just above the village.

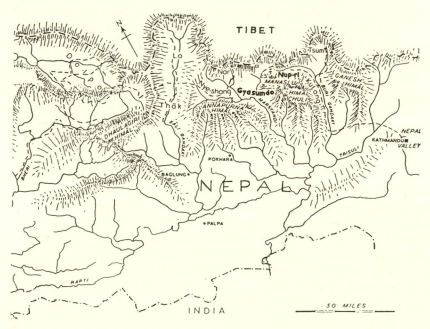

Figure 1. Map of the research area in Nepal

Many of the established families in the village had encouraged a son or daughter to become initiated into the Gompa community as a monk or nun. Monks and nuns are called *chos-pa,* meaning "religious ones." Village Lamaism was centered in the Gompa. The head lama and other *chos-pa* performed all of the household rites sponsored by the laity, but they also represented a monastic community that was expected to maintain orthodox practices, with strict ritual and textual training as well as the final initiation for lamas: the "three-year, three-month, three-day" retreat (*mtshams*).

Lama Dorje, considered to be the most learned and skilled lama of Gyasumdo, became my crucial informant. Although all the Gyasumdo lamas cooperated with the study, each giving me added perspective, it was this lama who gave the most numerous interviews, textual commentaries, and taping sessions after I had learned enough of his religious vocabulary. On the one hand, he was deeply embedded in his own village folk tradition so that he could not bend his interpretations to accommodate my prejudices. On the other hand, his intelligent and articulate mastery of the Nyingma texts was so complete that he could read and give immediate commentary in a manner that is rare among lamas in general, as I was to learn from educated Tibetan friends in Kathmandu.

After the first year a breakthrough occurred. By then I had observed rites and festivals and discussed them with lamas and helpful members of the laity, many of whom were quite well informed. But not until I had undergone the basic Tibetan Buddhist initiation could the lamas explain the texts used in the rites. The initiation lasted for six intense weeks during which I remained in the Gompa, where I also slept at night and carried out the required 100,000 prostrations to "purify the evil deeds of my past" while repeating a mantra with each prostration. Lama Dorje agreed that my initiation would be combined with his giving the textual commentaries that I had wanted. Hence it was also an initiation into becoming an ethnographer. On the one hand I was, according to the repeated mantra, dedicating myself to furthering the enlightenment of all beings. As an ethnographer, however, I was also preparing to learn from all beings. Was it a contradiction?

It was for most Tibetans, who thought that my dual project of receiving enlightenment from the lamas and also learning from the Gurung shamans would result in confusion or even insanity. The lamas thought me in danger of acquiring a divided mind (*rnam-rtog*), furthering the trend of this "evil age" (*dus-ngen-pa*). They assumed there was one certain truth that could be found in their sacred texts, and could not understand my ethnographer's notion of "reciprocal illumination" in which everyone learns something from everyone else.

When my initiation was finished and I emerged from the Gompa, the hard-working Tibetan householders told me that while I had spent six weeks secluded in the Gompa, my wife Maria had made far more merit than I had by giving medicine to the people. Further, Lama Dorje, noting how many tapes I was filling up with his commentaries, said I had become "too greedy for knowledge." It was, after all, a jest, for he loved the chance to record his interpretations and then have me play them for visiting lamas to get their reaction. When I later played the tapes to other Tibetans in Kathmandu they were astonished at the capacity of this village lama in the hills.

An ethnographic project that had first seemed overwhelming now appeared feasible. Other lamas in Gyasumdo became far more cooperative. Lama Nyima, the most expert lama of Gyasumdo in the *gcod* ("severance") rite would now give me a detailed reading and commentary on his *gcod* text. Everything started to fall into place. Taped commentaries were obtained on texts used for the main ritual performances I had observed: offerings made to serpent deities and guardian spirits, the exorcising of demons, soul-calling and the local Tibetan death rite, each commentary supplementing the tape recordings made of the oral performances.

Of particular interest was the discovery that extensive reference is made in each ritual to the symbolism of the Tibetan horoscope, the *rtsis*, which Lama Dorje was to explain in session after session. These data in themselves would make an important contribution to Tibetan ethnographic research. Taping the commentaries on the rites was supplemented by photographing most of the ritual texts so that they could be translated later in Kathmandu. The translation assistance came from Kalden Dingtsa, an educated Tibetan friend in Kathmandu. He is highly skilled in literary Tibetan and a member of a *chos-pa* family of Nyingma monks and nuns, who also helped in the translations.

It soon became clear that in Gyasumdo a full ethnography of Tibetan village Lamaism must incorporate the lama-shaman encounter. I would have to penetrate the shamanic regime in the Gurung villages as well. I had hoped to find a "pre-Buddhist" shamanism that would be contrary to Lamaism both ethically and philosophically. Present day Tibetan oracles (*lha-pa*) do not represent this older tradition, nor do the Bonpo, the non-Lamaist Tibetan sect that has been largely reformed. These are regarded as highly "Buddhist," since they also prohibit the "black" tradition of blood sacrifice that was defeated by the great lamas in Tibetan history. In Gyasumdo, however, the older pre-Buddhist shamanic tradition is still carried on by the Gurungs.

Gurungs in general claim to have had Tibetan origins centuries ago. Research scholars such as Pignède (1966:187–90) and Snellgrove and Richardson (1968:57) are convinced that Gurung shamans are probable carriers in Nepal of the pre-Buddhist tradition of Tibet. It is an identity that the Gurung shamans of Gyasumdo subscribe to themselves. The recent migration of Tibetans from Kyirong and Nupri into this region over the last century has instigated a contemporary clash between Buddhist lamas and Gurung shamans on the Nepal side of the border. The older, shamanic layer is still being challenged by Tibetan Lamaism, in a manner analogous to the confrontation that must have occurred again and again in rural Tibet in the past.

Earlier probes into the lama-shaman relation in Nepal have been done among the Sherpas by Robert Paul and Sherry Ortner. Paul (1976, 1982) found that in contrast to lamas, who are bound by the oath of Buddhism and represented the monastic ideal, shamans in Nepal are not bound by a formal religious code or doctrine, having a "this world" virtuosity based on their capacity to control spirits. The Tantric rites employed by many lamas, however, mediate *between* monastic and shamanic orientations (1982:88). Ortner (1978a) also found that even though the "defeat and subordination of the early shamans and their gods remains one of the central themes of Tibetan Buddhist myth and ritual," there has been an "appropriation of shamanic forms" on the part of the lamas.

Ortner's article and her book on Sherpa rituals (1978b) pinpoint a crucial distinction. She argues that in promoting a personal, "inner" religious path, Lamaist ideology tends to isolate individual identity from the matrix of social ties, while shamanic identity remains embedded in the world of relations, even accepting spirit penetrations into the self. In her provocative analysis of Sherpa ritual performance, Ortner further explicates how Buddhist individuation is contested by the "social stance" of Tibetan lay householders, who retain much of the relational world view found in shamanism.

These Sherpa studies portray Tibetan Buddhism as the historic antagonist of shamanism, the latter viewed as defeated and subordinated by the lamas. The problem for my own research was to find Tibetan Lamaism alongside a vital shamanic tradition that was still autonomous and free of Lamaist hegemony, so that a historic encounter between the two could be studied in depth as a process of both debate and mutual influence. Certain findings by other Nepal researchers suggested that such a contest has continued in various regions. Messerschmidt (1976a), for instance, found a clash emerging between shamans and lamas in his study of Gurungs in the Lamjung District. In the Thak Khola region, a Thakali legend recorded by Vinding and Gauchan (1977) narrates how a shamanic yak god that had been buried beneath the Buddhist stupas suddenly rose again during an earthquake, toppling the stupas and demanding that the people honor him again.

With these earlier research attempts in mind, I began to probe into the Gurung shamanic layer found in the periphery of the Tibetan Buddhist regime in Gyasumdo. Surrounding the Tibetan villages are Gurung communities, including the Ghale clan who, as the Gurung nobility, claim to have come from Tibet centuries before. Although certain Gurung households have become clients for the Tibetan lamas, the Gurungs as a people are deeply committed to their shamanic tradition. The two types of Gurung shamans are the same as those defined by Pignède (1966) in his studies of southwestern Gurungs. In Gyasumdo in the north, the practitioner that Pignède defined as "*Klihbri*" is called a *Ghyabrē,* and the one he defined as "*Pucu*" is called a *Paju.* The term "shaman" can be applied to both without hesitation. Their tradition is somewhat different from many of the spirit mediums called *Jhañkri* in Nepal (Hitchcock 1976). The ritual symbolism of the Ghyabrē and the Paju is that of the "classic" shamanism of the Siberian type.

According to Eliade (1964:499), "the specific element of shamanism is not the embodiment of 'spirits' by the shaman but the ecstasy induced by his ascent to the sky or descent to the underworld." This is precisely what the Ghyabrē and Paju shamans are eager to describe when explaining the meaning of their rites. Both have "bird" tutelary deities. In their imagination they visit *Khrō-nasa,* the Gurung underworld, going down the nine ladders. The upper world is also reached by nine ladders, arriving at a mansion in *Mu,* the Gurung term for sky. The "middle" human world is connected to the upper world by a tree in the sacred grove at Tapje village, and also by a rock dome called Oblē, the local Gurung land of the dead that is seen from the trail.

The Gurung shamans' descriptions of their ritual journeys to upperworld and underworld replicate the motifs found in Siberian ethnographies.[1] In Anisimov's "Cosmological concepts of the peoples of the north" (1963) we find descriptions of a world tree connecting the three worlds visited by Siberian shamans that are remarkably similar to Gurung shaman discourse. Both Siberian and Gurung shamans dramatize a "ritual hunt", and do animal sacrifices that are required for exchanges with beings in each realm (Alekseev 1984). Animal offerings given to other-world spirits have been central in the world view of the ancient shamanic-hunter: if human life is to be nourished one must give "life" in exchange (Siikala 1984). The Gurung shamans, like their Siberian counterpart, mediate between humans and the rest of the cosmos. Their visions do not emphasize a path of self-realization, but rather are meant to promote a world harmony that benefits the community (Gilberg 1984).

---

1. David Watters (1975:125) has noted many similarities between Siberian shamans and shamans found among the "Kham-Magars," a people living in Nepal southwest of Dhaulagiri Peak which he defines as carriers of the "classical" inner Asian shamanic tradition.

Gurung shamans have not been absorbed into either Hindu or Buddhist hegemony in Nepal. In Gyasumdo they may collaborate with certain Tibetan lamas who serve Gurung sponsors, but they regard themselves as representing all the services needed by the Gurung community. The Ghyabrē is a complete death cult specialist who guides the Gurung soul to the land of the dead in the manner of classic shamanism. The Paju is the specialist in exorcisms, and recalls the soul when it is lost or stolen through ritual journeys to the upperworld and underworld.

The problem for my research was how to break into this rich tradition after I had already so fully committed myself to the Tibetans and the lamas. Could both traditions be done in depth? Two factors opened up this possibility. The first was that my wife Maria had, against all expectation, performed extraordinary cures for kin members of influential Gurungs. The shamans, who were as appreciative of her medicine as the others, felt they should repay us with as much information as possible.

The second factor was that a close Tibetan friend and informant lived with his wife in one of the Gurung villages. The three Pajus and the main Ghyabrē that we worked with trusted him and approved of the manner in which he translated their Gurung into the Tibetan that I could understand. Most of the shamans also spoke a Tibetan that was difficult for me, but eventually I could converse with them more directly. Since half of the words in their ritual legends are in Tibetan rather than Gurung because, they explain, their forefathers "came down from the north," Tibetan seemed appropriate as the research medium.

When I first began to compare the Tibetan lamas with the Gurung shamans, the lay Tibetans with whom I lived saw that I was spending long hours in the Gurung villages in the homes of the Ghyabrē and Paju practitioners, whom they viewed as rivals to their own lamas. The Tibetan attitudes toward me went through three phases. First, they criticized me for learning "inferior" and "meaningless" talk of the Ghyabrē and Paju rather than concentrating exclusively on the truth of the Tibetan lamas.

In the second phase, they warned me that if I kept on learning the legends of the Ghyabrē and Paju I would "go crazy" (*smyon-pa byung*) from incorporating contradictory wisdoms. Beyond this, the guardian spirit of the Paju would become alarmed and attack me. In the third phase, the Tibetans' curiosity had become overwhelming, and they would beg me to play for them the tapes of ritual explanation that I had obtained from the Gurung shamans, which I did after getting permission from the latter. I had become a cultural mediator between the two communities.

Tibetan ambivalence toward the Gurung shamans was exposed in a new manner when a well-known Gurung villager died in Galantso and the family called the Ghyabrē shaman to conduct the soul to the land of the dead. In the ritual, the Ghyabrē injects the soul of the deceased into a pigeon which he holds by a string. It walks up to the living family members sitting in a circle, going up on their laps and appearing to recognize them.

It was a performance I didn't want to miss. I slipped out of the Tibetan village and went to Galantso to attend the funeral. When I climbed the ladder to the roof of the house where the rite was being held, I found scores of Tibetan lay persons already there ahead of me. They were ashamed that I had caught them. During the performance, Tibetan emotional involvement was apparent. Even though this shamanic act is explicitly criticized by their own lamas, the Tibetan laity harbored no doubt that the soul of the deceased had entered the bird.

That night I returned to the Tibetan village with my landlady, who had been there. As we sat around the fire eating, Nyima Drolma poured out her grief over the death of the Gurung man whom she had known, and expressed how she felt when she saw that he had entered into the bird to say farewell. Tibetan funerals have no miracles of this sort. She did not hesitate to admit her belief in the validity of the Ghyabrē shaman's practice, having seen the bird's strange behavior. The Tibetan lamas who had grown up in Gyasumdo before leaving for their training in Tibet or Nupri also had witnessed such events. They would not be able to erase the traces of such memories, even after becoming full lamas and rivals of the Gurung shamans.

Eventually, I gained access to numerous shamanic performances along with their legendary explanations (pe). Much of this northern Gurung material is not found in the classic study of southwestern Gurungs published by Pignède. To my delight I discovered that these shamans were not only willing to explain their rites and give the legends they chanted during performance, but also that each ritual type that I had studied in depth with the Tibetan lamas had an equivalent rite on the shamanic side. It would now be possible to publish together with analysis both Lamaist and shamanic versions of exchange with the underworld, the serving of guardian deities, demon exorcism, soul-calling, and guiding of the consciousness after death, all in a local historical context in which the two traditions were interacting as rival regimes.

The chapters that follow are written in a style that will interest both specialists and non-professional readers and students. The work undertakes the difficult task of interweaving textual materials with oral discourse. The rituals and legends regarded by most people of Gyasumdo as their established traditions will be fully explicated, while analysis of contending perspectives and dialogue will also reveal how the meaning of both traditions is unfinished, as it is in all cultures.

Chapter One

Unbounded and Layered Cultures

A HIGHLY REFLEXIVE MODE of cultural interpretation is emerging, as cultural anthropologists recognize the impact they have on societies they study and in turn find themselves being transformed internally by their informants. At the dawn of the twentieth century Durkheim noted that while global interdependence was accelerating, the old gods of bounded social memberships were dying. In our own time, distinct traditions are increasingly being depicted as unbounded. Like Pacific islands they lie upon a vast coral reef of interpenetrating layers of unfinished interpretation.

The process is not syncretism since such a term implies there were once self-contained, cultural completions that later become mixed with alien elements. Lévi-Strauss (1966) has shown that oral traditions are inherently relational. The fuller implications of his initial insight are coming into fruition. No tradition is exempted, since even those with doctrinal texts are thrust into a process of contending arguments and reinterpretations that are still emerging. Human cultural experience is coming to be viewed as a dialogue between partial truths.

The present study of cultural dialogue between Tibetan village Lamaism and its shamanic rivals in Nepal can provide a graphic example of this theoretical awareness. In Gyasumdo in northern Nepal can be found an earlier established shamanic tradition that has been challenged by Buddhist lamas coming in with Tibetan settlers. In the valley in which this research was carried out, the Marsyandi river divides the two main villages. On the northern hillside the Ghale clan nobles support their shamans in the Gurung village of Tapje. On the valley floor on the other side of the river, the Tibetan village of Tshap supports its Gompa (temple-monastery) with its two lamas, lama students, and nuns. Two additional Gurung villages that are strongholds of the Paju shamans lie just to the south of the Tibetan village.

In this study I describe sequences of rituals performed by both Lamaist and shamanic practitioners, in order to reveal the process of meaning crea-

tion as it occurs between them. Snellgrove and Richardson (1968) have noted
that in Tibet itself, "the slow penetration of Tibet by Buddhism must have
gone on continuously." In fact, they depict a history of interpenetrations:

> Not only were those who called themselves followers of Bon busy
> absorbing all they could of Buddhist doctrine and practices, but
> many of those who called themselves Buddhist were occupied in
> fitting the old Tibetan gods and indigenous rites into the framework
> of the new religion. Of this whole process we can expect to find no
> ready historical accounts. . . . (p. 108)

The research presented here will contribute to the filling of this ethnographic gap. For centuries, lamas have been crossing the border from Tibet
into Nepal attempting to establish Buddhist practices in competition with
the rival indigenous and shamanic traditions. Although the encounter on
the Nepalese side of the border does not precisely replicate Tibetan national
history, in Gyasumdo most of the Tibetan lamas' ritual texts are used by
the entire Nyingma sect of Tibetan Buddhism. In a manner similar to what
probably occurred in Tibet, the lamas have used their ritual discourse as
an opportunity to counter local shamanic arguments which they regard
as inferior or immoral, but which still tempt the Tibetan laity. The textual
language as such, however, cannot determine the meaning of these rites
performed in such a dynamic historical context. Each time they are enacted
and commented on they incorporate traces of local folk consciousness that
are embedded in the lived experience of the valley.

The textual learning and greater prestige of the lamas has been balanced
by the greater economic power of the Ghale noblemen and other Gurungs
who support the shamanic regime. This has allowed the Lamaist and
shamanic traditions to develop rival arguments, neither regime gaining
symbolic hegemony in the valley. In the past century Gyasumdo has in
this manner become a field of interpenetrating cultural layers.

When we study traditions in interaction, we cannot locate causal origins
or privilege one correct interpretation. Intentionality is pulled into a process
of use over time, as one keeps negotiating "what is meant," in light of
rival meanings. Analysis thus involves what Barbara Johnson (1980) calls
the "teasing out of the warring forces of signification." The strategy for
each chapter in this work will be to explicate a core of significance in each
ritual enactment, and then attempt to catch these practitioners and their
lay audience in the process of making up their minds about the meaning
of their rites.

To interpret this encounter, I will draw mainly on Mikhail Bakhtin's
model of "dialogic" interaction. In the past decade the contribution of this
powerful thinker in the field of literary criticism has spilled over into

ethnographic interpretation. His writings on the modern novel are, in fact, packed with analysis of culture as a temporal process. Anthropologists such as Crapanzano (1980), Dwyer (1982), Tedlock (1983), Basso (1984), Bruner and Gorfain (1984), Rabinow (1977, 1986), and Taussig (1987) have begun to apply Bakhtin's model. The time has come for an ethnography that draws more fully and explicitly on the broad synthesis of ideas found in Bakhtin's work. The present study of the lama-shaman encounter in the Himalayas is such an attempt.

Bakhtin's approach is found in the collection of translated essays published in *The Dialogic Imagination* (1981), but it is also developed in his earlier works such as *Problems of Dostoevsky's Poetics* published in Russian in 1929, revised in 1973, and translated in 1984, and *Rabelais and His World,* published in 1965 and translated in 1968. Further writings by Bakhtin, *Speech Genres and Other Late Essays,* were published in 1986. His focus on *discourse* portrays cultural communication as inherently emergent, a process of temporal becoming. Cultural meaning is not contained within social groups, persons, or linguistic terms, but rather it emerges *between* them:

> The living word . . . enters a dialogically agitated and tension-filled environment of alien words, value judgements and accents, weaves in and out of complex interrelationships, merges with some and recoils from others, intersects with yet a third group: and all this may crucially shape discourse, may leave a trace in all its semantic layers . . . [thus] the living utterance, having taken meaning and shape at a particular historical moment in a socially specific environment, cannot fail to brush up against thousands of living dialogic threads, woven by socio-ideological consciousness around the given object of an utterance; it cannot fail to become an active participant in social dialogue. (Bakhtin 1981:276)

The relational "betweenness" outlined in such a passage not only refers to contemporary influences that surround us on a horizontal plane, but also describes an ongoing dialogue over time between older and newer layers of tradition. Discourse that occurs in the past does not evaporate, but remains sedimented in discourse that occurs later, leaving a "trace in all its semantic layers." The notion of "decentered" meaning is fully incorporated by Bakhtin, who calls it "multi-centeredness" or "polyphony," and in his later essays "heteroglossia." Further, he is not referring to the entanglement of abstract ideas, but rather to contextualized discourse, the interaction of voices as historical events: "The idea is a *live* event, played out at the point of dialogic meeting between two or several consciousnesses. In this sense the idea is similar to the word . . . [which] wants to be heard, understood and 'answered' by other voices from other positions" (Bakhtin 1984:88).

A relational psychology is implicit in such a model. Consciousness is always co-consciousness; there are no isolated acts of consciousness; every thought is connected to others. The self is never finalized; it is forever pulled into the "intersubjective communion between consciousnesses." This does not, however, make the self merely coincidental with the world. One "goes out" to see the world through the other's eyes, but only partially falls prey to the other's horizon. By internalizing the voices of others, a hidden internal dialogue develops within each individual consciousness, an argument within the self.

In discourse between two persons there is a "partial coincidence between the borrowed words of one and the internal and secret discourse of another." Bakhtin graphically portrays this in a lengthy analysis of Dostoevsky's novel *The Brothers Karamazov*. Ivan has "two voices within himself," one wishing the murder of his father, the other opposed, arguing against it. His friend Smerdyakov, however, misinterprets Ivan's divided discourse. He assumes that the first voice is the "real" one, and that the second one is unreal. This is a monologic view that does not hear "Ivan's own rejoinder to himself." In Bakhtin's interpretation, Smerdyakov's conscious will "co-opts" Ivan's ambivalent will, turning it into the "Smerdyakovian voice" that commits the crime (Bakhtin 1984:259).

This intersubjective model has a temporal dimension, since the self is also penetrated by historical events. Caryl Emerson (1986) has examined Bakhtin's criticism of psychologies that are not historically contextualized. When the biological is seen as all-powerful and history is regarded as impotent, we eliminate time and social life from consciousness; we imagine our habits cannot be modified, but only satisfied or repressed. By showing how "outer words become inner speech," Bakhtin incorporates history and society back into the psychological. Drawing on Vygotsky's work *Thought and Language* (1934), he rejects laboratory data in favor of understanding historical events as the dialogized background of psychological events. The word is the most significant human event, as one fashions one's voice and inner speech by appropriation of the voices of others, which then undergo a retelling, to become "internally persuasive." In contrast to the view that personality is mainly acquired during childhood as a formative period, the historical model promotes an adult psychology, of what Bakhtin calls the ideological becoming of the unfinalized self.

Such a model of linguistically acquired identity by no means dismisses critical perspectives on social-economic stratification and political power. Bakhtin's writings are preoccupied with hierarchy in language styles and the manner in which hegemonic, "authoritative" utterances situated in a locus of power come to be undermined by counterhegemonic voices in the periphery, as illustrated in his study of Rabelaisian unmasking of aristocratic pretensions. Hegemonic discourse, having become "internally persuasive," is later "laughed out of existence" (Bakhtin 1981:240).

As we have noted in Dostoevsky's novel, the internal dialogue within the self can express many possible motivations and self-images. Identity is multicentered. In the process of discourse, however, one of these possibilities may become singled out and foregrounded. Hence, Ivan's internal ambivalence is narrowed into a single focus when it is pulled into the one meaning preferred by Smerdyakov. In Bakhtin's view, it is a "monologic" intrusion by the language of another.

Certain aspects of Lacan's analytic terminology can illuminate what occurs: A particular purpose or viewpoint selects one of the many metaphors of human aspirations, establishing only one signifier as the conscious one. This renders unconscious the full range of entangled motives and images that have evolved through discourse with others. A bar is thus placed over a repressed discourse by a manifest discourse, even though the latter is emotionally empowered by the rich diversity of linguistic experience that still lies beneath its surface (Davis 1983).

Vaihinger (1924) noted in his *Philosophy of "As If"* that our actual motivations can never really be accurately defined or disentangled from one another. When we impose a notion about our motives with a particular metaphor, it can serve as a useful fiction for a specific purpose. But if its fictional character is misunderstood (i.e., Vaihinger's example: the "economic" motive), that single purpose comes to displace the full range of human alternatives. In Bakhtin's (1984) model a monologic formula can "seal off" the rich complexity of dialogical experience:

> Dostoevsky constantly and severely criticized mechanistic psychology, both its pragmatic lines based on the concepts of *natural law,* and *utility,* and even more its physiological line, which reduced psychology to physiology. . . . (p. 61)

> The consolidation of monologism and its permeation into all spheres and ideological life was promoted in modern times by European rationalism, with its cult of a unified and exclusive reason . . . the monologic principle, ideology as a deduction . . . inevitably transforms the represented world into a voiceless object. . . . (pp. 82–83)

The contrast between monologue and dialogue is the fundamental point of departure. In the "monologic genre," whether it appears in religion, philosophy, literature, psychology, or ethnography, a formal doctrine or neutral principle draws a boundary line that stifles or masks the "dynamic chorus of languages" within us.

THREE LAYERS OF TEMPORAL IDENTITY

From the above standpoint, Bakhtin suggests a provisional history of three sociocultural periods, each having cultural genres that are defined as temporal identities, which Bakhtin often called "chronotopes." Each refers to the manner in which time and space are experienced, and the degree of dialogical awareness. The three periods can be summarized as follows from Bakhtin's work *The Dialogic Imagination* (1981):

   1. *The ancient matrix,* which is also called the "folkloric chronotope," is the most primal experience of time and space found in the ancient world and in folk traditions. For our purposes it epitomizes the shamanic world view. Personal identity is relational, defined in terms of connections between persons and the landmarks of local space. The sense of time in the individual is in harmony with cycles of nature. Everything in this matrix is "equally important" since "everything acts and takes part in the unified life of the whole."

   2. *The individual life sequence* is a new feeling of interior time, "sealed-off" from other subjectivities. It promotes a directional identity of "individual becoming" that seeks extrication from the world matrix, as in Christian or Buddhist religious destinies and economic individualism. The result is a bifurcation of personal time and world time.

   3. *Historical becoming* arrives after this vertical, individuated axis is questioned by a "Rabelaisian unmasking" that celebrates the future of the world rather than a destiny that is separated from the world. This transition unites the personal sense of time with historical consciousness. Images of the ancient matrix return in a reflexive manner, in terms of dialogue between diverse, interpenetrating cultural and ideological voices on a global scale.

With regard to the first transition, Bakhtin (1981:217) writes that "as class society develops further and as ideological spheres are increasingly differentiated . . . out of the common time of collective life emerge separate individual life-sequences, individual fates . . . nature itself ceased to be a living participant in the events of life. . . ." For Bakhtin, the problem of the monologic cultural genre develops acutely in this second period when the bifurcation of domains seals off the individual or the elite community from the remaining whole. Textual canons come to assert a "bounded" self and "finalized" truth, which are later replicated in total ideologies. The canon projects an imaginary community that vertically transcends the world matrix, within which a bounded subjectivity is also imagined, having correct belief or purity of intent.

These imaginary boundaries are drawn, however, in terms of an evolving reflexive awareness. On the one hand, a nostalgia for a time of "uncontested" truth is still expressed in the epic genre of the founding hero who inaugurates tradition in a timeless past (Bakhtin 1981:13). In the second period, however, the truths asserted are contestable, and "heresy" becomes conceivable. At this time only a few thinkers are aware of what will become generally known in the third period, that identities and ideologies are not self-contained, since they interpenetrate.

Such an explicitly dialogical orientation begins to emerge in the third period as a democratic reflexivity. It is expressed in the modern novel, and is generated by what Bakhtin (1981:11) describes as a "rupture in the history of European civilization: its emergence from a socially isolated and culturally deaf semipatriarchal society, and its entrance into international and interlingual contacts and relationships." The ancient matrix of inter-penetration thus returns, but now in terms of the "heteroglossia" of global communication.

Such a contemporary trend has been labeled postmodern, in the sense that it is postcanonical and postdoctrinal. Official languages that claim to encompass all human experience or to neutralize it are being decon-structed (Rorty 1979; Lyotard 1979). This is a sign that individually sealed off destinies are being decentered and absorbed back into the historical process. Identity does not collapse into a primitive or biological reduc-tion, however, but rather, as Bakhtin argues, we gain an identity of "becoming," in a world already filled with traces of ideological debris. The unmasking now forces us to recognize society as "locked in a war of meanings" (Barthes 1975). In contrast to the arguments of the ancient world, postideological dialogue becomes highly ironic, because traditions can no longer be grasped within finalized boundaries. As they interpene-trate, they become partial truths. The unbounded self and the unfinished culture emerge as an identity of *betweenness*. Bakhtin (1981:12) defines the process as "inter-illumination."

The above tripart sequence needs explication in terms of ethnographic studies and current trends in anthropological theory. Bakhtin's "ancient matrix" as a primal model has affinity with Geertz's (1973) analysis of tem-poral identity in Bali, where personhood is embedded in kin relations and natural time cycles that downplay the awareness of linear accumulation. Leenhardt's analysis of the "participatory personage" in Melanesia (Leen-hardt 1979, Clifford 1982) presents the tribal self as embedded in "socio-mythic relations," each realizing himself or herself "through the other" in a matrix that includes kin members, ancestors, totems, spirits of nature, etc. Identity is *decentered,* there is "no ego at the center of the converging lines." Mutual participation is experienced through mythic images of felt events rather than through bounded classifications.

As in Bakhtin, Leenhardt focuses on the distinction between this primal matrix and the bifurcation that emerges in the second historical period: boundary-drawing classifications that "seal off" individuals and different domains of life from their mutual participation. Granet's view of the emergence of bifurcations in China is remarkably similar: the ancient model of *yang* and *yin,* as interpenetrating male and female principles, gradually develops into a dogmatic system of classifications through the "rationalist spirit" of the Literati: *yang* becomes bounded so that it is not contaminated by *yin* (Granet 1977:107).

The bifurcations of the second period may be said to have fostered specific kinds of historical progress, but as these boundaries become unmasked, theoretical discourse returns again to models of interpenetration. A distinction must be made between the most "primal" unbounded identity, and that which is becoming postmodern. While the former is the least reflexive, locally embedded in nature and kin relations, the unbounding of identity in contemporary life is global, highly reflexive, aware of the provisional and ironic character of our symbolic images.

Victor Turner promoted this awareness in anthropological theory with his model of *liminal betweenness,* expressed in tribal rites of transition and in pilgrimage, but now emerging in creative experiences of betweenness in the world context (Turner 1974). Increasingly, the sealed-off cultural identity is found to be a mask that conceals its own process of becoming. Anderson (1983) and Handler (1988), for instance, analyze how the intricate overlapping of different cultural horizons in modern consciousness is still being denied in our own time by imaginary fabrications of the "national community" as if it were a separate and bounded entity. As Fernandez (1986) notes, such fabrications seal off the sense of belonging into a *simple* whole, while the real world is becoming a *complex* whole.

For Bakhtin, as this complex whole evolves it is inspired by the primal layer, an "ambivalent whole" which continues as an ancient trace that keeps returning in more reflexive forms. Certain trends in Asian cultural development, for instance, can be shown to undergo this process in religious consciousness and philosophical argument in a manner that leaps ahead of its global realization in our own time. Heesterman (1985) shows that in ancient India in the preclassical sacrificial system, the king and the Brahmin priest played alternating roles of "purity and impurity." As in Mauss's portrayal of reciprocity, each participated in the identity of the other. Heesterman notes how this ancient model was gradually repudiated in the caste hierarchy. At the vertical apex of the hierarchy the Brahmin became individuated, removed from the contamination of lower castes in order to strive toward renunciation. In the same cultural milieu, Buddhism promoted the ideal of individual karma as requiring purity of inner intent, as a merit path that would lead toward personal deliverance. A bifurcation was posited between the *samsāric* world and the goal of *nirvāna,* or as Dumont (1972) puts it, the "man-in-the-world" came to be opposed by the "world-renouncer."

Eastern subjectivity became highly refined in Buddhist religious philosophy. The doctrine of karma is well known to have democratized the sense of individual destiny (Obeyesekere 1980), even though Buddhist insight thrusts beyond the provisional karmic self, viewing merit-accumulation as only an interim identity. According to Paul Mus, the original Buddhist doctrine of "no-self" (Skt. *anātman*) should be interpreted as a repudiation of the *social* identity defined by the network of relations in ancient India (Lee 1967). The paradox is that the no-self doctrine signified a seizure by the individual of control of his own destiny. The no-self doctrine was later criticized as a "view" (a metaphor), and negated by the meta-argument that "no view" may characterize subjectivity or external phenomena (Collins 1982).

In the second century philosophy of Mādhyamika, the adept became aware of the relativity and interdependence of these metaphors, losing confidence in all of them in order to gain the intuition of "emptiness" (Skt. *śūnyatā*). In Yogācāra Buddhist philosophy, however, subjectivity is characterized as a "storehouse of consciousness" (*ālayavijñāna*). Such a storehouse can be viewed as a reservoir of the sum total of an individual's subjective experience through successive lives, but it also can be interpreted as the evolution of interpenetrating consciousnesses. The latter image has developed in conjunction with the Mahāyāna emphasis on the Bodhisattva, who seeks to experience the consciousness of all sentient beings so that all may be liberated together. Such visions are mystical in emphasis, in contrast to Bakhtin's communicational model, but they have remarkable affinity with his view of interacting subjectivities that emerge historically.

In his study of the Hua-yen school of philosophy in China, Francis Cook (1977, 1979) argues that while these early Buddhist philosophies served to negate attachment to the world of appearances, their evolution in seventh-century China, in Hua-yen, returned Buddhism to a this-world affirmation of the whole as an "interacting mutual-causal harmony":

> The Chinese Buddhist could find a place in his heart for everything just as it is: his "yes" of affirmation was unconditional and unbounded. Since everything, no matter how small, was a necessary

condition for the whole . . . this world, with its birth and death, joy
and sorrow, angels and devils, butterflies and cobras, disease and
health is itself the very body of the Buddha, the Pure Land. (Cook
1979:382)

In the view of Garma C. C. Chang (1971:xv) the Hua-yen model was a
shift away from karmic self-sufficiency, toward a "vast intermeshing of
events." For Winston King (1979), Hua-yen implies that all identities are
"mutually interpenetrative." Francis Cook finds here an historical process
of influence between cultural layers, the ancient matrix returning in later
modes of thought:

> There appears to have been a predisposition in pre-Buddhist China
> to see individuals as deeply involved in each other, and it is interest-
> ing to think of the Hua-yen cosmology as an extrapolation and
> more comprehensive version of the kind of relationship seen in the
> Chinese family which was considered a whole of dynamically inter-
> acting, mutually supporting parts. Harmony of parts is a desirable
> feature of both the family organism and the larger, cosmic family.
> (Cook 1979:381)

Such analysis of a dialogic process in Asia illuminates Bakhtin's western
example, eroding the outdated boundary between East and West. Max
Weber (1963) focused our attention on how prophetic thinkers in the West
promoted a unique trend of rationalization and science. The time has come,
however, to shift from Weber to Joseph Needham (1956), who finds that
while the East may have skipped the stage of Newtonian science, its ancient
model of intercausality is now coming into prominence with Einstein. The
question for Bakhtin is how the ancient view of interpenetrating influences
returns in a global communication field, as inner subjectivity matures to
discover its ground in intersubjectivity.

The complex whole that is coming into recognition is both spatial and
temporal (Mumford 1986). Cultural awareness accumulates as each experienced event incorporates the memory of prior events, as Bergson (1910)
has argued. This insight invites us to discover how dialogue occurs between
older and newer layers of culture. Walter Burkert (1983), for instance, finds
that Greek rites and mythic images must be interpreted in terms of their
changing meanings through numerous cultural strata. Present symbolic
meanings incorporate traces from each prior context of use.

New approaches to the study of cultural "memory" are exploring such
layers ethnographically (Obeyesekere 1984; Taussig 1987; Fischer 1986).
These studies employ the argument of Bakhtin that contemporary discourse
is "partly hidden," sedimented in older layers of language use that have
become traces of past experiences and images that are partially repressed
or denied. In Bakhtin's view of culture as a historical process, the first

chronotope—an identity embedded in the ancient matrix—gradually returns into a third model as we have noted above in the case of Hua-yen Buddhist philosophy in China. Bakhtin (1981:135) argues that in the West also, interaction between older and new layers begins to "resurrect the ancient wholeness" into a highly reflexive cultural identity, reconnecting the sealed-off individual sequences that had developed in the second model. It is most dramatically portrayed in *Rabelais and His World* (1968), and in other essays on the Rabelaisian "carnival sense of the world" as a literary genre:

> The ancient matrices are re-established here on a new and loftier base . . . Rabelais develops the authentic expanses of the folkloric world on a new base. Nothing fetters Rabelais' imagination, nothing within the given boundaries of the spatial and temporal world can confine him or restrict the authentic potentialities of man's nature. (Bakhtin 1981:240)

> Carnival is past millenia's way of sensing the world as one great communal performance . . . bringing the world maximally close to a person and bringing one person maximally close to another . . . into the zone of free familiar contact (with) joy of change and its joyful relativity . . . [as] opposed to one sided . . . official seriousness which . . . seeks to absolutize a given condition of existence or a given social order. (Bakhtin 1984:160)

As a literary genre, the carnival sense of the world continues to emerge after Rabelais in such writers as Shakespeare, Cervantes, Voltaire, Goethe, and Poe, Dostoevsky giving it a fully explicit, dialogic form in the nineteenth century. Such artistic works present a reflexive, communicational version of a former communal participation, inspired by the older model as a trace, a cultural underlayer.

In Bakhtin's historical approach, the carnival underlayer thus continues in festivals, pilgrim centers, morality and miracle plays, dialogues of the dead, etc., but also "resurfaces" in ever newer forms, infiltrating other cultural genres that carry it forward, particularly in literature. As occurs in yin/yang interpenetration, carnival dissolves the "either/or" and asserts "both/and." For instance, Rabelais unites life and death, the feast and the funeral, heaven and hell, crownings and decrownings. Such demasking of the bifurcated and bounded images have kept the potential for dialogue alive beneath the official monologue, making sure it would never "congeal in one sided seriousness or in a stupid fetish for definition or singleness of meaning" (Bakhtin 1984:132).

As this ambivalent whole becomes increasingly dialogical, it erodes the artificial barriers between artistic styles and between self-enclosed systems of thought, as seen in the novels of Dostoevsky: "In Dostoevsky's world, all people and all things must know one another and know about one another, must enter into contact, come together face to face and begin to talk with one another. Everything must be reflected in everything else, all things must illuminate one another dialogically" (Bakhtin 1984:177).

Bakhtin seems to wallow in such a prospect. He was undoubtedly influenced by Martin Buber's writings on "I-Thou" dialogue (Holquist 1984:27), and he often uses Buber's terminology: "The very being of man is the deepest communion . . . I become myself only while revealing myself for another, through another, and with the help of another . . . by a relationship toward another consciousness, toward a thou" (Bakhtin 1984:284–87). This intercultural identity emerges historically. People and their ideas "had broken out of their self-enclosed hierarchical nesting places, and had begun to collide in familiar contact" (Bakhtin 1984:167). The trend is postcanonical, postideological. His wager on the future was that as the doctrinal imagination erodes it will be replaced not with a "therapeutic" or "minimal" self (Rieff 1966; Lasch 1984), but rather with a dialogic imagination. There would be, however, a transitional phase of crisis, experienced in negative terms.

In the final sections of his book on Dostoevsky (1984:227–47) Bakhtin analyzes figures of "threshold discourse" who are caught in-between, in a time of historical turning. Stripped of all monologic barriers, they have "fully dialogized interiors," but they are not yet ready to live in the world that is coming into being. In *The Possessed,* the antihero Stavrogin confesses to imagined accusers whose judgment he both needs and rejects. "Irreconcilable voices interrupt one another, conflicting rejoinders overlap." As in Kafka's work, neither a guilty intent nor an accusing judge can be precisely located. In contrast to the ancient shaman who is possessed by spirits, the contemporary antihero is possessed by penetrative words and their hidden traces. Conscious awareness of this is a sign that the era of the monologic denial is ending, the third era beginning.

For Bakhtin, a sense of disassociation grows as we become aware of an "alien discourse" within us. Our words become double voiced, full of doubt about the implications of our own meanings. In Lacan's model of intersubjectivity, the contemporary self recognizes itself indirectly through such communication. Handwerk (1985) notes that in Lacan's model, self-awareness emerges through "ironic intersubjectivity" in discourse that must confess to a mutual complicity in constructing the self and the symbolic meanings that construct the world. In *Notes from the Underground,* Dostoevsky's Underground Man, personally insulted by the world order, speaks with ever sideward glances at someone else's words that continue to define who he is, seeking a "way out" through a final rejoinder. Bakhtin (1984:236) calls this the "confessional self-definition with a loophole."

In Bakhtin's theory of history, the confessional identity is a transition toward positive recognition that one's discourse is implicated in all other social discourses, which mutually reveal one another. He views history itself as an interplay between denial and confession of dialogical complicity in the world, but one in which "Rabelais," carrier of the ancient matrix, continues to resurface.

As a third temporal identity accelerates, the ironic interplay becomes conscious rather than unwitting. In the final pages of *The Dialogic Imagination,* Bakhtin describes a struggle between a dispersal outward, in which we consciously incorporate an ever greater variety of cultural voices, and a closure that seeks to escape from this complexity; desperate, latter-day attempts to "re-canonize and seal off" authoritative languages, to "remove them from dialogicality."

TEMPORAL LAYERS IN GYASUMDO

The cultural process described thus far is taking place in the small valley of Gyasumdo in the Nepal Himalayas. Bakhtin's tripart historical model encourages a new approach to cultural development, breaking with the two-part narrative of "little" and "great" traditions. It takes note of a "third" tradition, that of a process of interillumination. This process is emerging historically through unfinished dialogue between older and newer layers of culture, represented in this case by Gurung shamans and Tibetan lamas. Since this emergent tradition is unbounded and global, no one is excluded, not even the ethnographer.

A tripart narrative is more than an analytic model. All three periods appear to coexist in Gyasumdo, as a field of images and narratives in argument with one another. In the Gurung villages, the Ghyabrē and Paju shamans still seek to live out what Bakhtin calls the ancient matrix, an identity embedded within relationships of the community and the cosmos and signified in the local landmarks. The Gurung shamans offer no program of extrication from such a world. Their rituals seek to restore a balance, or harmony, within society and between the upper and lower worlds of their cosmos. They do not assert a religious or ideological truth. Rather they mediate between forces, images, and wills of various domains.

In contrast, the Tibetan Buddhist lamas' rites and teachings, based on written texts, thrust the theme of harmony into the background and draw to the foreground a highly individuating religious destiny. Tibetan rituals include an underlayer that deals with this-world concerns, just as do the shamans, but the lamas use their rites as an opportunity to introduce a Buddhist path of extrication from the world matrix. The main "doctrinal" teaching, karma as individual merit accumulation, promotes directionality

(Paul 1970) toward liberation (*thar-pa*). Merit making requires an internal ethic, that of purity of intent. At advanced levels this interiority matures through a series of renunciatory initiations that lead toward enlightenment.

We may equate both merit making and the renunciatory ideal with Bakhtin's second temporal identity: a bifurcation that promotes individual life sequences. While the Gurung shamans affirm the world matrix, the lamas devalue samsara as opposed to nirvana. They introduce binary discriminations such as inner/outer, merit/demerit, even though these terms must ultimately be viewed as "empty" (*stong-pa*). The shamanic matrix, however, cannot be ignored. Although Tibetan lamas of the Nyingma sect are highly trained in their texts, they draw on images that arise in primary relationships of folk experience, including the shamanic underlayer, to make their teachings persuasive to the Tibetan laity, including images of demonic affliction, communal sacrifice, and horoscope relationships that convey links between persons within the matrix of the natural world.

We may call this a method of "transmutation." Such a term is also employed by Tibetan scholar Lama Govinda (1969), who defines Tibetan Buddhism as a technique in which images of lived experience are transmuted into new planes of mental awareness. Bakhtin (1981:217) finds an analogous process in the West, noting that "when nature itself ceased to be a living participant in the events of life" it became a source of "metaphors . . . serving to sublimate individual and private affairs." Buddhist transmutations also individuate such collective antecedents by employing metaphors. Agricultural images of the ripening of fruit become karmic "fruition" in the individual. Sacrificial rites that renew the fertility of the cosmos become the "inner" sacrifice of the renouncer; the external ritual is refracted into an inner subjectivity (Collins 1982).

The promotion of the inner life is explicit in the definition which Tibetan Buddhists give themselves: *nang-pa*, "the inner ones," contrasting with the "external ones" (*phyi-pa*), which the lamas call the Gurung shamans of Gyasumdo. The Tibetan laity, however, are caught in the middle. They are urged on toward the inner life by their lamas, but feel much embedded in the external web of nature and social relations. They view their lay work as hopelessly implicated in samsaric compromises, in contrast to the nirvanic preoccupation of the lamas. Further, their own folk culture is only slightly removed from the shamanic layer of their own past, so that the rituals and arguments of the Gurung shamans are still familiar and persuasive.

The dialogic encounter in Gyasumdo has to do with this external-internal tension. It is made complex and dynamic by the particular kind of denial that is necessary in order to imagine oneself being extricated from the net of external relations. This denial can be noted most precisely during the Tibetan ritual fast (Nyungne), held each year in Tshap village. A group of the most committed of the Tibetan laity undergo the fast for two days in the Gompa, alongside the lamas, monks, and nuns. As a period of renunciation, it signifies temporary removal from the samsaric world. A tight imaginary boundary is drawn around the group of renunciates, within which it is said that inner intentions are pure ("virtuous mind" is *sems-pa bzang-po*), so that during the fast they are not implicated in the sins (*sdig-pa*) of worldly actions and relations.

We may call this extrication a denial, particularly since it is viewed as such by the Gurung shamans, who criticize it from a pre-Buddhist standpoint. An imaginary boundary of this kind should not be called false; rather it is a metaphoric truth which, as Bourdieu (1977:133) observes, operates to deny another truth. Lacan's model of denial is suggestive: within a bounded self-image, the subject can deny its complicity in the world of intersubjectivity that would otherwise make the idea of pure motives inconceivable.

In Bakhtin's analysis of the internal dialogue in Dostoevsky's characters, ambivalent motives within the self are penetrated by a monologic intrusion. The Tibetan lay mind, pulled in both Lamaist and shamanic directions, is indeed internally dialogized. During the Nyungne fast, the Tibetan lama's doctrinal monologue intrudes to provide the karmic metaphor of bounded subjectivity. Psychologically, it builds an ethic of intent, to motivate each Tibetan individually in a karmic career. It is provisionally useful, as Vaihinger has said of such metaphors, but as a partial truth it denies awareness of the relational world in which the self is still implicated.

The ambivalence promoted by this denial was immediately apparent when we started fieldwork in Tshap village. Tibetan Buddhists eat meat, but killing animals is prohibited. Pema, our landlord, pointed out that the yak meat being served to us was not from a "killed yak," but from a "fallen yak." Why a fallen yak? "Because there is no sin at all in eating a fallen yak." As time went on the supply of meat did not diminish, and we wondered how so many yaks were falling.

Eventually the dilemma was explained. Motivational closeness to the act of killing is the measure of the degree of complicity. To buy meat in the market involves no sin, since the purchaser has not personally willed the animal's death. To buy meat that is "still red" the day after it is killed implicates one partially in the act. To actually say "kill" is almost as sinful as wielding the knife, an act which Tibetan householders hire Gurung workers to do. Ideally, one would eat only the yak that "falls." In an unintended accident, no demerit is accumulated.

There is an interplay of denial and confession here, particularly since there is a middle region in the paradigm that is not agreed on. From a pre-Buddhist, shamanic perspective, there is no such dilemma. The minds of the Gurung shamans are already contaminated by the spirits that penetrate them during their rites. An ethic of intent for the sake of merit accumulation does not make sense to them, since they have no program for extricating the inner life from its relational entanglements.

Virtuous intent, as a metaphor that seals off subjectivity, may be viewed as historically emergent. It rises with the merit doctrine and intensifies further with religions having a truth or a faith that requires purity of mind. It then declines as global complexity overwhelms such boundaries. The Tibetan view of history portrays such a sequence. It predicts that the future will bring deterioration of the Buddhist project in the evil age (*dus ngen-pa*), since inner intent becomes decentered as it is pulled into a decaying world. Tibetan evil age discourse is similar to that of Bakhtin's third temporal identity, but takes a negative form, as in the threshold discourse of Dostoevsky's Underground Man.

In Gyasumdo, where historical events appear to be accelerating the evil age, Tibetans themselves say that their words have become "ironic" (*tshig-rgyab*) as the mental boundaries they have built around themselves erode from penetration by the multiple standards and distractions of the modern world now invading this remote region. The Tibetan lamas in Gyasumdo were dismayed. In the Nepal government village schools, "job training" was gradually replacing the Lamaist educational ideal of initiation into wisdom. Reports were being heard of a highly technological world "somewhere in the West," where inner thoughts were being caught up in the illusion of external appearances. It was, in the discourse of Gyasumdo, a further sign that the evil age was accelerating.

The above sequence replicates Bakhtin's three temporal models: first, the interpenetrations of the shamanic matrix; second, the bounded subjectivity of the individuated Buddhist path; third, the erosion of that boundary, viewed as historical decline. Each of these cultural layers has a different model of retribution: (1) For the Gurung shamans, retributions come as punishing afflictions, caused by disharmony in the matrix of relations. (2) The lamas shift the explanation of suffering into the individual sequence of karmic retributions: inner thoughts and actions having moral consequences in future lives. (3) The third layer introduces a postkarmic sense of retribution found in evil age discourse. Demonic afflictions are felt intersubjectively, the mind becoming divided by contradictory ethical demands. As in Dostoevsky, relational accusations invade from the sideward glance.

Tibetan Ritual as Transmutation

Evil age decline is not the intended outcome of Tibetan Buddhist culture. The temporal sequence toward enlightenment is meant to arrive at a positive "third" layer of identity beyond karmic individuation, to attain a higher intersubjective identity. Such a three-layered model was formulated by Atiśa (982–1055), whose coming to Tibet helped to inaugurate the later spread of Buddhism in Tibet during the eleventh century. The following quotations are selected from Atiśa's work *A Lamp for the Enlightenment Path and Commentary* (translated by R. Sherburne):

> In that they are Inferior, or Mediocre or Superior, persons should be understood as three:
>
> 1. One who by every means he finds seeks but the pleasure of samsara and cares but for himself alone, that one is known as the Inferior Person.
>
> 2. One who puts life's pleasures behind and turns himself from deeds of sin, yet cares only about his own peace, that person should be called Mediocre.
>
> 3. One who wholly seeks a complete end to the entire suffering of others because their suffering belongs to his own consciousness stream, that person is a Superior (Atiśa 1983:5).

The lamas in Gyasumdo view the three types as representing stages of religious consciousness as well as modes of ritual orientation. In their view, the local Ghyabrē and Paju shamans, with rituals focused only on this-world concerns, represent the inferior type, but so are those Tibetan persons who understand only the immediate and mundane benefits of the Tibetan rites. The second, mediocre type is found in the monks of earlier Buddhism, who became *Pratyeka buddhas* ("solitary realizers"), striving only for their own liberation.[1] The third, superior type is represented by the Tibetan lamas who practice the Mahāyāna Bodhisattva ideal as well as Tantrism, since here, discourse focuses on "the liberation of all sentient beings."[2]

---

1. Tibetan lamas in general do not have contact with present-day Theravada Buddhism and hence their image of it tends to be given only by this formula. It should be taken as a model rather than an accurate characterization.
2. The above three kinds of orientation should be differentiated from another tripart formula used to distinguish three levels as "vehicles" within Buddhist practice as such: (1) Hearer, (2) Solitary Realizer, and (3) Bodhisattva (Hopkins 1985:23).

The lamas' ritual sequence thus becomes a means by which persons may be brought gradually from the inferior condition into the second and then into the third type, by stages. It is a process of transmutation in so far as first-type motivations are acknowledged as a valid worldly concern that must be ritually addressed and then incorporated into the higher levels. Tibetan rituals can thus serve functions of abundance, protection, and healing as they do in the shamanic system, but for the lamas these mundane needs are not the final ends served. Ritual practice becomes an occasion for introducing higher human purposes.

We may call these rituals "reflexive," in that they incorporate new layers of meaning that comment on older layers. Turner (1974), Kapferer (1983), Babcock (1980), and Valeri (1985) have noted that certain ritual performances promote reflexive awareness. The Gyasumdo lamas are quite explicit in defining their rites as having higher teaching functions, and even classify certain rituals, such as demon exorcism and the death rite, as being particularly useful for this end.

The injection of more profound truth levels introduces a tension into ritual meaning. Lower, mundane orientations are to be transcended in the same sense that inferior persons may become mediocre and then superior. Beyond the first layer of pragmatic concerns, a second layer of individual commitment to Buddhist merit making and reflection is instigated, which in turn leads to a third layer, a Bodhisattva commitment to identify with the consciousnesses of all sentient beings in order to bring them toward liberation.

These stages are analogous to the three temporal stages of Bakhtin, but they are weighted somewhat differently. While Tibetan lamas view the first level of this-world pragmatism as inferior, Bakhtin's celebration of the ancient folkloric matrix is closer to a shamanic view. For the lamas, the middle level of solitary Buddhism is a mediocre attainment, as is Bakhtin's sealed-off individual, as a monologic transition. Both, however, fully celebrate a third stage in which all consciousnesses would ideally interpenetrate.

One may object that the western vision is more historical and communicational, the eastern more mystical. Yet we must keep in mind that each vision mirrors the other and has folk underlayers that incorporate the other, as well as having similar evil age type ironic discourses. Further, East and West each have theoretical insights that unmask the denials of the other, as do the Lamaist and shamanic regimes that are analyzed in this study.

As Tibetan lamas transmute what they view as lower modes of experience into higher wisdom, they shift images from mundane contexts to more "profound" (*gting ring-po*) contexts of meaning. This fusion of older and newer layers creates what Bakhtin calls "hybrid constructions." These are words or images that are saturated with contested and unfinished meanings, since they have been dragged through many different contexts of use over time. The hybrid meanings of these words may often be unconscious, but they become intentional hybrids when conscious use is made of their ambivalent nature.

Lamaist transmutations employ hybrid images in this manner, but they do not have full control of how they will be interpreted by their listeners, or the manner in which lower or older meanings may develop an underlayer different from the one expected. In Bakhtin's work, images of the ancient matrix likewise continue through time as a folk underlayer, expressing "carnival" or a "Rabelaisian" view of the world. While such images are reworked into precise concepts at the official level, the Rabelaisian use of these images retains the ancient sense of an "ambivalent whole," which resurfaces again and again as an artistic genre.

This seems to occur in the ritual transmutations of the lamas of Gyasumdo. Even lamas who have chosen to remain celibate (*dge-slong*) find themselves performing this-world rites for householders, renewing each year the fertility of the fields and sanctifying village stupas that symbolize a kingly world system of Mount Meru and the four continents. The image of an ideal cosmos of abundance is found in the Tibetan horoscope system. This is linked to the symbolism of the Universal Monarch, the Wheel-turning King who stands for the establishment of both the Buddhist dharma and an ideal prosperity. Each Tibetan rite thus communicates a hybrid fusion between an external world harmony on the one hand and inner enlightenment on the other.

In his analysis of the "two wheels" of the Buddhist dharma in Thailand, Tambiah (1976:35) notes that however personal and introspective it may seem, "Buddhism did in fact put together a picture of a world as a collective system . . . it used the constructs of Mount Meru as the axis and axle, and of world systems, their formations and reformations, in new arrangements with new implications." This underlayer draws on an ancient matrix that includes horoscope diagrams used by ancient kingship as well as the shamanic model of sacrificial offerings that renew harmony in the cosmos. Herrenschmidt (1982) argues that even in later traditions that repudiate external rites of world harmony on behalf of an internal, symbolic sacrifice, the ancient model of external harmony remains implicit. De Heusch (1984) notes that in addition there seems to remain in our historical memory an image of "indebtedness" that sacrificial rites acknowledge, and attempt to repay.

In Gyasumdo, images communicating such an ambivalent whole are retained as a ritual underlayer, even while the lamas transmute them into the karma ethic and inner awareness. Mundane concerns revolve around the natural cycles of seasons and years, as portrayed in the diagrams of the Tibetan horoscope. The lamas insert into each ritual performance various artistic images and effigies representing the horoscope, the universal kingdom, and sacrificial offerings. Beyond this primal layer of this-world concerns, the lamas add further layers of imagery, each being a mode of reflexive commentary on earlier layers beneath it.

The entire series of Tibetan rites reveals such a movement from primal worldly concerns to the most profound levels of Buddhist teaching. Fertility rites of exchange with the natural world lie at the base, beyond which guardian deity rites convey the historical construction of a Buddhist Kingdom. Beyond this, rites of demon exorcism convey the historical decline of the kingdom as well as the decay of the body. Finally, the rite of soul calling and the Tibetan death rite culminate the series. These Tibetan rites are all transmuted into higher Buddhist teachings, but as an entire ritual sequence they communicate Tibetan identity in the form of a historical narrative. This historicity will be noted in each chapter and examined explicitly in the final chapter and the conclusion.

LAMA-SHAMAN DIALOGUE

Central to the analysis is the way in which later ritual layers retain what Bakhtin calls the "ancient matrix" with its "carnival sense of the world" which lies at the base, and how that primal layer is transmuted into a historical consciousness that is experienced as dialogue rather than monologue. Such a development in Gyasumdo is furthered by the alternative regime of the Gurung shamans; their visible presence and their arguments continuing the lama-shaman encounter that began long before in Tibet itself.

A study of the attempt by Tibetan lamas to promote Buddhism in a Himalayan region long dominated by local shamanism provides insight into what may have occurred again and again in rural Tibet as Lamaism gradually triumphed over indigenous shamanic and later Bon practices. The comparison is valid in light of the observation made by Snellgrove and Richardson (1968:57) that in Nepal the Gurungs are most likely "peoples of old Tibetan stock who penetrated the Himalayas in pre-Buddhist times and have since escaped the full impact of the later Tibetan Buddhist culture. Thus from a Nepalese people like the Gurungs we can probably even nowadays gain some impression of the workings of such rituals in early Tibet."

According to Hoffman (1961:15), an original "animist-shamanist" religion in Tibet had once been widespread throughout the whole inner Asia region including Siberia, Turkestan, Mongolia, and China. What later became known as the Tibetan Bon religion has undergone developmental phases before and after the entry of Buddhism into eighth-century Tibet, with numerous foreign contributions. Whatever their sources, Bon and pre-Bon cosmological themes have persisted in Tibetan folk religion (Hoffman 1961, 1979; Tucci 1949, 1980). These images remain in folk layers that are still shared by both the Gurung shamans and the Tibetans who have migrated into Gyasumdo. Both, for instance, say there is a three-leveled universe containing an upper world, the human world, and an underworld. There are local "earth owners" which both communities call *sa-bdag* spirits, and both refer to *bdud* (demons) and clan guardian deities called *btsan*. Gurungs retain the image of the divine kingship that had once existed in pre-Buddhist Tibet, with the ancestral line of the Ghale nobility originating in the upper world.

Understanding the clash that occurred in Tibet between the pre-reformed Bonpo (followers of the Bon religion) regime and Buddhism when it was first introduced can aid our interpretation of the lama/shaman rivalry in Gyasumdo. The Indian Tantric master Padmasambhava, referred to by Tibetans as Guru Rinpoche, was invited to Tibet around A.D. 770 by King Khri srong lde btsan to subdue the demons and help establish Buddhism. With the building of the Buddhist temple at bSam-yas, he is said to have triumphed over a nonreformed Bon system that had become the state religion.[3]

In the autobiography of Lady Yeshe Tsogyel translated by Keith Dowman (1984:104–5), it is reported that despite the success of the Buddhist Padmasambhava, the king had retained the Bon rites of animal sacrifice; for instance, "a stag with fine antlers, a hind with a turquoise halter, a thousand yak, sheep and goats" would be sacrificed, and "nine kinds of grain," wine, clothes, and other items would be offered. The account then

3. Dowman (1984) in his translation and interpretation of the autobiography of Lady Yeshe Tsogyel argues that the Yeshe Tsogyel text portrays the eighth-century Bonpo as a mixed group of older and newer practitioners. The text describes many Bonpo as exorcist "controllers of spirits"; hence they may be regarded as representing the older, shamanic tradition (p. 324). The more ancient practices certainly continued in rural and frontier areas of Tibet (Hoffman 1979). In Milarepa's biography of twelfth-century Tibet we find that in the story of Milarepa's contest with the Bonpo at Mount Ti-se, the latter rides his drum to the top of the mountain. This motif is certainly shamanic. According to the lama scholar Chögyam Trungpa (1978), "until about the seventh century A.D. Tibet was referred to by its inhabitants as Pön . . . thus the name of the Tibetan religion was, at least archaically, synonymous with the nation itself."

reports that the Buddhist monks were horrified by such rites, and proclaimed: "One doctrine cannot have two teachers . . . fire and water can
never be allies . . . either the teaching of the Buddha is exclusively established in Tibet, or Bon is permitted to flourish. It is absolutely impossible
for them to co-exist."

The Bonpo regime is then said to have been defeated in a debate at
bSam-yas, which led to the conversion of those who were to become
reformed Bon,[4] and to the forcible exile of others into adjacent regions
such as Mongolia and Nepal. Dowman (1984:114) suggests that it was the
issue of animal sacrifice that led to the exile of such practitioners from
Tibet to "the border countries." At present in Gyasumdo in Nepal, both
Gurung and Tibetan informants use the term *Bon*. Sometimes they refer
to the local Paju shaman, a virtuoso sacrificer, as a "black" Bon (*bon-nag*).
The Ghyabrē shaman views himself as becoming a "white" Bon (*bon-dkar*),
even though he still performs animal sacrifices.

The incident at bSam-yas in eighth-century Tibet appears to mark a
shift toward a Buddhist regime that sought to establish a monologic truth
in place of views that are imprecise or unfinished. Further, the bSam-yas
incident introduces the Buddhist model of ethical retribution, in which
the act of ritual killing, called the "red offering," becomes a crucial offense.
In Gyasumdo, Tibetans say that the terms "red offering" (*dmar-mchod*)
and "sin" (*sdig-pa*) are interchangeable.

The Tibetan Bon rite described in the previous section is strikingly similar
to the spring rite of the deer sacrifice performed to this day by the shamans
in Gyasumdo. The deer sacrifice has been repudiated by the lamas who
have migrated into Nepal, as the Bon rite was repudiated in Tibet. They
think of the Ghyabrē and Paju as descendants of the unreformed Bonpos
who, in the Tibetan cultural narrative, had been exiled into this region
centuries ago. Thus in their view, the historic opposition in Tibet appears
again in the lama-shaman rivalry in Gyasumdo.

Across the river from the Tibetan village of Tshap where we lived, the
Gurung village of Tapje commands the valley from the hillside. In the center
of the village is an ancestral altar linked to the upper world, while below
the village is a sacred grove, thought to lie right above the underworld,
a tree in the grove representing a world axis. Beneath the tree is the altar
where the deer is sacrificed by the Ghyabrē shamans each spring, linking
the divine ancestor of the Ghale clan to the earth's sources of fertility.

In the Tibetan village across the river the Buddhist lamas condemn

---

4. The reformed Bon sect in Tibet is known to have flourished by the eleventh century and
   came to resemble Nyingma Lamaism (Stein 1972).

this cult of ritual killing as "sinful" (*sdig-pa*). But their own spring rite is a Lamaist reinterpretation of this older sacrificial layer. The Tibetans give substitute, vegetarian offerings to their underworld serpent deities (*klu*), as well as to their own community god (*yul lha*) who replaces the image of the king's divine ancestor. The lamas read texts and renew the village stupas, making their own spring ritual complex a Buddhist one.

Hence, two similar, but opposed cults are carried out at the same time in the same valley, the practitioners of each being critical of the other. They may be viewed as two historical layers formed on two sides of the river. The Gurung ritual system images the ancient sacrificial model for renewing the natural world; the Tibetan ritual system marks the historic break with that model. Recent local history has dramatically reenacted that break.

When the forefathers of these Tibetans came more than a hundred years ago, they at first compromised with the powerful Ghale lords in Tapje, who appointed the Tibetan village leader to perform a small-scale version of the blood sacrifice each spring. Even as lamas began to establish permanent residence in the village a few decades ago, the Tibetan laity continued to sacrifice a chicken in their communal spring rite, while their lamas looked the other way.

In the early 1960s, however, this formula was dramatically repudiated. A powerful Tibetan lama called Lama Chog Lingpa came down from Tibet into this valley and condemned the compromise. Lama Chog Lingpa subdued the local spirits and wrote a ritual text on the spot, which has been translated and explicated in this study. Informants throughout the valley testify to the rapid Buddhist reform that evolved after that extraordinary event. Hence in recent times in Gyasumdo there has been a historic shift analogous to the Buddhist turning point in eighth-century Tibet.

The present study examines the ritual regime established by the local lamas who carried through that reform, and the debate that continues with the Gurung shamans. The Gurung shamans still argue that the Tibetan laity have made a mistake, and that they will be punished by the local area gods for refusing to give them a blood offering. The Tibetan lamas argue the opposite in terms of the karma doctrine, that the laity would be punished in their afterlife in a Buddhist hell, if they do return to the red offering. The Tibetan laity are caught in the middle, obedient to their lamas yet half persuaded by the shamanic argument. Some admit to holding both views.

Two models of retribution thus collide. The older shamanic model, as Walter Burkert (1983) has outlined in his study of ancient Greece, is a system of reciprocal exchanges of "life for life" based on the ancient matrix of natural cycles. Retribution results from the failure to achieve harmony. The Tibetan lamas establish a retribution model with a very different project: the individual is to embark on a karmic career, accumulating merit and insight. The lama-shaman struggle for the mind of the Tibetan laity amplifies this contest between the two layers.

In Asian Buddhist cultures the two models are often found joined in a hybrid construction that bristles with dialogic tension. In Nowak's (1977) translation of *The Tale of the Nishan Shamaness* from seventeenth-century Manchu China, the shamaness, while retrieving the lost soul of a patient in the underworld, encounters her husband, who had died previously. He threatens to kill her for mistreating him when he was alive, a reciprocal retribution. The shamaness then enters another underworld region that appears as a Buddhist hell. Here, a Buddhist deity metes out karmic judgments for individual transgressions. As Obeyesekere (1981) points out, the initial layer of guilt expresses deep motives arising from the matrix of primary ties. The karmic guilt of the individual taught by Buddhism is a "consciously ethicized" retribution that overlays the primary one.

This results in deep psychological ambivalence as the two layers interact, the second layer gaining emotional salience from its links with the first. In a later chapter this dynamic process will be analyzed in more detail. Tibetan lamas, however, also teach a third layer of guilt awareness. It is the Bodhisattva identity which, as Atiśa put it, incorporates the suffering of all others into one's own consciousness stream. When Gyasumdo lamas teach the third model to their laity, they try to make it psychologically real by transmuting the previous two layers. As is done in Chinese Hua-yen philosophy, karma is reinterpreted in terms of a relational whole: "Every karmic fault has been committed against your mother, since everyone has been your mother at some time in past reincarnations."

Such a third Buddhist layer is comparable to Bakhtin's third temporal identity. It is also expressed in rituals, as later chapters will show. The Tibetan laity, however much embedded in the world, are still persuaded by the primary layer that is advocated by the Gurung shamans. It keeps returning, demanding recognition. The Lamaist project cannot ignore the shamanic images that are still clearly articulated in Gyasumdo. The more profound Buddhist layers contend with a folkloric matrix that still seems plausible.[5] The Tibetan lamas must somehow transmute that matrix, which belongs not only to the shamans but lies in the folk consciousness of their own system.

5. In the view of Tibetologist David Snellgrove (1980:19), "Most Tibetans are still *bonpos* at heart and they have recourse to Bon of all kinds, not only in their minds, but in words and acts as well." In his study of the conversion of Mongolia to Tibetan Lamaism in the seventeenth century, Heissig (1953) noted that the "newly imposed lamaist formulas were only substitutes for the shamanist functions."

The historicity of these layered meanings can be observed in the ritual performances of the lamas. The encounter with the local Gurung shamans is implicated in the creation of these layers. The lamas, having written texts which they define monologically as the only reliable truth, officially repudiate the shamanic contribution and work to replace the latter's ritual repertoire in Gyasumdo with a full set of Buddhist equivalents. In contrast, the shamans argue for ritual collaboration in which lamas and shamans would each make partial contributions to an unknowable whole.

By the time my research had begun in earnest in 1981, the Lamaist reform movement that started in the early 1960s had gained considerable ground. Backed by the prestige of their texts, the lamas' arguments had become increasingly persuasive and triggered a reflexive process among the Gurung shamans, some beginning to view their own scheme in a more conscious manner, as a rejoinder. This appears to have occurred in the development of reformed Bon in Tibet itself (Karmay 1972).

We may call this a "third" layer of meaning, emerging *between* rival regimes as an unpredictable process, in a manner that is dialogical rather than doctrinal. By examining such dialogue, one can view Tibetan Buddhist rites as a sequence of layers that are not fully worked out in ritual texts. Layers of meaning that are deeply felt signify critical events. The shamanic encounter is interwoven with these events, as contending memories about what they mean become activated in the ritual narratives of both practitioners. The result is a cultural process without boundaries.

We turn to examine the lama-shaman dialogue in Gyasumdo. I will introduce the encounter through a comparison of historical narratives which construct rival social hierarchies based on different models of retribution. I will then describe the Gurung deer sacrifice, as the powerful shamanic drama which the Tibetans have had to repudiate, followed by an examination of the local text written by Lama Chog Lingpa when he came down from Tibet in the early 1960s. The extraordinary document created by this lama was the inspiration for this research when I discovered its significance.

Events such as the 1960s turning point have become memory traces in the traditions of both regimes in Gyasumdo, informing the entire sequence of rituals that we will examine in the chapters that follow. I hope to show that ultimately, neither communal nor temporal boundaries can be drawn, since, as Walter Benjamin (1969:254–55) has stated, "nothing that has ever happened should be regarded as lost for history."

Chapter Two

Hierarchy and Narrative Memory

They looked like Tibetans and when I addressed them in that language . . . they replied in terms as close to the dialect of central Tibet as to make little difference . . . it was remarkable to discover that the children in this village were learning to read and write classical Tibetan, for one would have to travel a long ways northwards to find the same again. (Snellgrove 1981:239)

THE GYASUMDO TIBETANS

In Gyasumdo in northern Nepal, the communities of Tibetan-speaking peoples define themselves as *bod-pa* ("people of Tibet") to affirm their ethnic identity and Tibetan origin even though they have settled in Nepal. Snellgrove made the above observation regarding the "Tibetans of Gyasumdo" when he first passed through the region in the mid-1950s. There are several villages of Tibetans along the Marsyandi river, the village names Snellgrove reported being used by the inhabitants today: Tshad-med, Tshap, and Thang-jet (Tibetan names) are the main settlements. Darapani, and Tal (Nepali names) farther down the Marsyandi, and Tilje going north along the Dudh river are composed of half Tibetans and half Gurungs. The main Gurung villages are high up on the hillsides. Across the river from Tshap, the Tibetan village where the research was carried out, stands the Gurung village of Tapje, ruled by the Ghale clan, the Gurung nobility that still maintains political domination in the valley.

The Tibetan villagers and Buddhist lamas among whom we lived in Gyasumdo define their "tradition" (*lugs-srol*) as separate and distinct from that of the Gurungs and their shamans. Gyasumdo Tibetans view their Tibet origins as an ideal from the past, while they view their migration into Nepal as a falling into compromise with the ancient pre-Buddhist regime that had been repudiated in Tibet.

The Ghale nobles of Tapje are legitimated by the Gurung shamans. The Ghyabrē shamans chant the narrative of divine origins of the Ghale ancestors, to whom they perform animal sacrifices each spring. On the Tibetan side of the river in Tshap village, Lama Dorje tells the story of the triumph of Buddhist hegemony in Tibet. But when the Tibetans look across the river, they see the Ghale-shamanic stronghold of Tapje as an image of the regime that they were supposed to have defeated in their own narrative.

In this chapter I will examine the dialogue between the different narrative memories of these opposed regimes. The narratives of the two communities legitimate different conceptions of social hierarchy, and different models of retribution. The narrative of the shamans and Ghale ancestors represents the older layer. It remains as the more fundamental discourse, still hidden within the Tibetan narrative that has been constructed to oppose it (Bakhtin 1981:284). We must begin, however, by describing certain social-economic events in the recent history of Gyasumdo that have been incorporated into the stories that are told.

In an article referring to Gyasumdo, Nareshwar Jang Gurung observed that these "groups of Tibetans" have migrated from Nupri as well as from Kyirong and Tingri in Tibet (Gurung 1976:305). In my research in Tshap village I found a variety of origin points. Although there had been earlier arrivals in Tshad-med village, the first families to arrive in Tshap village had migrated from the Kyirong (*skyid-rong*) region in Tibet in the latter part of the nineteenth century. Since then, most Tibetans have come down over the last eighty years from Nupri, some claiming origins in Kutang and Tsum farther east. A smaller group of families have migrated from the west, their ancestors having origins near Mustang and, more recently, Muktinath. A few Thakali-speaking families from Thak Khola also settled in Tshap, but left during the 1960s.

After the Chinese consolidation of power in central and western Tibet a small influx of Tibetans in exile also settled in Gyasumdo during the 1960s, choosing to remain in the region rather than continue to Kathmandu or India. Among these are several households of Tibetan nomads or Drogpa (*'brog-pa*) who continue their traditional herding way of life, moving on a seasonal basis. Also counted as recent Tibetan settlers are Rüpa, people who had lived in Rü on the Tibetan side of the border above Larkya pass as intermediaries of the salt and grain trade.

The oldest Tibetans of Tshap village tell stories about their own fathers or grandfathers arriving in the nineteenth century when there were very few people in the region. As these settlers trickled in, they obtained land grants from the Ghale head at Tapje, who was the local administrator of land (N. *jimmawal*) and had jurisdiction over dispute settlement on authority from the Rana government. Those who settled in Tshap village gained ownership of their land by clearing the trees. Those who went to Tshad-med village worked first as tenant farmers until they could purchase their land, while in Thang-jet such tenant farming has continued even to this day.

Before 1960 these settlers divided their economic activity between farming, herding, and the salt and grain trade with Tibet; the trade route coming through Gyasumdo was a main factor in encouraging the earlier Tibetan immigration. Today, men from Tshap village still go every year on trading trips to Tibet, but the village is no longer the elaborate system of storage depots that it had once been. The memories they recall focus mainly on the oppression they suffered at the hands of the Gurung customs officer, called Subba, who regulated the salt and grain trade passing through Gyasumdo. Tibetans tell how the Subba forced the traders passing through to do labor for him, sometimes taking the salt away from them because they were indebted to him. "The people were terrified. None could raise a voice against him. He ate the wealth of the people."

Relations with the Ghale landlords of Tapje were less harsh, but corvée (unpaid labor) was required of all householders for three days each year, and extra services were required on demand. After the Rana government in Kathmandu fell in 1951, the Ghale leader in Tapje lost his previous title, but continued to oversee taxes on land and the sale of property, retaining the title of headman (Mukhya). The Tibetans now had the right to demand an end to the corvée system. The Ghale leaders agreed, but on condition that a certain dramatic form of subservience continue. Formerly, the Tibetans had been forced to deliver to the Ghale leader two sheep heads during the Dasain festival as an act of fealty. Today during Dasain, the Tshap villagers buy one sheep head from the Gurungs and deliver it to the Ghale leader of Tapje. They refer to it as "play-acting, to humor him." No one knows what consequences would follow if they were to stop the performance.

Ghale hegemony in Gyasumdo had been supported during the Rana period by the former Nepalese law code, the Mukuli Ain, established in 1854 and based on the Brahmin view of hierarchy. The law code had attempted to regulate behavior between ethnic groups throughout Nepal, defining everyone in terms of Hindu caste, even in this remote northern region of shamanic and Tibetan Buddhist persuasion. The code called Tibetans living in Nepal by the derogatory name *Bhotia,* a word which Gyasumdo Tibetans now reject with disdain since it signified low caste status. Because of their yak eating, regarded at that time as equivalent to beef eating, Tibetans were assigned to the low category of Shudra in the caste order as defined by the Brahmins (Sharma 1977:297).

During the first half of this century, the Gurungs in Tapje village dropped their own tradition of yak eating in order to maintain their higher status in the law code. After the fall of the Ranas and the introduction of the new law code of 1963 (Sharma 1978:11) the Gurungs began to view Tibetans as their status equals. The Ghale leaders in Tapje even joke about their own former caste pretensions, boasting of their return to eating yak meat as had been their custom in the past. They join with Tibetans in ridiculing the "arrogance of the Brahmins" who had formerly "come up from Bahundanda" to convince them of the Brahmin point of view.

While the immediate impact of the fall of the Ranas is thus evident, caste mentality as such remains in Gyasumdo. Both Gurungs and Tibetans have their own traditional clan hierarchies of birth, as I will note later. The continuing influence of the Brahmin view of hierarchy pertains mainly to groups at the bottom of the Hindu system. Blacksmiths and tailor castes, who are Gurungs in Gyasumdo, are both prohibited entry into Tibetan homes. While blacksmiths have been a low caste in traditional Tibet, the lowness of tailors was created by the Hindu law code of 1854.

The Tibetans who have migrated into Gyasumdo can in theory inter-marry among themselves, while marriage with the Gurungs, Tamangs, Thakali, and most Nyeshangpa in Manang District is conventionally pro-hibited. Tibetan polyandry, in the form of the marriage of brothers to a single wife, is still practiced in Gyasumdo by the Drogpa nomads and Rüpa Tibetans. Cross-cousin marriage is also practiced among Gyasumdo Tibetans, as it is among other Tibetan groups in Nepal (Goldstein 1975), even though it has long been prohibited in Tibet. The ideal is to form village units of intermarrying kin through bilateral cross-cousin marriage alliances.

Stein (1972:108) cites textual evidence that cross-cousin marriage may have been practiced in Tibet in rural areas in the past. In Gyasumdo, those who came from the Kyirong region in Tibet insist that this had been the marriage custom of their ancestors in Tibet. The Rüpa, who had previously lived inside Tibet on the border above Samdo prior to 1960, have also long practiced cross-cousin marriage. The Drogpas, however, coming recently into Gyasumdo from deep within Tibet reject this custom emphati-cally, saying they are disgusted to see "this incest" among fellow Tibetans. A few recent arrivals from Tibet, however, already seem to be changing their minds. "I won't marry my son to *a-zhang*'s daughter [uncle's daughter]," says Ibi Drolma, "I just can't make myself do it. But later on, if my son allows his children to do so, it's all right with me."

Thus among Gyasumdo Tibetans, marriage rules are in flux, in dialogue, promoting different aims. From the standpoint of patrilineal ideology, marriage alliance between relatives returns property back to the patriclan, and builds a strong communal boundary that preserves the quality of clan substance: the "bone" (*rus*) derived from the father and the "flesh" (*sha*) from the mother will not be diluted or dispersed. The same patriclans often continue to intermarry, forming local ethnic solidarities of families having "similar bone and flesh."

But there is another form of alliance which breaks out of this boundary. Ritual friendship, called Ro Gyab (T. *rogs-rgyab, grogs-pa rgyab*) and called the *mit* bond throughout Nepal, is widely practiced. It unites many Gyasumdo Tibetans with Nyeshangpas and Gurungs throughout Manang and Lamjung districts, and is used for a variety of purposes. Ritual friendship defines the participants and all their siblings *as if* they were consanguineal kin. For Tibetans it is not entirely metaphorical: they imagine that such friendships link them with other Nepalese who are potential kin members in past or future lives. The Tibetan lamas, after all, teach that ultimately, "everyone has at some time become the mother of everyone else."

This erasure of the kin boundary is also expressed in negative form. In the evil age, the envy of less fortunate beings is said to become manifest in demonic attacks on small children. If the child of an established Tibetan family is felt to be at risk, they may give the child temporarily to a Gurung family of low condition, making the child less attractive to fool the afflicting demons. After the deception has worked, the child is given back, but the two families regard themselves as having created an invisible kin bond, in a manner similar to the bond created in ritual friendship.

It appears, then, that kinship is also drawn into the dialogue between the drawing and erasing of imaginary boundaries. Some of the above examples might be called "kin strategies" rather than "kin rules" (Bourdieu 1977). But the ethical reasoning of Tibetans who felt that cross-cousin marriage was "sinful" cannot be so easily reduced to a monologic theory of kinship. Something else is being said when imaginary boundaries are drawn, something having to do with narrative memories. In this case it was the memory of those coming recently from a fallen Tibet, wondering whether the story in which they were the main characters was coming to an end.

ALTERNATIVE NARRATIVE MEMORIES

Alien penetrations were accelerating in the mid-1970s after the hazardous trail coming up from Lamjung was remade and access became easier. Only after that could a foreign researcher like me live in Tshap village. The trek up to the village was now only a matter of five days. The past decade had brought health centers and government schools. Tibetans no longer felt economically dependent on the Ghale aristocracy from whom they had first obtained their land, and they were becoming increasingly conscious of their Tibetanness.

During the 1960s, three extraordinary events occurred which become significant in local narrative memory. The first was the fall of Tibet, bringing streams of refugees down Larkya pass and into Gyasumdo on their way to Kathmandu and India. The crisis was aggravated by the Khampa soldiers from Tibet who, after their defeat in the north, caused havoc by trying to remain in the region. By 1975 they had left, having been cleared out by the army of the Nepal government. The second event was the coming of Lama Chog Lingpa from Tibet in the early 1960s and his condemnation of the compromises of local Tibetans regarding animal sacrifice, a crisis which will be explicated in a later chapter. The third event was the great landslide of 1968, which covered half of the homes in Tshap village, and was the third great landslide in this village since its founding over a hundred years ago.

These are *dialogical* events. Interpreting them has been a debate process that has involved not only the Tibetans but the shamanic voice as well, the narrative significance of the events remaining undecided. The fall of Tibet had thrust forward the issue of boundaries. During the first half of this century, the Ghale nobility had attempted to co-opt the story that Tibetans and their lamas tell about themselves.

The earliest Tibetan lamas of the region, particularly those from Nar in north Manang, had been far less orthodox than the current ones. They had been drawn into a system of collaboration with the animal sacrifices of the shamanic regime, headed by the Ghale lords. In the view of Lama Dorje today, the lamas of Nar had become "little better than Bonpos." Today the Tibetan laity tell jokes about these "failed lamas" of the past, but when the Gurung shamans remember the same past, they idealize that lama-shaman collaboration as the high point in their own narrative history.

The Ghale leader had hoped that these immigrants from the north would "become as children," under the cosmic umbrella of his own lordship. Had not the Ghale (G. *Kle*) ancestor been a divine nobleman (T. *jobo*) from Tibet itself in centuries past? The narrative told by the present Ghale head clearly states such a view. While his own divinity was, it seems, rapidly fading, he might still represent the ancient pillar that connects the three world levels. Whoever might settle in Gyasumdo could be incorporated into his own cosmic narrative that would weave all the strands together.

The crisis events of the 1960s, however, had challenged the Tibetans and their lamas to draw their own boundary, to seal off, as it were, their own story and the historic project it defines, and remove themselves from the base legend of the Ghale lords. As a result, very different narrative memories are found on the two sides of the river. They have become both interwoven and separated, projecting alternative models of social hierarchy and different models of retribution.

The Ghale legend begins with the divine birth of their first ancestor in Tibet. A woman who was a Jomo[1] was weaving when she saw a hail-stone fall in front of her. Being thirsty, she ate it, and later became pregnant. She was ashamed and hid in a cave, where she had the child.[2] Following the divine birth of the first born, the Jomo had two other children. As the first ancestors of the Jowo clan they migrated from Tibet into Nepal with their mother, later to become the ruling kings of Gyasumdo. The legend, as told by the present Ghale head, continues with their local exploits after they had established themselves at Tapje village:

> The two Jowo warrior-kings went to hunt in Nar [north Manang]. They saw smoke and knew there must be people there. So they returned and sent an army to conquer Nar. There was a lama in Nar village living in a Gompa. He foresaw that the Jowos' army was coming. The lama did sorcery [*mthu*] by pointing a Thangka [painting] at them. This brought a landslide down on the advancing army.

The Jowo kings then went by themselves and defeated the people of Nar. Today one sees the prints of their hands on the boulder "where they jumped over the Marsyandi river." The Nar villagers submitted to the Jowo when they "became convinced of their divine origin."

The narrative claims that the Ghale nobles migrated from Tibet.[3] It legitimates their rule over the region, as well as over Tibetan Buddhist immigrants, with images of divine birth and miraculous exploits that enable

1. *Jomo* (*jo-mo*) in Tibetan is the honorary title of a female head of a noble household (Jäschke 1977:173). The male term, *Jowo* (*jo-bo*), is the Tibetan nobleman's title of "Lord" which the Ghale claim for themselves.
2. It is striking that divine insemination through drinking also occurs in the Tibetan epic of Gesar of Ling, in which Gesar is conceived after his mother Gongmo drinks "heavenly water" (Paul 1982:251).
3. The Ghale have heard of the Hinduized account of their origin reported in studies of the southwestern Gurungs by Pignède (1966) and Messerschmidt (1976a), but they do not regard them as correct. Messerschmidt calls the latter account, contained in a written document called *Gurung-ko Vamsavali*, "a contrived explanation" of Ghale and Gurung origins that identifies them with high-status Hindus from the south (p. 13). In contrast, the Ghale account given to me contains much ridicule of the Brahmins living to the south of them, revealing anti-Brahmin sentiment. Opinion has moved to the view that not only the Ghale but the other Gurung clans as well must have originally immigrated from Tibet (Messerschmidt 1976b, Ragsdale 1979).

them to overpower even the "Lama of Nar." The legend then proceeds by describing battles between the kingdoms in Gyasumdo and Lamjung to the south, and telling how during the nineteenth century, the Jowo kings were defeated by the Rana rulers of Gorkha when the latter consolidated the Nepalese nation. Then, "four generations ago," the Ghale leader sought and obtained from the Nepalese rulers the title of landlord of Gyasumdo and jurisdiction over land, taxes, and dispute settlements.

The Ghale nobility's narrative thus begins with divine kingship and ends with their regional lordship, a jurisdiction they still retain to some degree as tax officials under the present Nepalese government. Their rituals and the accompanying legends performed and sung by the Ghyabrē shaman refer to their initial identity as divine kings. They enact the migration from Tibet and the local settlement at Tapje, and they portray the Ghale as uniting the upper world of their divine origin with the underworld by means of their marriage alliance with other Gurung clans, who originate "from below."

Their legitimacy derives from harmonizing upper and lower realms to bring rain and good harvests to the "middle" human world, just as in ancient Tibet the king was also lord of the three realms (Tucci 1955). In Robert Paul's (1982:36) view the pre-Buddhist kings in Tibet enacted "the part of metonymic representative of all his subjects." Among Gurungs in Gyasumdo, the marriage alliance between the Ghale clan and the Lamichane clan is the prototype of the union of cosmic domains. The Gurung name of the Ghale, *kle,* implies divinity. The Gurung name of the Lamichane clan, *khrō,* implies their origins in the Gurung underworld, Khrō-nasa.[4]

It is from this narrative base that the Ghale leaders of Tapje village say they had hoped to link all immigrant settlers within their jurisdiction. Their ancient ancestor-kings had, after all, protected the region and brought prosperity. But the lamas of Gyasumdo tell a different narrative for the Tibetans of Gyasumdo. It is well known in Tibet and was told by Lama Dorje in Tshap village as follows:

> The Tibetan people originated because an incarnation of Buddha Chenresig [Skt. Avalokiteśvara] came into Tibet in the form of a monkey Bodhisattva. He lived in a cave, vowing to remain celibate. But a "rock cliff demoness" [*brag sin-mo*] found him and begged

4. The local Ghale and Gurung clan names are summarized as follows: the four upper clans are *kle* (N. Ghale), *gono* (N. Gotane), *lam* (N. Lama), and *khrō* (N. Lamichane). Lower Gurung clans in Gyasumdo are called *thar,* which include the Paju and Ghyabrē shaman lineages. The four upper clans are referred to in Nepali as Charjat, and the sixteen lower clans as Sorajat.

him to take her as his wife, threatening to kill herself if he did not
do so. The monkey returned to the Buddha field of Chenresig. But
Chenresig said, "You should return and marry her to start a human
race that will have your Bodhisattva mind and learn the dharma."

The monkey Bodhisattva returned and married the demoness,
and they had offspring. But after a time they could not provide for
their own food in the forest. So the monkey again went up to plead
with Buddha Chenresig. "What will we do for food?" It was then
that Chenresig gave the five kinds of grain to the Tibetan people,
which grew spontaneously as crops for them to eat.

The story has certain features that appear equivalent to the Ghale
legend: divine incarnation of the founding ancestor, and the union of upper
world with lower world, symbolized by the encounter in the cave. The
result is food abundance for the Tibetan progeny of the union. The Tibetan
incarnational lamas, as Bodhisattva representatives on earth, substitute
for the divine king. However, while the Ghale legend establishes a sub-
stance-code hierarchy defining the Ghale clan as being of a different, divine
substance, the lama's story begins to erode clan differences, to incorporate
all Tibetans into an imaginary domain of "inside ones" (nang-pa), the
Tibetan term for Buddhist.

From there the narrative continues with the story of the coming of Padmasambhava to eighth-century Tibet to fully establish Buddhism, the story
of Milarepa's defeat of the Bonpo on Mount Tise (Kailash) in the twelfth
century and Milarepa's visit to this region of Nepal, and, finally, the
sequence of Tibetan lamas from the mid-nineteenth century onward, who
came to establish the dharma in Gyasumdo.

In narrating the original story, the lamas point out that the significance of incarnational penetration into the monkey domain was to bring
up a special people, who would have the mind of the Bodhisattva (byang
chub sems-dpa'), so that the dharma would be spread. All Tibetans can
thus define themselves as having the same ancestor-ancestress, and a
temperament that is "compassionate from the monkey Bodhisattva father
and quick to anger from the rock demoness mother." The lamas add that
"compassion should prevent Tibetans from performing animal sacrifices
like the Rongpa [the Gurungs] do."[5]

Tambiah (1976) has argued that when the past is used merely as a foundation for the present, it becomes a "Malinowskian charter," a handmaid
of authority seeking to conserve the present. The Ghale's shamanic legend
does serve such a function, but it is far more than this. As an ideal of cosmic

5. *Rong-pa*, meaning "valley people," is used to define all non-Tibetans in Gyasumdo. The
term originated in Tibet before immigration when they were still viewing lower-altitude
peoples in Nepal as non-Tibetan valley dwellers.

harmony, it expresses Bakhtin's ancient matrix, but one that is incorporated into a first hierarchy, legitimated by the epic hero. It masks the fact that the present is contested, by placing its meaning in a distant, uncontested past. Even though the story recognizes a competitor, the powerful Lama of Nar, he is mainly a magical opponent rather than an ideological one. Hence, "the epic hero . . . does not have a particular ideology that functions as one ideology among other possible ideologies" (Bakhtin 1981:334).

The Tibetan Buddhist narrative is also a monologic genre, but one that is ideological, drawing a boundary that evolves from the past, yet carrying an idea that is contestable. The narrative uses a series of closures: the Tibetan people (*bod-pa*) and in particular the religious specialists (*chos-pa*) become chosen or sealed off from the rest of the samsaric world as "carriers of the doctrine," the process culminating in the lama trainee's monastic retreat. The sense of closure within a mental boundary, missing in the Ghale's shamanic narrative, builds the shielded identity that can posit an individual ethic of pure intent. It is a boundary that is consciously chosen, reflexively directed to the future. As Bakhtin observes,

> As soon as a critical interanimation began to occur in the consciousness of [the] peasant . . . the ideological systems and approaches to the world that were indissolubly connected with these languages contradicted each other and in no way could live in peace and quiet with one another — then the inviolability and predetermined quality of these languages came to an end, and the necessity of actively choosing one's orientation among them began. (Bakhtin 1981:296)

The Ghale clan's narrative is told by the shaman as an "exemplary model" (G. *pe*). Here, a cosmic harmony is restored yearly by shamanic sacrifices, without which everyone would suffer affliction and poverty. The shaman's journeys mediate between the three levels of this cosmos, but the Ghale lords have appropriated the model by including their image of divine kingship as the mediation. The Ghale ancestral spirit originates from the upper world, establishes kingship in the human world, and enters into a marriage alliance with beings of the underworld. The Ghale clan substance is thus fundamentally different from the substance of those whose origins are in the earth or the underworld. His ancestral spirit protects, but also threatens retributional punishment if the ritual sacrifices are not performed.

The Ghale model does not provide a doctrine of extrication that would allow anyone to escape the cycles of interindebtedness. In contrast, the Tibetan lama initiates a Buddhist model of retribution: accumulation of merit or demerit as a moral career. Individual karma posits a social hierarchy that appears as a ladder of liberation (*thar-pa*). The shamanic, cosmic hierarchy is thus challenged historically by the alternative, Buddhist hierarchy in which individuals at the top are more meritorious than those at the bottom.

The two narratives are thus different historical layers, emerging as a dialogue between opposed models of hierarchy and retribution. The identity promoted by the lama comes "after" and argues against the original matrix. It becomes conceivable when time is experienced in separate individuated sequences that break free of the "base" cycles of reciprocity. The "contending memories" representing the two hierarchies are thus more than hegemonic charters: they are arguments for alternative ways of experiencing time.

Hierarchy of Liberation

In the canonical texts of Tibetan Buddhism, bad deeds (*las ngen*) are causes (*rgyu*) that bring eventual fruition (*'bras*) in each individual. In Tshap village this scheme is laid out for all to see in the Wheel of Life (*srid-pa'i khor-lo*) painted on the temple wall. The six kinds of rebirth destiny on the wheel are determined, one is reminded, by harmful motivations, particularly those of anger, greed, and ignorance pictured as the snake, the cock, and the pig shown in the middle. The rich images of reward and punishment on the wheel are retribution warnings that urge the villagers into a path of merit making.

Tibetan villagers thus view social-economic inequalities among themselves as signs of past deeds coming into fruition. This is interwoven, however, with an older Tibetan hierarchy of clan substances. Each rebirth places one in a clan having genetic qualities that reflect one's moral career at the time of birth. In Gyasumdo the Tibetan clan, called Gyuba (*brgyud-pa*), fosters the notion of a founding apical ancestor, often thought to have been an incarnate lama. A variety of sources have inspired these Gyuba names, such as *Lam-shag* ("path breaker"), *rDor-shong lha gi btsan-mo* ("goddess of the Vajra mountain ridge"), *bLon rig-pa spyang* ("clever minister").[6]

6. Two clans in Tshap village have names they have picked up inside Nepal since immigrating from Tibet. *Bista,* for instance, is a name used by a family that has migrated from Muktinath, but they say their real Gyuba name is *Sras-po,* a Tibetan term for "divine son." The name *Lama* is also used as a last name by many families in Gyasumdo even though they have their Gyuba name as well. *Lama* is a name to use in Nepal to signify ethnic allegiance to Tibetan Lamaism, but it has no Gyuba meaning.

The established landowning families intermarry and regard one another as having high status. They have similar "mouths," implying common substance and mental disposition, allowing them to share food from the same plate. These clans refuse intermarriage with recent Tibetan families "having no clan names," since new arrivals might be one of the three traditional polluted castes of Tibet: the *shen-pa* ("butcher"), the *mgar-ra* ("blacksmith"), and *yar-wa* ("beggars or scavengers"). During the research period, the son of a high family ran off to Kathmandu with a woman of low birth. When he returned, he had to take the ten-day pilgrimage to Muktinath and wash his mouth with the spring water (*chu mig*) as a purification, before he could "join mouths eating" (*kha yum zas*) with others of his status.

The lamas weave the Buddhist model of karma into this older hierarchy of clan substance. They place the Gompa itself and its full-time members, the *chos-pa,* at the top of the hierarchy of liberation on the basis of the lamas' texts, which define five "lineage types" (*rigs*)[7] into which the transmigrating consciousness may be born. Those who become *chos-pa* ("religious ones") are assumed to have done so from a psychological disposition inherited through good lineage membership.

The clan substance code thus overlaps with the liberation code. In Tshap village, Lama Dorje explains it as follows: "The top *rigs* give birth to persons of 'religious mind' (*chos kyi sems-pa*), the bottom *rigs,* such as blacksmiths and butchers, give birth to persons of 'sinful mind' (*sdig-pa'i sems-pa*)." Birth into an evil vocational role results from one's karmicly inherited mental disposition (*bag-chags*) to do such evil deeds in the first place: "Have you ever noticed how they love to cut up the animal, while we cannot stand to even look!"

Intermarriage between high and low lineages is thus viewed as a confusion of opposed mentalities: "If these *rigs* intermarry," the lama asks, "then what becomes of their child's mind? Is it religious? Or sinful? The result is a child of divided mind (*sems-pa gnyis*)." The concern is to distinguish and keep separate those who are directed toward a higher destiny from those who move only in a circle or spiral downward, the hierarchy repre-

7. Royalty (*rgyal-rigs*) and priestly (*bram-ze-rigs*) lineages are placed at the top, then come nobility (*rje-rigs*), common citizens (*dmans-rigs*), and the lowest groups (*gdol-pa'i rigs*). The lamas assume that the priestly category refers to lineages of married lamas. It is thought that Gyasumdo Tibetans are for the most part commoners or better, noting that some of their clan names imply noble birth (i.e., *sras-po*), but the claim is hard to validate. All polluted castes in Nepal, whether defined by the Tibetan or Hindu systems, are assumed to belong to the *gdol-pa'i rigs*.

senting a pyramid of degrees of extrication from a polluted base.

A hierarchy legitimated by individual karma can in theory break free from its former aristocratic entanglement. Among the Tibetan laity of Tshap village, however, "karmic progress" is culturally plausible in terms of an interpenetration of two discourses, the one hidden within the other: the "signs" of hierarchy constructed by individual merit are interwoven with clan substances that are predicated on an older vision of cosmic hierarchy, that is still projected by the Ghale aristocracy and their shamans on the other side of the river. The Tibetan narrative thus expresses a hybrid construction in which the former model continues as a trace in the latter one, the emphasis of interpretation being often left undecided in Tibetan discourse.

The interweaving of substance and liberation codes also includes a hierarchy of male over female. Tibetan women have independence of mind and relative autonomy (Aziz 1978), but in Gyasumdo they nevertheless view themselves as oppressed by what they call their "cooking stove births" (za-ma'i mi-lus). My tape recordings of statements made by the most articulate women of the village were often ironic diatribes complaining of male arrogance but finding no solution other than becoming a male in the next life.

Female birth is thought to be a sign of having committed more evil deeds (las ngen) in previous lives than did the males of the same lineage. In the death rite, lamas can be heard to urge the deceased to at least gain a "male rebirth" (pho gi mi-lus). Hence the laity regard a male birth itself as one level of thar-pa (liberation), women being regarded as more embedded in samsara than are men: "Men have more power, they are autonomous, they can easily travel, they are not stuck in the house at the stove like women."

The rich/poor distinction also signifies degrees of liberation, a meager birth assumed to have been deserved by one's past evil deeds. Tibetan villagers would often comment on how the poor haven't the wealth needed for merit actions and lack the leisure time required to develop their knowledge. The poor "can't even take time off to go on pilgrimage or to learn something from the lamas." The Nepali coolies coming up the trails carrying loads epitomize this condition: "They see only the trail, nothing else."

The leisure image is crucial for epitomizing the top of the liberation hierarchy. Lamas, monks, and nuns living in the Gompa compound are assumed to be enjoying a life of leisured learning, while the laity as a whole think of themselves as caught in the samsaric condition of work and distractions, defined as a trap, "like a fly caught in a flask of water trying to escape." My landlady Nyima Drolma often lectured her son Tashi on this distinction. He had entered lama training, but was thinking of dropping out and returning to lay life. "If you stay in the Gompa I'll make sure you are provided with all you need," she kept saying. "You'll never have to work again the rest of your life."

The term *thar-pa* ("liberation") should in theory refer only to nirvana itself, the lamas point out, "or at least it should mean reaching a Buddha field where enlightenment training can proceed without further suffering." But as was shown earlier, it is a contextually sensitive term with meanings that are not finalized, even in the minds of the Gyasumdo lamas. Various contexts of *thar-pa* discourse overlap, each informing the others, and further contaminated by traces of past use. The definition of *thar-pa,* even in its Buddhist versions, continues to emerge as a dialogic process.

"I cannot see the Buddha field. Maybe it is found only in the lama texts. So I prefer a better rebirth," asserted a Tibetan layman of low clan status.

HEGEMONY AND MEMORY: LAMA DUWANG TENDZIN

In the minds of most Tibetans, the merit hierarchy of karma and the cosmic hierarchy of the Gurung shamans are at least theoretically opposed, since their lamas have drawn a textual, "Buddhist" boundary between themselves and the shamanic regime. Since the lama's karma doctrine has developed as a critique of that regime, the Ghale clan origin legend and the lama's Tibetan legend have become opposed collective memories, each supporting an alternative model of retribution and hierarchy.

Foucault (1975) has noted how memory plays a role in hegemonic struggle: if one controls the content of a people's memory one controls their dynamism. In Gyasumdo there is a memory clash with regard to Lama Duwang Tendzin, the "first lama" of the region. Tibetans recall that he inaugurated opposition to the power of the Ghale lords over a century ago. It was a time "not seen by anyone alive today," when residues of the "good era" (*bskal-pa bzang-po*) were still present and great lamas had extraordinary capacities.

The legend of Lama Duwang Tendzin[8] is told and retold by the elders of the Tibetan villages of Tshap and Tshad-med, since he lived in a cave one can see today at Kota, half way between these two villages. Stories told about him appear to prove his power over each of the elements of nature. His magical flights reveal his power over air, and he is said to have hidden his texts that give instructions on flying high up in the cliff overlooking his cave.

8. The Tibetan spelling of Duwang Tendzin is 'Dus-dbang bsTan-'dzin.

His power over water appears in stories about his crossing the Marsyandi river riding on a goat skin, and his cursing the river to make all the
fish jump out in order to stop the people from the sin of catching them.⁹
Lama Duwang Tendzin's power over fire is signified by the huge boulders
lying on the trail in Tshad-med village on which *tser-ma* nettles are growing. While eating the nettles, the lama had hurled them as a fireball against
an enemy sorcerer, bringing down the boulders from the cliff overhead.

Lama Duwang Tendzin's power over earth forms the principal legend
told by Tibetans of Tshap village, since it was this village that was
destroyed by the landslide said to have been brought down by this great
lama's curse. The trauma still reverberates today and marks the first
Tibetan challenge to the power of the local Ghale lords that had ruled
over them. The best narrator of the story is Dawa Drolma, whose great-
grandmother was a principal actor in the episode more than a hundred
years before:

> When my great-grandmother was young, she was sitting here
> beside the hearth where I am now in this very house. Lama Duwang
> Tendzin came in and sat there at the head of the hearth. Then the
> Ghale lord, the great-grandfather of the present Ghale from Tapje,
> came into the house. He saw the lama at the head of the hearth,
> sitting there in his ragged clothes. The Ghale demanded that the
> lama move down so he himself could sit at the head of the hearth.
> Lama Duwang Tendzin refused to give place, so the Ghale said:
> "How can a yogi dressed in rags sit above me, a Ghale lord!" He
> struck the lama and went out.
>
> Lama Duwang Tendzin bore the insult in silence, and stayed for
> three days. As he left, he turned to my great-grandmother and said,
> "Because of your hospitality, your house will be spared." Then he
> left and made a *zor torma* ["weapon effigy"] out of dough. He
> threw the *zor torma* against the hill. A huge landslide came down
> and covered the whole village. Only this house was not destroyed.

Today, two landmarks remind the villagers of Tshap of that event. One
is Dawa Drolma's house, which survived; the other is a stupa (*mchod-
rten*) into which has been inserted a piece of cloth from Lama Duwang
Tendzin's robe as a relic to protect the village from further landslides.¹⁰
Tibetan lay persons admit they are ambivalent about the morals of a lama
who was a champion of their tradition and yet also destroyed their village.

9. The fish then all jumped out, the marks where some landed still seen on a rock near
the trail. Catching fish to eat is sinful because the fish themselves have already killed (flies,
worms, etc.). One eats the sin [*sdig-pa*] of the fish as well.

10. Two more landslides have occurred, however. Although this stupa itself has not been
destroyed by them, numerous homes in the village have been destroyed by the more
recent landslides.

Why did the great lama send the landslide down on the Tibetans of Tshap, when it was the visiting Ghale lord who had insulted him? "We deserved it," said Dawa Drolma, shaking her head after telling the story. "We Tibetans didn't really obey the lama either."

The ambivalence is not surprising. This flying lama from the legendary past who seems "half shamanic" had employed a mode of punishment that appears transitional between the retribution model of the shamans and the karmic retribution taught by lamas today. Lama Duwang Tendzin is for Bakhtin (1981:360) a hybrid image straddling two eras. He used magical power (*mthu*) over the elements to "retaliate" in the same manner that the ancestral spirits in the shamanic tradition return to punish their descendants in Gyasumdo. Further, his period, the "good era," is time-distanced, so that like the epic hero, it was not his "truth" that was contested but only his power. No one can recall anything he may have said.

In Benjamin's (1969:256) terms, this historical image "flares up" as an event marking a critical turning point between eras. For Tibetans today, the great lama's curse was directed against the Ghale lords who had dominated them after they migrated from Tibet into Gyasumdo. Narrators view the incident as proof of Lamaist superiority and of their first opposition to the Ghale lord's authority in the region, adding that the curse still returns today to punish those who oppose the dharma of the lamas.[11]

The present Ghale nobility, however, totally reject the Tibetan version of the legend. In their view the great flying lama supported rather than subverted Ghale authority. After I had tape-recorded the Tibetan version, which is the best-known "historical" legend among the villagers of Tshap, I played the tape in the presence of the Ghale leader when he was visiting a Tibetan home in Tshap village. When the tape arrived at the incident in which his own great-grandfather had insulted and struck the lama, the Ghale interrupted and loudly asserted that it was not so, that in fact the Ghale nobility at that time had a ritual friendship with the flying lama. The tape had to be turned off. The Ghale leader talked into the night about that lama's loyalty to his forefathers of the past. The Tibetans in the house sat in embarrassed silence.

LEGEND OF THE LAMA-BONPO CONTEST

My first project in collecting data on lama-shaman dialogue in Gyasumdo was to elicit comment on the famed legend of the twelfth-century contest

---

11. The legend replicates to a degree a prototypical act of Padmasambhava in Tibet during the eighth century when he demanded that king Khri srong lde btsan submit to him. He forced the king to prostrate to him when he summoned lightning and brought down boulders and turned the sky red, according to one chronicle (Ekvall 1964:208).

between the Tibetan lama Milarepa and the Bonpo Naro Bon Chung at the site of Mount Tise (Kailash) in Tibet. The legend had already been found to be prevalent among highland peoples in Nepal that have been influenced by Lamaism,[12] and in Gyasumdo both Tibetan and Gurung communities knew the legend well. The Ghyabrē and Paju shamans unhesitatingly identify themselves with the Tibetan Bonpo (practitioners of the Bon religion) who "lost the contest" to Milarepa. They and the Tibetan lamas agree on the main kernel of the story, which I summarize here from taped interviews:

> Milarepa went with his disciples to Mount Tise. He met a Bonpo who challenged him to a contest of magical power to see which of them should control the mountain. After a few preliminary contests of flying over the lake in which they were both equal, they decided to see who could reach the top of Mount Tise first on the morning of the next day.
>
> Early in the morning the Bonpo, riding his drum, flew up the slope of the mountain. Milarepa's disciple awoke his master and pointed to the Bonpo nearing the top. At that moment a ray of sunlight broke over the top of the mountain and beamed down into the window of the hut. Milarepa instantly rode the sunbeam to the top of Mount Tise, arriving ahead of the Bonpo.
>
> Defeated, the Bonpo fell back, dropping his drum which rolled down the mountain slope and split in half. To this day, the drum of the Bonpo has only one side, while the drum of the lama still has two sides.

Apart from this core of the legend, which is agreed on, there is a sharp divergence between the interpretation of the lamas, who tell the story as quoted here, and that of the Ghyabrē and Paju shamans, who make additions. For Tibetans the story proves the superiority of the lama. In the versions of the Gurung shamans there are two changes. First, they elaborate on the "preliminary contests" prior to the climb of Mount Tise. The Bonpo had, after all, "proved equal" to the lama in the magical competition over the lake (Manasarowar), since both contestants had "jumped over it."[13] Second, after the Bonpo was defeated on Mount Tise

12. The legend has been found among southwestern Gurungs (Pignède 1966), Tamangs (Holmberg 1980), Sherpas (Oppitz 1968), and Thakalis (Vinding and Gauchan 1977), as well as among Tibetans in general.
13. The written Tibetan Buddhist version of the legend found in *The Hundred Thousand Songs of Milarepa* (Chang 1962) can be used for comparison. It contains a number of preliminary contests, but in all of them Milarepa proves to be superior. The lama covers the whole lake with his body, the Bonpo can only straddle it. The lama throws a boulder

and dropped his drum, the version given by the Paju shaman adds the following:

> The Paju [Bonpo] was angry that he had lost the contest. In despair
> the Paju took all of his written texts and threw them into a fire,
> where they burned to ashes. Then he heard the voice of a god
> above: "Although you have destroyed your books you must do your
> rituals by remembering the knowledge that your books contained."
> The Paju ate the ashes of the burned texts and thus swallowed the
> knowledge. To this day, the lama has to read his texts, but the Paju
> chants his learning from memory.

The Paju knows that the lamas of Gyasumdo ridicule the Pajus for having no written texts. Hence when the legend is told in Gyasumdo, it comments on a present contest, as it were, an ongoing dialogue between rival practitioners. This becomes more obvious as the Paju shaman interprets his own version.

"How can the lamas perform exorcisms in the dark?" he asks. "Everyone knows that you must call your tutelary deity when it is dark, but the lamas can't even read their texts without light!" And what if the lama tries to chant in the dark? "Why, the guardian deity of the Paju might come and steal the lama's texts and run away," chuckles the Paju, delighting in the image of the lama whose knowledge evaporates without his books.

The Paju's discourse is double voiced. He is willing to tell the story of his own "defeat" by lamas. But the Bonpo and the lama in his version were initially "equal" in magical capacity. Only when the Bonpo is tricked by the lama's ride on the sunbeam, does the lama become superior, that is, in textual knowledge. On the other hand, the Paju retains another kind of superiority: "internal" memory from the swallowed ashes.[14] This "internality" of the Paju's knowledge challenges the lama's definition of Buddhists as the "internal ones" (*nang-pa*) and shamanic ritual practice as external (*phyi*). "After all," adds the Paju, "when knowledge is written down it loses its power because anyone can read it," thus explaining why, in his view, the lamas have lost their ancient magical powers and the Paju shamans have not.

---

through the air twice the size that the Bonpo can throw. Milarepa can build a stone wall of his hut by magic, but the Bonpo cannot lift the stone to make the roof, etc.

14. At this point my Tibetan aide Phurbu, who is himself not literate and lives among Gurung people so that he has become sympathetic with the shamanic viewpoint said: "Perhaps he means it is like the knowledge of the Tibetan laity who sing their 'knowledge' in the songs they have learned by heart."

Another Paju from Rangu village tells the legend of the contest in a
similar way, but adds a further appendix to show that the lama and the
Bonpo did not after all become unequal, but rather became differentiated
only in function:

> Originally the lama, the Ghyabrē, and the Paju were all equal
> brothers. Having the same mother and father, they all had texts.
> After the contest on Mount Tise, however, they decided to have
> different specializations. The lama chose to perform rites of fortune
> expansion [gyang khug]. The Ghyabrē chose to do the death rite
> and deliver the soul to the land of the dead. The Paju decided to
> recall the wandering soul of the living and to expel demons, dealing
> with rites concerned with the earth and the underworld.

The Rangu Paju's appendix not only gives these specializations equal
status, he even awards the prestigious death cult to the Ghyabrē shaman
rather than to the lama, reversing the expected allocation of pragmatic
rites to the shaman and rites of afterlife transcendence to the lamas.[15] Here
the Paju is well aware that he is countering an argument that the Gyasumdo
lamas present to Gurung villagers, that "the Gurung funeral gives no merit
to the deceased's consciousness" so that it "does not find the path." Such
intrusion by the lama into the shamanic domain was not, in the Rangu
Paju's view, the original agreement. If some of the wealthier Gurung families now call the Tibetan lama after the Ghyabrē's death rite is finished
it is "only for prestige."

The two Paju versions of the Milarepa contest legend demonstrate the
rivalry that underlies lama-shaman dialogue in Gyasumdo. The lamas
assume that the story proves that they stand at the apex of a vertical hierarchy of ritual knowledge. The Pajus prefer to speak of a system of knowledge specializations, with collaboration along a horizontal plane. The
shamans thus appeal to a memory: that of an initial equality in magical
capacities.[16] The Paju in Rangu refers to a time in this region of Nepal
when "lamas and Pajus competed" to demonstrate their magical capacities,
just as they did in the Milarepa contest legend. There was in Nepal, they
claim, a "competition place" in Lubra (T. klu-braġ, a Bonpo monastic
center near Muktinath), where the forefathers of the Pajus and Ghyabrēs

15. The allocation of "pragmatic" healing rites to the shamanic practitioner is more typical
    of the Tamang, whose Tamang Buddhist lamas specialize in the death cult while the
    Lambu and the Bombo (Holmberg 1984) specialize in exorcisms and recalling the wander-
    ing soul. Among northern Gurungs, however, the Ghyabrē and Paju still regard Lamaist
    inroads into the Gurung funeral as an intrusion.
16. A lama's knowledge of "mantras" (sngags) is equated with a capacity for "sorcery" (mthu).

had once been trained after migrating into Nepal from Tibet.[17] For these Gurung shamans, Lubra is an image of past equality in magical contests with lamas.

In describing Lubra, the Paju paused to demonstrate for me the kind of contest held between practitioners of that time. He constructed a small canopy of paper stretched out over the fireplace, held up by sticks stuck into the ground on each side. Then with great concentration he whispered mantras and blew the incantations into the paper. "If the mantras are powerful enough, the paper cannot burn," he said, lighting the fire. "Each Paju, seated around the fire would take a turn to see whose mantras could stop the paper from burning." Unfortunately, his mantra for the demonstration was not powerful enough that day—the fire rose higher and burned the paper to a crisp. But he added, "These days, if a lama were to compete with us like this the Paju would surely win."

The Paju's memory of the past was supported by an additional legend. It refers to a time when his Paju forefathers and the lamas both had extraordinary magical capacities which they stole from one another. Chanted during one of his exorcisms, the legend describes competition between brother and sister Paju shamans of the past, and portrays how the girl Paju steals the corpse-raising secret from the lamas in order to raise her dead brother.

> The sister passed through the eye of a needle, but when the brother tried he got stuck half way through and died. The girl cut open her dead brother's body, tore out the heart, and hung it up in a basket. She sent her mind into a cat's body. The cat seized the heart and ate it. Then her mind entered into a vulture, which flew north [to Tibet]. The vulture looked down and saw nine lamas making the medicine used for raising corpses [*ro langs*]. The vulture swooped down, seized the medicine, and flew back home. Becoming herself again the girl Paju applied the medicine to her brother's corpse. He came to life, and they both used the new knowledge.

The legend portrays a magical tradition shared in the past in a lama-Paju rivalry. Here it is the *ro langs* ("corpse raising") technique that is stolen. People in Gyasumdo say the technique is no longer practiced, but

17. Both in the tradition and in the legends of the Ghyabrē and Paju, Lubra was a past training ground. Even if this were true, it is no longer the case, according to Charles Ramble (personal communication) who studied the Bonpos in Lubra during 1981–83. The Bonpos of Lubra appear to have repudiated all associations they might have had with Nepali shamans, identifying themselves fully with reformed Bon and becoming ritually almost identical to Nyingma Lamaism.

there is evidence that it was thought to be practiced at one time at least in Gurung villages. Informants point out that the low door frames on the oldest homes were made that way to prevent *ro langs* zombies from entering (they cannot bend over).

For the Paju, such narratives recall a time when lamas had magical capacities similar to those which the shamans still have in diminished form. Lama Duwang Tendzin, who brought down the landslide, is said to have employed the supernatural power which Tibetans call *mthu*. The Paju shaman claims that while he himself cannot match this today, landslide sorcery was practiced by his recent forefathers. The Paju collects feces of a human, a dog, a cow, and a pig and puts them into the horn of a bull. He covers this mixture with copper coins. Then he digs a hole and buries the horn along with a Paju's trident and the drawings of *btsan* and *bdud* demons. Over the covered hole he places a dough effigy of his tutelary deity and chants an incantation, starting a severe downpour of rain and hail. This in turn brings down the landslide that covers the houses of one's enemies.

The Gurung shamans thus remember a past in Gyasumdo with a very different significance from that of the narrative told by the Tibetan lamas today. The lamas' story may begin with magical power, as did the story of Lama Duwang Tendzin's landslide, but the narrative of Lamaism in the region becomes one of increasing textual orthodoxy as the Nyingma lamas become different from and "superior" to the Gurung shamans. In the lamas' story, even the lamas of Nar, who had once been "little better than the Bonpo," gradually become more orthodox and rid themselves of their earlier compromises. In the most recent episode of this narrative, sacred lama refugees fleeing from Tibet during the 1960s passed through Gyasumdo and gave impetus to a trend of Buddhist reform and monasticism among the local lamas.

In this narrative of progress there is a gradual decline of the *mthu* ("supernatural powers") of the "first lamas" (*bla-ma dang-po*). The memory, however, includes a transitional period in Gyasumdo, during which progress in Buddhist ethics and orthodoxy is still interwoven with magical powers used to defeat the local shamans. A few decades ago, a lama called Gelong Nyompa ("crazy monk") was a prototype of that period. The name refers to his constant drunkenness and womanizing, suggesting the hybrid that he was: a married monk.

All of the elderly in Tshap village remember him. He came to Gyasumdo after leaving Tibet as a celibate lama, but the Tibetans of Tshap enticed him to settle in their village by offering him a wife, stealing a girl for him by force from one of the recent Tibetan immigrant families. Ibi

Lhamo, the bride who was stolen at the time and who is now an aging widow, still recalls the shock of that night, when she was seized from her parents' house in a neighboring village, "carried naked into the night," and taken to Tshap where she then became the wife of Gelong Nyompa.

Gelong Nyompa is now passed away, but Ibi Lhamo has described for me in many hours of taped interviews his heroic efforts to institutionalize the Tibetan ritual cycle in Tshap village. He established the Nyungne (*smyung-gnas*), the yearly fast of atonement in which the laity participate, and he founded the system of rotating lay stewardship (*gnyer-ba*), in which each household takes its turn in organizing communal festivals and rituals at the Gompa.

Ibi Lhamo and other lay persons insist that despite his ethical laxities Gelong Nyompa had "more knowledge" than current lamas because he could perform extraordinary rites that present lamas cannot match. He could stop a thief on the trail through mental concentration, bring or stop rain, make others sick through his *mthu,* etc. In her recollections, Ibi Lhamo describes magical conflicts that Gelong Nyompa had with the Paju of Rangu. Each would afflict the other with his powers:

> The Paju used to send sorcery at Gelong Nyompa and make him sick. But the lama always knew who had sent it, and he would just return the harm to the Paju without saying any more about it. One time when the lama was doing a Jinsek [*sbyin-rseg,* "fire offering"], the Paju sent sorcery into his body. The lama knew what had happened. He kept meditating on his tutelary deity, chanting, and he recovered. Then he returned it, sending *mthu* against the Paju. The Paju got sick and came to the lama and cried, "What have you done to me!"
>
> Gelong Nyompa replied: "You got sick from your own deed!" Then the Paju knew that the lama knew what he had done, and prostrated before him, begging him to heal him.

Although Ibi Lhamo's description is a personal account that cannot be substantiated, it portrays a fundamental Tibetan model similar to the lama-bonpo contest of Milarepa: the lama initially shares the same magical tradition as the Paju shaman, but uses it to subdue the shaman. In the end the lama claims both ethical and textual superiority. This becomes clear toward the end of Ibi Lhamo's account:

> Gelong Nyompa had agreed to let the Paju help him perform the *dge-ba* [Tibetan funeral rite]. During the rite, Gelong Nyompa began to ridicule the Paju. He handed the Paju his text and said, "Read it!" The Paju had to admit that he could not, because he was

not a lama, and they began to argue. Later they agreed that the
lama would only do the lama part and the Paju would only do the
Paju part. They became friends again, but the Paju would kill a
chicken during his curing rites. Gelong Nyompa would say to him,
"Don't do the red offering! You are a killer!" Thus they could not
do exorcisms together because the Paju would always kill a chicken.

One lama is left in Gyasumdo who represents the same transitional
period. He is regarded as a *sngags-pa,* a "mantric exorcist," and lives
among Gurungs in the village of Rangu. Tibetans regard him as ethically
compromised because he does not object to the Paju shaman killing a
chicken "just outside the door" of the house in which he performs Buddhist
rituals. As the last local lama assumed to have *mthu,* he is regarded with
awe, and Tibetans fear his retributional anger: "You have to stay on his
good side or he will harm you. You say, *'La so! la so!'* when you meet
the Rangu lama."

This description of opposed narrative memories in Gyasumdo leads us
back to our original comparison. The shamanic cosmic hierarchy promoted
by the Ghale nobility and the karmic liberation hierarchy of the Tibetans
compete on the two sides of the river. The Tibetans themselves, however,
retain a hybrid image that incorporates both shamanic and Buddhist
models of retribution in their narrative memory. In the legend of Lama
Duwang Tendzin the Tibetan laity recall the older mode of reciprocal retribution, expressing as well a nostalgia for a past when lamas had shamanlike powers. The Gurung shaman's "harmony" requires collaboration
between such powerful practitioners. The earlier domination by the Ghale
must have maintained that collaboration as long as possible.

It is clear, however, that the lamas have deliberately seized on these
memories in a different manner, to construct their alternative scheme. Padmasambhava and Milarepa had defeated the Bonpo with shamanlike
powers, just as Lama Duwang Tendzin's magical powers "defeated" the
Ghale lords. But in the hands of the lamas, these recollections empower
the model of karmic retribution. By promoting a merit hierarchy that leads
toward liberation, they extricate themselves and their laity from their earlier
collaborations. In place of a cosmic scheme of high or low birth, the lamas
offer a democratic invitation to enter what Bakhtin views as the second
cultural layer: the "interior time" of the "individual life-sequence."

As later chapters will show, the Gurungs and some of the shamans
are gradually being influenced by the Lamaist ethic. The Tibetans themselves, however, cannot escape the intertextuality of a folk tradition that
is evolving between the two communities. They are still half-convinced

of the older cosmic hierarchy, while being committed to the promise of individual liberation. Their ambivalence extends to their own legendary figures whose hybrid images remain dialogical, pulling in both directions.

Caught in the middle, the Tibetan laity are making up their minds about a shamanic past that still tempts them. That temptation in its most anti-Buddhist form is displayed every spring when the red offering sacrifice is enacted in the village of Tapje, reminding everyone that Lamaism has not triumphed here as it had in Tibet. The significance of this shamanic drama must now be explicated.

Part II

Rituals of Life

Chapter Three

Shamanic Sacrifice and Buddhist Renunciation

As TIBETANS CAME DOWN from the north into Nepal and settled in Tshap village, they saw that across the Marsyandi river, the Gurung stronghold of Tapje was far more than a political center. It was a cultural layer from the past, still full of vitality on the Tibetan periphery that had not been subordinated to Lamaist hegemony. The extraordinary rite of shamanic sacrifice they encountered then is still enacted today. As Tibetan Buddhists they deem ritual killing, the "red offering," to be the highest form of transgression. Today they do not take part, but during the first half of this century they could not escape being implicated, because the Ghale lords of Tapje, backed by the persuasive arguments of the Gurung shamans, required them to participate.

In the folk layer of both communities, everyone "knows" that to bring the spring rains that nourish the cultivation cycles of wheat, buckwheat, barley, maize, potatoes, and beans, first-fruit offerings must be given to the spirit agents that guard the land and own the underworld. In the shamanic system, two historical layers pertaining to fertility are activated: one has agriculture as the immediate focus; the other has as its focus an older hunting world, which is disappearing but which remains vital in the minds of the Gurung shamans.

In the following pages I will examine the ritual and legendary significance of the Ghyabrē shaman's spring sacrifice. It is the matrix which the Tibetan lamas must repudiate, but which they also transmute into the Tibetan Buddhist alternative. That alternative will be introduced by comparing the shamanic sacrifice to the renunciatory cave of Milarepa, a Tibetan pilgrimage center. I will attempt to show how the Lamaist intrusion into this region has penetrated the Gurung shaman's ritual discourse, but also how that discourse, in turn, triggers an internal dialogue in the Gyasumdo Tibetans.

Each spring in the Gurung community of Tapje the harvest celebration culminates in the sacrifice of a deer. A wild deer is caught alive in the wilderness by a male cult of "hunters" and returned to the village. After the Ghyabrē shamans perform a series of rites, they take the deer down to the sacred grove where they cut open the deer and tear out its heart, offering it to both the underworld and to the ancestral deity of the Ghale nobility.

Ritual use of a deer in relation to the hunting cult is well known in Siberian shamanism. The Russian ethnographer Jochelson (1926:210–11), reporting on Yukaghir shamans of the 1890s, noted that after the shaman enticed a deer's spirit from the "owner of the earth," a real deer would be found by a hunting party. If the shaman stole the deer from the earth owner, however, the result would be misfortune and infertility. Anisimov (1963), reporting on the Siberian Evenki, describes a "spring rite of renewal" in which hunters would "chase" a deer into the upper world. After the deer is shot, it "miraculously comes to life again, and hence all of nature comes to life again." In Gyasumdo, both deer and bird are central legendary motifs for the Gurung shamans and, as in the Siberian tradition (Jankovics 1984:155–60), the Gurung shaman's drum is also made from the skin of the deer and from the tree which connects upper and lower worlds, the bird coming down from the branches in the upper world.

The Ghyabrē shaman calls the Ghale ancestral deity to whom the deer is given "Drong," which is also the Tibetan term for "wild yak" (T. 'brong). Deer and yak may have been interchangeable among early nomadic carriers of inner Asian shamanism. The mode in which the Gurung shamans tear out the heart of the deer is strikingly similar to a practice of animal sacrifice in western Tibet that has persisted well into the twentieth century.[1] Robert Paul (1982:273–86) has explored the significance of the sacrificial killing of a wild yak in pre-Buddhist Tibet. The Ghyabrē shaman's equating of the wild yak with the Ghale divine ancestor supports Paul's contention that yak sacrifice seems to have been a communal incorporation of the patrilineal father, linked with royal succession.

In Tapje village the festive occasion begins when the deer is caught alive in the wild, bound and carried back into the village by the male cult who have, for the period, purified themselves by sexual abstinence. Excitement mounts to fever pitch as the struggling deer is brought. Word is sent

1. Asboe (1936:75–76) observed: "In various valleys of Western Tibet the sacrificial customs, though different in detail, are uniform in principle. The method of sacrificing animals is that of making a deep incision sufficiently large to permit the introduction of the hand, and then tearing the heart out, after which that organ is offered to the local deity."

out to surrounding villages that the deer sacrifice is about to begin. Tibetans across the river in Tshap village also receive the message, since in the past they had been expected to replicate the rite in a simpler manner on their side of the valley. The Tibetans no longer obey the Ghale in this regard, but some Tibetans own land on the Ghale side of the river and still take interest in the outcome of the rite. To maintain good relations, Tibetan households send barley to Tapje for making beer (chang) as part of the "first fruit" that is presented and then drunk by all those in attendance. No Tibetans, however, attend the deer sacrifice in the sacred grove, for that would implicate them in the sin of ritual killing.

As night falls, the main Ghyabrē and his shaman assistants gather around the ancestral altar set up in the meeting house. On the altar is the dough effigy of a bird, the god Kle-Nyima,[2] the tutelary deity of the Kle clan (Ghale); the Ghyabrē says the tutelary was obtained in Tibet before the Ghale migrated into Nepal. The deer sacrifice serves to unite with the underworld the bird coming down from the upper world. These worlds are also united by marriage between the Kle clan and the Khrō clan of the Ghale-Gurung community. The two clans as well as upper and lower worlds are united by the tree that grows up out of Khrō-nasa, the Gurung underworld. As a result of the union, rain falls from the sky, and vegetation, symbolized by the tree, sprouts from the underworld.

The Ghyabrē sings the first part of his ritual chant:

> The bird, Kle-Nyima, is the Kle [Ghale] ancestor who originated from above. He first fell down into a cloud, the region of the gods [*lha*].
> He then fell farther into midspace, the region of the *btsan*.
> Then he came down to earth, landing on a mountain peak, then on a rock cliff, and finally came down to the grass plain.
> Kle-Nyima unites with the beings of *klu* [serpent deities] of Khrō-nasa in the underworld that is beneath the earth. [The bird unites with the serpent.][3]
> The Khrō-nasa people came up from the underworld and united with the Kle people. The Kle brought rain down from the sky. The Khrō brought vegetation up from below. From above send rain from the sky, from below may vegetation grow.

2. *Kle* is the Ghale name for the Ghale clan, while the term *nyima* is the word for "sun" in Tibetan, associating the Ghale nobility with an origin in the upper world. The Tibetan name of the Ghale clan is Jowo (T. *jobo*).

3. The Ghyabrē identifies the *klu*, the serpent deities in Tibetan Bon cosmology, with the Khrō-nasa people in Gurung cosmology, even though the descriptions of these underworlds differ. This is not surprising since the Ghyabrē claims that half of the terms used in this chant are Tibetan.

The chant legend, which in Gurung terminology is called the *pe,*
meaning "model" or "example" (T. *dpe*), is recited as the Ghyabrē shamans
beat their drums, as the mode of requesting rain from the sky. They alter-
natingly beat the drums and cymbals, then chant while dancing in a circle,
now joined by the live deer which has been tied on the back of a Gurung
man who dances with the shamans, the deer struggling to get free. This
is repeated several times in the village, the entire Gurung community of
Tapje watching as night closes in.

When it is totally dark the Ghyabrē shamans, the deer, and the cult
of male helpers plunge down the steep trail toward the sacred grove in
a procession lit by torches. We come to the underworld of Drong ama
("mother yak"), which the Ghyabrē calls the "mother's house" and "Khrō-
nasa." We must enter it, give offerings, and emerge above it before reaching
the sacred tree that is said to grow out of the underworld. We take off
our shoes and the Ghyabrēs prostrate several times, chanting to the "mother
in the house":

> Open the golden lock of the north. Open the silver lock of the east,
> Open the iron lock of the south, open the copper lock of the west.
> The doors must be opened. Open the golden door, the silver door,
> the iron door, the copper door. Open the doors, we are coming to
> make the offering. Open the doors of your home.

Now the Ghyabrē shamans enter the house (a tree-covered area) and
beg forgiveness for mistakes in the rite and for offenses committed in the
past. The mother Drong ama is then offered the barley grain as the first
fruit of the harvest. Nine handfuls of grain are sprinkled over the area,
but even after the nine are removed from the basket the supply is not
depleted. "No matter how much is offered it never runs out," the Ghyabrē
observes, a sign that Drong ama blesses the harvest.

Emerging above on higher ground, we enter farther into the grove and
arrive at a huge tree. The tree has "grown up out of the underworld" we
had passed through, and its branches are occupied by Kle-Nyima the bird
tutelary, who is also identified with Drong awa, the Ghale ancestor. We
are now in the middle world, where the tree unites upper and lower worlds.

The union of above and below must be effected by the deer sacrifice.
The male cult slowly circles the tree three times, the struggling deer
included, each member bowing to the root of the tree where there pro-
trudes a branch having the appearance of a phallus, and identified as such
by cult informants. The deer is laid on the ground, and the ropes are untied.
The deer no longer struggles, but with eyes open, lies on the ground. "The
god is holding it now," the Ghyabrē says, "a good sign that the offering

is accepted." At that moment he pours water over the deer's head, "as a purification" of the sacrifice before it is offered.[4]

The cult members seize the deer, and one of them thrusts a knife into its abdomen, then plunges his hand into the hole reaching up toward the heart, which he quickly tears out of the deer's body and puts on a rock altar beneath the tree. Clanging his cymbals, the main Ghyabrē chants and watches the heart that is still pumping up and down. This is the moment of divination, for if it jumps strongly, Drong awa will bless the harvest this year. The heart beats well and long. Everyone appears satisfied.

The heart is the offering. The rest of the meat is roasted, some of it shared out among the participants in the grove, the remainder stored for later distribution to every household in the village. It is the "leftover" of the offering after the first portion is given to the deities, and the Ghyabrē compares it to the "rain that falls from the sky to nourish the soil."[5] While the meat is shared among the cult members, the Ghyabrē shamans recite in a long singing chant the origin legend of the deer sacrifice:

The legend is the "model" of how it came to be that the Ghale ancestors Drong awa and Drong ama settled in the tree grove below Tapje village. The "descent of the bird into the tree" is made homologous to the divine origin of the Ghale ancestor, born of the Tibetan woman Jomo when she swallowed the hailstone that dropped from the sky. The legend tells how the two brothers, now called by the Tibetan name Jowo, settled in Tapje village in Nepal; how the elder became the guardian deity of the village and made his home with his mother in the sacred grove.

One of the brothers, Timu, arrived first and established Tapje, becoming the king of the region by conquering the people of Nar.[6] The other brother, Drong, went farther with his mother into Gorkha (east of Gyasumdo and Lamjung). The chant names each village they arrive at as they go down the trail, most of the names identical to the village names of today. In Gorkha he married and had a daughter, but when the daughter died he decided, from grief, to return back up the trail with his mother, "to return to Tibet." Drong carries the dead daughter up the trail. It is

4. In other sacrifice contexts, such as when the Paju shaman offers a chicken, pouring water over the head of the victim is a mode of divination to see if the animal and hence the god agrees with the offering. Here, the Ghyabrē interprets the calming of the deer and the condition of the heart taken from the deer's body as the divination, the water being a removal of pollution.

5. The Ghyabrē compares the meat sharing with the Tibetan lama's distribution of *tshogs* (Skt. *prasad*) that is distributed after each Tibetan ritual, and also compares it to the lama's Chinlab (*byin-rlabs*): elements he has blessed that are distributed among the laity.

6. Details of the defeat of the Nar people have already been given in chapter two.

the same trail along which the Ghyabrē guides the soul after death, and
again each village is named in the chant. It should also be noted that it
portrays a yak leading the deceased spirit to its ancestral destiny, a tradition
similar to that of pre-Buddhist Tibet (Stein 1972, Paul 1982:282).

In the Ghyabrē's chant the funerary travelers finally arrive at Galantso,
pass through Tshap village and then Timang, and stop at Nangdo. Here
they meet the Jowo brother Timu, who has just returned from defeating
the people of Nar.[7] Timu knows his brother Drong has magical powers
that are needed for protecting Tapje village, and invites him to remain as
its guardian warrior-king. At first Drong refuses, but the chant continues:

> Then a wild deer appeared across the river. Drong saw it and said,
> "If you can catch such a deer and sacrifice it to me every year, I will
> stay. No other animal is necessary, only the wild deer."
>   They agreed, and Timu said, "If you can protect me from
> enemies and from landslides as well as from sickness and hunger,
> then I will sacrifice the deer to you." They agreed to the contract.

The Ghyabrē uses the Tibetan term g'am-rgya, "bond of agreement,"
to describe how Drong awa is taken on as the guardian of the Ghale clan,
and thus becomes the protector of the people of Tapje. It typifies the ancient
tradition of encountering a spirit which is taken on as the guardian deity
of a clan. Yearly offerings must be given, if protection rather than angry
retribution is to result. The bond of agreement cannot easily be broken.
The chanted legend continues:

> Then they had to find a place for Drong awa and Drong ama[8]
> to settle in Tapje. The Jowo (Timu) said: "Stay here in this place"
> [to the left above Tapje]. Drong awa replied, "No, a lama lives
> there, and it is a place for white offerings. Because I need red offer-
> ings [the deer sacrifice] I will not live there."
>   Then Timu offered him a place above Tapje on the right. Drong
> said, "No, I can't stay there, there are klu [serpent deities] there.
> The klu get angry if we pollute their area with red offerings."
>   Then Drong chose his own place to stay, below Tapje in the tree
> grove. But Timu warned him: "It is dangerous there. Landslides
> come there and enemies attack there." Drong replied, "I can stop
> landslides. I can stop enemies. I'll live there."

7. The legend adds that Timu had powers which he used to raise from the dead the warriors
   of Tapje who had fallen at Nar. He thus combines in himself both king and shaman.
   Drong is also a shaman ancestor since he delivers the soul of his daughter up the trail.
   In the death cult the journey goes on to arrive at the Oblē dome located one day beyond
   Tapje village.
8. The mother and wife of Drong coalesce into one female image: Drong ama.

So Drong awa and Drong ama lived in the tree grove, the tree
becoming their body.

The Ghyabrē explains that the bird tutelary that descends into the tree
can be thought of as the Drong ancestors, who, after they died, became
the protecting deities. The chant makes clear that the Ghale protector is
not congenial to the Tibetan lama who appears in the legend, and further,
serpent deities as the lama defines them are regarded as antagonistic to
the tradition that is being celebrated. Hence the meaning of the Ghale
guardian is already partially defined in the Ghyabrē's chant dialogically,
being in contention with the perspective of Tibetan lamas in Gyasumdo.

In telling and explaining the legend, the Ghyabrē feels compelled to
defend the deer sacrifice which he knows the lamas condemn. He argues
that Drong awa is "stern," using the Tibetan term *kyong-po,* and hence
there is "no choice" but to go against the lama's view on ritual killing.
Drong awa cannot be satisfied without the deer's heart. When the agreement was first made, the people of Tapje at first tried to substitute a sheep.
Then Drong awa, through the mouth of the Ghyabrē, said: " 'If you don't
give the deer as promised, everyone will become sick, wild animals will
attack the cattle, and they will die, and landslides will come.' Since then
the people of Tapje have caught a deer each year. No landslide has ever
come down into the sacred grove area as they had before then."

At this point in his exposition, the Ghyabrē pointed out to me certain
evidence of what happens if they do not please this guardian spirit. Several
years before, some of the deer meat was eaten by a dog by mistake. The
dog died immediately. It was proof that such mistakes during the performance bring punishment. "Apologies must be made immediately for ritual
errors," he added.

SACRIFICE AS REDOING THE PAST DEBT

Two kinds of offering are given during the deer sacrifice we have examined.
Initially, a first-fruit offering of grain is thrown out nine times from the
basket into the underworld "house." Later, the heart of the deer is offered
at the tree. Both of these can be shown to be a remaking of a past deed,
paying the debt owed by the first hunter. For Gurungs, mankind broke
an original primal harmony. The result is the present evil age of suffering
and death.

The image of the primal era is seen in the first marriage of alliance:
the Khrō clan from Khrō-nasa below emerged and married with the Kle
clan from above. Sociologically, the two clan groups still intermarry, but
only the Ghyabrē and the Paju can still enter Khrō-nasa in their ritual

imagination. The Ghyabrē cult can, however, reenact the past—when the break first occurred—doing right what was done wrong. Why, then, must the nine measures of grain also be given to the underworld?

The answer is found in the main legend chanted by the Paju shaman, during his rites. It concerns the Khrō-nasa underworld and the "first" shaman, a Paju named Khrō. He had originated in Khrō-nasa, but had come up with his mother to live in the human world, establishing for the first time the rites that would prevent sickness and bring abundance. Each rite was expensive, requiring offerings of nine measures of grain:

> Khrō Paju had nine apprentices. One day they complained and said, "Our teacher demands too much expense." So they reduced the offerings from nine measures of grain to one. When Khrō Paju had done the rites with nine measures, the effect of the rite would last twelve years. When the apprentices reduced it to one, the effect lasted only five or six days.
>
> Khrō saw what they had done and became angry. His mother said to him, "Don't stay here any longer!"
>
> Khrō Paju did as his mother said and they both went back to Khrō-nasa. On his way down he untied the mouths of all the area gods that caused harm, the *lha, klu, btsan,* and *bdud.* Then he cursed the people of the earth, saying: "Before, there had been abundant food, health, and long life. Now, may your crops fail, sickness come, animals and humans die, may your food not be tasty, may your clothes be shabby and look bad. May you suffer hardship."

The story does not finish at this point, even though it explains the human condition and the decay of the present era. Out of desperation, two of the Paju's former apprentices decided to call the first Paju back by going down to the underworld:

> They found the door in the earth and went down. When they arrived they saw that Khrō-nasa was different from the earth. The people were very small. They could rest their carrying loads on the dung of a sheep. They could carry water in a barley stem, and they had to build bridges over the footprints of the chickens. There were four lakes, one blue, one red, one white, and one black.
>
> The two apprentices saw the Paju plowing his field, but he could not see them. To get his attention they burnt incense. Khrō Paju now heard them after smelling the libation. His mother invited them into the house.
>
> The two apprentices entered and gave an offering, and begged Khrō Paju to return to the human world. The mother said, "Since they have brought offerings you may go back with them." So he went.

> When Khrō Paju emerged into the human world he saw the
> suffering that his curse had caused. Many people had to eat ashes
> instead of food. There was no meat, only spinach. There were
> hardly any grains to offer in the rites. He heard many sad stories.

The Paju shaman explains that on his return, Khrō Paju reestablished
his ritual system. Now, however, there was not enough grain in the world
for offerings of nine measures. He had to make do with one measure.
Further, no longer could nine animals be sacrificed. Only one animal could
be offered. The Paju pointed out that the decrease in the number of
sacrificed animals is a sign of historical decline from the good era. His
view was the exact reverse of the Tibetan lama's view that ritual killing
is itself a sign of the decline.

In the performance of the Ghale deer sacrifice at Tapje we have seen
that prior to the sacrifice, the "house" of the mother guardian deity is entered after doing a libation. In the house, nine offerings of grain are given,
a replication of the ideal of what should have been given in the first era.
The huge animals and tiny beings in Khrō-nasa in the Paju's legend dramatize the food abundance that can be tapped if the original mistake can
be corrected. When the male cult reaches the tree to give the deer's heart
to Drong awa, there is a similar redoing of a past mistake. Here the myth
association draws on another legend told by the Paju shaman, concerning an ancient hunter who was chasing a deer:

> The hunter saw a golden horned deer and shot it, but the arrows
> bounded off the jewels in its body. Discouraged, he lay down to
> sleep. He saw in a dream an earth-guardian spirit, who said, "I am
> the owner of the deer. You can have it only if you give me a fish
> from the southern valley and a bird from the northern mountains."

The hunter woke up, gave the offerings. He then found the deer tracks,
which led down to the underworld. He went home first to get his dog,
and put his son into a wooden box so that the boy would be safe until
he returned.

> The hunter now plunged down into the underworld with his dog,
> chasing the deer. He climbed down nine ladders and entered Khrō-
> nasa. His dog ran ahead and he could not find it. He saw the tiny
> people and asked them if they had seen his dog and the deer. They
> replied, "If you stay down here three days you may take the deer,
> but only if you give a share of it to us in exchange."
>
> After three days the hunter found the dog and killed the deer.
> He promised to leave the exchange gift at the door that leads out of
> the underworld. But reaching the door, he escaped into the human
> world without leaving a share for the people of Khrō-nasa.

> On the earth the hunter took the meat of the deer and rushed
> home to share it with his son whom he had left in the box. On the
> way he saw that the sun was extremely hot and saw dead rotting
> animals. He went into his home and opened the box. His son was
> dead from the heat. The hunter thought, "The people of Khrō-nasa
> have taken their offering in exchange for the deer."
> It was the curse of the people of Khrō-nasa. "Burn and die,"
> they had said, causing nine suns to appear in the sky. Animals died,
> crops burned, and humans went hungry.

Up to this point, the story has explained how the original reciprocity
between humans and the underworld was broken, the result being the
present degeneration. But with the nine suns, the upper world is implicated as well. The hunter had to find a way to remove the extra suns,
and found a bird that could do the task:

> The bird said, "If you allow me to make my home atop the great
> Wishing Tree,[9] then I can remove the other suns." Everyone agreed
> and offered the bird gifts of barley, corn, wheat, buckwheat, all
> kinds of grains. With these the bird built its home in the tree where
> no humans could disturb it. From there he danced all night, reduc-
> ing the nine suns to one.

The two legends taken together represent a past break with the good
era of harmony "when humans could go and return from Khrō-nasa" main-
taining the relation of abundance and well-being. The break comes when
humans fail to keep the rules of reciprocity. The legends also reflect the
two economic concerns, that of hunting and agriculture, showing how
offerings are required for each. For Gurungs as well as for Tibetans the
good age can be conceived as being still in operation a little over a hundred
years ago. The decline into the present begins for many Gurung informants
with their great-grandfathers. These men were great hunters, using bow
and arrow; in contrast, the present Gurung hunter uses a gun, and hunting
has become a sport instead of a way of life in a Nepal of rapidly diminish-
ing wildlife. "In those days the hunter always gave an offering to the
animal's spirit-owner [*bzhi-bdag* or *sa-bdag*], but today we just kill with
the gun and forget the offering," admitted a Gurung informant.
    The guilt of having offended the primal owners of the earth living in
the underworld, who must still be placated to gain abundance, is linked
to the sense of decline from former rules of reciprocity set by their hunter
forefathers. In the same manner, the grand offerings of grain given by a

9. It appears to be the same Wishing Tree of the Tibetan tradition called *dPag-bsam shing,*
   which is well known in Hindu cosmology in India as well as throughout inner Asian
   cultures.

former nobility are said to have decreased to smaller amounts (from nine measures to one) over the same historical period. In both legends the "curse" of the beings from Khrō-nasa that ends the good age is punishment for a collective past offense that recurs in the present.[10]

The deer sacrifice, then, returns to the past and attempts to repair the breach portrayed in the two legends; at the same time, the heart of the deer is given to Drong awa the guardian deity. In the Ghyabrē shaman's dramatic performance, it is the "mother" in the underworld house who receives the nine measures of grain, just as in the Paju's rites, apologies are first made to the mother of the underworld, since it was she who had urged the first Paju to curse the human world. Then, arriving at the foot of the tree where the bird resides, the Ghyabrē offers the heart of the sacrificed deer to make sure the debt from the past is paid. The distribution of meat ensures that all beings will now receive a share. The past debt is ritually redone. The primal harmony, broken by the first hunters and the first agriculturalists, is partially restored.

The legends of the Paju recall the first era. The legend of the Ghyabrē regarding the Ghale ancestral migration from Tibet into Nepal, however, has an historical reference and is contextualized as a particular noble clan's charter. Hence, the earlier underworld theme concerning the harmony of humanity as such with the natural world, is overlaid by the story of a particular noble clan. The latter story, however, incorporates the image of the primal human condition. It is a model found throughout Asian cultures: kingly legitimacy depends on the capacity to restore harmony with the natural world to gain timely rains. The Ghale accomplish this by merging their own narrative—a "contract" with their guardian deity—with a more fundamental narrative that is pan-human and universal.

CAVE OF RENUNCIATION

The Ghale clan legend and the deer sacrifice can be understood as a commentary on a more primary mythological text. The Ghyabrē's legend of a ruling noble clan draws an older theme into a new use. Different versions of the theme of the hunter and the deer can represent historical transformations over time, rather than being merely synchronic structural variations. When a legend becomes a later comment on a prior statement it takes into account the earlier story in its reformulation. The two overlap, but the later one, in dialogue with the older version, becomes more

---

10. The Paju from Galantso elaborates the "break" from the original harmony by illustrating with another offense committed, this time against the bird that became established in the tree. "One day a boy took an egg from the nest in the tree of this bird that had warned humans not to disturb it. After that humans could no longer talk with animals."

reflexive. Tibetan Buddhist vesions of the story of the hunter and the deer
in Gyasumdo illustrate this diachronic process. The twelfth-century
Tibetan lama Milarepa came to this region of Nepal for a period of time
and stayed in a cave in Nyeshang, two days' walk northwest of Gyasumdo.
Informants from all of the Tibetan villages make a pilgrimage to the cave
each summer. The site is called Khyira Gonpo Dorje, the name of "a hunter
who chased a deer into Milarepa's cave" centuries ago. I joined in one
of these pilgrimages, and the oral version given to me was as follows:

> A hunter in Nyeshang with his dog was trying to hit a deer with
> his arrows, but failed. He chased the deer up a steep hillside and
> arrived at a hermit's cave. The deer entered first and saw Milarepa,
> meditating. Milarepa sang to the deer, inviting it to seek refuge with
> him. The deer was calmed and sat beside him. Then the hunter's
> dog entered the cave, and it too was calmed and sat on the other
> side of the saint.
>
> The hunter charged into the cave, became enraged by what he
> saw and shot an arrow at Milarepa. It could not touch him. Then
> Milarepa sang to the hunter, asking him to kill the passions within
> rather than kill sentient beings without. He invited the hunter to
> remain and practice the dharma.
>
> The hunter threw down his bow and repented of the sin of
> killing sentient beings. The deer and the dog were sent to a Buddha
> field,[11] and the hunter himself stayed with Milarepa until he had
> obtained liberation.

This core version is sometimes elaborated with details regarding the
dialogue between the hunter and Milarepa: "Milarepa asked the hunter
to renounce his former life and remain in the cave. But the hunter said,
'If I don't hunt, what will my family eat?' Milarepa offered him roots and
nettles to eat and sang to him that he must renounce his family for the
sake of gaining liberation. The hunter stayed and gained liberation."

A huge wooden bow, said to be the one which the hunter threw down,
is seen hanging on the cliffside by pilgrims as they arrive at the site. The
Gompa below contains a large painting of the story, showing the deer
and the dog on either side of Milarepa and the hunter kneeling in front,
the bow thrown aside. Only a few pilgrims have the strength or courage
to climb all the way up to the cave, but most circumambulate the saint's
footprints and hang prayer flags on the spots where he meditated, cooked
food, etc.

11. Some of the pilgrim informants said that the deer and the dog then "fell dead" and their
consciousnesses were sent to a Buddha field by the saint. Others argued that no animal
should be said to obtain liberation directly without first becoming a human.

Tibetans say that it is important that men who have killed animals in the past should forsake their hunting and come to this spot just as did the hunter Khyira Gonpo Dorje. Here one repents of one's sinful past of killing sentient beings, and virtuoso laity and monks meditate for months in places of retreat, since more than most pilgrimage centers the theme of this site is renunciation. The ordinary pilgrim who reaches it becomes committed to the path of enlightenment.

The legend of Milarepa and the hunter shares the same myth core with the story of the Gurung hunter who chased a deer into the underworld, but the message is clearly reversed: renunciation of the world rather than harmony with the world. It is not a reversal within a structure of symmetrical oppositions (e.g., life and death), since it is a repudiation of an initial harmony model by a new layer of conscious reflection on human destiny, analogous to Bakhtin's second model: the interior time of individual life sequences. A dialogue represents the earlier standpoint by giving the hunter's initial objections: "If I don't hunt, what will my family eat?" Milarepa's reply (to eat roots and nettles and forsake his family) is outrageous for a Gurung shamanic understanding of human purpose, while it makes good sense to the Tibetan lay pilgrims with whom I trekked to Milarepa's cave.

Other common themes are utilized to dramatize this reversal. While the Gurung hunter who went to the underworld was asked to give a share of the deer to the Khrō-nasa owners as an exchange, the hunter in Milarepa's cave gives the deer to the saint, who communicates the Buddhist message to it, liberating the deer. This itself offers an "answer" to the loss of the good age brought about by the primordial hunter's mistake, but an answer far different from the solution of the Ghyabrē shaman's deer sacrifice, which returns aspects of good-era benefits on a temporary basis in each yearly cycle. Milarepa's Buddhist answer is to forsake the cycle altogether, while his shamanic capacity to communicate with the animals through singing hints of a nostalgia for the lost era: for instance, the Ghyabrē shaman says that singing and dancing during the deer rite reestablishes communication with the ancient legendary beings. Milarepa thus transmutes the primal shamanic images into his "higher" teaching.

The hunter who offers a deer to Milarepa in that cave is also redoing the primal hunter's mistake, but for the Tibetan pilgrims, the hunter's conversion to Buddhism is a commentary on the Ghyabrē shaman's deer sacrifice. This is accomplished by imagery that merges the deer and the Buddhist saint: they both become "hunted." The arrows that are first aimed at the deer are then aimed at Milarepa. Animal and human become mutually identified as members of the same domain in the Buddhist sense of "sentient beings" (*sems-can*) whose killing becomes a sin.

The shaman's sacrifice equates the animal and human in one domain in a quite different sense: both are metonymically identified as "food," exchanged in a cycle of life for life. Milarepa on the other hand merges the animal upward into a humanlike status, now having a different temporality: their nature is defined by their "becoming," their potential to be transformed into something other than what they are: liberated beings. This long-term directional goal equates the two separate species in terms of having a shared temporal destiny.[12] To kill an animal, the lamas say, is like "killing your mother or your father" because, through time, every sentient being has had a turn at being the parent of every other being.[13]

The Gurung hunter story is quite explicit in noting that if the hunter does not give back a share of the deer, then he has to give his own son, who must die to satisfy the exchange requirement. It is a hunter's world view, found in many parts of the world. The narrative of Milarepa's cave repudiates this model even as it transmutes the same theme: Milarepa's temporal identification of human and animal overcomes the broken harmony of the "first-era," by going forward ethically rather than exchanging lives in a cycle.

The transmutation appears to utilize a method of transference found in the Jataka tales of previous incarnations of the Buddha. When the hunter enters Milarepa's cave, he finds that to kill the deer he must first try to kill a Bodhisattva. From there the transmutation can proceed: he must now kill only the impulses and ignorance within himself.

The argument, however, cannot end there. The Tibetan pilgrims cannot, after all, renounce their families, but must return to their homes. They share the same need for abundance in the world, which is what the shamanic regime's spring sacrifice seeks to accomplish. We have seen how the Ghyabrē shaman reopens the door to the underworld to gain access to its wealth, uniting it with the upper world. Rain flows down from above, vegetation grows up from below if the first fruits of the harvest and the heart of the deer are offered each spring. Does Milarepa's cave of renunciation have anything equivalent to offer?

12. On the one hand, the Tibetan Wheel of Life showing six realms of existence (gods, demigods, humans, animals, hungry ghosts, and hell beings) differentiates the human from the animal spheres since only the human is capable of religious aspiration. On the other hand, it equates them in terms of their common destiny.

13. This is hammered home in lama sermons constantly by means of a shift from metaphor to metonymy on a temporal scale: "Even the lowest worms are not to be killed because they are *like* humans, having their own kingdom. But over time they *have been* our mothers and fathers through past millennia."

The Ghale lords and their shamans to some degree replicate the king-Bonpo alliance in pre-Buddhist Tibet. The Buddhist transmutation must somehow provide an alternative to this model of abundance in the world as well as point beyond it. Even in the Milarepa pilgrimage site, hybrid images merge the Buddhist alternative with the ancient model of the divine king. Milarepa, despite his renunciation, takes on kingly functions. His blessing, called Chinlab (*byin-rlabs*), guarantees long life. It flows down from his cave as a spring of water under which a number of Tibetan women in our group stood until their clothes became soaking wet. This Chinlab, in the form of water or earth or herbal medicines, can be gathered from such a sacred spot (*gnas*) to serve as relics of the sacred lama associated with it. The sacred substances are brought back to the village to empower the health of the family or to be put into the fields to make them more fertile. Most important, such relics can be inserted into the village stupas (*mchod-rten*), to bring abundance and protection to the Tibetan community.

The sacred lama at the pilgrimage site thus provides an equivalent image of the ancient matrix as a source of kingship, and is often made to stand for the Universal Monarch as defined in the Tibetan Buddhist tradition. The Lamaist transmutation thus proceeds through a hybrid image: a world with which exchanges are made, and a world that is renounced. In Gyasumdo, the image of the lama as a king thus makes it possible for Tibetans to challenge the lordship of Ghale rulers in Tapje.[14]

The argument between the shamanic and Lamaist kingly regimes is far from completed in Gyasumdo. We have seen that in the ritual legend of the Ghyabrē shaman, the Ghale ancestor-protector refuses to settle where the lama lives, since no red offering is allowed there. The chant itself takes into account a critical lama commentary already being made on its own theme. Looking over his shoulder as it were, the Ghyabrē is already becoming self-aware through dialogue with the lamas of Gyasumdo.

This particular Ghyabrē has himself begun to take into account the lama's ethical arguments. He has given up many of the red offerings that his own father used to perform, except that of the deer sacrifice. He has, he claims, brought his tradition from being "black Bon" (*bon-nag*) a little

14. In Chang's (1962, 1:290–91) translation of Milarepa's songs it is reported that during Milarepa's stay in Nepal the Nepalese king of Ko Kom (Bhaktapur in the Kathmandu Valley) invited the yogi to visit him. Milarepa refused to go, replying: "I am the great universal emperor. There is no other emperor who is happier, richer and more powerful than I. If the worldly kings will follow my Royal Way, each may also become the Supreme Emperor."

closer to being "white Bon" (*bon-dkar*) in one generation,[15] thus partially replicating the historical process of Bonpo reform in Tibet.

In this manner the Ghyabrē continues a dialogue with the present lamas, first accommodating them, then opposing them. I asked why he had retained the deer sacrifice. His answer was immediate. This particular guardian deity had already shown that he would not tolerate any change in the original agreement. To give up the deer rite would bring suffering on the whole community. Far more was at stake here than a personal ethical decision. In any case he would prefer not to define the giving of the heart of the deer as a "killing." "Only its heart is torn out and then it dies naturally."

Later, when the lamas in Tshap village heard me report this argument, they scoffed at such a rationalization. In their view the Ghyabrē is trying to skirt around the Buddhist critique. The Ghyabrē's dilemma and reflections reveal an argument going on not only between the two traditions but within the conscience of the shaman himself. He is troubled by the lama's ethical stance. But the Tibetan laity face a similar dilemma, torn by the same internal dialogue. They agree with the Ghyabrē shaman that many of these pre-Buddhist area gods in Gyasumdo are indeed "stern." Such gods demand a red offering, and may punish those who refuse it. But most of these Tibetans have made a pilgrimage to Milarepa's cave, and have given up ritual killing. How is the dilemma to be resolved?

The lama's transmutation shifts the meaning of the anger that punishes. The Tibetans are burdened with the memory of having compromised with the red offering in their past. If they return to it they may be punished again by the curse of Lama Duwang Tendzin, who brought down the first landslide over a century ago. The Tibetans of Thang-jet village, however, openly complain that they cannot satisfy such conflicting moral demands. Different historical layers of their past contend within their minds.

Together, the Gurung and Tibetan communities of Gyasumdo have constructed an intertextual folk system of indebtedness, comprising the following legendary images: (1) The primal beings of the underworld, who demanded the deer exchange payment and cursed the world with the nine suns; (2) The "first Paju" and his mother from the underworld, who cursed the human world when the nine offerings were reduced; (3) The Ghale ancestor-protector Drong awa, who threatens to afflict the Gurungs of

15. In Tibet, those who did not accommodate themselves to Buddhist teachings and continued animal sacrifices were "black Bon" (*bon-nag*), and those who became "white Bon" (*bon-dkar*) assimilated Buddhist ethical teaching by giving only "white" offerings. Unlike the Tibetan reformed Bon, however, this Ghyabrē in Gyasumdo remains without texts and his chants continue the shamanic themes of the past.

Tapje if they stop the deer sacrifice; (4) For the Tibetans, the curse of Lama Duwang Tendzin, who destroyed the village of Tshap with a landslide; (5) Milarepa's cave of renunciation, where the bow thrown down by the hunter can still be seen.

These sources of retribution from the past have become a layered sequence through time from the most primal to the more recent ancestors and lamas. In the coming chapter I will examine how the Gyasumdo Tibetans have recently experienced an historical turning away from the shamanic layers. I will then show how the lamas transmute those layers so that rituals concerning fertility of the underworld, ancestral guardian deities, and demonic afflictions come to subserve the ethic and enlightenment path of the Tibetan Buddhist project.

Chapter Four

Repudiation of the Red Offering

IN THE EARLY 1960s a rapid cultural transformation took place among the Tibetans of Gyasumdo. As the Chinese consolidated their power over the whole of Tibet, refugees poured into Nepal along the southwestern border, streaming down over the passes at Mustang, Larkya, and Tsum. Great lamas from the Tibetan monasteries were among them, and as they made their way to Kathmandu and India they found temporary refuge among the pockets of Tibetans who had long before established themselves in Gyasumdo.

Lama Chog Lingpa, an incarnate lama, was among them. He was shocked to find that although the Gyasumdo Tibetans had lamas of the Nyingma sect in every village, had built Gompas, and had followed the Tibetan ritual cycle, they had nevertheless compromised with the Gurung custom that is most critical: the red offering of animal sacrifice (*dmar-mchod*). Outraged, Lama Chog Lingpa thundered condemnation in sermons as he gathered the Tibetans to receive his initiations (*dbang*). Tibetan lay leaders in every village except Thang-jet threw out the yearly spring communal sacrifice they had practiced for generations under the domination of the Ghale lords.

In this chapter I will examine the nature of that compromise with the Ghale system and the manner in which it was broken by Lama Chog Lingpa. Then I will analyze the Tibetan text which he wrote at that historic moment and left behind, as a basis for redirecting the ritual life of the Tibetan Buddhist community. We have here a case study of the Lamaist method of transmutation, which in certain ways replicates what may have taken place over a long period of time in rural Tibet during past centuries, as Buddhism triumphed over the Bon regime.

It was noted in the second chapter that the first Tibetan immigrants were absorbed into the Ghale system of dependency, serving the lords from whom they obtained their land in a variety of ways, including corvée labor.

The Ghyabrẽ shaman of Tapje and the Ghale lords that he supports have viewed this dependency as a ritual complex, the sacrificial system enacting the model of divine kingship. The king's relation to the ancestor ensures union between the upper and lower worlds, while the commoners offer their first fruits to the king and share in the distribution after the sacrifice is made.

The spring rite has been examined as one expression of this complex. The Tibetan community in Gyasumdo were for decades forced to participate by enacting a smaller but equivalent red offering of a chicken on their side of the river. Tibetan complicity was based on the Gurung conviction that *all* area gods of the valley should be placated. The Tibetans were also enacting an oath of fealty to the Ghale lords, analogous to what the annals of the T'ang dynasty in China have described as the Tibetan oath of fealty to their king, in which sheep, dogs, monkeys, and other animals were offered every three years in order to "propitiate the gods of Heaven and Earth" (Bushell 1880:441).[1]

During the fall harvest the sociological aspect of this oath swearing was more explicit. As was noted previously, each village was expected to kill two sheep and deliver their heads in a ritual manner to the Ghale in Tapje.[2] In the spring rite the complicity that the Ghale lords had demanded of Tibetans was as follows. The Tibetan community of Tshap village was required to choose among themselves an "area god master" (*lha-dpon*) who would make a yearly animal sacrifice to the local "regional god" (*yul-lha*). In Tshap, the sacrifice was made to the regional god called Akyenedong, to coincide with the deer rite performed by the Ghyabrẽ shaman in Tapje. Pasang, the present village leader in Tshap, was the last *lha-dpon* of the village who had to perform the red offering. He recalls how the tradition began and how he had inherited the position from his father:

> When Tibetans first settled here we tried to maintain our customs. But the Rongpa lord [Ghale] had power over everyone—the fields, trade, everything. Not only did we have to give grain to Tapje for their deer offering, we had to sacrifice a sheep or a chicken in Tshap village also. My grandfather's father was the first to do it. Then the *lha-dpon* custom became inherited in our lineage.
>
> When my father died, my older brother was supposed to become the *lha-dpon,* but he was retarded [*lem-pa*]. I was then only thirteen and my mother said, "He's too young!" But the community said that

1. Hoffman (1961:22) notes that when the Buddhists forbade the practice, the Bon priests substituted "representations" of yaks and sheep, and "carvings of deer heads."
2. Informants say that the sheep's "head" symbolized the "headship" of Ghale rule (N. *mukhya*).

I had to be the *lha-dpon*. Each year I sacrificed two chickens, one
up to the gods, and one down to the serpent deities.[3]

Informants note that during this period of complicity, similar *lha-dpon*
roles developed in the other Tibetan villages as well; the lamas "kept silent"
because they knew that their condemnation of the red offering would go
unheeded. The lamas did not participate and were conspicuously absent
during the enactment. The degree to which the tradition became engrained
in the Tibetan laity can be studied currently in the village of Thang-jet,
the only Tibetan village community that has failed to repudiate the red
offering after the arrival of Lama Chog Lingpa.

Each spring, while Lama Dawa "looks the other way," the Thang-jet
Tibetan males sacrifice a sheep to Devi Than, the local goddess (N. *devi
than,* "shrine goddess"), distributing the meat to each household in a
manner similar to that practiced by the Gurung male cult in Tapje.[4] The
participants admitted to me that they are ashamed of what they are doing,
and some of them, after washing the blood off their hands, rush over to
the Buddhist Gompa to help Lama Dawa prepare for the rituals of the
Tibetan Nyungne fast. "What else can we do," they plead. "If we don't
sacrifice to the goddess she will attack us, destroy our crops, ruin our
trade!"

But couldn't Devi be tamed just as Padmasambhava had tamed such
goddesses in Tibet? I put the question to Tashi Drolma, one of the nuns
who lives in the Gompa on the hill above Thang-jet village. She pointed
out that the compromised laity in this case are poor tenant farmers who
carry on the old habits even after their Gurung landlord has moved to
Kathmandu. Beyond this social reality they honestly fear the goddess. The
only way to break their custom would be to convince them that Devi Than
is "in fact" a manifestation not of the goddess Durga, but rather of the
Tibetan goddess dPal-ldan Lhamo,[5] who was tamed by Gurung Rinpoche
(Padmasambhava) in Tibet. Then they would have confidence that Lama
Dawa's incantations (*sngags*) could control her.

3. The reference to sacrificing in the direction of both the upper world and the lower world
   shows that harmonizing the levels of the Bon cosmos in Tibetan lay discourse is important,
   just as it is in the local shamanic scheme. Further, even though for Tibetans the lower
   world is the region of serpent deities (*klu*), the Gurung shamans insist that the Gurung
   Khrō-nasa is "the same" as the Tibetan *klu* underworld.
4. The use of the Nepali-Sanskritic term *devi* suggests Hindu influence, the local goddess
   being a manifestation of Durga. The Thang-jet Tibetans say they took over the name
   of the local Goddess used by the cult of the landlords they worked for as tenant farmers.
5. dPal-ldan Lhamo, who is a Tibetan equivalent of the terrifying Hindu goddess Durga,
   is regarded as the patron goddess of the Tibetan people as a whole. In her legend she
   first becomes the queen of the "evil king of Sri Lanka" (Schlagintweit 1863) who had become

The dilemma felt currently by the dependent Tibetan farmers of Thang-jet gives insight into how other Tibetans in Gyasumdo have interpreted their past compromise with the Ghale sacrificial regime, and why the break with that custom two decades previously required a charismatic lama presence that would replicate the taming and oath binding performed by Padmasambhava in Tibet.

The event in the early 1960s took place as follows. When the incarnate Lama Chog Lingpa entered Gyasumdo after leaving Tibet, he announced that he would give an initiation (*dbang*) to the assembled Tibetans of the region. In the village of Tshap were gathered hundreds of lay persons, as well as a smattering of Gurungs, including the Ghyabrē shaman from Tapje, to receive the great lama's blessing. Unexpectedly, he preached a powerful condemnation of Tibetan complicity in local animal sacrifice. Informants say waves of shock and dismay went through the crowd. He proclaimed that not only those who wielded the knife but all those who ate the meat of the red offering were destined for the Hell Realm (*dmyal-ba*).

Pasang, the village leader and *lha-dpon* of Tshap, testifies to the transformation within himself that occurred at that time:

> With great anxiety I went to Chog Lingpa Rinpoche and asked how we could dare to give up the red offering. "Would the area gods harm us or not?" I asked. He replied that we must indeed give offerings to the area gods, but these must be "white" (vegetarian) offerings only. Then we built a stupa [*mchod-rten*], and Lama Chog Lingpa bound the area gods to the oath [*dam-bca'*]. He told us how to do the white offering. Then he wrote a text for our lama to use in the rite. If he had not written the text the gods would not have obeyed after he left.

THE TEXT OF LAMA CHOG LINGPA

The text, written on the paper of its original composition two decades before, is in the Tshap village Gompa today (it is translated in appendix A). Each spring it is taken out and chanted by Lama Dorje, performing the annual fertility rite in a Tibetan Buddhist manner. It is both an instruction to the local Tibetans and a recitation addressed to the area gods. The

---

the enemy of the Buddhist dharma. She kills her own son in order to destroy the succession to the throne. Hence she repudiates her kin role as a mother in order to become a terrifying destroyer of those who oppose the dharma. If a goddess who demands the red offering can be defined instead as the terrifying goddess who brings retribution to those who do the red offering, Buddhist transmutation occurs.

following is an analysis of selections from the text that was photographed and later translated, with interpretation based on a taped commentary given by Lama Dorje of Tshap village.[6]

In the first paragraph is stated the purpose of the composition: "This is written to benefit ignorant beings of this existence, since those who perform the red offering [*dmar-mchod*] will go to the Hell Realm; and in compliance with the Buddhist scriptures to aid in the petition offering to the area gods who are *klu, btsan,* and *bdud.*" The purpose is further summarized at the conclusion of the text: "This text is written by gTer-chen Chog Lingpa[7] in the locality of Tshap in the land ruled by the Gorkha king [of Nepal] in order that the people of Tshap may renounce their earlier practice of the red offering and correctly follow Buddhist teaching. With this in mind it has been written."

The text reflects the view of the visiting incarnate lama as well as the local Gyasumdo Tibetans that a radical break with the red offerings of the past was possible because, first, a powerful lama could openly say what the local lamas had been afraid to say; second, he could subdue and bind the "stern" local area gods to the Buddhist oath; and third, he had the mental telepathic power (*ngo she khyen*) to "know" and classify the types of harming agents so that the right offerings could be used to placate them. Finally, unlike the local lamas, he had authority to write a text for ritual practice, to remind the area gods yearly of the oath under which they had been bound.

The remainder of the text can be analyzed under the following headings: (1) the classification of area gods and their required offerings; (2) the model of Padmasambhava's oath binding; and (3) the transmutation from lower to higher awareness.

Area God Classifications

The three categories of area gods mentioned in the text, *klu* (serpent deities), *btsan* (warrior guardians), and *bdud* (demons), are defined in a highly standardized way both in Bon cosmology and in Nyingma Tibetan Buddhist ritual. These are also terms used by the Ghyabrē and Paju shamans in their own imagery as part of the mythological consciousness of Gyasumdo. Lama Chog Lingpa seeks to reclassify them in a Buddhist manner, transmuting the older layer of meaning to convey a higher ethical distinction.

6. The text is called *Tshap kyi yul lha bdud btsan klu sum gsol mchod* ("Petition offerings for the three area gods of Tshap village: *bdud, btsan,* and *klu*"). A full text translation can be found in appendix A.
7. The title gTer-chen refers to his capacity to "find hidden texts" (*gter-ma*).

His text describes the gods physically so that the listeners will know how to make their images as dough effigies for the yearly offering:

klu The king of *klu* [serpent deity] is white, wearing a white cloth. His two hands hold a wish-fulfilling gem. Surrounding him are countless spirits of the eight regions. The effigy [*gtor-ma*] of *klu* is white, and the tip is decorated with a blue turquoise dragon.

btsan The *btsan* [warrior spirit] chief is red with a red shawl wrapped around his body. In his right hand is a fire sling, in his left the power of deluding [*shed-gar*].[8] The effigy of the *btsan* is red and triangular, and the tip is decorated with a snow lion.

bdud From a high cliff comes the demon king [*bdud rgyal-po*]. He is colored black with tiger and leopard skin tied below the waist and human skin wrapped above. In his right hand is a demon's sling and in his left is a jewel of demon origin. The effigy of the *bdud* is black, and the tip is decorated with a Garuda bird [*khyung*].

The three images, quoted here from the text, have been painted on the Gompa walls in Tshap village exactly according to the above descriptions. In Lama Dorje's commentary he points out that each harming agent's supernatural power is represented by a threatening animal aspect of the natural world. The *klu*, serpent deities of the underworld, are associated with the dragon thunder clouds in the sky that can either bring timely rains or ruinous storms. The *btsan* warrior spirits of the middle world often dwell on mountain passes, their power represented by a snow lion who may seize the unwary traveler. The power of the *bdud* demons, who are initially fallen deities dwelling in high cliff regions, is represented by the extraordinary Garuda bird of Indian mythology.

The three colors white, red, and black may represent the three realms, the upper, middle, and lower worlds of Bon cosmology; and in some schemes, white signifies the *lha* ("gods") of the upper world, red the *btsan* who dwell in the middle region, and black the demonic beings emanating from below.[9] Here, however, the three colors refer to the temperament of each harming agent and the kinds of offerings that must placate them.

The *klu* (serpent deities) are "from below," but since they are the most allied with Buddhist teaching and are vegetarians, they demand white offer-

8. The phrase *shed-gar* also means the "power of the dance" [of existence].
9. In the color associations used in Tibetan horoscope diagrams, black is associated with demons, white with gods, red with *btsan* warriors. This leaves the colors of a middling nature to represent a variety of underworld beings and earth owners: *klu* serpent deities being blue, *sa-bdag* earth owners being green, and *gnyen* spirits, who are not well known in Gyasumdo, being yellow.

ings. The *btsan* remain red as the spirits of roaming warriors and kings of courageous but ambivalent temperament, who demand offerings of beer and meat. The black *bdud* demons are inherently malicious and always demand flesh and blood, which is often called the red offering (*dmar-mchod*) but here is equated with blackness.

According to Lama Dorje, one function of designating distinct colors is to demonstrate the importance of distinguishing area god "types" as Buddhist classifications. This is meant to undo the "confusion" of mixing categories as is done in the shamanic system. In imitation of the Ghyabrē and Paju, the Tibetan laity had been making red offerings to all area gods, but these "wrathful" offerings should have been appropriate only for the demons. This had particularly angered the serpent deities, who are vegetarians, and caused them to retaliate. On the other hand, since an actual red offering is ethically prohibited by Buddhism, the great lama's oath binding would make even the demons accept substitutes for the wrathful offering they demand.

Figure 2. Tibetan dough effigies, *tormas,* of the three categories of area gods, shown left to right, *bdud* (demons), *btsan* (warrior guardians), and *klu* (serpent deities)

The spring rite performed today by Lama Dorje corrects the previous error. Using Lama Chog Lingpa's text as an instruction, Lama Dorje makes the three effigies described above. He faces the great boulder where the main community god Akyenedong is still assumed to reside. He then invites the *klu, btsan,* and *bdud* to enter the dough effigies, *tormas.* But nowhere in the text, nor in Lama Dorje's chant, is there mention of the name Akyenedong, whom the lay Tibetans assume to be the main receiver of the sacrifice. It is part of the transmutation method. The Buddhist text displaces the pre-Buddhist local god names, and provides instead universal categories. Lama Dorje himself admits to using this strategy. When he consecrated a stupa in a Gurung village, the Gurungs thought he was addressing their area goddess. Lama Dorje deliberately avoided her name and instead summoned the Buddhist protectors.

Hence in the text written by Lama Chog Lingpa, the area gods are invited to come into the effigies "from anywhere": "Because your only bodies are your minds, come hither by your power of manifestation [*rdzu-'phrul*] and come sit in the soft seat [*'bol-den*] we have prepared for you."

While the Ghyabrē shaman's spring rite particularizes the local ancestral guardian Drong awa, associating him with a clan and a place within the folkloric matrix (Bakhtin 1981:105), the lama's text consciously universalizes, concealing the identity of local beings under general classifications, each standing for the "chief" of the *klu, btsan,* or *bdud,* who have been bound by the oath to control their local manifestations.

The Model of Padmasambhava's Oath Binding

Once the area gods are present, the performing lama is imagined to become Guru Rinpoche (Padmasambhava), who subdued the area gods in Tibet for king Khri srong lde btsan around A.D. 770. By becoming Guru Rinpoche in this textual chant, Lama Dorje also replicates the coming of Lama Chog Lingpa to Gyasumdo in the early 1960s:

> I myself am Pema Chungne [Guru Rinpoche, the "lotus born"], who has traversed the nine levels and holds a Dorje [Vajra] in his right hand and looms over the sky of all envisioned existence. Everything that is visible in the existing world is subdued by his glorious power . . . gods and demons of this land, you are gathered here without power since you have been subdued, so yield now to these orders: give up harming thoughts and develop compassion and fulfill without deviation the duties to which you have been entrusted.

This is a model that is presented in numerous ritual texts used by the Nyingma lamas of Gyasumdo. Tucci (1955) has pointed out that more is at stake in this model than the ritual message. In Tibet the feudal aristocracy of local kings had been responsible for harmonious relations between the social order and the beings of the natural world. The Buddhist "Tantric master" must not only encompass the area gods, he must also encompass the particular kingship with a universal dharmic kingship, as a "subjugator of the gods of the soil and mountains" (p. 179). In the text, Guru Rinpoche incorporates the image of such a king; seated on a lotus seat of sun, he "looms over the sky of all envisioned existence." As a sub-jugator of the local gods, he holds (as do the Gurung shamans) a "trident decorated with colorful cloths."

The Tibetan lay informants often say that "only the coming of a great lama such as this" allowed them to break their former allegiance to the Ghale nobility's sacrificial system. A complete shift of allegiance from the old regime to the Buddhist one is possible if there is assurance that exchanges with the spirit owners of natural domains can be accomplished in the Tibetan lama's ritual system. The text thus provides for a first-fruit offering that is equivalent to the one offered by the Ghyabrē shaman in Tapje, promising return benefits that are also similar: "May all lands but particularly this land have rain on time so there will be a good harvest and increase of grains. . . . May causes of disharmony that bring deaths to domestic animals, infection of the land by insects, hailstorms, or land-slides: may these be removed. . . ."

To receive these benefits, another ritual act is necessary, that of apology for offenses against the earth and underworld beings. It is somewhat equivalent to the Ghyabrē shaman's apology to the underworld for a primal mistake of the past. Hence in Lama Chog Lingpa's text we read: "We beg forgiveness for anything we have done against your wishes such as killing wild animals, bringing pollution, digging up the earth, breaking rocks, and stirring up the waters." However, the definition of the offense is different. The Ghyabrē shaman apologizes not for "killing wild animals," but for the past failure to make the proper exchange when doing so. In the Tibetan apology there is a greater historical connotation, implying a violation of the earth in the building of civilization rather than, as the Paju says, a failure to give "nine measures of grain."

Transmutation from Lower to Higher Awareness
The text of Lama Chog Lingpa provides fundamental models for analysis of the transmutation of lower to higher levels of awareness. Basically, it finds solutions for pragmatic concerns in a manner that elevates them to subserving the dharma and the enlightenment process. First, the text deliberately intermingles two definitions of *increase:* "May the truth of

the dharma spread, may those who uphold it have long life, may all lands, particularly this land, have good harvest and increase of grains, and may all sentient beings practice religion."

The style of the text weaves the two concerns together to show they are interdependent modes of increase. Further, as a Buddhist visualization, the small effigies and the beer and grain libations become a *total* offering, and the participant hopes for a total return:

> . . . our homes, clothes, farms, belongings, our animals both
> domestic and wild such as yak, sheep, horse: all these including all
> the wealth that you can see in the existing world without
> ending. . . . [Since] this offering given to you has the quality of
> bringing about all that you desire without ending . . . so accept it
> with gratitude and benefit us and our property and the people of
> this land.

The Ghyabrē shaman of Tapje also employs the phrase "without ending" as he gives the nine measures of grain and the heart of the deer, but he does not, like the lama, give the whole world. Further, while the Ghyabrē's strategy for attaining the renewal of abundance is to attempt to return to an approximation of the "original" harmony, the lama's strategy, since he is aware that there is no going back, is to thrust forward to complete the Buddhist project. The original model of exchange reciprocity still holds, but at the far end of an historic totalization: all is given, all is to be gained in return. It is the same expansion that occurs in the lama's directional aspiration for "all sentient beings," going far beyond those of the local community. Hence the text asserts: "I prostrate before the Buddha, the dharma, and the sangha and to all sentient beings of the six realms who are my parents, and whom I would lift up to the Buddha field."

The goal of enlightenment as the final transmutation in this sequence appears in considering the origin of *bdud* demons in the text, drawing on the fundamental Buddhist distinction between two truth levels. The text identifies ultimate truth (*don dam bden-pa*) with the "beginning" and the fall into ignorance by the demons as the lower, conventional truth (*kun-rdzob kyi bden-pa*) that must be overcome in the process of time. The description involves an interplay between ontological and psychological epistemologies that are central to Tibetan Buddhist transmutation. Addressing the demons, the text asserts:

> In the beginning there was only self-originating transcendent
> wisdom. Then there arose the thought of samsara and nirvana, and
> you became gods and demons devoted to benefit and harm. . . .

> You are space wandering ghosts [*yi-dvags*] with mind forms only
> [*yid kyi lus*] so that your mental inclinations [*bag-chags*] become
> your imagined enemies and you feel pain from your own thoughts.
> Hence you become divided into good and evil spirits by your
> inclinations and arrogance. You wait around for offerings and for
> chances to seize the life essence of humans. . . .
>   So listen to my words of truth and ponder its meaning: the
> result always follows the cause [*rgyu-'bras*] without fail.

The passage instructs both the demons and the Tibetans for whom
the text is written. It is assumed that Lama Chog Lingpa as an incarnate
lama knows ultimately there is no dual division of gods and demons, benefit
and harm, friends and enemies. But the spring harvest rites are concerned
with this conventional truth level, as are demon exorcisms. Hence at this
level the text is concerned to "make distinctions" by correctly classifying
the area gods. The term used implies deliberate discrimination (*dbyen phye-
ba*) in contrast to the less reflexive process of dual thinking (*rnam-rtog*)
that suspects the presence of demonic harm. Reflecting on ethical distinctions to promote meritorious action is the first step that will eventually
lead beyond the conventional level.

In Lama Dorje's view, the "confusion" of the laity before Lama Chog
Lingpa arrived was typical of the present "evil era." The manner in which
they viewed the *bdud* demons had become the model of classifying all other
realities. To instigate merit accumulation, the lama first overcomes this
confusion with ethical distinctions. Persons are directed beyond the theme
of harmony that is promoted by the Gurung shamans, into a Buddhist
project that is future oriented. The lama's classifications within the conventional truth level are thus made to subserve movement toward the ultimate truth level. Unconscious dual thinking, once turned into conscious
ethical reflexivity, is led gradually and programmatically toward the
removal of dual discriminations altogether.

A sequence of layers is necessary. First the mundane goal of food abundance is brought into a Buddhist ethicization of the offering, and those
who regress back into the pre-Buddhist model are warned that they will
suffer retribution. In this manner, correct ritual action promotes both a
good harvest and ethical merit. The moral principle that negates ritual
killing moves beyond the shamanic emphasis on cycles of ritual exchange;
the teaching of the karma doctrine moves into the foreground.

Thus the text completes the lesson to the demons with the merit
principle that "the result must follow the cause." This puts the area gods
on notice that they too are now subject to the same law: they can be
punished in hell, but may also advance up a merit scale. While the Ghyabrē
assumes that he is making the same offerings every year to the same earth

owners and ancestors, the lama now makes offerings to beings who them-selves can change year by year as they move toward Buddhahood. This shifts personal identity into what Bakhtin calls the time sequence of the sealed-off individual. It redefines the "three worlds" of the shamanic (and Bon) universe (underworld, human world, and upper world) into a tripart moral universe of (1) hell and animal realms, (2) samsaric human births, and (3) Buddha field.[10]

However, the earlier view, which stresses the theme of harmony, is not fully replaced. The two tripart schemes continue to overlap as a dialogue between two discourses. The Lama Chog Lingpa text encourages this inter-pretation. It does begin with an ethical hell warning for those who practice the red offering, but then moves into the image of exchange with the gods of fertility along with apologies to the underworld, drawing on shamanic and Bon cosmology. Then, again, a Buddhist merit-enlightenment path is asserted. As the Lamaist imagery becomes more grand it gathers the area gods themselves into the domain of sentient beings destined for a Buddha field. In the earlier image the earth beings who are sources of fertility are like parents on whom humans depend. In the latter image they are among universal parent beings who move toward a realization.

Expanding the Meaning of the Text

When Lama Chog Lingpa arrived in Gyasumdo and wrote a text for the Tibetan community, he accelerated a historic process of dialogue between Lamaist and shamanic regimes. As a lama who had just arrived from Tibet, he wrote a text that he could have written upon discovering a shamanic enclave in Tibet itself; thus it is a fully Tibetan document. The local lamas insist, however, that the particular Gyasumdo area gods were the ones telepathically recognized by the great lama, so that his classifications were precisely correct for the region. The local lamas themselves regard the text as a locally generated creation, not a standardized model imported from Tibet.

The text is now chanted in the same manner every spring by Lama

10. This conception must be distinguished from the wheel of six realms of existence in which hell is included in samsara. In the folk conception which the lamas share, the three lower realms of the wheel of existence are regarded as a general region of punishment, from which one is "liberated" (*thar-pa*) into human births as an intermediate level of merit opportunities. The next aspiration is arrival in a Buddha field, since the fifth and sixth realms of the wheel, regions of demigods and gods, are not psychologically real aspira-tions, and are never mentioned as goals. Merit accumulation is directed to better human births, while the higher religious life is directed to a Buddha field where progress to full nirvana can proceed without falling back into samsara.

Dorje in Tshap village before the large boulder where the main area god still resides. When the text refers to *klu, btsan,* and *bdud,* it summarizes the three categories of beings addressed throughout the year in other rituals of the lama's repertoire. The definitions of these beings and the rites addressed to them are implicated in the historical events of Gyasumdo that have been triggered by the repudiation of the red offering. The text left behind thus provokes further meaning expansion. Each time it is chanted, there is fresh awareness that the categories of beings placated are no longer the categories that were thought to demand a red offering before the text was written.

A written text drives a wedge of reflexivity between Gurungs and Tibetans in the folk matrix that both share in Gyasumdo. This provokes a linear trend of ethical self-consciousness. But the prior layer continues to voice its argument, particularly through the mouth of the shamanic presence. The shamanic system itself had a long development prior to the arrival of the Tibetans. Iconically embedded in the local region, these images resist the universal classifications represented in the lama's text. The Ghyabrē and Paju do not classify, rather they juxtapose local events and images that are remembered and reenacted (Leenhardt 1979).

Lama Chog Lingpa's ritual text decontextualizes these prior images in order to claim universality. As the lama-shaman dialogue continues, the meaning of the text further expands beyond that which was intended when it was written (Ricoeur 1971). Its meaning accumulates historically, gaining fresh associations that again evoke new responses (Bakhtin 1986:170). The later interpretations do not replace the earlier ones, but rather develop a sequence of layered meanings. It is within this model of understanding that I will examine other Tibetan rituals enacted in Gyasumdo, chanted from texts that were written in Tibet and brought into this region by the lamas.

In the three chapters that follow I will examine three types of rituals now performed regularly by the lamas of Gyasumdo, each concerned with one of the three classifications found in Lama Chog Lingpa's text: (1) reciprocal exchange with *klu* serpent deities of the underworld; (2) rites of defense that serve the *btsan* guardian deities; and (3) rites of exorcism that expel the *bdud* demons. I will examine each type with the awareness that each represents a different layer of Tibetan Buddhist transmutation, and each expresses a turning point of historical consciousness. Toward the end of each chapter I will further show how each rite serves as an idiom through which the lama-shaman dialogue continues after Lama Chog Lingpa's repudiation of the red offering.

Chapter Five

Reciprocal Exchange with the Underworld Serpent Deities (*klu*)

WHEN LAMA CHOG LINGPA "bound the local area gods to the oath" in the early 1960s in Gyasumdo, the Tibetan relationship with the underworld serpent deities (*klu*) became more fully Buddhist. The alliance with the underworld established by the Ghale lords and their shamanic regime in Tapje was felt to have been replaced on the Tibetan side of the river by the lamas of Tshap village. Their Tibetan version of alliance with the underworld would now pertain.

Who are the serpent deities of the underworld? In the text of Lama Chog Lingpa, the most primal of the area gods demanding ritual offerings are *klu*, the text describing them as serpent deities holding a "wish-fulfilling gem." In Tibet, when Guru Rinpoche conquered the land for Buddhism in the eighth century, he also subdued the *klu*. They became allies, supplying wealth for the building of the great temple at bSam-yas. In Tibetan villages in Gyasumdo, the local stupas (*mchod-rten*) replicate bSam-yas, symbolizing the establishment of a Buddhist kingdom. Beneath the stupas live serpent deities, who contribute rain and abundance in general.

In this chapter I will explicate the ritual relation with the *klu* of the underworld, including the *sa-bdag* ("earth owners") who personify the natural elements. The analytic problem is how the lamas employ these images to establish a Buddhist kingdom of this-world abundance, in opposition to the Ghale regime. To accomplish this the lamas must somehow overlay the shamanic retribution model, based on reciprocal exchange, with a model of karmic retribution. On the other hand, reciprocal exchanges with the underworld are retained, but in Buddhist terms. This will be shown by analyzing the ritual performance which enacts such a model. Further, the harms and benefits of this ancient matrix can be made calculable through the Tibetan horoscope system (*rtsis*), which will be introduced later in the chapter. I will conclude by showing how the Tibetan Buddhist version is contested by the older shamanic layer that it had sought to encompass, in terms of a dialogical model.

I first encountered Tibetan folk awareness of serpent deities in the home of our landlady Nyima Drolma. She told us that her son had died from a malevolent *klu* attack a year before our arrival. The same dangerous serpent deity "still lived in the stream below our stairway." My wife Maria complained one day of a rash on her hands while washing clothes in that stream. Nyima Drolma became instantly alarmed. She rushed Maria back to the stream, carrying offerings to placate the *klu*. She burned juniper leaves as an incense offering (*bsang*) and poured over it roasted barley flour (*tsam-pa*), butter, sugar, and milk, sprinkling water over the burning leaves to increase the smoke so that the serpent deity could consume the offering through smell.

For Gyasumdo Tibetans, the *klu* live in a kingdom beneath the earth or at the bottom of lakes and streams, and they also may reside in the hearth inside the home. They are polluted by people spilling food into the fire or by muddying the waters where they reside or by throwing human waste under rocks. Consequently, the *klu* become angered and retaliate, sending diseases of the skin such as boils, rashes, and leprosy. When humans cut trees or split rocks for house building, serpent deities residing there can be injured and will strike back with afflictions or withhold abundance. The burnt offerings that are sent down to their realm must include herbal medicines to heal the *klu*. It is a mutual exchange of healing: the humans who are afflicted should also recover, on the basis of the ancient model of reciprocal harmony.

Closely associated with *klu* are the *sa-bdag* ("earth owners"), who control surface territories and the basic elements of nature.[1] Gyasumdo Tibetans assign a *sa-bdag* goddess to each element—earth, air, fire, and water—called the "four-element goddesses" (*'byung-ba bzhi gi lha-mo*). Our landlady Nyima Drolma used lay remedies to placate *sa-bdag* goddesses as well. When her daughter had a toothache, she concluded that it was the goddess of water (*chu gi lha-mo*) living in the stream who had caused the affliction.[2] She seized a stone in the stream and tied a string

1. Although *klu* and *sa-bdag* are often referred to as having different kinds of domains, the *sa-bdag* category (*sa* is "earth," *bdag* is "master") can also encompass the *klu*, the latter being regarded as a type of *sa-bdag*. Another general category is the term *bzhi-bdag*, "masters of the four quarters."
2. If the symptom had been an external sore, she would have assumed that the harmer was a *klu*. Internal swelling and a burning pain—here caused by the toothache—is a symptom of *sa-bdag* goddess attack.

around it, gradually pulling it out of the water and saying, "If you feel *this* pain, then don't *send* pain!" Nyima Drolma interpreted this to mean, "If the water goddess agrees to stop causing the toothache, we will stop doing the same to her," using the model of reciprocity in negative form. The model was dramatized by hanging the stone over the hearth (to feel heat) and wrapping prickly leaves around it. After a few days the goddess seemed to get the message: the toothache subsided, and the stone was put back into the stream.

THE UNDERWORLD AND BUDDHIST KINGSHIP

There is an ancient relation between Buddhist societies and serpent deities of the underworld, called *klu* in Tibet (pronounced "Lu") and *naga* in India. In the Jataka tales the *nagas* dispense nature's gift of abundance, both as fertility and gems, and they punish those who violate the earth. The alliance between kingship and these underworld beings was considered essential in ancient times, and involved reciprocal exchange. The ancient king's ordination was often held at the site of the shrine (*caitya*) where serpent deities were honored and given offerings, since they could make or break the kingship by sending or withholding timely rains (Bloss 1973).

Alliances appear to be of two kinds: reciprocal exchanges through offerings, and the king's marriage to the serpent deity maiden. Throughout Asia, Buddhist societies have transmuted this ancient mythic layer (Tambiah 1976). In the Tibetan folk epic of Gesar of Ling,[3] the hero-king Gesar is born of the marriage between an incarnate god and a serpent deity maiden. The marriage is "arranged" by Lama Padmasambhava. He first poisons the river leading to the underworld so that the serpent deities become ill, and must then invite Padmasambhava to enter their realm to heal them. When he enters, he is lavishly entertained by the wealth of the *klu* kingdom: "Magnificent carpets, richly embroidered tapestries, seats and tables of gold and silver, vases ornamented with jewels, and a thousand other precious articles were brought out from the state treasury" (David-Neel 1959:62). After healing the serpent deities of the poison, Padmasambhava demands a return payment: a *klu-mo* serpent deity maiden must come up to the human world and unite with a divine king, to become the mother of the hero Gesar, who will save Tibet from further decline in the evil age.

This version of Gesar is one in which the older folk layer has been transmuted by Tibetan Buddhist lamas (David-Neel 1959) and reveals two kinds

3. The Gesar epic is sung by the Drogpa nomads in Gyasumdo. Here I am referring to the Buddhist version translated by David-Neel (1959).

of discourse, each within the other. "Marriage with the underworld" is the ancient matrix that is not yet bifurcated: the "below" is not a Hell Realm of punishment. The image is highly shamanic: we have noted how the Gurung shaman's legends celebrate the marriage between the ancient Ghale king and the beings of the underworld. It is highly visible in the Tibetan Bon tradition, and also in Tibetan folk consciousness in Gyasumdo.

The image is also that of the pre-karmic model of reciprocal retribution: offenses committed by humans against the natural world require human apology and renegotiation of the original reciprocity. Each side, humans in one domain and nature's *klu* and *sa-bdag* spirit agents in the other, can harm or benefit the other. When humans disturb the underworld, they damage both the bodies and the "kingdom" of its inhabitants. Harmony with that primal layer is required in Buddhist kingdoms.

The six stupas (*mchod-rten*) in Tshap village establish a "Buddhist kingdom." The model of reciprocal harmony is the fundamental layer. The stupas are thought of as "Buddha residences" (*Sang-rgyas khang gnas*), signifying Lamaist hegemony in the village as a kingly presence of the Buddha. My observations made during the construction of one of these stupas in Gyasumdo show how it incorporates the serpent deity underlayer. Before the first stones are laid, a hole is dug in the center into which is put a "treasure vase" (*bum gter*) that has been prepared with (1) five kinds of grain for the underworld kingdom, to return as rich harvests; (2) five kinds of treasures to fill the serpent deity treasury; (3) five kinds of cloth which provide them with fine clothes; and (4) five kinds of herbal medicines to heal serpent deities of human-caused illness. Over the top of the vase is stretched a white cloth on which is drawn the wheel of the Universal Monarch.[4]

The vase is buried in the hole, representing the underworld. Over this is constructed the "Tree of Life" or "Life Tree" (*srog-shing*), consisting of a half-meter wood pole carved from the branch of a pine tree. Small twigs of other trees are tied to the sides of the pole. Tibetan mantras are written on each side, pointing to the four cardinal directions. Around the pole are wrapped five colored cloths representing the five kinds of cloth as well as the five elements.

While Lama Dorje prepared the vase and the Life Tree, he gave the following explanatory lecture to the lay persons who were gathered:

> If we wrap around the Life Tree the five kinds of cloth, then we will
> in the future become wealthy with clothing. By inserting the five
> kinds of grain we will have abundance of crops, even in a period of
> famine. By inserting five kinds of treasures we will obtain fortune

4. Also known as the "Wheel-turning King" (*stong 'khor-lo sgyur-ba'i rgyal-po*).

and long life. By putting in five kinds of medicines we will not become sick in the future.

The exchange can be effected only if the lama magnifies the bits of wealth into a kingdom of wealth through his imagination. The Life Tree, which in the view of the Gyasumdo shamans unites the three worlds, becomes for the lama the Wish-granting Tree that has its roots in the underworld treasure store and grows up through Mount Meru (*ri-rab*), emerging at the top to provide fruits and medicines for the gods. When the stupa is completed it replicates this image. A branch is installed on it as the Life Tree growing through the top.

The resulting union of upper and lower worlds brings fertility and abundance. The Buddhist transmutation is finally achieved when the lama inserts into the completed stupa the Chinlab (*byin-rlabs*) elements that he has gathered at pilgrimage spots (*gnas*). The term can be translated as "supernatural blessing" (Jäschke 1977:376). Tibetans compare Chinlab to rain, but the source is the Buddha or the incarnate lama; for example, the water that flows down from the cave of Milarepa is Chinlab. Lama Dorje had brought earth and water as well as herbs from Milarepa's cave in Nyeshang and from Muktinath (*chu-mig*), from Bodhgaya in India and from Lumbini, the birthplace of Buddha. In his commentary, Lama Dorje explained:

> During the good age the whole earth was Chinlab. Now, during the bad age [*bskal-pa btsog-pa*] there is deterioration [*nyams-pa*] of the nutritious value of the earth. Thus the fortune of humans also deteriorates. But the Buddha has established sites [*gnas*] where deterioration from the good age does not occur. In Muktinath the original fire burns in water in harmony, and there the rocks and soil are as they were at the beginning of time. We collect these and bring them back so we can insert them in our Chortens [stupas] and in the soil of the fields to delay deterioration, restoring to some extent the qualities of the good age.

The Tibetan Buddhist stupa thus becomes a container of such Chinlab, temporarily holding back the historical decay. *Chinlab* can be defined as traces left over from the primal era. Hence it is not surprising that the conception is closely related to the *klu* serpent deities and *sa-bdag* earth owners, who are also "traces" of the primal time.

Upon completing the stupa, the lama performs a special rite of offering to the *klu* before inviting the protecting Buddhas to reside in it. The image of the link between kingship and the underworld is the first layer at the bottom. Subordination of that layer by Buddhist hegemony is represented by "relics of great lamas," also called Chinlab, inserted at the top of the stupa.[5] Then the "three protector Buddha-lineages" (*rigs-gsum mgon-po*) are invited to occupy the altarlike hollow near the top in which butter lamps are lit: (1) Avalokiteśvara (sPyan-ras-gzigs), (2) Manjusri ('Jam-dpal-dbyangs), (3) Vajradhara (Phyag-na rdo-rje).

CIRCUMAMBULATION OF THE TEXTS (*YUM 'KHOR*)

This Tibetan synthesis is dramatized each spring, when the Tibetan stupas in Gyasumdo are reconsecrated (*rab-gnas*). The lamas and their monk and nun aides follow the circuit of village stupas, which they reconsecrate while lay persons, mainly women and children, circumambulate the agricultural fields, carrying the main texts of the Gompa. They do this "circumambulation of the texts" (*yum 'khor*)[6] after the lamas have spent five days rapidly reading them in the Gompa. The serpent deities hear the words of the texts while they are carried on the backs of humans, delight in the words of the Buddha, and bring rain.

On the other side of the river, however, the Ghyabrē shamans are carrying the deer on their back. When they give its heart to their underworld beings, they also bring rain to the same valley. The lamas regard the textual mode of bringing rain as the Buddhist answer to the Ghyabrē's sacrifice. As the Tibetan lay carriers of the texts go around the fields on the Tibetan side of the river, they can hear the excitement of the Gurungs of Tapje across the valley where the deer is being brought back from the wild. Tapje is on the sunny, more fertile side of the valley, which gives the shamanic rite the appearance of greater success.

On the Tibetan side, an older layer of meaning suddenly appears during the circumambulation. The carriers arrive at a pond. The children strip off their clothes and "play in the water" (*chu-brtse*). This also encourages rain they say, since serpent deities are found in ponds.[7] The lamas play down the importance of *chu-brtse*, arguing that the serpent deities really cooperate with the human world because they "hear the texts." Further, they insist, "It is not only to bring rain, [since] the serpent deities themselves are led toward liberation." The sources of underworld fertility thus subserve the dharmic regime. As long as the shamanic argument is still voiced in Gyasumdo, however, the two layers of meaning are in contention.

5. Lama Dorje identifies three types of Chinlab at this level: (1) the relics of sacred lamas inserted in the stupa are the "body" (*lus*) of the Buddha; (2) texts inserted in the stupa are the "speech" (*gsung*) of the Buddha; and (3) the three protectors present are the "mind" (*thugs*) of the Buddha.
6. The term *yum* ("mother") here refers to the Abhidharma Buddhist scriptures.
7. The water play resembles a similar spring fertility rite found in ancient China (Granet 1977).

The lamas' argument together with their reconsecrations of the stupas dramatizes that there is far more at stake in the Tibetan spring rite than the problem of rain and abundance. The additional message is Buddhist hegemony on the Tibetan side of the river. The stupas, containing both the wheel of the Universal Monarch and the presence of the three Buddha protectors, provide an image of an absent king. While on the Gurung side of the river the meat of the deer sacrifice is distributed among the Gurung villagers, on the Tibetan side the *tshogs* (Skt. *prasad*), the leftover food of the offering made to the Buddhist deities, is distributed to the Tibetans.

Tibetan lamas "renounce" the world and yet establish a "kingship" in the world, replicating the ancient king-underworld link that is celebrated in the Ghale's shamanic regime. The Ghale lord's divine ancestor descends from above to fertilize the earth below, but likewise when Tibetan incarnate lamas visit Gyasumdo and give *dbang* ("empowerment") to the assembled laity, they throw grain to the people as Chinlab, the same supernatural substance that is inserted into the stupas.[8] The purpose shifts, however, to the dharmic project of the lamas. The lamas are the source of both long life (*tshe-ring*) and enlightenment. It is their image of the ideal kingdom.

RITES OF EXCHANGE WITH THE SERPENT DEITIES (*KLU*)

Exchanges with serpent deities occur in rites of healing as well as stupa consecrations. The ritual texts used reveal how a healing ritual incorporates images of kingdom construction. The following is an analysis of the *klu-gtor* rite (serpent deity torma offering) along with selections made from the texts used[9] which are standard for Nyingma Lamaism.

The lama first makes a small "*klu* king" torma surrounded by seven lesser *klu* kings, making eight in all. These are put in a circle on a plate and decorated by flowers representing the "*klu* palace in the *klu* kingdom in the ocean." The *klu* kings and his retinue are called into the tormas. They receive the required offering of three white and three sweet items, along with the five cloths and herbal medicines.

As the ritual arena becomes filled with serpent deities and their close relations, the *sa-bdag* earth owners, Lama Dorje imagines that he, as the performing lama, becomes Buddha Chenresig (Skt. Avalokiteśvara), from whose heart

8. The throwing of grain to the people by the incarnate lama replicates the origin legend in which Buddha Chenresig (T. sPyan-ras-gzigs, Skt. Avalokiteśvara) sends grain to the first Tibetan humans.
9. The names of the texts are *Klu 'bum dkar-po, Klu 'bum nag-po, Klu 'bum khra-po* ("100,000 white *klu*, 100,000 black *klu*, 100,000 mixed *klu*").

a light shines on all the *klu* and *sa-bdag* as they arrive. He pours water on a ritual mirror (*me-long*) to purify them. An incense (*bsangs*) burning of juniper leaves is started, and the reading of the text begins: "May the *klu* and *sa-bdag* be alerted by the smoke of the *bsangs* and come immediately by your emanation powers. . . . In the oceans, rivers, waterfalls, hills, rocks, earth, stones, in wind, fire, water, and air, in all of these elements are the *klu* that exist in them. . . ."

Defining them in terms of the elements in the natural world, they are the eight serpent deity kings of the underworld kingdom and their eight chief ministers, followed by a list of *klu* commoners defined by their capacity to harm or benefit.[10] A priestly caste of *klu* is called, but no specific names are given. The entire serpent deity kingdom appears to consist of a hierarchy from natural elements at the base through animals that are controlled by *klu* or *sa-bdag* as their "animal-headed" owners, through human being-like creatures, to *klu* kings at the top. Lama Dorje notes that this kingdom has the "same four or five Gyubas" (clan groups) that human society has. He further classifies them as harmers, the ritual performer wearing a cloth on his head to stave off their attacks: "Some *klu* send poison just by looking at you. Others send poison that hits you when they say, 'Haa!' Others poison you if you touch them, and still others send poison just by thinking evil thoughts. That is why one must immediately chant: 'May all your minds be purified so that you don't harm.'"

The arriving *klu* and *sa-bdag* are told to submit to the word (*bka*) of the Buddha embodied in the performing lama. But suddenly, a reversal occurs. Even though the lama has already "become" the Bodhisattva Chenresig, he puts this identity aside and prostrates (in imagination) before the *klu* king (Gabo) who has arrived, begging him for forgiveness for human transgressions against the serpent deities and their domains: "I myself and the sponsors prostrate before Gabo the king of *klu* to apologize (*bshags-pa bul*) for sins (*sdig-pa*) committed against *klu,* both in this life and in past lives."

It is important to define the nature of human offenses against the *klu* and *sa-bdag* to understand why apology is necessary. Further in the text we find:

> The palace of the *klu* is in a large ocean with nine kingdom
> areas. The *klu* meadows are blue. Red cows and bulls run here and
> there . . . peacocks spread their feathers and there is the sound of
> bells and drums. . . .

10. The *klu* kings are led by their leader dGa'-bo 'Jogs-pa, the best known. The eight chief ministers have names such as Mirror-Faced One, Snake-Headed One, etc. Commoner *klu* have names such as Dragon Sounder, Fruit Ripener, Harm Doer, *Klu* Residing in Wind, Water, Trees, Hills, Rocks, and Earth.

> But we in our ignorance, by stirring up and muddying the
> water, have destroyed their wealth. . . . We ask for forgiveness for
> cutting trees, for digging the earth, for turning over rocks, for
> breaking boulders, for killing sheep and goats that are owned by
> *klu,* for baiting birds owned by *klu,* for cutting up snakes' bodies,
> for hooking the mouths of fish, for cutting the limbs of frogs, for
> destroying the palaces of the *klu* and emptying their wells, for
> blocking their springs, and for harming the *klu* themselves. . . . I
> beg forgiveness for these acts.

The list of offenses portrays harms against the *klu* underworld social
system (destroying its wealth, its palaces, its wells, etc.), offenses against
sentient beings of nature "owned" by the *klu* (both wild and domestic
animals of the three realms of air, land, and water—particularly water
beings, such as fish, frogs, and snakes), and further, offenses that have
directly hurt *klu* "bodies," such as cutting or burning trees and breaking
rocks where they reside, as in the following passage: "Forgive us for making
fire on hills, for rolling boulders, for poisoning lakes or digging earth,
for cutting trees, for whatever acts have harmed the *sa-bdag* and *klu* race."

Two types of offenses must be examined in greater detail: acts that
harm the bodies of the serpent deities and acts that destroy their natural
kingdom. The early part of the text is preoccupied with reciprocal exchange
as a method for healing the *klu* bodies harmed by humans, so that they
will reciprocate and heal the human bodies they have afflicted with diseases, usually skin sores, limb diseases, or leprosy. The text matches each
type of harm that humans cause the *klu* with a medicinal remedy that can
be given to them through the burnt offering. For instance:

> To cure *klu* afflicted with damaged skin, burn a snake skin . . . to
> cure *klu* with damaged palms, burn the palm of a crocodile . . . to
> cure *klu* with damaged skull, burn the foam of the ocean . . . to
> cure *klu* afflicted with paralyzed hands and feet, burn *wang-po lak-pa* (a
> tree glue) . . . to cure deteriorated flesh, burn curd and loin of meat. . . .

The *klu* with these disabilities are called up to receive their remedies one
by one as each ingredient is put into the fire, thus: "The king of *klu* whose
hair and mustache are damaged, be healed by . . . , etc." Clearly, all the
ingredients are not available to Tibetans, and Lama Dorje admits there
must be a selection of items to show a proper ritual attitude. Nevertheless,
the exchange rule allows the ritual sponsor to expect that the equivalent,
klu-caused human ailments such as boils and leprosy will be healed.

The text then moves quickly to the issue of the wealth of the natural
world identified with the serpent deity kingdom itself. The ingredients

offered are now of this domain: "To the *klu* king and his attendants we offer fruit-bearing trees with scented leaves, flowers, incense, grains, and clothes as well as herbal medicines." These benefits are represented by bits of tree wood and other twigs representing the trees which humans may have cut and which must be restored, along with the wealth ingredients noted before: five kinds of grain, five kinds of cloth, five kinds of treasures, five kinds of herbs. The entire serpent deity world is to benefit:

> By offering all these may all the *klu* have wealth, brightness, fame, glory, and power. May the *klu* king and his attendants have prosperity. May blind *klu* see, may hungry *klu* eat, may poor *klu* have plenty, may great *klu* have lands, may *klu* suffering from fire, water, theft, thunderbolts be freed from these dangers. . . .

The above list well summarizes human aspirations. Serpent deities share with us these sentiments so that a return gift from them can be anticipated. Such a list of wants also allows the lama to heal the serpent deities in terms of restoring body parts rather than having to give them a life as the Gurung shamans do in their sacrifices. Bodily ailments and their cure are incorporated metaphorically into rebuilding the social and natural environment.

The centrality of the "tree" (*shing*) is striking as an iconic sign to effect this shift of domain. Individual serpent deities have their bodies cut by the "chopped tree," but the same act also causes ecological ruin and poverty in their kingdom. Twigs of various kinds of trees are put into the burnt offering while the lama chants from the text: "By offering different kinds of tree branches may this pay all debts for cutting trees. May these debts be taken back."

The twigs referred to in the text are the same as those that are wrapped around the Life Tree pole inside the stupa during its construction, as we have noted. They are part of the tree mediating the three worlds in Bon cosmology as well as the tree growing atop Mount Meru in the Tibetan Buddhist cosmology. These images join to represent both harmony in the natural world and abundance in the social world, which are in turn linked to healing the "cut limb" of the body of the *klu* when the tree was cut.

For instance, in the imagery of the serpent deity text, the twigs put into the burnt offering cure the nose of the *klu,* and in return, cure the nose of the human who was afflicted by these *klu.* From there, larger results follow: the same twigs replace the cut trees in the valleys and hills, replenishing the natural universe. The grander exchange benefits the *klu* kingdom and then returns in full to the human world. The serpent deities are told:

By obtaining these things, now confer upon us—myself, the lama, the sponsor, and all his dependents—the same benefits. By offering you flowers, may those who are ugly become beautiful. By offering you incense, may we receive good smells; by offering you medicines, may we be cured of diseases that come from the four elements. By offering you the five kinds of grain, may we be freed from famine. By offering you gems, may we have long life, power, useful goods, clothes; may we have crops without having to work; and may our animals not die. By offering you alms, may we both gain wealth.

Lama Dorje summarizes the agreement in his personal commentary:

If the *klu* are poor, humans become poor; and if the *klu* become rich, so do humans. If *klu* get sick, so do humans. So we must look after the *klu*. Further we must understand that benefit comes not merely to the sponsor of the rite but to the entire world (*'dzam-bu gling tshang-ma*). This is what the lama must imagine. He must expect that the fields will grow and that no one will suffer famine and that this will bring harmony (*mthun-pa*) between us all.

The text ends by underlining the need for rain, which the *klu* are also asked to provide during circumambulation of the texts in the spring rite: "May the king of *klu* send timely rains to ripen the crops. May you and we have rain at the appropriate times." The ripening of crops as an image of fruition allows metaphoric shift: the more fundamental layer of *reciprocal* retribution is turned into *karmic* retribution: "As you sow, so shall you reap. Mind is the essence of religion. . . . Don't commit sins. Do meritorious acts. One's mind should be purified. This is what the Buddha dharma is."

A reciprocity model again returns. This time, however, it has incorporated the Buddhist ethic: "Now imagine that the *klu* have accepted your apology and you should imagine that all your transgressions have been dissolved (*sdig-pa tshang-ma sbyang*)." The ritual ends. The lama takes the serpent deity tormas and places them in the area where the *klu* are known to reside.[11]

The ending of the serpent deity text makes explicit a dialectic in the Tibetan rite. First, one apologizes to the serpent deities for harming them

11. When Lama Dorje performs the *klu* rite at the Gompa, he places the tormas behind the Gompa beside a stream where a powerful *klu* is known to reside. His commentary on the *klu* text was obtained after he had performed the rite. In this case, one of the nuns at the Gompa had developed a skin rash. Then Lama Dorje said he "dreamed of this *klu*," and so he had to perform the rite. The commentary on the *klu* text was taped after this particular performance.

to instigate a mutual healing, defined as "exchange" (*tshong rgyab*). Second, one instructs the *klu* in the ethical career of the karma doctrine. Finally, there is a dissolving of all debts at both levels of concern. The dialectic can be compared to the Ghyabrē's "apology" to the mother Drong ama of the Gurung underworld, the difference being that the shaman does not move beyond the reciprocal retribution model.

TIME CYCLES AND THE TIBETAN HOROSCOPE SYSTEM

The *klu* text includes an appendix, a chart explaining how the proper timing of ritual exchanges with serpent deities over a twelve-month period can take advantage of time cycles operating in the underworld. Offerings are made to coincide with the times that serpent deities are predisposed to make particular exchanges with the human world. Each month has auspicious days for types of *klu* activity and the benefits made possible by ritual exchanges.

The monthly cycle in the text can be summarized as follows. In the first month serpent deities "listen to religion." In the second month they retain the ability to "remember" and become willing servants. In the third month they have discussions among themselves. In the fourth month they renew their laws. In the fifth month they do summer work. In the sixth month they search for fruits. In the seventh month they gather fruits. In the eighth month they "wear their clothes." In the ninth month they "gather juice from trees." In the tenth month they are dormant. In the eleventh month they do "winter work." In the twelfth month they guard their material wealth.

In commenting on the above schedule, Lama Dorje advises that one should correctly time one's serpent deity rites to gain the return benefit corresponding to that period's *klu* activity. This is better understood in the context of the additional schedule given for the *sa-bdag*. An apology (*bshags-pa bul*) is added after each ritual action for each period. For instance, there is an apology for building a house at the "time of the horse" during the day, or building a house on the sixth, sixteenth, or twenty-sixth of any month. Four time cycles are referred to: the four seasons, the twelve months, days of the month, and times of the day. In each period a type of activity is disallowed that is associated with the natural element activated during that season: in spring, wood activities are disallowed; in summer, fire activities are disallowed; in autumn, certain metal activities are disallowed; and in winter, water activities are disallowed.

It is the same model found in astrological calendars in China, still enacted today in Taiwan in the Taoist rite of Tao Chia Yüan Liu (Saso

1972). Needham (1956) describes the cycle enacted by the Han Dynasty of the third-century B.C. China as follows: In spring, wood presides in the east as a sign of the growth of plant and animal life, hence the king is to avoid cutting trees and he forbids killing animals. In summer when fire predominates in the south he is to avoid "haste" that would lack respect for the hot season and thus cause epidemics. Between summer and autumn the element earth predominates in the center, and thus the earth should not be disturbed with building projects. During autumn when metal reigns in the west, all mining is forbidden, but, reversing the prohibition for spring, trees may now be cut and armies can be sent out to kill. In winter when water reigns in the north, no water may be stirred up by removing dykes.

The schedule corresponds to the agricultural cycle practiced today by Tibetans in Gyasumdo. Tree cutting is done only in autumn (when metal reigns), to collect firewood for winter, but not in spring (when wood reigns) since new plant growth is respected. Bridge building, which alters waterways, is done only in summer (when fire reigns), but not in winter (when the element water has primacy and is not to be abused). The *sa-bdag* ritual text reinforces this model of timing in order to maintain harmony (*mthun-pa*) between the human domain and the natural world.

Such scheduling is required, in the Chinese view, because human civilization has broken the initial harmony with the natural world. Harmony can be provisionally restored through proper timing of social-economic projects along with ritual apologies to spirit owners of each domain. Hence in Michael Saso's (1972:71) study of the model in Taoist rites, offerings are made to the "Lords of the Soil" in each direction in the appropriate season "to restore the five elements and their ruling spirits to the pristine state of nature." Tibetans of Gyasumdo likewise make timely apologies to the local *klu* and *sa-bdag* spirit owners. In the *sa-bdag* appendix, if a corpse must be burned in summer—the wrong time—this can be negotiated. If disturbing the waterways becomes unavoidable in winter, this mistiming too can be resolved through ritual apology. The model employed by ancient kingship is thus transmuted into the Tibetan Buddhist ritual system.

To clarify the centrality of this model of harmony between human and natural worlds I will introduce the Tibetan horoscope system of calculation, called *rtsis* ("calculation"). It underlies not only the time cycles of reciprocal exchange explored thus far, but is fundamental in all of the Tibetan rituals to be explicated in later chapters. In Gyasumdo, Nyingma Tibetan lamas acknowledge that the horoscope system they use is called the "Chinese calculation" (*nag-rtsis*). The principal *nag-rtsis* text,[12] which

12. The name of this text is *Nag-rtsis sngon-'gro'i lag-len* ("Introduction to Chinese calculation practice").

I have had translated by Tibetans in Kathmandu, was explained at length to me by Lama Dorje in Tshap village in Gyasumdo. His commentary is the basis for the introductory summary that follows.

Horoscope calculation, which includes texts on divination (*mo rgyab*), employs various cycles of time reckoning. The most important is the well-known twelve-year cycle (*lo skor bchu gnyis*) identical to the Chinese twelve animals that recur in the same order.[13] The twelve animals can also be used to designate the twelve months of the year and the twelve periods of a full day (a two-hour period is used for each phase of the sun starting at eleven P.M.). Two other time frames include the seven days of the week, represented as the five planets, plus sun and moon, and the thirty days of each month, based on the lunar cycle.

The importance of each time cycle for the Tibetan laity as well as for the lamas is immediately apparent in such a Tibetan village ethnography. Lay persons are aware of their own inauspicious days of the week, their own birth year in the twelve-year ritual cycle, and numerous images of relationship in the horoscope. These are not only learned in local discourse and ritual participation, but adult members of a village sooner or later request a horoscope reading from the lama for illness diagnosis, birth calculation, marriage matches, and after-death prognosis.

The twelve-year cycle is the cycle most referred to. Each animal year is correlated with one of the "five elements" (or "processes"): wood, fire, earth, metal, and water, as in the Chinese system. A person born in 1944 would be "monkey-wood," a combination that is repeated only every sixty years since the five elements, each repeated twice in succession, form a ten-year cycle that is juxtaposed to the twelve-year animal cycle, resulting in a sixty-year cycle.

The animal year–element link reveals the basic premise of the Tibetan *rtsis* system. Events that occur in each time cycle correspond to a conjunction of natural forces, as a spatialization of time. As time moves across the spatial plane of the natural cosmos, the five elements clash and harmonize. Calculation is possible because each element is linked not only with planets and stars but also with the cycle of the four seasons and the midyear, the four cardinal directions (plus the center), and the five colors: wood (*shing*) is linked with Jupiter, spring, east, and green; fire (*me*) is linked with Mars, summer, south, and red; earth (*sa*) is linked with Saturn, midyear, center, and yellow; metal (*lchags*) is linked with Venus, autumn, west, and white; and water (*chu*) is linked with Mercury, winter, north, and black.

13. The twelve animals are the rat, ox, tiger, hare, dragon, serpent, horse, sheep, monkey, bird, dog, and pig.

Periods calculated within each time cycle are auspicious or inauspicious for the well-being of a person or for the starting of a project, depending on whether the five elements as configurations of forces in the cosmos at that moment are in conflict (*'khrug-pa*) or harmony (*mthun-pa*). Different combinations come together and disperse as they move through the cosmos. In Tibetan Lamaism these configurations include spirit forces. Hence the need for ritual dialogue with them.

The Five Elements: Conflict and Harmony

The *nag-rtsis* text elaborates in great detail the various element combinations. The village stupas represent a hierarchical image of the natural elements. The usual four elements (earth, water, fire, air) are topped by a tree at the summit of the world mountain (Meru) representing all plant vegetation, and beneath the stupa are metal treasures in the underworld. Hence if we subtract air and add wood on top and metal underneath, we have the five elements.[14]

Jupiter	Mars	Saturn	Venus	Mercury
SPRING	SUMMER		AUTUMN	WINTER
East	South		West	North
Wood	Fire	(Earth)	Metal	Water
Green	Red	Yellow	White	Blue/Black

Figure 3. The diagram of seasonal correspondences

Clash or harmony in the process is based on the assumption that the element that "nourishes" the one above it is its "friend." Going from top down, earth is the friend of the wood (vegetation) growing upon it. Water is the friend of the earth above it, which it fertilizes. Fire, often pictured in Tibetan cosmology as emanating from below water, is the latter's friend since its heat vaporizes water to form clouds. Metal below fire is the friend of fire as "the iron stove that contains it," human civilization intruding at this point.

The "enemy" relation begins a reversed sequence. Metal, taken from the earth can be made by human civilization into an axe: metal, now coming down from above becomes the enemy of wood since it cuts down trees. Going in the same direction from top down, wood becomes the enemy of earth since it ruins the soil that is covered by fallen trees. Earth

14. Air can be subtracted in the short list of five, since water can become rain-bringing clouds. Air is added back into the list along with "heaven" (*gnam*) and "mountain" (*ri*) in the longer list of eight elements.

then overpowers water as landslides that muddy the rivers. Water in turn extinguishes fire, and fire, the agency of the blacksmith, melts metal, again lying at the bottom.

Not all lamas give the same interpretation as Lama Dorje, and explanations of why there is conflict or harmony of elements can differ in varied contexts.[15] With regard to the main consideration of this chapter—the timing of human projects to avoid conflict with the natural world—the diagram of seasonal correspondences shows how the five elements, far from being matter, are processes and qualities of nature going through transformations during the yearly cycle. Each element below, corresponding to its planet above, becomes dominant by turn during the four seasons, the element earth appearing during the harvest season during the fall equinox.

Eight Trigrams (spar-kha) *and Nine Numerical Squares* (sme-ba)

The relations I have outlined above are overlaid by two additional diagrams on Tibetan horoscope charts, again derived from the Chinese system: the eight trigrams, called *pakua* in Chinese and *spar-kha* in Tibetan, and the nine numerical squares, called *lo shu* in Chinese and *sme-ba* ("nine blots") in Tibetan.

The trigrams on Tibetan charts are always called the eight *spar-kha,* and are modeled on the trigrams of the Chinese *I Ching,* consisting of broken and unbroken lines. The trigrams are thus sign indicators of yin/yang balance changes that recur through the time cycles, and which affect human projects and relationships. In the Tibetan *rtsis* chart shown, the eight trigrams and nine numerical squares overlay the more basic diagram of elements, directions, and seasons.

The eight trigrams (*spar-kha*) are matched with eight directions going around the seasons, while each direction in turn is linked to one of eight elements, the original five expanded by air, heaven, and mountain. Again, the elements in this expanded form, in conflict or harmony, determine the trigram influences in horoscope calculation,[16] and all eight directions and seasons can be represented as element relations. In Tibetan calculation, the trigrams usually define a type of "element threat" in a particular time and place. Hence the trigram called *da* indicates the danger of being

15. The "friend" and "enemy" series are the two extremes. A middling relation is called "mother-son," which combines elements as follows: water is the mother of wood (it nourishes plants); metal is the mother of water (melted iron turns into a water fluid); earth is the mother of iron (the earth is the bosom of iron ores mined in the earth); fire is the mother of earth (ashes are transformed into earth); wood is the mother of fire (it is the burning fuel for fire). The series in this case conveys dependency, but also the manner in which elements are transformed into one another. A final middling series simply reverses the above, calling water the "son" of metal, and so on.

16. The Chinese model of yin and yang forces underlie the Tibetan trigram system. Seasonally, the male element yang is in ascendency during the summer; in the Tibetan system it

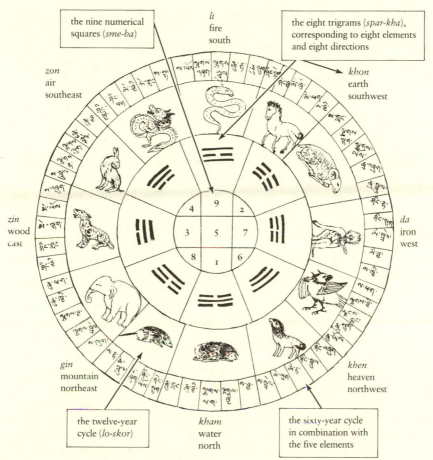

the nine numerical
squares (*sme-ba*)

li
fire
south

the eight trigrams (*spar-kha*),
corresponding to eight elements
and eight directions

zon
air
southeast

khon
earth
southwest

zin
wood
cast

da
iron
west

gin
mountain
northeast

khen
heaven
northwest

the twelve-year
cycle (*lo-skor*)

kham
water
north

the sixty-year cycle
in combination with
the five elements

Figure 4. The Tibetan *rtsis* (horoscope) chart

cut by metal in the west, while the trigram *zin* warns of harm coming from
wood (a falling tree, etc.) in the east, and so on.

The final diagram is that of the nine numerical squares, each square
having a number associated with a color. Originally, they mirrored the
nine provinces toured by the ancient Chinese emperors as well as the nine
rooms of the king's ritual temple; but Tibetans simply regard the *sme-ba*
as the numerical calculator in the *rtsis* system, a time grid for locating
periods of conflict or harmony.

Gyasumdo lamas often refer to the *sme-ba* numbers and colors to
indicate years that are dangerous, every nine years replicating one's year

is called *spar-kha li* and indicates fire, south. The female yin is in ascendency in winter;
it is called *spar-kha kham* and indicates water, north.

of birth, and each of the nine squares representing the intensity of conflict. The most harmonious squares are 1, 6, and 8, all white; 3, 4, and 5 are middling colors—blue, green, and yellow. The squares 7 and 9 are the dangerous color red, and finally square 2 is black, the worst color.[17] Each year of the calendar is assigned to a numerical square in a recurring cycle of nine years. A person born on 1-white has a very auspicious birth but a person born on 2-black (for example, in 1944) lives under the sign of a demon configuration.

Klu (serpent deities) and *sa-bdag* (earth owners) have become interwoven with each of these diagrams for the sake of scheduling particular human projects as well as the agricultural cycle. For instance, the popular ritual text used when starting a house-building project is the *Nang dgye*. In the text, various *sa-bdag* are explicitly identified with the "incompatibilities of years and elements, *spar-kha* and *sme-ba*." The world foundation is pictured as a huge golden turtle lying in the ocean. On the turtle's body are the eight *klu* kings and on the limbs and tail are the "*sa-bdag* along with their element combinations" considered as the "owners of the elements, the mountains, cliffs, lakes, springs, house roofs, foundations, and hearths." Inside the nine numerical squares are eighty-one *sa-bdag* who are imagined to roam, changing locations in the squares as the stellar and planetary configurations, as twenty-eight lunar mansions, roam through the heavens.

It is clear that the horoscope system of cycles of underworld and earth-owning deities is the same fundamental model of "harmony" (*mthun-pa*) employed by ancient kingship. It is also an intermingling of what Ahern (1981:9–15) calls "interpersonal versus noninterpersonal transaction." The noninterpersonal calculation of the Tibetan horoscope predicts certain configurations. The harms predicted can then be undone through interpersonal ritual apologies and offerings to the beings conjoined with each configuration.

The text used by the lama for appealing to earth owners is called "libation for opening the doors of the *sa-bdag*."[18] The model presented is that of "opening the doors of the four directions" controlled by the *sa-bdag*. The four doors are imagined to be found in a "mandala" (*dkyil-'khor*) of the four cardinal directions, around which revolves the *sa-bdag* king along with his royal court. At each point around, the king

17. In Tibetan horoscope diagrams the various area gods are associated with the squares, their natures revealed by the colors. The white squares are *lha* (gods). The red squares are *btsan,* and the black square is reserved for the *bdud* demon. *Klu* and *sa-bdag* occupy the squares colored green, blue, and yellow.

18. The name of the text is *Sa-bdag sgo bye gser-skyems* ("*sa-bdag* door partition libation").

is identified as the owner of the element of that season, and his *sa-bdag* retinue represent the horoscope conjunctions. The end of the text states: "The *sa-bdag* hold the jeweled keys to the four doors of wealth and send rain on time."

This ritual text is recited whenever libations are given to *sa-bdag* by Tibetan lamas, but it is clearly modeled on a royal system. More important in the context of Gyasumdo, it has a striking resemblance to the chant of the Ghyabrē shamans on the other side of the river as they carry the deer to be sacrificed and stand before the sacred grove and request entry into the underworld. For comparison I repeat here a relevant section of the Ghyabrē's chant, an oral tradition having no written text: "Open the golden lock of the north. Open the silver lock of the east, open the iron lock of the south, open the copper lock of the west. . . . the golden door, the silver door, the iron door, the copper door. . . . Open the doors, we are coming to make the offering. Open the doors of your home."

The image of four doors matched with four directions allows the Ghyabrē to link divine kingship of the Ghale nobility with fertility sources in the earth. In my taped commentary by the Ghyabrē, he notes that the earth spirits that he placates can also be called *sa-bdag,* a Tibetan name that is fundamental in the Gurung shaman ritual vocabulary. The Tibetan *klu* and *sa-bdag* rites performed by the Buddhist lamas thus overlap with the cosmology which they found already developed in Gyasumdo when they migrated into Nepal. The oral layer chanted by the shamans, however, continues to interact with the textual layer recited by the lamas.

The Dialogue between Harmony and Liberation

The Tibetan horoscope is a map of a total intercausal system. It remains embedded in a model of recurring "harmony" (*mthun-pa*) which is primarily the shamanic ideal. The lamas promote harmony as a layer in their folk culture, but graft onto that layer the karma doctrine of merit accumulation, which promotes the ideal of personal "liberation" (*thar-pa*). The Tibetan laity are caught between these two layers. More involved in the round of reciprocal relations, the Tibetan laity view the rites for serpent deities that we have explicated mainly in terms of a harmony ideal similar to that of the shamans.

In Gyasumdo the lamas formulate the karma ethic in opposition to the shamanic tradition, seeking to convince the laity that they should focus on the merit path. The lama's central institution for teaching merit is the Nyungne fast (*smyung-gnas*), during which the most committed Tibetan laity of the village join the lamas, monks, and nuns in the Gompa for a two-day period. Nyungne promotes reflexive comparison between the liberation ideal and the harmony model epitomized in folk rites such as serpent deity reciprocity and the horoscope. On the other hand, Nyungne aggravates the Tibetan lay dilemma, and instigates counterarguments by the Gurung shamans, which will be examined below.

The Tibetan lay persons who participate in Nyungne are temporarily removed from the samsaric round of work. I myself attended a number of these fasts. As a select group, we would take a vow (sdom-pa) to set ourselves apart to live a faultless day (sdig-pa med-par), to "wipe out" (sbyang) our past demerits through a rigorous series of prostrations and to accumulate merit (dge-ba bsags-pa) for the future through turning prayer wheels, counting rosaries, and circumambulating the Gompa. During the second day the fast becomes total: no food or drink, no speaking to anyone, no impure thoughts are allowed.

During the recesses, with hunger pangs growing and exhausted from merit making, we would sit silently on the rooftop of the Gompa compound and look down the hill upon the village below, as if peering down from a Buddha field upon a distant world we had left behind. We could see the rest of the laity who had refused to come, going about their daily rounds. The farmers who were plowing were, it was assumed, killing innumerable invisible creatures in the soil, dragging the farmer himself farther down into the samsaric cycle, while we, by not eating the produce of this work during the fast, were not being implicated in his deeds.

To make sure of our virtue we kept our eyes to the ground while circumambulating the Gompa to catch sight of small insects that might be unwittingly trampled. This is because sdig-pa, as demerit, can be done without personal motive to commit the offense, like the plowman who does not see the worms under his plow. In contrast, dge-ba, positive merit, can only be made with good intent (bsam-pa bzang-po). For that reason, any admitting to feeling hungry by the Nyungne participant is taboo, for that would indicate regret for having fasted, a sign of impure intent. For instance, as a joke, after Nyungne is over, those who attended for the first time are often tricked into admitting a "regret." One is asked, "Did you feel hungry?" A simple yes answer brings the immediate retort: "Then you got no merit because you regretted doing it!" I soon learned how to deny my impure intent.

On the first day, when speaking is allowed, the lama gives a long lecture on the meaning of the fast, and tells illustrative legends. In Tshap village one of the most popular illustrations given by Lama Dorje is the legend concerning a serpent deity or klu who gained liberation through Nyungne merit making. In the story there is a kingdom with a beautiful garden, in the middle of which is a lake in which lives a *klu*. The king's gardener has a dream in which the serpent deity appears, saying:

> I am the *klu* in this lake. My birth as a *klu* is a punishment for my having broken a Nyungne vow in my previous life. In my previous life your king and I were ritual friends, and we attended a Nyungne fast given by a lama. The lama had us take a vow that during the fast we would not sleep with our wives. My friend kept his vow, but I broke mine when my wife made me sleep with her. As a result, my friend was rewarded by being reborn king, while I was punished, being reborn as a serpent deity. Now I am suffering down here, and I must find a way to be liberated.

At the conclusion of the story a solution is found: the king sponsors another Nyungne fast. While the ritual texts are being read, the merit accumulated by the fast is transferred down to the serpent deity in the lake. This enables the *klu* to "ascend up to a Buddha field" to gain liberation.

Lama Dorje's Nyungne tale transmutes the serpent deity underworld into a Buddhist retributional model. To the older layer of reciprocal harm and benefit is grafted on a new layer of merit making and the reading of the Buddhist text, which transfers the merit to the serpent deities below. It lends support to the cultural revolution brought to Tshap village by Lama Chog Lingpa, defining the serpent deities as Buddhists who repudiate the shamanic mode of exchange through animal sacrifice. This is dramatized during the Dasain fall harvest. A special Nyungne fast (*gso-sbyong*) is held by Tibetans in Tshap village to protest the animal sacrifices being performed in the Gurung villages. The lamas transfer the merit made in the fast to the sacrificed animals, so they might gain liberation, as is done in the above story of the serpent deity.

How do the Gurung shamans of Gyasumdo view this Nyungne protest? The Paju shamans in Gyasumdo are particularly outspoken in criticizing the Nyungne, calling it hypocritical. "They say they are making merit, but they can hardly wait to finish their fast and return to drinking beer," comments the Paju in Galantso, questioning the "pure intent" for merit accumulation claimed by Tibetans. This Paju is particularly bitter about the symbolism of counteracting his own blood sacrifices. "They say we are sinning by killing the animals, but after their fast they come to our village and buy the meat for food."

The Paju shaman's sacrifice is a fundamental commitment to reciprocal exchange as the mode of harmonizing separate domains. In Mauss's (1954) theory the gift is made under the rule of reciprocity, with an expectation of equivalent return. In the spring rite of exchange with the underworld, the offerings of both the deer and the grain are identical equivalents of the return gift: the deer increases the abundance of animal food and the grain increases the crops which "grow up from below." Further, the shamanic exchange legitimates the "Ghale kingship," because a "real marriage" is required between upper world and underworld, through inter-clan marriage alliance in the Gurung system.

The arguments of both lamas and shamans often resemble critiques of ideology, an "unmasking" that is not newly invented with modern social theory. Lama Dorje openly asserts that the Ghyabrē shaman's legend about the Ghale ancestor's divinity is "not true," and serves "to praise" (stod-ra gtang) the Ghale whom they support. With regard to the shaman's blood sacrifice, the lama ridicules the naive epistemology of the Paju, who in offering a real animal, falsely rejects the validity of a symbolic substitute. The Ghyabrē and Paju, for their part, counterargue that without an ancestral link between sky and underworld, abundance is inconceivable and that the lama's imagined substitutions are unrealistic: mere symbolism which can never become the real offering required in valid gift exchange. While Evans-Pritchard (1956) found that the Nuer can substitute a cucumber for an ox in Nuer sacrifice, in a dialogic model one may dis-cover, as we do here, an argument about whether substitution is valid at all.

The Gyasumdo lamas transmute and overlay the older system of the shamans but they cannot fully encompass the shamanic argument. Earlier and later layers evolve dialogically between shamanic and Lamaist voices. When the debate process is highly explicit, Bakhtin uses the term inter-illumination. It propels dialogue into reflexive awareness of the other, and the alternatives that the other represents. At a less reflexive level, however, the process may also involve an implicit interpenetration of images, in which the polemic is hidden,

> only indirectly striking a blow at the other's discourse, with the result that the other's discourse begins to influence authorial dis-course from within. . . . The hidden polemical discourse is double voiced, with a special interrelationship of the two voices: the other's thought is reflected in the discourse, and begins to determine authorial discourse in its tone and meaning, as if acutely sensing alongside itself someone else's word speaking about the same object (Bakhtin 1981:196).

An implicit dialogue emerges in the Tibetan laity. For them the wealth-bringing serpent deities of the underworld subserve their lama's project, but the image retains the older trace of an underworld interlinked through marriage with divine kingship. After I had been convinced that I had obtained everything that could be said about serpent deities in Tshap village, Lama Dorje unexpectedly admitted to me that his own mother told an older, different story that had long survived in this Tibetan family. It was about a marriage between the upper world and underworld that was to have occurred in the primal era:

> In order to bring humans into the world and provide them with abundance, a god incarnated into the world as a prince. He went to the underworld and obtained a bride among the *klu-mo* (serpent deity maidens), who returned with him to the human world. Before the marriage could be consummated, the *klu-mo* said: "I must return to my home in the underworld for a period of three years. If you can wait for me that long I will return to you from below and bring with me all the wealth necessary for our offspring to live in abundance forever.

The serpent deity maiden decides to make for him a substitute girl to serve him while she is gone. She uses gold, silver, copper, and iron but these cannot talk. She picks up chicken excrement that is on the ground, and makes a girl who can talk, and returns to the underworld. After three years the prince tires of waiting and marries instead the chicken-excrement servant girl.

> Then the *klu-mo* returned and saw that the prince had married the excrement girl she had made. She took all the treasures and grains she had brought with her and returned to the serpent deity kingdom below, saying, "Now the people of the human world will not have the abundance they could have had. Instead they will be poor and hungry." That is why humans are poor, instead of having the world of abundance which they could have had.

There is a striking resemblance between the light-hearted, scatological imagery in this story and the Gurung shaman's underworld (Khrō-nasa), in which the inhabitants lay their loads down on the "excrement of goats." Bakhtin (1981:224) would detect here the "Rabelaisian laughter" that begins to restore the ancient complex.

Was there supposed to have been a marriage between a divine king and a serpent deity maiden? An ancient mythical consciousness in Gyasumdo claims that the present age of decline began when a curse upon humanity broke an original harmony with the underworld. It is a hidden premise in the Tibetan lama's rituals of reciprocal exchange with serpent deities. The image reappears in the lamas' *sa-bdag* texts that refer to an earth goddess as the source of all well-being, and to the "goddesses of the four elements" (*lha-mo 'byung-ba bzhi*).

The relational implications of this trace arise as ambivalence felt by Tibetan lay persons who are caught between the shamanic and Buddhist arguments. Nyungne merit making makes highly visible a selection of people extricating themselves from "the rest," who are caught in samsara. Tibetan householders who refuse to attend the Nyungne fast, however, complain that lamas are hypocritical and do not understand the lay dilemma. These lay persons describe the inevitability of transgressions inherent in lay "work" (*las-ka*): farmers must kill worms when they plow, traders must lie to make a profit, women kill tiny insects when they make chang (beer), and so on.

The tone is double voiced, an ironic view of liberation given by those who cannot escape from contamination. Lama Dorje opposes this lay protest, stating that the yearly Nyungne fast is designed as a "first step" out of samsaric complicity.[19] That first step is to draw an imaginary boundary around the participants and around their motivations, to imply that individual merit actions can be counted up.

But the lama's own serpent deity rite acknowledges the dilemma of labor complicity. As we have seen, the ritual enacts a relational way out by imagining an ideal world rather than promoting extrication from the world. The Gyasumdo lamas dare not ignore the dual image found in their ritual texts, their village stupas, and their oral tradition. The ritual construction of a "kingdom" promotes dialogue between liberation and harmony with the natural world. The lama must restore the "body parts" of the serpent deities in recognition that their realm has been violated, and then finds that he must expand the visualization by rebuilding an underworld utopia to which humans above ground can also aspire.

19. While karmic merit itself does not extricate humans from samsara, it can be viewed as initiating a *process* of extrication, as Heesterman (1985:199) has argued in the Hindu context.

Chapter Six

Rites of Defense: Serving the Guardian Deities (*btsan*)

T H E G H A L E L E A D E R S and their shaman supporters in Tapje had assumed that the immigrating Tibetans who settled in Tshap village would be incorporated into Ghale rule. Tibetans were included under the protection of the divine ancestor of the Ghale, viewed as the guardian deity of Tapje (Drong awa) who resides in the tree in the sacred grove. In his article on kingship and mountain gods in Tibet, Kirkland (1982) describes how this worked in Tibet: migrating families would "reassociate their traditional holy mountain [or lake, tree, etc.] with one in their new territory." In Tapje village one can observe this formula of incorporation: each Gurung family that has settled in Tapje has brought its own clan guardian spirit, who is then identified with that of the Ghale leader.

This model would have worked for the Tibetan settlers if it had not been for the intervention of the lamas, beginning with the great magical lama Duwang Tendzin, who "challenged the Ghale nobility over a hundred years ago," and recently when Lama Chog Lingpa repudiated the red offering sacrifice of the deer in the sacred grove. This chapter will focus on the guardian deity complex as a dialogic process, triggered by Lamaist intervention and still going on when the research period ended in 1983.

Incoming Tibetans of Tshap village have indeed brought their family guardians with them, defined as *pho lha* (patriline "male god"), or *srung-ma* ("guardian deity"). The Srungma may retain the image of an apical ancestor, similar to the Ghale leader's divine ancestor, but Tibetan informants also recall how their Srungma was probably "picked up" by their forefathers. A powerful spirit of some locality, for instance, would speak through an oracle (*lha-pa*) who was a member of the family. In one such account: "When they migrated here they did not know where to settle. They stayed across from Temang. But Ibi *lha-pa* ['grandmother god-possessed one'] was visited by the Srungma in a dream. She woke up and said, 'Don't stay here, go up the river until you come to the great cliff and settle there.'"

Some recall how their family Srungma had been a "community god" (*yul lha*) of an area in Tibet. Two informants in Tshap who had arrived as orphans are now saying that their sons will take on the local community god Akyenedong as their family Srungma.[1] Another informant has changed his Srungma through choice, holding a rite of apology to dismiss the one inherited from his patriline and acquiring a new one suggested by Lama Dorje.

The above examples in Gyasumdo illustrate how the changeability of guardian deities makes them susceptible to the lama's intervention. In the following pages I will describe the lama's intrusion into two Tibetan folk traditions, in which the warrior aspect of the guardian deity is incorporated into a Buddhist conception. In the first example, the guardian deities of all households in Tshap village are joined together to form an army around the local community god Akyenedong of Tshap village, to protect the Tibetan community and, in the lama's view, to protect Buddhism as such. In the second example, the guardian deity of the family group is transmuted, through a yearly household ritual, into a protector of the dharma.

In the Tibetan ritual sequence, there is a shift from the primary model of exchange with the *natural* world, which we examined in the previous chapter, to a model of protection of the *social* order in the human world. The shift is signaled by a change in the ritual discourse from an emphasis on "exchange" (*tshong-rgyab*) to an emphasis on "service" (*zhabs-phyi zhu*), implying service to the guardian deity of the clan or the community. The shift reflects feudal social relations and a new historical period, in which the epic of the Tibetan kings is glorified rather than the primal past. Srungma rites thus introduce historical consciousness, affirming a civilizational project.

In Lama Chog Lingpa's ritual text, the guardian deity or Srungma is the second of the Tibetan area gods, called *btsan* (pronounced "tsen"), who is red. The *btsan* are fierce warriors, spirit residues of historical kings and heroes. A *btsan* painted on the Gompa wall in Tshap village is a fierce, red, helmeted warrior dressed in kingly robe. *Btsan* are usually found

---

1. All males are born with certain deities within their bodies: a "male god" (*pho lha*) residing under the left armpit is directly inherited as the patriline's guardian deity. A "warrior god" (*dgra lha*) residing on the right shoulder is regarded as the fierce, protecting aspect of that same guardian. However, the birth god residing in the forehead is the "area god" (*Yul lha*) where one happens to be born, but it is sometimes identified with the guardian deity as well. To these three indwelling gods is added a fourth,, the "mother's-brother god" (*zhang lha*) which is inherited as the guardian deity of the mother's patriline. Men insist that only males have these gods within, a view that women, tight-lipped, refuse to comment on. Tibetan males of low birth are also said to have no gods within them, a view that low-status males themselves openly reject.

located atop red cliffs, waterfalls, or mountain passes.[2] Most Tibetan householders view their clan Srungma as having a *btsan* character. The Srungma protects the kin group against enemies, its "victory banner" (*dar-lcog*) raised on the roof of the house, topped with a yak tail.[3]

The Tibetan Srungma is often remembered to have had shamanic origins, having spoken through a "god-possessed one" (*lha-pa*) in the past. Tibetans in Gyasumdo also remark that their Srungma "protects us from the Srungma of the Gurung Paju." The ultimate prototype of the Srungma is not the divine ancestor of a king, but rather the spirit tutelary of the shaman, a model that is appropriated by the guardian spirit complex. I will thus begin with the Paju shaman's guardian spirit, and then shift attention to the Tibetan Srungma. The analytic problem is not only how the lama transmutes that complex into the "protector of the dharma" (T. *Chos kyong;* Skt. *dharmapāla*), but also how the prior, shamanic layer returns, particularly in moments of crisis.

THE PAJU SHAMAN'S GUARDIAN DEITY

We begin with the Paju shaman's tutelary guardian, which Tibetans call the The'u-brang demon. The Paju described his The'u-brang to me using Tibetan names, even though he has a variety of Gurung names used in his chants.[4] The Paju's own drawings of male and female The'u-brang are shown in figure 5.

The male image, holding the trident as a weapon of defense, is often seen pinned over the door of Gurung households after the Paju has finished an exorcism. The image is meant to be fierce for the same reason as guardian deities are fierce in Lamaism: to threaten and subdue evil power with the controlled demonic protector. The Paju claims that it has seven forms in all, sometimes appearing as an animal, a child, a man, etc., all named in the Paju's chant.

During the Paju's ritual performances, the male and female The'u-brang who aid him often operate as searchers to find the sorcerer enemy who

2. Mountain passes are often the seat of a *btsan* which resides in a *lha tho* ("stone pile") on which travelers put juniper branches and hang prayer flags.
3. The red-white combination implies that the Srungma is part god (*lha*) and part *btsan*. A few households having a purely *lha* guardian display only a white flag, but without *btsan* fierceness it is regarded as less effective. Laymen who do not own the house they live in hesitate to put their banner on the roof, and instead put it up in a *lha tho* ("stone pile") on a nearby hillside. Stein (1972:206) has observed that the Tibetan *lha tho* is often called *btsan mkhar:* "castle of *btsan*."
4. Tibetans use the term The'u-brang, Kang-pa gcig-pa (One-Legged One), Ber-ka 'sug khen (Cane-Using One). The Paju uses the latter two names, but in rituals he often refers to The'u-brang as Badza.

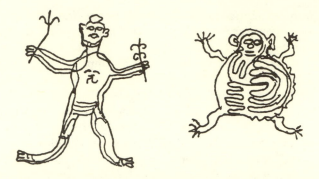

Figure 5. The male and female The'u-brang demons as drawn by the Paju shaman

has stolen a personal item or wealth from a client. Before the rite begins, two small effigies of the male and female The'u-brang are made. If they are elaborated, they carry a bag and stick and their feet point backward. At a minimum, they must have stuck into their bodies "wings" (chicken feathers) so they can "fly out and search." When they fly out, they are accompanied by porcupine quills called *dung-shing* that are "shot" from the quiver held by the Paju. The quills are said to light the way during the search by sending sparks of flame.

The following is a selection from the chant that the Paju recites while the The'u-brang fly about searching. The chant begins with the Paju's calling spirits of ancient "guru" Pajus into his body to give guidance during the rite, his body shaking as they enter. Then all fires in the house are doused so that nothing is seen. The Paju beats his drum and chants while he and the audience imagine that the The'u-brang effigies are flying, first inside the house and then out the door, led by the flaming quills that have been "fired" out of the quiver. In the following chant they search for a witch who has stolen and hidden something belonging to a client for the purpose of sorcery:

> Search around the fire hearth and in the four corners. If anything is hidden in one of the corners, find it.
> Then go to the house of the blacksmith. See if anything is hidden among the blacksmith's tools—his tongs, his hammer and billows. If it is hidden in his furnace, take it out with his tongs.
> Go to the fields and look in the earth in four directions. If it is hidden in the earth in the fields, then dig it up, using a pick.
> Go to the rivers and lakes. Go into the water and meet the fish. If it is hidden at the bottom, the fish will go down and retrieve it and bring it to you.

Search at the waterfall. It may be hidden behind the waterfall.
Ask the bird that lives there to fly behind the waterfall and retrieve
it for you.

Go up the high cliff on the mountain. If it is hidden there, then
ask the deer that lives on the mountain to get it for you.

Go to the crevasse between the cliffs. If it is hidden there, send
the small chepari [froglike animal] to retrieve it.

It may be hidden in a tree. A woodpecker in the tree will
retrieve it for you if it is there.

Go to the Gompa where the lama lives. It may be hidden in a
hole under the lama's house, or the nun's house. Ask the lama's nine
monk students to dig under the house and find it. The lama will aid
you by doing a libation, saying, "May there be no sin by digging
under the house."

It may be hidden on the great mountain [Mount Meru]. Only
the lama's ritual dagger can find it there. The lama will cast a spell
and send the dagger to retrieve it.

Now go below to Khrō-nasa. Get the lightning from the sky to
crack the earth and enter the underworld to retrieve it.

The chant ends with a quick journey to Khrō-nasa, the Gurung underworld, which is typical of all of the Paju's chants. Someone then relights
the fire, and the audience looks to see if the two The'u-brang (the flying
effigies) have returned from the search. The effigies are seen surrounded
by numerous quills that have been "shot" in the dark. The witch-stolen
object may now appear on the stick of one of the The'u-brang. The helping guardians are rewarded with "flesh and blood" of a sacrificed chicken,
but, "If they don't retrieve anything they get nothing," the Paju assured me.

In his commentary on the above chant, the Paju emphasized that his
mind follows the The'u-brang aides. They are mediators, since they are
both "of the wild" and domesticated—even their appearance is half beast,
half human. This gives the Paju access to otherwise inaccessible regions,
and he communicates with the natural residents of all domains—the
fish, bird, deer, frog, woodpecker, etc.—who then retrieve the stolen
object.

The oral chant, without textual guidance, explores the elements of
nature in a sequence that is practically identical with the ancient Chinese
geomantic diagram used in the Tibetan horoscope (*rtsis*). Beginning with
the fire of the household hearth, it moves out to metal (the blacksmith),
the earth in the fields, water, mountain tree, before arriving at the lama's
Gompa, then ends with a search at the top of Mount Meru and below
in the underworld.

The Paju is not aware of this underlying pattern, but he is eager to point out that the search process returns him to the primordial period "when animals and humans could converse," and all beings "cooperated as equals." The section referring to the lama is important to the Paju, since it shows the lama willing to cooperate with the The'u-brang and hence with the Paju himself. For the Paju, the chant thus returns him to the "good age" when lama-Paju collaboration was included in all of these intercommunicating domains. The present view in Gyasumdo, that the The'u-brang demons are the "enemy of the lama and the friend of the Paju," is a sign of the current degeneration.[5] The chant recaptures the model of primal cooperation, just as the cure of a patient or the recovery of stolen objects is achieved through cooperation of all domains in the natural world.

The paraphernalia of the Paju shaman are weapons used by the tutelary guardian, but they are also iconic signs of the "first era." Much of the preliminary chant tells how each item originated from elements whose harmony is essential for the success of the rite. The drum is made from the wood of a juniper tree, which is equated with the original tree connecting the three worlds. The drum skin is that of a *thangsar* (deer) killed by a hunter. These are necessary, says the Paju, "because the juniper tree and the *thangsar* are friends, even like relatives. Their minds are harmonious. If this were not so, the right drum sound would not come out." On the handle of the Paju's drum is a carving of a monkeylike claw. "It is the claw of a The'u-brang demon."

The appropriation of harmonious elements from the first era is then replaced by the use of these elements as weapons of destruction. In the Paju's chant, the offending witch or demon is often lured by the The'u-brang with false promises, so that it comes into the house. Once there, the enemy spirit is confronted by the Paju, who is armed with a full range of weapons and techniques for destruction.

In a basket half filled with corn are the main weapons: a ritual dagger for stabbing, two trident spears (*berung*), which are held in the Paju's hands and which "eat the flesh and blood" of the demons, along with numerous quills (*dungshing*). Placed in front of the Paju are two small stones. The first is the "father stone," a "meteorite from the sky" which strikes the enemy from above with lightning. It is used mainly to kill sorcerers. The second is the "mother stone," a volcanic rock from Khrō-nasa underworld. It is sent out "from below" to roam the earth in four directions, destroying

5. The Paju claims that the chant celebrates an earlier, open relationship. For him to go today to the Gompa and ask to dig under the lama's house for stolen objects would be unthinkable. The development of monastic celibacy which Tibetans regard with pride has for the Paju accelerated the decline from the good-age sense of equality between practitioners.

enemies. In order to terrify demons, the Paju has at his disposal four dog canine teeth, with which he conjures up the image of a mad dog. There is also a tiger whisker for conjuring up a wild tiger, from which the demon or witch flees in fear.

The Tibetan clan guardian spirit, or Srungma, must be understood in conjunction with the above shamanic layer. J. F. Rock (1959), who has studied Srungmas of the *btsan* type, notes that shamanic oracles representing each Srungma acted as sorcerers, "casting spells on insurgent enemies." While shaking in trance, the oracle would shoot off arrows at the invisible invaders. Heissig (1980), studying pre-Buddhist traditions among Buddhist mongols, found that every warrior male had a protecting champion spirit, its insignia carried on a banner and identified with the "warrior god" (*dgra lha*) of the male. He notes that these guardians probably originated with nomadic hunter-warriors, the deity guiding its owner's arrow to the target, whether a hunted animal or an enemy, whose heart would often be torn out and offered as a sacrifice to the warrior god.

In Gyasumdo as well, the Paju shaman's tutelary aide is a prototype of the warrior guardian gods acquired by the patriclan. We have noted that the ancestor of the Ghale clan Drong awa was such a warrior spirit and then became the protector of the village of Tapje. For Gurungs and Tibetans alike, the guardian deity develops from shamanic origins into a clan protector, and from there into the champion god of a village community.

THE TIBETAN ARROW-SHOOTING FESTIVAL

Every spring the Tibetan males in every household must participate in an arrow-shooting festival called Da Gyab (*mda' rgyab*). All household heads bring the Srungma guardian deity banner of their own patriline to the huge boulder on which lives the communal god (*yul lha*) of Tshap village. He is Akyenedong, the same god to which sacrifices had once been offered before the arrival of Lama Chog Lingpa two decades previously. Lama Dorje performs the Buddhist rite, reading Lama Chog Lingpa's text in front of the boulder. Then the males place their banners alongside that of Akyenedong atop the boulder, becoming warriors who join his retinue to defend the village. A gun is fired and they begin the arrow-shooting competition which defeats the demonic forces for that year. It is here that the warrior aspect of the lineage guardian is most prominent.

On two large board targets thirty meters apart the lama draws two figures of male and female demons, called *ling-ga*. They are naked and their sexual organs are prominent. The lama's ritual chant coerces the demonic force into the *ling-ga* image that gives it a form, so that when the arrow strikes, it will be subdued. There is much banter about the phallic nature of the arrows, implying sexual conquest as well, particularly when the arrow hits the naked female demoness.

In ritual exchange with the serpent deity underworld, reciprocal harmony with the earth was prominent. Here, that older layer becomes repressed, overlaid with a new layer: the historic theme of subduing for the sake of defense of the social order. When the demonic images are hit, the target boards are crushed to the ground and trampled down by the triumphant warriors. The village goes wild with excitement. The men who hit the demons are given honorific scarves and money and carried through the village to be met by women who greet them with songs and beer. Everyone dances through the night.

In his work on Tibetan folk songs, Tucci (1966) refers to arrow-shooting festivals in Tibet. He regards them as pre-Buddhist rites which Lamaism must have incorporated into the Buddhist scheme. Tucci notes that folk songs that glorify archery contests refer to wild yak hunting, even after being synthesized into herding and agriculture. In Gyasumdo, while the Tibetan men shoot the arrows, the women serve them beer from the barley harvest, while across the river in the "deer hunt" of the Ghale male cult, Gurung women also serve beer from their own barley harvest. In both cases a more ancient warrior-hunter image reinvigorates the defense of a social order built upon agriculture.

These thematic layers are ignored by Lama Dorje, whose main concern during the arrow-shooting festival is to incorporate it into the Tibetan Buddhist project. He links the warrior theme to the Tibetan legend of the battle between the gods and demigods over the wish-granting tree at the beginning of time. The demigods (lha ma-yin) living at the base of the tree attack the gods at the top who enjoy exclusive use of the fruits of the tree's branches. In the legend, the gods always win, but the battle must be fought every year, Lama Dorje argues, in the arrow-shooting festival in which local Tibetans aid the cause of the defending gods.

This interpretation promotes the importance of the lama's ritual chants, but the lay males are ambivalent regarding the lama's contribution. They argue that if the arrows that strike the two demons do not hit squarely, the demons are not fully subdued for the year. Lama Dorje scoffs at this view: "It is the mantric chants, not just the arrows" that ensure victory. The definition of the evil that is subdued is also dialogized. Laymen define it as the demonic forces that thwart abundance and health for the year. Lama Dorje does not deny this, but prefers to call the demons "those of opposed view" (log-lta) who harm Buddhism. They are the "real" target, he insists, lifting the meaning of the arrow-shooting festival into a higher battle for the establishment of the dharma.

TRANSMUTATION OF THE TIBETAN SRUNGMA: THE CASE OF SHUGS-LDAN

Prince Peter (1963) has argued that Tibetan clan membership based on allegiance to a guardian deity may represent a shift from a former unity based on blood ties to the imaginary unity of a cult. The "male god" (*pho lha*) often turns out to be "a mythical figure who demonstrates the unity of the lineage or clan group" (Brauen 1980). In the present study I am interested in how the lama seizes on the cult nature of the Srungma, in order to transmute its former ancestral image into the image of the Buddhist protector.

To do this the lamas advocate dropping non-Buddhist lineage ancestral protectors and taking instead those recognized by the texts as Buddhist protectors (Srungma). An aspect of this process of Lamaist intrusion is their writing of Srungma texts for Tibetan families. Most of the Tibetan family guardians in Gyasumdo are described in ritual texts which had been written for that family at some point in its Tibetan past, the text having been brought with the forefather that first migrated into Nepal. In the following pages I will examine the most popular Srungma in Gyasumdo, rGyal-po Shugs-ldan, along with the text used in the ritual that honors him by the households that serve him.

The Tibetan guardian deity called Shugs-ldan (or rGyal-po Shugs-ldan, rDo-rje Shugs-ldan, etc.) provides a special case study of the Tibetan Srungma and its transmutation. He is extremely popular, but held in awe and feared among Tibetans because he is highly punitive. Dawa Tshering, a wealthy merchant of Tshad-med village, has done very well with Shugs-ldan as his guardian deity. He gave the following oral account of Shugs-ldan's origin:

> Long ago in Tibet, rGyal-po Shugs-ldan was a powerful, learned lama who was more popular than the Dalai Lama himself. Other lamas envied him and tried to kill him. They shot at him but could not hit him. They tried to crush him under a rock, but he did not die. They tried to burn him in a fire, but he was not burned. Shugs-ldan called his enemies before him and said: "You want me to die. All right, I will." Then he stuffed a scarf down his own throat. Thus he died by his own hand.
>
> The spirit of the dead lama became a demon. He attacked his own former enemies and they died. The people asked the Dalai Lama to send a lama to exorcise the demon. A Jinseg [*sbyin-seg*: "fire exorcism"] was prepared. But when the fire was lit, it burned the lama instead of the demon. The people called another lama. Chanting mantras, the lama tricked the demon into entering his

body. Then the lama himself entered the fire and died. The demon
part of Shugs-ldan was destroyed, so Shugs-ldan became a god.

The above is a Tibetan villager's version of the Shugs-ldan legend.
Tibetans in Kathmandu who know the story say that after the Jinseg (fire
exorcism), the fifth Dalai Lama of that time (seventeenth century) invited
the still-wandering spirit to become a Srungma of the Gelugpa order,
with the result that Shugs-ldan became one of the most popular Srungmas
in Tibet. With the encouragement of local lamas, kin groups all over Tibet
took on Shugs-ldan as their lineage guardian, many substituting him for
the pre-Buddhist one they had before.

For Gyasumdo Tibetans, Shugs-ldan is similar to the previous century's
landslide-causing Lama Duwang Tendzin. Both images are hybrid constructions, combining the punitive power of the shamanic sorcerer with
that of the Buddhist lama. Both lamas had been dishonored by the people,
resulting in a curse which destroyed, but which now works on behalf of
those who serve him. Moreover, both lamas are viewed as historical per-
sonages who were rejected or unrecognized at a specific period, unlike
the serpent deities or earth-owning *sa-bdag* who exist from the beginning
as chthonic beings. What these Srungma lamas do have in common with
the nature deities, however, is the first model of retribution: that of
reciprocal vengeance.

Shugs-ldan participates in a folk belief that is regularly transmuted by
the lamas: a historical person who dies a strange, sudden death is likely
to become a dangerous wandering ghost having "unfinished business,"
often regarded as a vindictive *btsan* warrior spirit. Such a warrior may,
like the Ghale ancestor, become the protector of a noble clan and its
dependents, but when bound by the oath of the Buddha it becomes a protector of both the kin group and the Buddhist dharma. Lamaist authority
is particularly strengthened when the warrior spirit is also, like Shugs-ldan,
a historical lama.

In Gyasumdo, each Tibetan household has its altar on the male (right)
side of the hearth. The image of Padmasambhava is seen, but household
heads admit that the altar is thought of primarily as that of the lineage
Srungma. Those who take this relation seriously perform offerings on a
regular basis. The merchant Dawa Tshering for instance does an offering
once a month, but at high risk:

> If I forget, then he'll make me sick. But if I do not neglect him he
> will aid me wherever I go. When I travel I pray to him, "May
> sickness not come." When I cross a bridge I ask, "May the bridge
> not fall." If I do not serve Shugs-ldan he will get angry. He will kill
> my animals and I will lose my wealth and the members of my
> household will fight.

Many lay householders who serve Shugs-ldan in this manner also have a Shugs-ldan "text" (*lha-gsol*) which was written by a lama in the family's past. The text is read when the local lama comes at least once a year to the house to perform the *lha-bsangs* rite, which can be translated the "smoke offering to one's god." I was able to photograph one lineage Shugs-ldan text in Tshap village, which was later translated in Kathmandu. It was the only Shugs-ldan text that could be photographed, for other laymen feared Shugs-ldan's wrath if they were thus to reveal his secret.

I will analyze sections of the text in conjunction with the lama's *lha-bsangs* rite that is performed in the house while the text is read.[6] The warrior function of Shugs-ldan as leader of an army against enemies is boldly proclaimed in the text, which at first pleads with him *not* to follow Buddhist principles. Instead, "partiality" (*nye-ring*), "hatred" (*zhe-sdang*), and "arrogance" (*nga-rgyal*) are deemed to be the necessary qualities of the protector:

> rDo-rje Shugs-ldan,[7] the time has come to display your power and
> talent. The force of your *btsan* army and four garrisons: command
> them to be harsh! Gather more force, don't hesitate. Don't be
> impartial. Repel the hated enemy and harming agents by the spirit
> of religion. Resort to wrathful acts! Blow fire of red and black.
> Cause a strong wind, in the midst of which reveal your most angry
> and arrogant form. . . . Destroy the enemy completely . . . kill them
> immediately!

The passage lends support to Ortner's (1978b) view that certain Tibetan Buddhist rites seek to magnify the fierce (*drag-po*) aspect of the protector deity. Since Shugs-ldan is supposed to have made progress toward Buddhahood, he may not always be sufficiently partial and wrathful, and so must be induced to become so, for the protective function. Shugs-ldan's iconographic image in the text portrays the wrathful aspect in the extreme:

> From the syllable *Thi* arises the protector of the dharma, the great
> king rDo-rje Shugs-ldan. The color of his face is dark red, he has
> two hands, the right raised to the sky, the left holding a skull con-
> taining a human heart. . . . He rides a black horse. His emanations
> are unimaginable. . . . From the mists of emptiness emerges a
> palace. The walls are built from terrifying human heads and from
> intestines, lungs, hearts of humans. Their bone marrow is burned as

6. The yearly *lha-bsangs* rite, performed in the sponsor's house by the lama, is held between the new moon and full moon period, the first to the fifteenth of the month (usually the tenth month). The most beneficial dates are the third, the eighth, and the fifteenth.
7. Both *rDo-rje* and *rGyal-po* can be used as first names. The Shugs-ldan text for this household is called *Rdo-rje Shugs-ldan mchod-thabs gsol-kha* (Method of offering-petitioning rDo-rje Shugs-ldan).

an offering, and in the midst of its smoke sits the proud and
arrogant Shugs-ldan and his retinue.

The palace of slain enemies represents the sacrificial offering presented
to Shugs-ldan: the slain bodies of the enemies killed in battle are payment
for the warrior service.[8] The enemies' flesh and blood, together with their
hearts, are made into an image of a huge offering torma, which together
with animal effigies is given to Shugs-ldan and his retinue by means of
the smoke offering (*bsangs*):

> May these offerings of blood fill the ocean . . . may the meat and
> marrow, burned as smoke, fill up the space like a cloud . . . the
> external offering of black yak, sheep, bird, dog, etc. . . . . The flesh
> and blood of enemies repelled from the ten areas is built up into a
> large red torma like a hill. I offer them whether they are obtained in
> reality or in the imagination. . . .

The phrase suggesting that the flesh and blood may be offered either
in reality or in the imagination is difficult to interpret. Lama Dorje insists
that whenever such phrases appear in his texts it can only refer to a substitute, not an actual red offering, otherwise it would not be a Buddhist
ritual.[9] It is possible, however, that this hybrid image permits a degree
of slippage into the pre-Buddhist mode, in such a text that may have been
written in a frontier region in Tibet over a hundred years ago. The phrase-
ology can also refer to actual war, since later passages suggest that Shugs-
ldan had become a tutelary spirit of military campaigns. The meaning of
the text can thus shift in later historical contexts of performance.

The huge hill-like torma, representing the Srungma, is constructed by
Lama Dorje and placed on the householder's altar, with a warrior retinue of
small tormas surrounding its base. On twelve sticks that emerge from it are
put tiny dough hearts of the enemies. At the bottom are three small effigies:
a yak, a sheep, and a goat, the domestic animals that would be sacrificed if
it were a pre-Buddhist rite. In addition are block-printed animals that crawl
underground, roam the earth, and fly in the air: the three-world cosmos
and hence the totality of all wealth, including the five kinds of cloth, grain,
and treasures similar to those offered to the underworld.

In contrast to underworld exchanges, however, is the bold foreground-
ing of conquering apparatus: at the base of the householder's altar are

8. According to Hart (1975) the identification of the slain enemy in battle as a blood sacrifice
was common in ancient Tamil poetry. This is also the case among pre-Buddhist protector
deities in Mongolia (Heissig 1980).
9. Certain texts, for instance, refer to a "bloodstained" offering, in which case Lama Dorje
assures me it only means the red coloring on the torma.

put "weapons" (*mthson-cha*) made available for the Srungma's use, consisting of whatever is available: bow and arrow, spear, gun, knife, even a saddle. The entire offering is then magnified in the lama's imagination to make it equivalent to reality.

Historical kingship gained through conquest is the image that soon emerges in the text, conquest being equated with the spread of the dharma: "May we overpower the kings of India, Tibet, Mongolia, and their kingdoms, ministers and subjects and wealth as well as their Srungmas. By doing so, may we spread the dharma to people with inferior faith . . . with no opportunity to practice the dharma. May all their minds be directed to the dharma."

While such a statement appears to justify imperial conquest with a religious cover, it is not so interpreted by Lama Dorje. His main strategy is to transmute the narrow, particular cause of the householder's clan to the universal cause of a dharmic king. The householder is identified with the Tibetan king Khri srong lde btsan, who built the great temple monastery at bSam-yas in the eighth century. The performing lama is identified with Padmasambhava, whom the king invited to Tibet to subdue demonic forces and bind the local area gods to serve the Buddhist cause. The *lha-bsangs* rite is thus a reenactment of this historic event.

No longer is the focus on primal harmony with the natural world, as it had been in the rite of exchange with serpent deities of the underworld. Instead, all area gods, including the serpent deities, are inducted into the Srungma's army: "May the *sa-bdag, klu, yul lha* and their retinue come through their power of emanation. You owners of space, land, and water . . . reduce to dust the hated enemy and hindering demons." Once the "owners" of natural phenomena are oath bound, nature itself becomes controllable beneath the Srungma umbrella of command.[10]

At this point the householder goes to the roof of his house and calls for victory to his warrior god, here referred to as the *dgra lha* (pronounced "da lha"). Every Tibetan male is thought to have a personal warrior god, born with him on his left shoulder. It may be interpreted as the warrior aspect of the family Srungma. The householder circles around the burning incense (*bsangs*) altar on top of the roof, blowing a conch shell. He yells out "*Lha rgyal o!*" ("victory to the god!"), by which he means his own Srungma's victory.

While the layman circles above on the roof, the lama performer reads the text below the smoke hole at the hearth. Lama Dorje is highly ambiva-

10. This is done with the aid of three prototype Buddhist Srungmas who were known to have been subdued by Padmasambhava in Tibet: (1) rDo-rje legs-pa, (2) Thang-lha, and (3) Ten-ma chu gnyis, all of a higher order than Shugs-ldan.

lent about this section of the rite. He feels that the layman misunderstands the meaning of the text. "He is thinking only of the victory of his own family Srungma. He should be thinking of all Srungmas together, defeating the enemies of the dharma."

It is not surprising that the Tibetan householder is pulled toward the pre-Buddhist layer. The tiny dough figures put on the sticks coming out of the huge Srungma effigy are "hearts," and in the Shugs-ldan text they are hearts of "enemies." As the Tibetan layman goes to the roof to light the incense, he can look across the river and see the sacred grove in Tapje village, where the Gurung shamans sacrifice the real heart of a deer each spring. There, the life-for-life exchange with the ancient hunter's underworld is fused with the historic layer of the Ghale clan's ancestor, a divine warrior-king who demands hearts of enemies. The underworld offering as the more primal shamanic layer is translated into the historic battle.

Such a merging of layers is also evident in the Tibetan Srungma rite. In the Shugs-ldan text, the additional layer of the Lamaist transmutation is clear: the protection of a particular Tibetan clan is to be incorporated into the historic defense of the universal Buddhist dharma. Such a message is found nowhere in the legend of the Ghale nobles. By having Shugs-ldan lead armies in Tibet and India to "spread the dharma," the lay sponsor of the *lha-bsangs* rite becomes a "religious king" (*chos kyi rgyal-po*) with a universal mission on the world stage.

Once a Srungma is thought of in this way, the identity of the Tibetan patriline begins to shift away from its biological clan narrative to its "inner" narrative. Each Tibetan family gives allegiance, not to the Ghale lords of Tapje, but rather to a "temple community" gathered around the village Gompa. This trend has accelerated in Tshap village over the past few decades, and particularly since the reform movement instigated by Lama Chog Lingpa. The *lha-bsangs* rite with its reading of the householder's Srungma text is a crucial aspect of this transmutation. It shifts the narrative from the "story of nobility" to the "story of lamaization."

Contending Models of Retribution

A pre-Buddhist model of guardian deity acquisition—a spirit-possessed oracle—is thus being replaced by the lama model. The Tibetan householder comes to say that his ancestor "must have been a lama" who received initiation to serve a "Buddhist" deity. Tibetans in Gyasumdo contrast this image with what they call the "Srungma of the Paju," the The'u-brang demon. But they also refer to a time in the past when various householders, even some Tibetans, would "keep a The'u-brang in their home" in a back room, where it would be fed, going out at night to bring back stolen wealth from neighbors.

At present, only Gurung shamans are said to harbor such The'u-brang aides, but the The'u-brang demon is thought to have been prominent in Tibet before it migrated into Nepal along with the Bonpo exiled from Tibet. It is as if the tutelary spirit of the shamans in Gyasumdo belong to the Tibetan past, a pre-Buddhist guardian deity of sorcery and secrecy. The'u-brang guards the Paju's secret lore, and "will harm" those who try to penetrate it, as I was warned by concerned Tibetans. The Tibetan layman's own Srungma, no matter how Buddhist it has become, retains some of this older mystique. They had genuine fear that if I photographed their Srungma text, retribution would fall upon them.

Ambivalence toward the Srungma is interwoven with the Tibetan concept of pollution (*grib*). If a Srungma is polluted by events that disrupt social harmony, its anger will bring retributional attack. As the lama incorporates the Srungma into the project of Buddhist destiny, two retributional layers appear to be in dialogue. On the one hand, the Srungma is angered when he is polluted by "impure persons" (*mi-gtsang-pa'i grib*) who enter the house, such as a widow soon after the death of her husband, or one who has just been near a corpse (*ro grib*), or one who helped to give birth (*pang grib*). The blacksmith, who is also impure by birth in Tibet, also angers the Srungma if he enters and thus he is kept at the door, outside the house.[11]

But on the other hand the Srungma is also angered when polluted by "bad persons" (*mi btsog-pa'i grib*) such as the butcher (*shen-pa*), a doer of evil deeds (*las ngen*). Indeed, anyone who has just killed an animal and then enters the house can anger the Srungma, as can the eating of red meat on the same day that it has been slaughtered. The shift from "impure" persons to "bad" persons suggests that a new layer of ethical reasoning is emerging in the Srungma model of retribution. Quarreling or fighting among people (*'khrug-pa*) also pollutes the area gods and clan Srungmas, triggering their angry reprisal. When such fighting is defined in a Buddhist sense as involving anger or hatred (*zhe-sdang*) it implies a karma model of retribution.

11. Tibetans in general have ethical explanations as to why a butcher is polluted, but give ambivalent answers regarding the blacksmith. While many just say that blacksmiths have always been impure in Tibet, others attempt to ethicize the judgment in Buddhist terms: "He makes the weapons that soldiers use for killing," or "His hammer, tongs, fire, and bellows are like the hell realm." Unfortunately, the issue is further confused by the fact that in Gyasumdo the Gurung tailor (N. *damin*) is also not allowed in Tibetan homes. Certain informants admit honestly there is no Tibetan precedent for this, and that to call the tailor impure is to compromise with a Brahmin caste view in Nepal.

The Srungma's vengeance does not arrive at full Buddhist ethicization, however, since it does not judge an act as "sinful" (sdig-pa), a term that can only apply to individual demerit and its fruition over a long period of time. The Srungma's retribution is immediate and implicates collectivities; it is similar to the curse of the flying lama Duwang Tendzin, who brought the landslide down on Tshap village, or to Shugs-ldan's massive revenge on his enemies.[12] These Srungma types of retribution images are then pulled toward Buddhist ethicization by *later* interpretations. Some of the dialogue heard among Tibetans is precisely about this process. Was Lama Duwang Tendzin's punishment ethical? Or was it spiteful revenge?

Tibetan lay persons understand that the lama's transmutation pulls the Srungma image away from the older, sorcery model.[13] There is a dilemma, however. As Tibetan Srungmas become more ethically principled, they become less effective in obtaining immediate results for their sponsors. Lama Dorje complains about this lay ambivalence: "They would rather win (nga-rgyal) than become a Buddha."

This dialogic tension is reflected in the lama's divination text, called the *Lha-mo brgyad rtsis*. The contents are well known by the Tibetan laity since it is read to them repeatedly during the lama's diagnosis of illness. It is based on the time cycles of the horoscope (rtsis), but with Lamaist redactions. Certain selections, for instance, repudiate the "Srungma of the Bonpo" and reveal ethicization of the pollution concept. The following selections are pertinent examples:

> If you are ill on the monthly dates of the second, tenth, eighteenth, and twenty-sixth, these are times of the goddess Tenma. The Srungma of the Bonpo is angry with you. But your own *pho lha* [Srungma] is also angry . . . for you have eaten bloodstained [just slaughtered] meat . . . the symptom is pollution sickness and pain, vomiting, sores.
>
> If you are ill on the dates of the sixth, fourteenth, twenty-second, and thirtieth, these are the dates of the goddess Chema. You may have been seen by a Bonpo or there were people

12. A bus loaded with pilgrims returning from India, some of them Tibetans from Gyasumdo, hurtled over a cliff, killing most of the people. Survivors testified that the bus driver and the bus owner had been fiercely quarreling just before the bus plunged over the side. Many Tibetans believe that the guardian deities of the passengers had been angered and polluted by the quarrel. Since the pollution had contaminated the whole bus, the retribution had punished everyone.

13. My landlord owned an old sorcery text which had been handed down in the family from the lineage past, but which had not been opened for over a generation. I was given permission to take it to Lama Dorje for evaluation. He found that it contained a string of magical Sanskrit formulas translated into Tibetan letters. Lama Dorje expressed disgust that such a text should be found in a Tibetan home, and showed no further interest in it.

fighting and you went to witness it. The symptoms are pollution sickness, sluggishness, fever and headache, gall bladder pain.

If you are ill on the dates of the eighth, sixteenth, twenty-fourth, these are the dates of the goddess Khyong Dhema. Your illness was caused by *dam sri* and The'u-brang. . . . You may have eaten from the hands of a Bonpo. . . . While walking you experience coughing, aching of the heart and bones. . . .

If you are ill on the weekday of Saturday, it is because you were unable to perform the worship that you had previously been doing to the Srungma of the Bonpo. . . . For a remedy, read your *lha gsol* [Srungma text].

If you are ill on the weekday of Thursday, you are being harmed by a demon that your forefathers used to worship long before. . . .

In the above selections, "higher" Buddhist doctrines are absent, but an ethical trend is represented in certain types of pollution that anger the guardian spirit of the client. The "Bonpo Srungma" is interpreted by local Tibetans as a threat emanating from their past, and from the Paju shaman in Gyasumdo. For instance, in the third selection the term *dam sri* signifies a recurring harm (*sri*) emanating from a broken "vow" (*dam-bca'*). This implies that a pre-Buddhist Srungma of the past is causing present retributional harms.

By juxtaposing "Bonpo type" and "Lama type" Srungmas, the text reflects the dilemma posed by the Lamaization process: a past ancestor may have made a vow to a guardian spirit that continues to harm descendents after the vow has lapsed. Latter-day ethicizations of the Srungma image do not fully erase this *trace,* emanating from the lineage past. The divination text sorts out past from present Srungma anger and appears to distinguish the more lama-approved retributions from "amoral" demonic afflictions. Once the harming agent is matched with the time of its attack, then it can be known whether a straight exorcism is needed, or whether the lama should be called for a reading of the family's Srungma text, such as the one we have examined above.

The Tibetan *Lha-mo brgyad rtsis* divination method is based on three time frames: dates of the month, days of the week, and the twelve times of the day. The client tells the lama the date, day, and time of the start of the illness. The lama then consults all three time frames, each equating a set of symptoms with specific social events: the arrival of a traveler in the house, a fight, the eating of polluted food, failure to worship the Srungma, etc. Within each configuration the harming agents are identified and a ritual remedy advised. The client usually recognizes at least one of the configurations as his actual experience.

In the divination text, the causes of pollution and retribution clearly differ from those we have seen in the serpent deity rite of the previous chapter. Serpent deities punish when human actions disrupt the harmony of the five elements in the *natural world*. In the divination text, the Srungma and other area gods bring punishments for disruptions of the boundaries between *social groups* that have been historically constituted.[14] Both are concerned with threats of disharmony, but in different layers of time. Serpent deity retributions recall humanity's primal break with nature. Srungma retributions recall historically situated contracts, and focus on the warrior's defense of the established kingdom.

In neither case does retribution fully become extricated from a collective or relational base. Further, the punishing agent is still regarded as partial toward the domain or social group it guards in the samsaric world. The configurations that are read in the divination text thus represent the totality of relational causes, as does the horoscope system (*rtsis*) on which they are based. They do not single out an individuated chain of karmic causes and effects.

THE SRUNGMA DIALOGUE

We have analyzed Shugs-ldan's immense popularity as a Srungma, explained by his dual nature as a *btsan* warrior-king and a lama of Tibet. The problem of transmutation for the lamas in Gyasumdo is to find a formula by which such a family guardian can be both partial to its particular clan and oriented toward religious universality. The local Shugs-ldan text we have explicated does not really solve the issue. Shugs-ldan's identity is in process, not finalized.

An argument has been raging about Shugs-ldan, not only in Gyasumdo but also among Tibetans elsewhere. Is this Srungma really a Buddhist protector or is he, after all, more like the pre-Buddhist ancestral guardians of the past? Recently, the Dalai Lama, as leader of the Tibetan people, has made a historic judgment. He has determined that the guardian deity called Shugs-ldan not only is too dangerous, but he also has promoted a vicious factional rivalry between the Gelugpa and Nyingmapa religious orders. In a written statement sent to every monastery and to numerous

14. While social-order pollution encompasses a variety of threats from low or bad persons who intrude into the kin group, it refers also to the order of the social system as a whole. For Lama Dorje, an underlying concept is *skor nor k'yi grib:* "retinue error pollution." It implies that a reversal of hierarchy pollutes the social group, for instance, when servants act like masters.

Tibetan families in Kathmandu, the Dalai Lama has urged that Shugs-ldan as a guardian deity be dropped.[15]

News of the statement has filtered up the Himalayan trail to Gyasumdo. A new factor has now entered the Srungma dialogue. How can these villagers abandon so easily the guardian protector they inherited from their own fathers? I asked Lama Dorje of Tshap village if *he* could forsake Shugs-ldan. "I'm afraid to," he replied. "Look what happened to Lhagpa Tshering! Should I take that risk and be ruined as well?" Lhagpa Tshering's case is well known. Several years before he had tried to repudiate Shugs-ldan. After he had raised a new banner over his house to his new Srungma, Shugs-ldan struck it down with lightning. Because of such events the older punitive image of the lineage god continues in the internal dialogue of these Tibetan villagers, even for Lama Dorje, who is the most learned lama of Gyasumdo.

Another far more dramatic controversy, however, continues to transform the Tibetan Srungma image. We have noted that each spring the males of Tshap village join their family guardian deity banners into one community Srungma. As warriors they defeat all enemies of the village by shooting arrows at demon targets. They replicate the hunter-warrior motif, but they do it without performing the animal sacrifice that had once been performed in Tshap village before they repudiated the red offering. Just before the arrow shooting begins, Lama Dorje reads the local text written by Lama Chog Lingpa in the mid-1960s. The orthodoxy of this text, however, cannot repress the warring forces of signification that swirl around the text in oral discourse.

The Paju shamans in the Gurung villages openly argue that the Tibetans have made a tragic mistake by failing to offer flesh and blood to their community god. When the Tibetans of Tshap stopped their communal red offering, the Pajus predicted that terrible consequences would follow. A few years later, the prediction came true. In 1968 a great landslide roared down the mountainside and covered half of Tshap village. Many of the homes were destroyed, some villagers were killed. Most of the personal biographies of Tibetans collected during the research refer to this traumatic event.

The tragedy seemed to confirm the Gurung shamans' view, triggering

15. Tibetans in Kathmandu regard Shugs-ldan as a guardian honored by those who adhere to the Gelug sect, while members of the Nyingma sect think of Shugs-ldan as their enemy, sent against them by the rival sect. But in the villages these sectarian differences are not well understood. In Gyasumdo the lamas are all Nyingmapa, yet most of them honor Shugs-ldan as a lineage guardian picked up in Tibet in the past by their patriline.

a crisis of confidence among Tibetans. Had their lamas been wrong? In the community debate that followed, half of the laity argued for immediate return to the former sacrificial cult. It is not surprising that Tibetan villagers should make such a plea. We have seen that in the family Srungma rite torma effigies of the goat, sheep, and yak are given as sacrifice substitutions. The imagery makes the shamans' argument plausible: Could it be that the guardian deities require real rather than symbolic offerings?

The lamas and their lay allies were able to prevail in the debate, but only by shifting the explanation of the landslide to another source of anger, a memory trace from the past that could teach a Buddhist lesson rather than a shamanic one. It was recalled that the first landslide to cover the village over a hundred years ago had been caused by the legendary lama Duwang Tendzin, who had destroyed Tshap village because Lamaism had not been respected in Gyasumdo. Was the curse of Lama Duwang Tendzin still recurring? There had been a second landslide twenty-four years before, falling on the year of the monkey, and this third landslide had also been on the year of the monkey (1968). It all suggested a recurrence of the ancient lama's curse every alternate twelve-year cycle.

This argument was plausible because it could be equated with the theory of recurring harms, or *sri,* in which the untimely death of a member of the household continues to recur as a curse, striking other kin members later on as each reaches the same age as the one who suffered the first tragedy. Hence to this day, Tibetans of Tshap village refer to the *sri* of Lama Duwang Tendzin that recurs every other year of the monkey.

However, another Tibetan alternative to the shamanic view was offered during that debate. In this argument, the community god had indeed been angered, but not for the reason given by the Paju shaman. It was remembered that just before the landslide, a visiting Tibetan exorcist (*snags-pa*) from Nupri had been asked to stop the constant rain that was ruining the crops. He performed a libation (*gser-skyems*), but to the horror of those who were watching "he suddenly threw disgusting things into the burnt offering" calculated to pollute and anger the area gods: "old shoes, dog excrement, and the like." The wicked exorcist is said to have fled toward Nupri and died on the Larkya pass, but his act had "angered the area's guardian deity, who then caused the rain to pour in torrents," bringing the landslide down on the people.

Both arguments, heard by various factions today, shifted blame away from the issue of animal sacrifice, and enabled Tshap village to remain loyal to the Buddhist text of Lama Chog Lingpa. But Lama Dorje was not fully satisfied with these explanations. He visited Lama Dunjom Rinpoche in Kathmandu, the reincarnate head of all Nyingma lamas. Dunjom Rinpoche suggested another explanation. The landslide had occurred because of the four *sa-bdag* goddesses of the elements (*lha-mo 'byung-ba bzhi*). They had been angered by the killing of creatures in their domains, both through hunting and sacrifices. Only if the killing of these animals were to stop in Gyasumdo would the recurring landslides cease.

Lama Dorje returned to the village and painted the images of the four *sa-bdag* goddesses on the walls of the Gompa. These earth goddesses would now become more representative of the dharma, and he would present them as guardians of Buddhist law opposed to both hunting and the red offering. The landslide event had driven him to a further ethicization of the local mythical consciousness.

The Paju shamans, however, continue to predict future disasters. They smile knowingly and warn of the next landslide that will come because of the Tibetan abandonment of the red offering. Many Tibetans inside Tshap village remain ambivalent. Householder Phurbu's home lies directly in the way of the landslide predicted to come in the next year of the monkey (1992). "If only I could persuade our village to offer just one small chicken each year," he whispers. "Otherwise I'll have to sell my house and move out of here as the time approaches."

In the meantime, Lama Dorje is sure that his Buddhist argument will prevail, saying, "Another landslide would come *only if* the communal sacrifice were to be resumed." Everyone is waiting in anticipation. The lama is confident. "Let us see what happens," he says. "We will find out who is right."

DIALOGICAL IDENTITY AND NARRATIVE EVENTS

Dialogical analysis that is genuinely temporal must note how ambivalent images evolve within personal consciousness as well as in public discourse. Serpent deities of the underworld represent an image that subserves Lamaism, but they carry memory traces of an older, shamanic underworld. In the next ritual layer, the guardian deity (Srungma) becomes a Buddhist protector, but the Srungma is also a clan group's defender emanating as a trace from the ancestral past.

On the one hand, the Srungma himself is progressing up the karmic ladder toward Buddhahood. On the other hand, his retributional anger operates in the same manner as that of the Srungma of the Gurung shamans. The two retributional models interpenetrate. A Tibetan lay informant puts it as a dilemma. He himself might not mind if a black-smith (*mgar-ra*) were to enter his house, but his clan Srungma would be polluted and would send afflictions. It is what the divination text of the lama predicts.

The older layers are thus only partially transmuted by the lama's project. Opposed intentions within the same linguistic terms are present when such terms are used, and only contextual analysis can locate which intention is predominant. It is more than a question of language use, however. The mind which speaks these dual terms is itself divided, in Ricoeur's (1970) view, between "prior" and "anticipatory" tendencies. Prior relationships pull the self from the past; anticipatory ideals pull toward a future realization. The prior self is implicated in primary family ties that influence deep motivations (Obeyesekere 1981). The anticipatory self incorporates alternative possibilities from contemporary voices which, as Bakhtin puts it, become "internally persuasive."

Since internal dialogue is thus pulled between prior and anticipatory voices, analysis is incomplete that does not take into account influences from both time frames. The Tibetan rituals of the *klu* serpent deities and the *btsan* guardian deities instigate such an internal dialogue since these images are transmuted by the lamas from past recurrence into aids to future liberation. But destiny or utopian images are highly problematical. They have the character of metaphorical approximations of the unseen, unlike the unquestioned and felt presence of recurring events and authorities from the past.

Psychologically indeterminant future possibilities are for many Tibetan villagers *less* internally persuasive than the voice of the past: the persecution of a neglected lineage guardian, an area god that may punish with landslides, or the visible certainty of a real offering rather than an imagined substitute. Each Tibetan personality has a different relative weighting of past or future-pulling images within the self. Either may be foregrounded in different contexts. The transformation from one to the other involves intersubjective dialogue.

Tibetan ritual transmutations construct different layers of the Lamaist narrative, but in Gyasumdo these layers remain in contention with the alternative of the Ghale regime and the shamanic cult. In the most primal layer of exchange with the underworld, the lama's horoscope and divination texts attempt to displace the shaman's divination of the jumping heart of the deer. The Lamaist claim to build a Buddhist kingdom of well-being challenges the older divine kingship that had been established in Gyasumdo. In the rites of "defense" involving guardian deities, however, the historic stage of kingship and social order is introduced into the narrative. While the Ghale's ancestral guardian merely defends, the lamas celebrate the triumph of the king who defends Buddhist precepts against the "opposers of religion" (*log-lta*).

The narrative meaning that is built up, however, cannot be fully controlled within the texts or even in the lama's commentary upon them. No one can predict how or when a particular image in this field will suddenly flare up. Extraordinary events trigger new clashes of interpretation in unexpected ways. The recent fall of Tibet brought powerful lamas into the region, forcing local Tibetans to rethink their Buddhist commitment. The tragic landslide a few years later reactivated the older shamanic argument. Two models of retribution again clashed. The Tibetans were partially convinced by their lamas, but the shamanic interpretation of that event is remembered as a discourse that is hidden within the rituals of the Tibetan community.

The lamas of Gyasumdo are not unlike Walter Benjamin (1969), who viewed the past as historical layers waiting to be evoked, in order to awaken a future-oriented consciousness. Like Benjamin, the lamas seize on past critical moments to remind the people of their historic project. The recent landslide brought a panic to return to the red offering of the past. So the lamas evoked another past, the memory of the flying lama's curse, to incorporate the crisis into the Buddhist narrative rather than the shamanic one.

But the lamas do not have hegemony over the memory of Tshap village. In Tapje village across the river an alternative hegemony over memory is still asserted. To the dismay of Tibetans in Tshap village the Ghale leader denies that Lama Duwang Tendzin had ever sent any such landslide. The Tibetans on their part recall numerous events of oppression by the Ghales which the latter have "forgotten." The Paju shamans recall events which many lamas have also forgotten, such as lama-shaman collaborations in the past.

The events thus may be called dialogical events. They do not instigate "adaptations," but rather argument, reflection, and moral choices which become turning points that can be recalled. The lama's memory transmutations have been a deliberate weaning of the Tibetan laity away from the Ghale-shaman narrative, replacing it with a sequence of lama events. In this manner the Lamaist narrative emerges in the layers of ritual we have examined thus far.

Chapter Seven

Rites of Exorcism: Expelling the Demons (*bdud*)

Long lips reaching out from where one hundred males gather send envious talk [mi-kha] like an arrow; where one hundred females gather, it is like spun wool . . . where one hundred demonesses gather, it flows like water. . . . In Tibet the dharma is dying out, like living beings who are near death. Oceans are drying up, the Life Tree is falling. The big lips of the nine mi-kha *brothers are coming . . . (from* mi-kha'i lto bsgyur bzhugs so).*

THIS QUOTATION from a Tibetan demon exorcism text communicates the sense of decline felt by Gyasumdo Tibetans who came to settle in this valley. Many say they moved from the "good age" (*bskal-pa bzang-po*) in the Tibet they left at the beginning of this century to arrive at the "evil age" (*dus ngen-pa*) in contemporary Nepal. Further, Padmasambhava had predicted that toward the end of the evil age, the "nine Gongpo brothers" (*gong-po spon dgu*) would overrun Tibet. They are demonic manifestations that take a number of forms, such as "envious talk" (*mi-kha*).

Before my arrival in Tshap village, Mao's China had destroyed the monasteries in Tibet. For most Tibetans of Gyasumdo, such news from refugees coming down the trail were signs of evil-age acceleration. Lama Dorje asserted that Mao had been a returning manifestation of Langdarma, the demon king in ninth-century Tibet who had overthrown the first establishment of the dharma. As refugees poured down the trail in the 1960s, they reported that some Tibetans of low birth had cooperated with the Chinese in making accusations against families of high birth, just as the evil-age texts had predicted.

The metaphor of demonic return well fits the paradigm of exorcism. Gyasumdo Tibetans recall that in former Tibet, local landlords would sponsor grand exorcisms, in which a scapegoat in the form of a beggar would be exiled from the village. Carrying gifts of clothes, he would also

140

carry away communal impurities and afflictions, as if to play the role of the demon being exorcised. Had such beings now come back to bring a return retribution? In Gyasumdo, other kinds of aliens were entering the region, including alien discourse.

The demon is the third spirit agent defined in the text written by Lama Chog Lingpa. We may think of all three agents as making accusations against the human world. The *klu* (serpent deities) make accusations against those who destroy harmony with the natural world. Emerging historically, the middle *btsan* (warrior spirits) seek revenge for their heroic deaths, as did Shugs-ldan, analyzed in the previous chapter. The *bdud* (demons) are the third agents of affliction, harbingers of personal and historical decay. They represent a host of alien penetrations and half-forgotten traces as all boundaries begin to erode. Tibetan discourse in Gyasumdo implies that they are the third layer in a tripart narrative.

In demon exorcism the use of ritual by Tibetan lamas as a means of ethical and religious reflexivity becomes more explicit. At the same time, the dialogic rivalry with the shaman practitioners also accelerates because the Gurung shamans still claim to have the only sure means for dealing with local demons. For Tibetans in Gyasumdo, demons are the chief cause of death: the destruction of the *srog,* or "life force." The fear of this presence among Tibetan informants was first evident to me when the woman of a neighboring household said her child had been seized by a demon who had "ridden into the village on the back of a visiting relative, Drolma." How had Drolma got the demon on her back?

> When my sister was gathering wood at night she felt a tug on
> the sack behind her. She turned and saw a woman wearing a dress
> but her back was hollowed out. She knew it was a demon and ran,
> but it followed behind her. When she met our mother on the trail,
> the demon seized our mother instead. She got sick and died. Then
> the demon must have climbed on my back before I came to visit
> Tshap village.[1]

Tibetan exorcisms begin with such suspicion (*rnam-rtog*) of demonic affliction and proceed on the assumption that they can be ritually expelled or destroyed. Two years before the start of the research, there had been an epidemic of demon attack in Tshap village. Divination confirmed that

1. The image of the demon entering on the back of a traveler is called *'grul-'dzul,* and is widely held among Gyasumdo Tibetans. Once the demon enters a village in this manner, it attacks the weakest member of the first house the traveler enters. A family with a small child may put a sign in front of the door, warning all travelers not to come into their house first. The sign is a leaf rake sticking out of a basket, with a girl's trouser hung over the top.

the ghosts of two recent strange deaths, a drowning and a death during childbirth, had turned into demon killers. The most extreme Tibetan tantric exorcism, the Jinseg or "fire offering" (*sbyinseg*)[2] had been required.

I was able to attend one Jinseg. Inside the home where the villagers gathered, the performing lama drew a four-directional mandala on the floor colored red, green, black, and white, to represent all types of area gods.[3] A fire was lit over the mandala on which the performing lama boiled a pot of oil to a great heat. While chanting mantras, he suddenly poured in alcohol. A blazing pillar of fire shot up and spread out to every corner of the ceiling; the audience was surrounded by flames as if trapped in a burning house. After several seconds the fire was gone. The demons had been burned out, to be released into a higher rebirth. "If the lama had not chanted the mantras, the house would have burned down," the people in the audience assured me.

For Tibetans the *bdud* as "demon" is the summarizing figure of all harming agents. The demon pantheon includes the *gShin-rje,* messengers of death who emanate from the hell region; *rGyal-po Pehar,* the chief of demons who was subdued by Padmasambhava in Tibet and now controls lower-order *bdud;* and two types of *dre* demons: the *gShin-'dre,* wandering evil spirits of the dead (Skt. *pretas*) who have failed to find rebirth, and *gSon-'dre,* living sorcerers and witches. While some *bdud* such as the *gShin-rje* hell beings originated in the beginning of time, wandering ghosts or *gShin-'dre* are dead humans who have "not found the path," usually because their sudden and strange deaths have left them with motives of unfinished business and revenge.

For Gyasumdo Tibetans, the The'u-brang demon is particularly identified with historical degeneration. The The'u-brangs are thought to have come down into Nepal when the Bonpos were expelled from Tibet centuries ago. Everyone in Gyasumdo assumes that because he has tamed a The'u-brang as his aide, the Paju shaman is far better at dealing with this demon than the Tibetan lamas. A severe remedy is required to get this demon out of a dying child. The lama's own divination text, for instance, suggests that when a child falls ill from The'u-brang the best remedy is "beating."[4] The lama, however, can beat this demon only in his mind, while the Paju shaman sets fire to a broom and slams it down over the patient's head several times.

2. The Jinseg is the same exorcism that is said to have been used on the guardian deity Shugs-ldan in Tibet before he became a Srungma.
3. In this case, white is *lha* (gods), red is *btsan* (warrior spirits), black is *bdud* (demons), and green is *klu* (serpent deities) or *sa-bdag* (earth owners).
4. The *Lha-mo brgyad rtsis* text says the following under the "time of day" section: "The agents of harm are . . . The'u-brang and a she-demon coming from your mother's lineage. The remedy is to beat these demons."

THE PAJU SHAMAN'S DIALECTIC:
LURING AND EXPELLING

In chapter six, in examining the Paju shaman's use of his The'u-brang demon aide, we noted an alternation between harmonious cooperation among powers of the world while searching and enticing and then fierceness. This pattern underlies all of the Paju's demon exorcisms.

I will examine the Paju's Zor ("weapon") exorcism to reveal the basic pattern. The analysis is based on an exorcism performed in the home of a prominent Gurung householder. The performance played to a packed audience, the lay sponsor seizing the opportunity during each ritual sequence to explain into my tape recorder the legends chanted by two performing Paju shamans.[5] In the Zor exorcism, they entice the demon into an effigy. The Pajus then curse and destroy it, but they also expel it out of the village into a long cyclical journey so that it cannot return for a whole year. The double sentence of both death and exile allows for uncertainty in the outcome of the rite.

A row of tormas representing animals and humans are put on the effigy, to entice the demon into it. Once the demon is caught in the trap, he is cursed and then taken in the effigy out of the village, where he is shot with arrows and thrown over a cliff. The two legends in the chant provide models for the violent actions. As warnings and threats, they are persuasive both for the demons and for the audience in the house watching the performance.

In the first legend, a brother and sister go hunting. They kill a deer, but as night closes in they must stay together in a hut in the forest. To avoid incest, they make a vow to sleep back to back. The boy breaks the vow, however, when he turns over to grab some meat from the fire. At that moment a tiger enters the hut and eats the boy:

> His sister heard the sound of jaws chomping meat, but refused to break her vow and turn over, thinking, "My brother is eating the meat." In the morning she awoke and saw what had happened. She pledged to get revenge and crossed nine passes and nine valleys to find the killer. She saw a tiger and aimed her arrow, saying, "If this tiger is indeed the one that killed my brother, may my arrow hit its heart." She let loose the arrow. It struck the tiger and it fell dead.

When this chant is finished, a chicken is sacrificed and its blood is

5. The sponsor was the village leader of the Gurung village of Galantso. His extraordinary help was gained after my wife cured his wife of pneumonia. He spoke Tibetan, and during the Zor rite his commentary in Tibetan was understood by the Gurung audience. Later the tape recordings were gone over with the help of the two performing Pajus for corrections and additions.

poured over the effigy so that the demon will be lured into it, just as the tiger is lured into the house by the bait of the boy and his sister in the story. This red offering is a ransom, a substitute for the sponsor and his household. "Take the meat and go," the Pajus chant. When the ransom effigy is taken out of the village, the Paju aides aim a bow and arrow at it just as the sister had done.

The second legend chanted replicates the landslide that will cover the demon after he is thrown over the cliff:

> There was a boy who had no wife and no one would give a
> daughter to him. So he jumped into a lake and married a beautiful
> fish wife. The fish warned him: "During the rains the landslides will
> come, and since you cannot swim like a fish you will be carried
> away." The boy scoffed: "I can jump just like a fish! I'll stay." When
> the landslide came, the fish escaped, but the boy was carried away.
> Fishermen came and found him dead.

In the enticement part of the chant, the Paju says, "Come swim in the lake." In the destructive part he chants: "May you be carried away in the landslide!" The demons, after being lured, are thus destroyed like the "examples" (*pe*) in the chant. The disastrous outcomes also warn humans against defying the incest taboo or the rules of marriage. They warn that when established human rules are violated, the breach of social harmony brings demonic attack. But they also imply, as suggested in the model of Lévi-Strauss, that in the process of achieving the contemporary social order, humans broke the original, idyllic harmony between the natural world and themselves, and the breach was the ultimate source of demonic affliction. While the demons are at first lured through the image of idyllic harmony, the historical decay of that primal harmony which now requires humans to kill demons is dramatized in the climax of the exorcism.

This interpretation is supported by the Paju's exorcism of "pressing the Sri demons," which was also performed that same evening. The Sri are the demons that were released from the Gurung underworld (Khrõ-nasa) in the primal era. In the Sri exorcism, they are "pressed down," sent back into the underworld through a hole dug in the earth. The Sri demons are first lured into a tray of small dough animal effigies. Their footprints are detected by sprinkling a thin layer of white ash on the tray, covered by a black ash layer. At the head of the tray is put the skull of a dog into which the Sri will be put as an imprisonment.

All fires are put out as the Paju calls the Sri demons. When the chant is finished, an aide rushes to the door and lights a lamp to see if there are footprints in the ashes. No, there are no footprints. Again the room is made dark and the Paju repeats the chant. Again there is nothing. The audience grows impatient, and the Paju notes that he may have forgotten part of the chant. He tries again. This time the aide brings the tray before the audience, showing that the footprints, tiny wavy lines, have appeared. The ashes are put inside the dog skull.

Now the Paju, beating his drum, marches out of the house; his aides carrying the skull and followed by the entire audience. They come to a hole that has already been dug in the ground. The Paju peers down through the hole into the Khrō-nasa underworld. He lowers the skull into the hole, which he covers with ashes, rocks, watered sand, and finally wood. Over that a fire is built. The people rush forward and stamp furiously over the hole eight times, pressing the Sri into the underworld, while the Paju beats his drum and chants: "You are pressed down by earth and stones, drowned by water, burned by fire!"[6]

The performance makes clear that the Paju can only try to plug the breach through which underworld harms leak yearly into the human world, for there can be no real return to the harmony of the first era. The two main Gurung legends about Khrō-nasa examined earlier explain the retribution model of this breach: (1) A hunter goes to the underworld, but is punished for failing to share the deer with the inhabitants. (2) The "first Paju," who is from Khrō-nasa, curses the human world because his disciples reduce the share of grain offered to the underworld. In both legends, an idyllic harmony is broken by the refusal to share food according to the model of reciprocity. The human order and the underworld separate into antagonistic worlds.

The failure to share food with the underworld becomes a model for the failure to share food in the human world. As a breach in social harmony, it is linked with demon exorcism, since the envy caused by lack of sharing generates witchcraft. The witch enters a house during a meal but is not invited to join, and then leaves with envious and resentful thoughts that cause harm. Gurungs assume that malicious thoughts arise from unfortunates who resent not sharing in the food of the fortunate. Hence there is an affinity between demons emanating from the initial failure to share food and demonic afflictions emanating from contemporary social envy.

The primal era's retribution is understood within a model of reciprocal justice: the world was cursed by the first Paju, who let the Sri demons come up "from below," after humans refused to share their food with the underworld. In the present degenerate era, the model of reciprocal harm still applies. It is assumed that suspicion of unfair wealth accumulation

---

6. The stamping "eight times" signifies the "eight dangers" from eight elements of the natural world, a well-known formula in Gyasumdo, and represented in the eight trigrams (*spar-kha*) of the Tibetan horoscope.

is accelerating. Gurung villages protect themselves from the envy of outsiders by hanging a string of wooden knives across the village entrance
each spring to prevent the ruination of their crops. Thus in exorcism, the
Paju beats back contemporary envy while he forces demons back into
Khrō-nasa. It is a provisional measure, filled with uncertain outcome,
dramatized by the "mistakes" the Paju admits to making during the rite.

SHAMANIC COMPLICITY AND THE ETHIC OF INNER INTENT

The performance of terror through the shamanic curse deserves special
consideration as the mode of retribution, since the Tibetan lamas distinguish their own exorcisms from that of the Gurung shamans precisely on
this issue. The curses are "meant to kill," the Paju explains. It is the method
of dealing with the demonic in the degenerate era. The head Paju dons
a hideous headdress with "tiger's canine teeth" hanging down around his
face, and holds his trident in one hand and his ritual dagger in the other.
The assisting Paju shakes violently, beating his drum furiously and scream-
ing curses at the demon trapped in the ransom effigy. Commentary from
the Paju regarding his curses revealed three kinds.

The first type threatens violence as such:

> If you are the one that harms, the arrow will strike your heart. It
> will rip out the blood of your heart, your lungs, and your kidney!
> You will be stabbed with the dagger, your eyes will be torn out,
> your mouth ripped open! May the other harmers in your household
> die completely! May your father, mother, sons, and daughters die!
> May your animals—goats, sheep, horses—all die!

The second type of curse attempts to turn back the demonic harm
emanating from envious talk, turning it back against the demons themselves: "May you and your fields be ruined by envy and slanderous talk!
May you be harmed when people see ornaments and things in your house!"

The third type of curse turns back demons that were sent from the
Gurung underworld (Khrō-nasa) by the "first" shaman Khrō Paju. The
Paju reverses this primal curse by reciting idyllic images of the Khrō-nasa
underworld: "Go to the place where the radishes grow and where the *sisi*
fly stays! Go to the place where the leaf is like a plate, and where rain-
drops stay on the leaf without spilling! Go build a bridge over the footprints of a chicken!"[7]

7. In Khrō-nasa, radishes and the "sisi" fly originate. People are so small they use leaves
   for plates to eat off of and for vessels to carry water. They also build bridges over animal
   footprints to get over them. The giant-size crops and animals suggest total abundance.

In each case, the Pajus interpret their curses as an intent to kill, a motivation which distinguishes the Pajus' violence from the mode of intentionality in the Tibetan Buddhist exorcisms of the lamas. In Nyingma Tibetan Buddhism there are, in fact, ritual texts used for "pressing down the Sri" (*sri gnen*), counted among the highly "wrathful" Tibetan tantric exorcisms. Only two lamas in Gyasumdo, regarded as magicians (*sngags-pa*), attempt to press down the Sri. One of the texts used[8] has been written recently by Dunjom Rinpoche, the head of all Nyingma Tibetan lamas, and apparently is a summary of older *sri gnen* techniques. I will quote a few selections translated from the Tibetan text to show how its imagery represents ethical transmutations of the terror found in Paju shamans' exorcisms.

> Imagine you are holding their hearts with a hook and you have a
> sling around their necks, their hands and feet bound with chains.
> Visualize that they dissolve into the drawn figures. . . . Then
> imagine that butchers appear on the platform. As they utter
> wrathful incantations, flames like cutting knives shoot from their
> mouths. They cut up the bodies of the demons, whose power and con-
> sciousness flick out, like crops destroyed by a hailstorm. Imagine they
> are reduced to dust as water and sand are poured over them. . . .

As is done in the Paju's Sri rite, the Tibetan model is to press the Sri demons down a hole dug in the ground. In the text, the ground is imagined to "crack open" when the lama stabs it with his ritual dagger. He peers down into the underworld below: "Through the crack you see nine levels.[9] Below that is an ocean in which there is a nine-headed serpent demon (*klu gi bdud*) who is a prisoner of his evil deeds. . . . He has a crocodile's body and a dark, ugly face with his open mouth emitting poisonous vapors."

The lama lowers the imprisoned demons into the hole, imagining they are "pressed down into the mouth of the serpent demon." The huge crocodile mouth is then itself "tied" and the serpent "sent back" into the ocean depths below the earth.

In the lama's Sri pressing, the violence done to the demons occurs only in the lama's imagination, not in outward performance. The lama distances himself from the work of violence that is required. He not only uses an underworld serpent as an executioner, but he also conjures up butchers to chop the demons to bits so that the lama himself is not directly impli-

8. The name of the text is *Bdud gdon dbang gto grol log.*
9. The reference to "nine levels" indicates a Bonpo source in the text. A later passage referring to the underworld leaves out the nine levels, substituting a more standard Tibetan Buddhist conception: "Below Mount Meru there is an ocean in which resides the black serpent demon."

cated in the killing. The detachment is made possible in the same manner that Tibetans distance themselves from the killing required to obtain meat for food, the butcher caste (*shen-pa*) in Tibet functioning to absorb the sin (*sdig-pa*) of wielding the knife.[10]

In contrast, the Paju's terrifying gestures show that he himself is committing the violence, the shaking and shouting dramatizing the wrathful intent. Lama Dorje is particularly outspoken regarding this distinction. His view emerged when I challenged him to explain the seemingly violent threats that appeared during his own commentary on an exorcism text. In the popular exorcism *za-'dre kha sgyur* that is performed against death demons, the performing lama's threats appear at first identical to those of the Paju shaman: "If you disobey Phyag-na rDo-rje, he will split your head! He will chop up your body and send down a rain of weapons and turn you to dust! Instead of this it is better for you to leave!"

In contrast to the Paju, however, Lama Dorje was eager to deny any personal intent to harm even in this case. For one thing, it is the wrathful Buddha form Phyag-na rDo-rje (Skt. Vajradhara) who threatens, having manifested himself in the performing lama. The lama's own intentionality must contain no personal enmity while reading the text, no change of tone or facial expression. Further, the purpose is to "threaten," to warn the demon of karmic retribution so that it will "turn to the Buddhist path."[11] If the Tibetan exorcism does characterize the demon as being killed, he is "sent immediately into a higher rebirth."

In contrast, when I pointed out this "higher" Buddhist goal to the Paju, he had a quick rejoinder: "I only try to kill the demons, there is no thought of liberating them." The Paju further argued that the Tibetan lama's "higher ethic," in fact, prevents the latter from carrying out the violence which he, the Paju is willing to do.[12] The shaman regards his own exorcisms as more effective for that reason, justifying his own violent rites as the only effective way to expel demons from the community.

The shamanic and Lamaist styles of demon exorcism thus provoke a dialogue between opposed models of retribution, while at the same time they interpenetrate and mutually define one another. It is also clear that

10. Gyasumdo Tibetans agree on this general premise with varying opinions about degrees of complicity. When it comes to ritual killing, by conjuring up "butchers" to do the chopping, the lama's complicity is minimal.

11. Even in the extreme Tibetan Sri-pressing exorcism examined earlier in the chapter, the demons are pressed into the jaws of the underworld to punish them for their evil deeds "until they have obtained the Bodhisattva mind."

12. It is assumed that Lama Dorje as an unmarried lama (*dge-slong*) is more restricted than the married lamas who call themselves *sngags-pa* ("mantraists") and employ relatively more violent methods such as the Sri-pressing exorcism.

at the very point at which a Buddhist lama is most implicated in the life in the world—the performing of exorcisms—his personal extrication from the world is still ensured. This requires a denial: the lama's motivational purity is not contaminated. This is precisely what the Paju shaman does not deny.

TIBETAN EXORCISM: EXPELLING DEMONIC TIMES

One of the most popular Tibetan Buddhist rites of demon exorcism in Gyasumdo is expelling the three-headed demon, referred to as "the black three-headed one" (*Nag-po mgo gsum*). Like the exorcisms of the Paju shaman, this Lamaist version employs what Nebesky-Wojkowitz (1956) has defined as a "scapegoat" effigy (*glud*), which the lamas view as a ransom substitute for the sponsor. The three-headed demon is trapped in the effigy where it is subdued and threatened. The effigy is also shared out among all the demons as a substitute for the sponsor before it is cast out of the village.

The ransom consists of a huge effigy of the three-headed demon and smaller ones representing the sponsor and his household members, the entire structure substituting for the householder's wealth. On top are "thread crosses" (*mdos, gnam-kha*) consisting of five colored threads strung in concentric designs around crossed bamboo sticks. The purpose is to lure mGo gsum, the three-headed demon, into the ransom and trick him into accepting it as a substitute for the sponsor's household. Once inside it, the demon is captured by a fence of wooden knives stuck around the effigy and will be paraded out of the village by a crowd of lay helpers who whistle and shout to scare the demon away. The effigy is then put at the crossroad where it faces outward, now a "weapon" (Zor) aimed at alien demonic forces.

The effigy is usually constructed in the home of a lay sponsor. The three heads are carefully crafted by the lama and colored with dyes. The middle head is a red ox of "passion" (*'dod-chags*), the yellow tiger head on the left is "anger" (*zhe-sdang*), the blue pig head on the right is "ignorance" ("mental torpor" or *gti-mug*). These three basic vices can be extended to become the five poisons by identifying the ox as jealousy, the tiger as arrogance, the pig again as ignorance, the upper body as anger, the lower body as passion.

At the base is a long serpent deity tail colored blue. Hence the bottom represents a "serpent demon" (*klu-bdud*), the middle of the body colored red is the "*btsan* demon" (*btsan-bdud*), and the upper body colored black is the demon as such (*bdud*), an indication that here the three kinds of

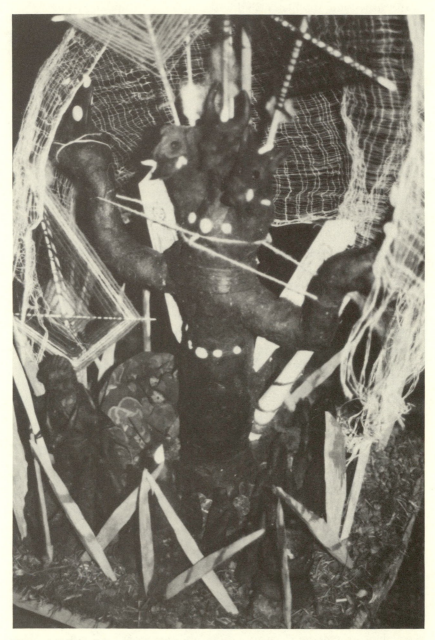

Figure 6. Effigy of the three-headed demon *Nag-po mgo gsum* used in Tibetan Buddhist demon exorcism

harming agents can all be characterized as demonic forces. The long arms are stretched out, palms facing up, each carrying a Zor, the magical weapon appearing as a long spike that will be turned against external enemies. Lama Dorje carefully defines this enemy as *log-lta*—persons of "opposed view" (those who oppose the dharma)—and teaches the lay audience this lesson while putting the effigy of a human corpse of a *log-lta* into the mouth of the head of the pig.

In the exorcism text, called "expelling the three-headed black one" (*Gto nag mgo gsum*), the legend that is chanted teaches the orthodox lesson of karma. It also dramatizes the capacity of the lama to represent the Buddha Manjusri, who transforms himself into a wrathful form in order to subdue the demon and bind it to the oath of the dharma. In the legend a three-headed demon child is born to an old woman because of her unnatural lust. Her aging husband accuses her in terms of karma· " 'This terrible child was born because of the accumulation of your evil deeds!' The old woman retorts: 'It must have been from both of our evil deeds accumulated from past lives.' The old man replies, 'No! it was from your evil deeds!' "

The husband tries to throw the child into the sea, but it protests: "If you throw me into the sea I will eat your flesh and blood! I'll kill living beings! If I don't get flesh, blood, pus, urine, then I'll eat my mother and father and all my relatives instead."

Then Buddha Manjusri (T. 'Jam-dpal-dbyangs) speaks from above, advising that since the child is really a flesh-eating demon (*bdud*) he must be "subdued." Manjusri then takes a fierce form, that of Yamantaka "with twenty-one bull's heads and forty-nine hands holding weapons with eight legs and tongue protruding." He swallows the three-headed demon, forcing it to submit to the law of the Buddha.

When Lama Dorje tells the legend, he dramatizes the "karmic" cause of this demon manifestation, and adds that it also represents "the present era of degeneration" during which the five karmic poisons become magnified. Extraordinary wrathful means are thus needed to subdue it. Further, since the Tibetan lamas of Gyasumdo condemn the red offering used in the shamanic system, the ransom effigy must be turned into an imaginary offering. It has the renunciatory significance of giving "everything" in contrast to the Paju shaman's chicken or sheep. The lama's visualization must trick the demon into thinking he is getting "the totality of all wealth."

The property of the sponsor is thus represented on the huge demon effigy as a part of the offering, magnified into "all desirables of visible existence"; the sponsor himself is defined as the Wheel-turning King. A square foot of grass placed in a huge concave iron pan resting on an iron grid is the foundation: the base of Mount Meru rises out of the ocean.[13] The demon effigy, the Life Tree, and the totality of offerings rise above, filling all of space with desirable things through the thread crosses on top.

The five colored threads of the thread crosses take on the significance of a garden paradise, the main illusion that will attract the demon into the trap.[14] The green threads are the trees of the garden, blue and black are sky and lake, yellow are the fertile earth, red are the cliff sides, white are the clouds in the sky. Rounding out this utopia are small block-printed effigies of wild and domestic animals. In the midst is the kingly "palace" of the sponsor, drawn on a wood tablet.

While these images are at first visualized metaphorically, Tibetan lamas claim that knowing the hidden meanings is not enough. The Nyingma lama's three-year, three-month, three-day retreat is meant to develop a capacity to visualize metaphorically, but also to transform the images metonymically into an actual reality. The levels of meaning are represented as a three-tiered semiotic system: (1) The "external" (*phyi*) level is naive realism (*ngos*) which only sees the iconic resemblance between effigy and offering. At this level the demons would not be fooled and instead would demand real flesh and blood. (2) The second, "inner" (*nang*) level is that of reflecting on the metaphorical meanings of the effigy with pure intent, a level achieved by lamas of "middling" (*ting*) capacity. (3) The "secret" (*gsang*) level of meaning is achieved through mantras (*sgnags*) which actually transform the visualization into a reality that is efficacious.

The lama first "beguiles" (*bslus*) the demon into seeing what he is visualizing in his mind and tricks him into entering the effigy to receive it rather than seizing the life of the sponsor. To do this, the lama makes the effigy of the sponsor and his wealth appear deceptively more grand than the sponsor himself.[15] The male sponsor and his wife are represented by an effigy of a man with a bow and arrow and an effigy of a woman with a spindle. Two sticks (*khram shing*) are stuck into these effigies on which

13. The text begins with this cosmology: "Out of empty space [*gnam-kha stong-pa*] there arises the earth and grass of Mount Meru [*ri-rab*] in the midst of the ocean. From this arises the four elements which comprise the turtle."

14. The thread crosses were originally Bonpo devices in Tibet. Here, their earlier function as demon traps carries into Lamaism, but with a great deal of added symbolism. The lamas call the thread crosses *gnam-kha* which can be translated "mouth of heaven" with the implication that all the desired items represented in the effigy fill the whole of space.

15. In the *brgya-bzhi* exorcism text this is spelled out as follows: "The ransom effigy (*glud*) of the sponsor is very beautiful, dignified, expert in talk, high in intelligence, dressed in fine clothes and beautiful ornaments . . . appearing as a warrior setting out for marriage. . . . This marvelous *glud* is even better than a human! So please accept it."

male and female figures are drawn, with their ages marked on the back, a check for each year. Over the male sponsor's effigy a smaller thread cross is stuck, the five threads representing his personal horoscope, the inner thread being the color and element of his birth year, the other colors filling out the five elements, fire, water, earth, iron, and wood. The threads are also to be interpreted as parts of the "sacrificed" body of the sponsor, drawing on another element combination: fire being the heat of the body, water the blood, earth the flesh, air the breath, and "space" (*gnam*) the mind.[16]

We have noted how the Paju shaman correlates demonic attack with the failure to share food. This is also assumed in Tibetan exorcism, a good part of the text carefully detailing the "sharing out" of the entire effigy as food given to the demons. The distribution is described as a dialogue between the three-headed demon and Buddha Manjusri. The demon asks for the "name" of each part of the effigy, and as Manjusri identifies the parts, they are assigned systematically to each type of demonic agent who must receive a share. It is the distributional emphasis that requires transformation of the effigy into a "real offering" by the mantras.[17]

Expelling Envious Talk in the Degenerate Era

In his analysis of the Underground Man depicted by Dostoevsky, Bakhtin portrays the emergence of the "fully dialogized consciousness" as a confession with sideward glances. One's own discourse and motives are penetrated by the voices of others. Such awareness accelerates in the ritual discourse of Tibetan demon exorcism, which focuses on the Tibetan term *mi-kha* ("people-mouth"): the manifestation of demonic attack from "envious talk." It can be contextualized in current social relations and historical conditions in Gyasumdo.

While the demons see the grand vision projected by the lama, the lay audience can see only the bits and pieces that go into the construction of the gigantic effigy. Among these are pieces of cloth called "rubbish bits" (dzara dziri) which the lay sponsor gives to represent his own clothing. While the lama's mantras change these bits into an attractive wardrobe

---

16. Other Gyasumdo lamas add an alternative series, using only the colors of the threads: red is the flesh and blood, green is the hair, white is the bones, blue or black is the heart. In this case the "external" (*phyi*) sacrifice is the five elements, and the "internal" (*nang*) sacrifice would be the five-colored body that is offered.

17. The mantras work a series of transformations. The first mantra makes the demons see the illusion of the total offering. The second turns it into a reality. The third prevents the demons from fighting over it. The fourth ensures an "exact" distribution. The fifth pacifies their minds and the sixth prevents the offering from running out so that all are satisfied.

for the demons, what are the ordinary Tibetans in the audience thinking? They are reminded of their decaying historical context.

According to lay informants, in the good age of the Tibetan past the nobility did not give rags but entire garments of fine quality which were taken by beggars or low-status persons who received them in playing the role of the "ransom" exiled from the village. Nowadays when the audience sees the cloth bits (with no human ransom) they interpret it as a meager distribution that stingy sponsors provide in the present degenerate age. While the traditional share-out to low-status persons who were exiled used to take place as a grand social drama, now it occurs only in the lama's imagination. While the cloth bits may satisfy the demons in the imagined world, they communicate to the audience the decline of their visible social world.

The lamas themselves complain of the refusal of even the wealthiest sponsors in Gyasumdo to add real clothes to the effigy. The complaint draws attention to the sponsor's impure motives. In theory the lay sponsor is an "offering master" (T. sbyin-bdag, Skt. danapati). He gains merit by commissioning the exorcism, but only if there is pure intent (bsam-pa bzang-po). If the sponsor is relatively poor, the lama's imagination can turn the meager offering into a magnificent one in any case.[18] But if the sponsor is wealthy, the throwaway rags are viewed as stinginess and lack of good intent. It is a sign of the "degenerate" historical context in which the visible social hierarchy no longer appears as an "inner" hierarchy of religious motivation. Ironically, when a newly wealthy lay household tries to spend lavishly as a ritual sponsor, this too is suspected as a false display, lacking pure intent.

Another "rubbish" element is added to the effigy, consisting of food leftovers and impurities such as used tea leaves, beer-making yeast, garlic, onions, black radishes, and a chicken bone, all dumped into a tiny carrying sack along with a few coins. They signify the provisions of envious talk, that is, mi-kha, which the demons will take away with them when they are exiled. This too triggers suspicion of the "sideward glance," for the wealthy sponsor has provoked mi-kha from the less fortunate.

We have noted how the Gurung Paju shaman curses such envious talk in his expelling rites. The Tibetan term, mi-kha, takes on the extra meaning of interpenetrating subjectivities that befall after Buddhism has focused

18. The text of the brgya-bzhi exorcism makes explicit the lama's capacity to "make up" for a poor sponsor's meager offering. Each of the four offering categories can be reduced to fifty, or to twenty-five, or for the very poor, even one item. A grand offering can still be attained if the sponsor has pure intent and the lama has the highest (rab) visualization capacity to expand the meager amount into the required gift of a "hundred each."

on the importance of inner intent. It is well understood as a demonic symptom of the degenerate era. Lay sponsors who stand out ahead of the rest of the community are talked about, making them susceptible to *mi-kha* harm. The lama's power of visualization attempts to turn the *mi-kha* into tasty traveling provisions distributed among the envious demonic agents, who will take them away. Epitomizing the envy of the unfortunate, these demons will be satisfied and "turn their mouths away" (*kha sgyur*) from the sponsor.

The displacement is homologous to the Tibetan folk custom of giving a child believed to be under demonic attack to low-status persons, who in turn give the child back the next day. It tricks the demons into thinking the child is not worth attacking,[19] but the metaphoric giving of the child to the lowly also appears to placate the source of what Taussig (1987) calls "counter-hegemonic envy." This too is part of the sideward glance that accelerates in the evil era. The Tibetan lama regards exorcism as a more comprehensive solution: he imagines a distribution of equal shares to *every* source of envy. Perhaps it will delay the effects of the decay a little longer.

Expelling the Cycles of Bad Times

When the Paju exiles a demon from a Gurung village, he assumes that it will "cycle back" the following year. This model is greatly elaborated in the lama's demon-expelling tradition. In the Tibetan horoscope (*rtsis*), complex cycles of harming influences are calculated precisely so that each household in the village knows when their member's "rough" (*rtsub*) periods are due. The Tibetan term *gto* ("expel") is associated with expelling inauspicious times. The opening lines in the text of the three-headed demon exorcism present the issue in terms of the horoscope paradigm: "Among the eight trigrams [*spar-kha*] some have become friendly, others enemies, and the planets and the nine numerical squares [*sme-ba*] are fighting. By doing so they send harm to us. Fighting then develops among us and property deteriorates."

These bad configurations are expelled with the ransom effigy, so that inauspicious times of every member of the household are exiled for at least one year. We have noted earlier that the sponsor's effigy contains a smaller thread cross of his personal horoscope. The lama also places twelve small animal tormas around the demon effigy representing the sponsor's twelve-year cycle. The nine numerical squares of the astrological chart

19. Low castes, the poor, and widows are considered crucial sources of "envious talk" (*mi-kha*). If a girl child is given to blacksmiths, she is called *gar-mo* ("blacksmith girl"). Since the low name is retained for a while after the child is returned, the name usually sticks as a nickname.

are also block printed and stuck onto the effigy, as are the eight trigrams and the seven planets.[20]

Each animal of the twelve-year cycle is associated with one of the five elements. The tiger year holds a plant (wood) and the serpent holds fire, the bird holds an iron wheel, etc.[21] The combinations dramatize the clash of incompatible time periods that can occur for different persons. Each person's birth year that recurs every twelve years poses a threatening configuration that weakens the self so that demonic harms can easily penetrate. Every household member's "unlucky year" (*lo-skag*) must be expelled with the effigy. In the textual chant each of the animal year tormas to be cast out is identified, beginning with the year of the rat: "The year of the rat: a human form with a rat's head, holding a ladle with water. Bring this ransom for the death year of persons having that year, expelling their unlucky year."

As the chant proceeds through all twelve, the lama has the option of mentioning the names of individuals in the household who are endangered by the coming year. The impact on each individual is predicted by the individualized cycles of the personal horoscope. These reveal the waxing and waning of the strength of one's life essence (*srog*), soul (*bla*),[22] body (*lus*), power or destiny (*dbang-tang*), and luck (*rlung-rta*), each factor having "periods of deterioration" (*nyams*) that invite demonic attack. In addition, the year just before and just after the unlucky year are partially dangerous. The birth year danger is further extended to another model called the "three ruinations" (*pung sum*), defined as every fourth year starting from the individual's birth year, giving three additional unlucky periods in each twelve-year cycle.

Added to the inauspicious years are the other two models, the nine numerical squares and the eight trigrams, also printed onto the effigy of the demon. We have introduced these categories before to illustrate the horoscope system. Here, we may note how these periodic disharmonies hit individuals at different times. Every nine years there is a danger calculated for each person from the numerical squares counting from the birth year.[23] The block printing of all nine numbers expels the dangerous times

20. The reader is referred to chapter five for an explanation of these categories.
21. In the text these combinations are arbitrary since in the horoscope chart the year and element combinations change throughout an entire sixty-year cycle, the twelve animals recurring on a different cycle than do the five elements.
22. The *bla* is the soul that can wander or be stolen while one is alive, while the *srog* is the force of life that is destroyed at death.
23. Persons born on *sme-ba* "2-black," the worst possible planetary conjunction and the most associated with the *bdud* demons, are the most endangered. Women born on 2-black are particularly inauspicious. One woman in Tshap village who was born on this date is assumed to have been a demon in her previous birth, and further, since it means that

for all household members. In the case of the eight trigrams, each household member's birth year is associated with a type of threat emanating from the natural elements that may strike that year. The eight trigrams are also printed onto the demon effigy to be expelled together.[24]

But another type of recurring harm may be expelled as well. These are the Sri demons which, as was already noted, are exorcized by both shamans and lamas in Gyasumdo. Tibetans equate them with extraordinary events, usually a "bad death."[25] The Sri continue to pull down other members of the same household as they arrive at the age of the one who suffered the first tragedy. Since any number of past ancestors may have suffered untimely deaths, Sri recurrences are numerous; and are often equated with different periods of the life cycle: they may call from the grave (*dur sri*), bring wealth deterioration (*phung sri*), or destroy bonds of relationship (*dam sri*). Any initial disaster may return again.

When the ransom effigy is paraded out of the village by the lay audience, all inauspicious times for the year are expelled from the self and from the community, and harmony is restored. In the final paragraphs of the text there is a summarizing statement. All "disharmonies" (*ma-mthun-pa*) that typify the evil era (*dus ngen-pa*) are expelled from the community: the clashing of elements, such as deer fighting in the forest, fish fighting in the rivers, birds fighting in the air; social conflicts; such as fist fighting, marriage incompatibilities, sorcerer's competitions, envious talk, hidden anger, and blasphemy.

The intercausal matrix of events that impact on each person is thus built into the demon image and articulated in the lama's text and his oral

---

she was born under "three stars" she is expected to have three husbands, bringing ruin to each one. During the research period she acquired the third husband and brought him misfortune as she had to the previous two. All that had been predicted seems to have come to pass.

24. If the trigram (*spar-kha*) *zin* which is associated with the element wood is due, then Lama Dorje warns of the possibility of falling off a tree, harms emanating from the "place of a carpenter." If the trigram is *da,* the element iron is threatening, and danger may arise from iron weapons, from "the place of the blacksmith." Lama Dorje's summary of the dangers represented by each trigram are as follows (see the diagram in chapter five): (1) *li* (fire), danger from any fire that is near; (2) *khon* (earth), danger when digging earth and from landslides; (3) *da* (iron), danger from knives, axes, iron weapons; (4) *khen* (sky), danger from things falling from above, or from falling oneself; (5) *kham* (water), danger from drowning in rivers; (6) *gin* (mountain), danger of injury while climbing up mountains; (7) *zin* (wood), danger from trees or wood weapons; (8) *zon* (air), danger of penetration by wind causing mental depression.

25. For effective exorcism of Sri afflictions, the horoscope texts usually recommend the extreme Sri-pressing rite described earlier in this chapter. Lama Dorje avoids doing that dangerous rite and instead recommends expelling the three-headed demon Nag-po mgo gsum as a summary exorcism.

commentary. Beyond this is added what Bakhtin (1984:162–63) calls a Rabelaisian "carnival sense of the world," with its "crownings and decrownings" that bring reversals and scandalize all pretensions. It is found not only in the extraordinary features of the effigy, but also in the climax of the performance. When the textual chant is ended, a carnival atmosphere erupts. Laymen from every household come and parade the three-headed demon through the village in the dark of night, clanging cymbals, beating drums, howling to terrify the demons trapped in the effigy. Other householders come to their doors to watch in a grand moment of village conviviality. After the demon is expelled, they throw white flour over each other in wild exhilaration. All become "purified" (dag-po).

In Gyasumdo, the demon exorcism of the Paju shaman, whatever its earlier transformations may have been, can be regarded as the base model. The Paju does not deny complicity in his terrifying methods of expelling and restoring, which at the same time keep alive an idyllic image of primal harmony as the ancient matrix. The Tibetan lama's denial through mental distance maintains a sense of personal directionality. It moves him out of such samsaric complicity. Yet he also retains the primal matrix in the horoscope images inserted into the base of the demon effigy, enacting as well the drama of restoring human harmony in the village.

In Bakhtin's view, this "folkloric matrix" returns in various forms even after the experience of time has been bifurcated "into separate individual sequences." This is explicit in Lama Dorje's commentary after finishing the above exorcism: "If the exorcism were totally successful, the evil era itself would be expelled, and the village would become like the 'hidden land' [sbas-yul]." The "hidden land" is the idyllic image of communal harmony prior to any differentiation, "in which everyone is equal and all land and food is shared." For Bakhtin, however, such imaging is not enough. In addition, the carnival sense of the world carries forward the dialogic potential of the primal matrix, as an underlayer that emerges in ever newer forms until it "bursts forth" as explicit interillumination between cultural voices. It is this betweenness, not found in the lama's texts, that we must try to unpack in rites of demon exorcism.

RIVAL EXORCISMS: DEBATE AND INTERILLUMINATION

What do the Paju shamans in Gyasumdo think of the lama's Tibetan exorcism? We have seen that the Pajus must add a blood offering to their own exorcisms to make sure that the demons are satisfied. The Pajus argue openly that in the case of demons there is simply no alternative. Only flesh and blood will placate them; otherwise, the exorcism is merely symbolic and ineffectual.

It is here that the clash of the two perspectives is at its sharpest. The lama's elaborate thread cross construction must somehow become a convincing answer to the Paju's challenge, so that real flesh and blood are not thought to be necessary. Thus the lama transforms the *glud* effigy through the power of his visualization (*dmig-pa*) into a cosmic totality that includes *all* animals and wealth of the world.

But here the lama's visualization teeters precariously on the question of his own transformational powers. The *brgya-bzhi* ("four area") exorcism text, for instance, states explicitly that a mediocre lama will fail to effect the transformation required. How then can a lay sponsor have confidence that his lama has sufficient power to twist the mind of a powerful demon who demands flesh and blood? Some Tibetans, while respectful of their lama's textual superiority, regard the Paju as more adept at the intersubjective struggle with the demonic powers, for the Paju knows their names and local histories. Such a lay person may secretly call the Paju to heal a patient after a lama's exorcism has failed.[26]

The Paju for his part argues for the superiority of his own exorcism as the solution to a moral dilemma, since he, but not the lama, is willing to take the risk of committing the transgression of ritual killing, both through blood offerings and by the curses that kill the demons. Further probing into his position reveals an ironic paradox. The lama's ethical message does penetrate the Paju shaman's consciousness. He partially accepts the lama's doctrine that the blood offering is a moral offense, but rejects the lama's view that he accumulates karmic demerit each time he ritually kills. "I commit an offense," he says, "but when I do it, I benefit the people. Therefore my bad deed is immediately erased, and we are the same as before."

When the Paju shaman's exorcism fails, the fault, he says, is partly his own because of his ritual errors, and partly the fault of the local community for not fully gathering around the patient for ritual protection. While the Paju respects the lama's ethical message, he reincorporates it back into a shamanic perspective of diffuse guilt that is taken on for the sake of the community and then removed through communal healing. This emphasis is consistent with the theme of relational complicity that is celebrated throughout Gurung customs, not only in the sharing of the meat of ritual sacrifice, but also in the death cult in which cooperation between

26. The use of the Paju by an individual Tibetan household may occasionally involve allowing the Paju's red offering as a last resort. This private compromise in extreme circumstances is not considered to affect the communal Tibetan decision to repudiate ritual killing. It does, however, illustrate the continued belief in the efficacy of the older practice. When this compromise is made, the householder will light butter lamps in the Gompa in order to make up for the demerits that are sure to follow.

intermarrying clans is necessary to ensure the proper destiny of the soul. Within this framework, however, the lama's ethical message can be seen to be gradually transforming the shamanic perspective.[27]

The Tibetan lamas perform exorcisms mainly among Tibetans. But when they compete with the Gurung shamans for wealthy Gurung sponsors, their transmutations of the shamanic ideology of Gyasumdo into a Tibetan Buddhist form become acutely dialogical, since they must answer counterarguments. This is highly explicit in transmuting the shaman's reciprocal retribution into the karmic model, as we have seen in the lama's attempt to ethicize the shamanic curse and turn the blood offering into an imagined offering.

Analysis of Tibetan uses of demonic imagery can clarify the epistemological shifts (Kapferer 1983) involved in moving from one retributional layer to another. Lamas exorcize demons even though they say that from the standpoint of ultimate truth (*don dam bden-pa*) demons do not exist. Lama Dorje argues that the essential value of exorcism is to transmute into the karmic path the experiences which the laity have in the cycles of demonic affliction. It is an opportunity for the lama to teach the doctrine of karma, the basis of Buddhist ethics.

Tibetans are eager to point out that Gurungs "do not know" the doctrine. It is known textually and then transmitted through Lamaist teachings. Only then does karma appear "evident," as a sign of observed inequalities in society. The lama employs the iconic images of exorcism to transmit a doctrine based on this textual epistemology. The *rtsis* horoscope diagrams printed on the demon effigy organize "primary events" which have first impact on awareness. Horoscope epistemology becomes a bridge between what is felt to be known experientially and universal Buddhist conceptions, which are not so known. The horoscope predicts the times of suffering for each person. The lama's exorcism seizes on these crisis points and links them to an ethical causal sequence. Critical events of suffering that recur in cycles are turned into visible signs of a linear series of karmic retributions.

The key to this transmutation is a temporal distinction made by the lamas between "timely" and "untimely" demonic attacks. After exorcism has expelled all "untimely" demonic attacks, only the "timely" karmic fruition is left in the patient. If the patient then dies, the performing lama assures the laity that it is from the patient's past evil deeds. The trauma itself becomes proof of the invisible karmic reality. This contrasts sharply with the discourse of the Paju shaman, who blames his failure to heal a patient on his own ritual mistakes and other influences of uncertainty.

---

27. This will be examined in a later chapter on the Ghyabrē shaman's death cult.

Tibetan lay discourse on this matter when the lama is not present indicates that indeed the Buddhist lesson "takes." The model of comparison is "recurrence" (*'khor*). When a family has a series of deaths of its young children, some lay persons interpret this as Sri demon recurrence, in which the demonic affliction causing the "bad death" of a first child automatically returns to pull down each additional child arriving at the same age. Others, however, will speculate that it may after all be *lan-chags* ("karmic retribution") coming into fruition. In this manner the model of time cycles is incorporated into the karmic sequence: it now becomes a return of the "creditor," coming back to demand payment from a harmful deed committed in the past. The shift is achieved by extending the primary experience of suffering into the secondary, metaphoric model of Buddhist retribution.

The transmutation becomes internally persuasive dialogically. When Tibetans employ the term *lan-chags* ("karmic retribution"), they are aware of what they are *not* saying, *bar-cad* ("hindrance"), a term used in contexts in which the speaker wants to imply that the demonic harm is undeserved. Tibetans understand that the Paju shaman's explanations are always that of hindrance, while Buddhist retributional discourse is viewed as ethically superior. When the lama uses the exorcism to "teach karma," his perspective and the shamanic perspective contend for primacy in the mind of the Tibetan laity. The lama's ethical transmutation in Gyasumdo thus emerges through the critique of the prior model of shamanic exorcism.

In what sense then does the shaman's perspective influence the exorcism of the lama? In the above exorcism of the three-headed demon, the lama performer becomes Yamantaka, a terrifying form of the Buddha Manjusri, in order to subdue the demon. It is strikingly similar to the Paju shaman's use of a terrifying appearance in the costume he wears and the weapons he wields. The Gyasumdo lamas refuse to admit that their technique may be even analogous to that of the Pajus, arguing that the terrifying form joined with mantras is the tantric method to counteract the acceleration of demonic power in the evil age.

There is another mode, however, in which the lamas can be said to incorporate a shamanic model into their uses of demonic imagery. In the ransom substitute exorcism the lama draws a boundary around the community and expels the demonic threat beyond it. Gyasumdo lamas defend this model as part of the Nyingma textual canon, but they admit that to draw such a boundary is a compromise within the conventional truth level. There is a more profound model, however, which ironically is the most shamanic appearing of the lamas' rites. It is the famous *gcod* ("severance") rite.

The severance rite in Gyasumdo is more than a private meditation.

It is found in a local text called *Gcod kyi tshogs las kyi cho-ga*, which refers to the accumulation of merit that benefits the householder who sponsors the rite. Here, no boundary is drawn and no ransom is cast out. Demonic beings are not expelled but are invited to fully penetrate and feed on the body of the ritual performer. The severance rite visualizes a fierce manifestation of the goddess Ma-cig lab-dron (*Ma-gcig slab-sgron*) cutting up the performer's body. The flesh, blood, and bones are distributed to swarms of demons and other sentient beings who come to the feast. At the same time the severance cuts away anger, passion, and ignorance as a meditation of ego negation.

We have seen that for both the Gurung Pajus and the Tibetan lamas, exorcisms are concerned with satisfying and expelling demonic harm emanating from envy by sharing out the ransom effigy. The *gcod* severance rite is said to carry the distribution to a higher plane by sharing out one's own body as a self-sacrifice. The distribution pays back the karmic "debt" (*bu-lon*) of the sponsor owed to those whom one has wronged in previous lives. The demons of affliction are defined as creditors who demand retribution (*lan-chags*). At the climax of the rite, the merit accumulated by the performance is shared out to all sentient beings in a grand vision of karmic intercausality.[28]

The emphasis of the severance rite in Gyasumdo became clear when Lama Nyima allowed me to tape-record his reading of the *gcod* text, translating each phrase into colloquial Tibetan along with comments given to local monks and lay persons who were present. When he came to the demons who rush into the feast as "uninvited guests," he joked with the audience: "It's like those people we all know who come to your house uninvited, that's what it means!" Everyone laughed, but the point was made: the principle of nonpartiality is crucial in severance ideology, the text saying repeatedly: "All must receive their share, no one is to be left out."

"What, then, is the most important meaning of the *gcod* rite?" I asked at the end of the reading. The lama did not hesitate. "It is the distribution. It is turning one's body into the merit offering and distributing it to all the guests." To illustrate why the food distribution should include

28. That *gcod* (severance rite) practiced in Gyasumdo is derived from the tradition developed in Tingri in Tibet (Aziz 1979), which is not far from Kyirong. When it is performed, the altar contains a torma holding a card painting of the twelfth-century Tibetan woman adept Ma-cig lab-dron who has become the central goddess of the rite. There is also a painting of her teacher, the Indian born Pha-d'am-pa Sangs-rgyas. The rite developed during the time of Milarepa when the shamanic tradition within Bon was still strong in Tibet and may well be a synthesis of Tantric practice brought from India (Van Tuyl 1979) with an earlier rite of Tibetan shamanic practice that is well known (Norbu and Turnbull 1972:129).

all sentient beings, the lama held up his two arms and revolved them in a huge circle. "Each of us has become the child as well as the parent of every other being at some time in the past."

The *gcod* rite itself appears to have been derived from both Tibetan and Indian sources (Van Tuyl 1979), but the Gyasumdo lamas say it is the "most Tibetan" of all their rituals and that it unites samsaric and nirvanic concerns in the same ritual act. It also appears to incorporate part of the shamanic argument that we have noted. As Samuel (1985:387) has noted, lamas "who have the highest status within the Tibetan system do so as much because of shamanic as clerical qualifications."[29]

The severance share-out is conceived as taking place "at the end of the age" when demonic power has become so prevalent that giving one's body to all beings becomes the most effective practice for gaining enlightenment. Lama Nyima was eager to place the significance of the rite in such a historical context. He left the gathering where he was explaining the rite and returned with a paper on which he had written a personal *gcod* declaration some years back. I quote here part of the final paragraph recorded on tape:

> Ma-cig lab-dron has combined both the Sutra [Mahayana] and the Tantra into one [*mdo-sngags zung-'jug*]. She is an external manifestation of Drolma. . . . Lord Buddha promised that at the end of the age when you find only selfishness, the victorious Mother will emanate as Ma-cig lab-dron from a northern city. From the beginning she has embodied the truth of emptiness within herself. She will make all beings—gods, humans, and demons—ripe for liberation.

THE THIRD MODEL OF RETRIBUTION

The above uses of the demonic idiom can thus be interpreted as a series of transmutations, displacing felt afflictions into images of self-transformation. Gyasumdo lamas explain that the laity's "scruple" (*rnam-rtog*) about demonic affliction is a level of reality that is useful for proceeding to higher levels. Transmutations build on the epistemological confidence gained at one level to promote confidence in another. In this sense, reality is a metaphorical ladder of what Vaihinger (1924) calls "as if" construc-

---

29. Shamanic initiations throughout inner Asia have enacted dismemberment of the body in which the "parts" are identified with various demonic afflictions and powers of nature (Eliade 1964, Halifax 1979). In Eskimo shamanism in North America there has also been recorded such enumeration of body parts in initiation (Bogoras 1928:441–44), suggesting ancient, pre-Tantric origins. In other regions of Nepal, the Jañkri's death is viewed as a dismemberment shared out into various species of the land (MacDonald 1975:124).

tions. One sees the illusory character of lower rungs only as one climbs to further rungs, even though it is clear that lower-level images still contend with higher-level intuitions, even in the minds of the lamas.

Such epistemological layers have an implicit temporal sequence in the narrative communicated through the performance of Tibetan demon exorcism. In the huge three-headed effigy, first, the primal era is Mount Meru with the horoscope diagrams printed onto it. Second, the historical, royal period is the demon as king with honorific umbrella overhead. Third, the contemporary evil age is the demon itself, but in particular, the *mi-kha* ("envious talk") that he carries away in his bag of travel provisions. As the narrative lumbers toward thirdness, there is a shift from natural element clashes and social sources of affliction toward psychic, intersubjective modes of affliction.

This implies a third model of retribution: *Mi-kha* is no longer mere envy, but is that which emerges in the era of decline, after the karmic model has already been internalized. This is supported by the fact that the lamas transmute *mi-kha* into "antireligious" demonic attack (*log-lta*) giving it a postdoctrinal interpretation. It is an intersubjective sense of retribution. The lamas observe that in the evil era, demonic attack is instigated both internally and externally, using the Tibetan term *rnam-rtog* to mean "scruples, doubt, suspicion of the divided mind." It is an intuition of how our wills interpenetrate, a reflexivity that is dialogically self-aware. In Gyasumdo, such betweenness is recognized not merely through meditation but in dialogic interaction with both the prior shamanic regime and the modern world.

A third model of retribution thus begins to emerge in the Tibetan ritual sequence, after an individual ethic has been internalized, but experienced as the decay of the individual in a decaying world. The advanced, severance (*gcod*) rite's method of dealing with the demonic threat, however, expresses an attempt to transmute this negation into a positive acceptance of ethical interindebtedness. Its universal distribution of wealth is a liberation technique that is both individual and collective. For Lama Nyima it is more than a ritual meditation, for when the goddess of the severance appears, she comes historically.

Part III

Rituals of Death

Chapter Eight

Soul Calling and the Shamanic Matrix

WE HAVE NOTED that Gurung shamans and Tibetan lamas have equivalent "rituals of life" that are layered in an increasingly reflexive manner. The base rites concerning underworld fertility are commented on and incorporated into rites concerned with kingly guardian spirits that protect the human order. The rituals of demon exorcism signify historical decay of that human order as well as decay of the individual.

While the rites of both traditions reveal progressive awareness, the Tibetan lamas explicitly transmute the entire series into a higher teaching. They begin by using each ritual layer to teach a path of karmic merit and inner awareness. To do this they reinterpret the images generated by the shamanic matrix—such as sacrifice, horoscope, kingdom, soul guidance—into what Bakhtin calls the "sealed off individual sequence." This promotes a bifurcation between personal time and world time. This second level of temporal identity, however, does not fully escape the shamanic matrix. That matrix, as a carrier of what Bakhtin calls the "carnival sense of the world," keeps returning in "Rabelaisian" forms, deconstructing the bifurcation and drawing the individual back into the world.

The enlightenment path which the lamas teach seeks to transcend the shamanic vision. It culminates in the highly elaborated guidance of the consciousness in the Tibetan death rite. We have noted in our analysis, however, that in Gyasumdo the shamans continue to argue back, triggering a reflexive process that cannot be controlled in such a programmatic way. The lama's technique of illumination cannot guide or predict the historically emergent dialogue, a process of interillumination.

Like other lamas in Gyasumdo, Lama Dorje is drawn into such dialogue in two directions, with the shaman from the past, and with the contemporary world of the future. In Bakhtin we have a thinker who seizes both ends, celebrating both kinds of decentering. From the past is the participatory personage (Leenhardt 1979) at home in the matrix of relations and possessed by spirits that are dangerous, but not ideological. At the contemporary end is the highly dialogized consciousness, "possessed" by overlapping ideological fragments that lead to a homeless mind.

The Gyasumdo lamas were not at ease with either of these modes of influence. They repudiated the Gurung shamans, but they also warned the Tibetan laity against modern ideas that miss the "root" spiritual causes. The lama's rite of soul calling in particular was caught in this double bind. From the past could be seen the shamanic model, viewed as a miraculous performance and appearing more convincing than that of the lamas. At the same time, the lama's soul calling was being ridiculed by the Nepal government school teachers who were sent up from Kathmandu, the most recent having scandalized the village by eloping with a Tibetan woman of Tshap village.

Both the ancient matrix of the shaman, and these modern penetrations, were becoming sources of soul loss. In the shamanic model, the soul would be frightened out of the body and snatched by spirit agents emanating from the past. In the modern context, soul loss resulted from distractions which Tibetans equated with the evil age.

For both practitioners, soul calling as a healing rite mediates between the rites of life and death, and involves what Eliade (1964) calls the "psycho-pomp" guiding of the consciousness that has been the hallmark of inner-Asian shamanism. In this chapter I will focus more on the rite of the Gurung Paju, to reveal in striking detail the shamanic matrix that has been the base model of this study, and to prepare the reader for the death rites that come in the next chapters.

The Tibetan text used by Nyingma lamas is named *Bla bslu,* which means "luring the soul." Textual versions have been translated by Lessing (1951) and Bawden (1962), but they do not illuminate these Tibetan Buddhist versions with an ethnographic study of the shamanic equivalent. The data presented here finally allow such comparison. The essential issue is the degree to which the textual chant of the lamas is decontextualized from the local space and time in which the shaman is embedded. I will begin with the lay version of soul calling practiced by families in both communities. I will then present in detail the oral rite of the Paju shaman, and follow it with the Tibetan lama's textual performance, so that the two versions of this ancient healing rite may contend side by side in the mind of the reader.

Gurung and Tibetan families share a similar folk tradition in Gyasumdo which in this case clearly resembles the shamanic model. I was first introduced to such soul recalling in a Tibetan household. A mother recalled the wandering soul of her infant child, whose lethargic look was taken as a sign that the *bla* ("soul," pronounced "la") had been taken away. She placed flowers in a jug of water and took it with a plate lined with rice and a short length of string to the small stream outside the house. It was assumed that the soul had been hidden by one of the area gods in a location defined by the elements of nature. The mother called to the soul as follows:

> Don't stay under the water,
> don't stay under a rock or tree or under the earth,
> from all of the directions please come!
>
> If you are caught by a *klu,* escape from it,
> If you are caught by a *btsan,* escape from it,
> If you are caught by a *bdud,* escape from it!
>
> Escape from any direction. Your mother, your father,
> your relatives are all here. We have food for you here.

When she felt that the soul might have returned, she took the string which the soul should enter, and tied it around the flowers. She went into the house and asked the household members, "Has the soul returned yet?" "No, it has not," they replied. She returned to the stream and repeated the above. Again she went in and asked the question. They sent her back to repeat the calling for a third time, viewed as the last chance. This time they said, "Yes, it has come back." She removed the flowers and dropped kernels of rice into the water jug one at a time as a divination. When the kernels began to float rather than sink, it was a sign that the soul had returned. Then she tied the string around the neck of the infant.

This family soul calling is fundamentally shamanic. It appeals to natural relationships inherent in each domain: the harmony among elements in nature, between the child and the parental home, and between the alienated soul and the human body to which it returns. This restoring of the proper balance of agents within and between each domain is the basis of the final divination.

SOUL CALLING OF THE GURUNG SHAMAN

The soul-calling techniques of both the Gurung Paju and the Tibetan lama build upon this folk model, but it is the Paju shaman who elaborates its basic ideal of balancing relationships. When the Gurung Paju recalls the soul, he calls it a *pla;* the pronunciation "pla" suggests a common origin with the Tibetan term (*bla*). The Paju first takes the pulse of the patient to locate the mode of spirit attack. If the pulse flows very slowly in the right arm, it means the soul has been stolen by one of the invisible gods or demons of the three worlds. If the pulse flows extremely fast in the left arm, a living witch has stolen it.[1]

The Paju then hangs a huge garland of golden flowers gathered in the wild from the ceiling of the patient's house, calling it a "golden ladder" which ascends to the upper world of the gods. Beneath are prepared dough effigies into which the Paju's tutelary and other spirit aides are invited. They will join him in searching for the lost soul. The largest effigy also represents the mountain that connects the underworld, human world, and upper world. Four twigs stuck into it represent the tree on the mountain, and effigies of four birds are stuck on their ends.

The birds thus "sit on the branches of the tree growing out of the mountain," but they are also sent out in four directions ahead of the tutelary searchers, later to become goddess dancers who lure the soul. The patient is marked with soot on the forehead, with a string led to a finger so that the tutelary searchers can claim, during their search, that the soul they demand back is indeed the one belonging to the patient.

Before the journey begins, the Paju's main ancestral spirit is called from his home in the land of the gods above Tibet. He travels down the ancient migration trail, enters the large effigy, and enters the Paju shaman's body. The Paju shakes during the jolting penetration. He is now empowered to undertake the journey back up the trail with his spirit retinue, which will lead up the mountain and the tree, then up the nine ladders to the upper world, called Mu gi Gompa ("sky" gompa), to arrive at the palace of the gods. If the soul of the patient is not found there, he will have to search for it in the Gurung underworld, Khrō-nasa.

This cosmology is not only created in the mind of the Paju shaman. Much of it is a locally experienced matrix of relations and landmarks. In the Paju's chant the journey goes up the trail running through Gyasumdo that is used by everyone. The chant-song of the journey, called *pe* ("exemplary model"), begins when the house is darkened. The audience of Gurungs crowd around the Paju and the patient. Hearing the drum and the chant, they imagine the Paju's mind is following his tutelary spirit aides up the trail. The Paju holds his trident to protect the group from demon attack, while his porcupine quills (*dung-shing*) fly in the air above to light the path with sparks of fire.

The search begins locally, the Paju calling out the names of goddesses of rock, soil, rivers, and trees to ask if the soul has been taken and hidden

---

1. Pulse taking by the Gurung Paju can also identify other kinds of disease-causing spirit attacks. If the pulse goes forward and backward, a live witch is sending sickness into the body. If it jumps up and down, the attack has been made by a The'u-brang demon, and so forth.

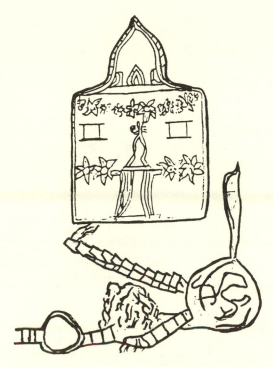

Figure 7. Drawing by the Paju shaman showing the palace of the gods and the ladders leading to it

in these regions. It might be found here, but the rite invariably goes on to every cosmological domain, covering all possibilities. As the Paju and his aides proceed up the trail, the chant names local villages in Gyasumdo: Donague, Temang, Dzangyug, Kato, Tshad-med, rTa-rLung, Drak-Thang. At midway point they pass the pond called Black Water, regarded as one of the doors to the underworld.

Farther on, they arrive at the top of the gigantic rock dome called Oblē, near Pisang, a well-known landmark in this region of Nepal. It is the Gurung land of the dead. They call it Sa yi Gompa ("earth temple") and imagine that it mediates with the "sky Gompa" of the gods. In the Gurung death rite, the soul of the deceased is led up to the top of Oblē dome by the other shaman, the Ghyabrē. The Paju shaman, recalling the soul of a living patient, travels the same route to bring a stolen soul back down, rather than deliver it upward.

At the top of Oblē dome they encounter a barking dog barring the way to the land of the dead, a classic shamanic image (Eliade 1964:203,

417). The Paju chants: "Tie up the golden dog, tie up the silver dog." This is only to humor the dog and its owners, the Paju has assured me, for it is not really beautiful and golden. The occupants of the land of the dead tie the dog to the rock hitching post, a thin column of rock which sticks out at the top of the dome, and is easily seen from the trail below.

If the soul of the patient has been stolen by a spirit of the land of the dead, it can be retrieved at this point, but the chant quickly moves beyond it in order to reach the heavenly palace in Mu gi Gompa. New terrain is crossed northward, the chant taking note of four villages that are identified with ancient Gurung clan names,[2] and which may have been way station settlements of early migrations coming into Nepal through Nar and Phu.

The search party, now apparently in Tibet, begins to ascend to the sky. The climb is made up a "tree of the gods" that is "atop a mountain" that links earth and sky. The Pajus call the tree raja dong-bu ("king tree"), and its white, red, and black leaves are identified with the Tibetan classifications lha, btsan, and bdud, here representing the upper, middle, and lower worlds. Above the tree a series of nine ladders reach up to a divine palace.

Arriving at the palace, the shaman loudly announces that he has come to retrieve the lost soul of his patient, whom he names. But the gates are locked. The Paju shouts to the gods inside, "Give me the golden and silver keys!" These are thrown out to him, and he and his tutelary aides unlock the gates and enter. They gaze at the beautiful golden and silver pillars. The Paju says, in a smooth, luring voice to "bend the minds" of the inhabitants inside, "I have come for the soul of that one there, who has the mark of soot on the forehead and a finger tied with a string." The palace gods are conceived as a divine family, so the Paju begins by asking the children whether they have taken the soul. He pokes around in the stove as well, but does not find the soul.

The Paju has a final strategy. The birds who have come with him now turn into "seven goddesses." They begin to dance, putting on a show that will attract all of the inhabitants of the divine palace. As the crowd gathers to watch the beautiful dancers, the Paju searches among the onlookers to see if the patient's soul (pla) has been tricked into coming. "Dimly" he sees it and goes to speak to it in a "pleasing voice" to lure it back to the human world:

> If you come with me I will give you gold and silver. I'll give you
> golden earrings, I'll give you gold bangles. I'll make you wealthy

2. These settlements are called: (1) village of Trul, (2) village of Gyab-btsan, (3) village of Khrō-btsan, and (4) village of Jowo.

with a share of the inheritance. Look there at your home. See the
domestic animals, the things in the house, the beautiful clothes,
tasty food. And see, there is a beautiful garland of flowers for you!

In his commentary, the Paju confirms that these are words of bride
enticement. They may be used when a boy courts a girl in the Rodi (meeting
house), in which Gurung youth dance and sing through the night. The
Rodi tradition in these northern Gurung villages still flourishes, and its
dancers are famous in the region. When they put on all-night shows, each
young man may search among the crowd for the girl of his choice who may
have "come to watch." He may even form a "groom party" that seizes
her on the edge of the crowd and takes her to his home in the hope that
she will be his bride. There he must further lure her with gold earrings
and bangles; otherwise, she will run away and return to her natal home.

From the point of view of the parental home, luring in the Rodi is
equivalent to the theft of the soul.[3] "Bride luring" is legitimate when parents
arrange to have their daughter seized by a groom party that takes her to
her marriage destiny in another village. The most popular song for girls
in the Rodi bewails having to leave her Rodi lover, being forced to return
home and go with these parent-arranged captors.[4] The latter must also
entice her favor with gold earrings and bangles.

Shamanic soul recalling, as a metaphoric luring of the bride, draws
on such emotional correspondence between soul loss, marriage elopement,
and captivity. If the thief-spirit can use techniques of the Rodi lover or
groom party, so can the Paju in luring back. The dancing goddesses and
the Paju's soothing voice begin the enticement. As the soul (*pla*) draws
near, he tries to seize it against its will and put it in his drum. As he grabs
it, the god who has stolen it may hold on; a tug of war results. When
the Paju finally succeeds, he trembles, showing that the soul has been captured.

Now the captors rush out of the palace and back down the ladders.
When they arrive again at the land of the dead on Oblē dome, the guardian
dog again bars their way, but the Paju throws it a bone and curses it: "May
your legs be broken." It is no longer necessary to sweet-talk the dog, calling
it "golden and silver" as he had when seeking access to these domains.

3. In the *Nine Songs,* written around the third century B.C. in China, the shamanic calling
   is portrayed in terms of sexual enticement, in which a human is lured by a spirit of the
   opposite sex (Loewe 1982:105–6).
4. Bride seizure as a regular practice in Gurung marriage is confirmed by Ernestine McHugh
   in her research among southwestern Gurungs: "The woman is forced to leave her home
   in an arranged marriage about which she is not consulted or even informed until the day
   of the event when the groom's party comes and carries her away in a mock kidnapping"
   (McHugh 1986).

The reversal from peaceful luring into wrathful cursing is repeated down the trail as the Paju fiercely scares away harming spirits that reside in certain areas, each trying to grab the patient's soul away from him. As every Gurung knows, there is a vicious demon agent who lives below Kato, and a malevolent *btsan* ghost of a deceased shaman who resides above the waterfall at Donague.

Arriving back at the village in front of the patient's home, the Paju must again entice the soul, to get it to go into the house and to enter the body of its owner. He shows it the ladder to the roof of the house: "Please climb the golden ladder to your house. Inside is your family, your possessions," he chants. Once it has reached the roof, the Paju adroitly removes the ladder in his imagination so that the soul now has no choice but to come down into the flower garland hanging from the ceiling inside the house. The audience inside stares intensely at the flowers as the Paju beats the drum, chanting. Suddenly the flowers flutter in the air. It is the sign that the soul has returned.[5] The garland is put around the patient's neck.

The Paju's work is not over. If the patient's soul is not retrieved up to this point, he must go down into Khrõ-nasa. He will go in any case, since the ritual formula includes visitations to both upper and lower worlds to restore their harmony with the human world. In one of the observed sessions there were two patients, one having her soul recalled from above, the other from below. After the flower garland was presented to the first, the Paju continued the chant, following his tutelary aides down nine ladders into the underworld. Here, they encounter the spirit people of Khrõ-nasa. As was noted in a previous chapter, these spirit beings are very tiny, but their underworld is so fertile that their crops and animals are of an enormous size, Gurung tradition regarding Khrõ-nasa as an alternative land of the dead. Among northern Gurungs the Ghyabrē shaman's death rite depicts the deceased as dwelling there only temporarily before being taken up the trail to the ancestral home on top of Oblē dome.

The search party reaches the underworld, and again a dog barring the way must be tied up. The Paju repeatedly appeals to "ama, awa," who are the mother and father of Khrõ-nasa. At this point his chant briefly refers to the Gurung legend of the "first Paju" who had come up from Khrõ-nasa in the first era to serve the human world. Because he had later cursed the human world and returned to Khrõ-nasa, souls can be stolen from below and must be retrieved there by Pajus of the present time.

Here, the Paju must plead with the Khrõ-nasa owners to prove that one of the spirits in the underworld is in fact the soul of his human patient.

---

5. The flower garland really does flutter. There was no way of knowing whether a waft of air had been caused by the Paju or by anyone else in the sessions observed.

His chant asserts that the divinations done before this rite were done "by the lama." The Paju relies on such an argument because he recognizes that in Gyasumdo his Gurung patients often go first to the Tibetan lamas to ask for a reading from the "more reliable" Tibetan divination text. If it indicates soul loss, they go to the Paju for the shamanic rite. It is a subtle form of collaboration that is not admitted by the lamas. For the Paju shamans, however, it is an ideal of pragmatic harmony, interweaving the different contributions of the two practitioners.

The Paju quickly obtains the soul from Khrō-nasa and returns it to the human world. This time it comes up, underneath the mountain effigy on the floor of the house. The soul enters into the four bird effigies on the tree branches, and then into the strings which have been tied to them. The strings are removed and tied around the neck of the patient. The rite is finished.

SOUL CALLING OF THE TIBETAN LAMA

When a Tibetan adult suspects the loss of the soul (*bla*), he or she visits the lama to have a diagnosis and to have the soul recalled in the ritually prescribed manner, using the text called the *bla bslu* ("soul luring"). First the patient tells the lama of the "signs" (*rtags*) of loss that have been experienced. Beyond the usual symptoms of lethargy and melancholia, the patient may be able to remember an experience of sudden fright which occasioned the loss, or a period of deep despondency that has given a spirit agent a chance to seize the soul.

These signs are supported by dreams which the lama analyzes. If one dreams of walking naked in a strange land or in a wide open field or along a river or of having one's clothes pulled off or of having a fight with an enemy, there probably has been soul loss. The testimony of one informant reveals a variation on these themes, including the factor of repressed guilt. "Years before, I had failed to provide the best funeral for my mother when she died. At the time of my soul loss, I dreamed that many great lamas had come to perform the funeral as it should have been done. Then I saw myself climbing a high cliff with my mother, looking down over the cliff, and then falling off."

Soul Luring

Dream signs of this type convince the lama of the need to perform the *bla bslu* ritual, and he warns the patient that if this is not done, death may follow, perhaps within a year. The textual scheme for soul recalling develops the folk layer into a Tibetan Buddhist model that retains the female caller in the form of the Tibetan Dakini, who can be interpreted as a mother and female figure that mediates between the lost soul and the performing lama. The patient's body is represented by an item of his or her clothing placed in a basket, a tiny piece of turquoise (*bla gyu*) as the seat of the soul, and the leg of a sheep (*bla sha*) as the flesh of the patient.[6]

At a certain point during the rite a male relative of the patient goes to the roof of the house and holds out the basket of clothes, the sheep's leg, and the turquoise, along with an "arrow flag" (*mda dar*) of long life. He calls out, "Soul, come here!" (*bla gugs o!*) repeatedly, while the lama and his aides chant the text and perform the rite below, inside the house.

The soul is thus "lured" (*bslu*) to return, but also the taker of the soul is induced to take a ransom substitute (*glud*) for letting it go. In this case the ransom effigy is simple, consisting of four small tormas with human figures block printed on each, along with other animal figures, grain, herbs, pieces of cloth, and a few hairs of the patient. The lama visualizes offering this ransom to the "black one [*bdud* demon] holding a black sling and led by a black dog with a black bird flying over." The chant names a series of demonic harmers, including Ma-mo, gShin-rje, The'u-brang, Dre, Dre-mo, gNod-sbyin, to cover a range of possible thieves, asking them not to pass the soul over to the worst of the *bdud* demons, and to release it in exchange for the ransom: "Today I offer to you a bloodstained ransom (*khrag gi glud*) for the sponsor. Don't send the soul to the *bdud*! Release the captive that you have bound! Accept this ransom . . . and bring back the soul and the life. . . ."

The lama assumes that the ransom effigy will substitute for the "bloodstained" offering mentioned in the text and that it will be accepted. The second technique involves luring the soul back to its home. The luring is done by five peaceful Dakinis (*mkha-'gro-ma*), "sky-going" goddess-mediators in Nyingma Lamaism. The Dakinis are sent out to search in the five directions:

> To lure back the soul from the east direction is Dorje Khandro . . .
> To lure back the soul from the north direction is Rinjen Khandro . . .
> To lure back the soul from the west direction is Pema Khandro . . .
> To lure back the soul from the south direction is Le gi Khandro . . .
> To lure back the soul from space is Sangye Khandro . . .

Following these five peaceful Dakinis, the five wrathful Dakinis are

6. Gyasumdo lamas regard the sheep's leg as optional, since to kill a sheep for the rite would be tantamount to animal sacrifice. If a sheep has already been killed for food, then a leg with the meat still on it is included in the rite. If there is a sheep's leg, the turquoise is embedded in it; otherwise, the turquoise is placed with the clothes in the basket.

called. They are associated with elements of nature, and are thus asked to lure the soul from fire, water, earth, air, and the Jungpo[7] ghost.

Divinations of the Returning Soul

The lay relative doing the calling on the roof might notice a sign of the returning soul if the clothes and the turquoise appear to shine. But the real test is by the lama inside the house in a series of divinations. Three tests are performed. In the first, an aide draws three stones from a covered bowl of water in which three white and three black stones have been placed. If two out of the three are white, the test is positive. If two black stones are drawn, the relative is sent back up to the roof for more calling, while the lama chants again for the help of the fierce Dakinis.

As soon as the first test is positive, the second test begins. A small animal effigy made of butter (*bla lug*)[8] denoting the animal year of the patient's birth is placed in a dish, which is then twirled in a large bowl of water. The effigy spins around slowly as the lama and the aides again do the chant calling for the Dakinis to lure the soul. If it stops facing the patient or the lama, the soul has returned. If not, again the male relative returns to the roof to call, and again the animal effigy is spun in the water.

Now the lama must go further into the text, where the chant appeals to even more wrathful Dakinis who will strike terror into the demons holding the soul. They are pictured as emerging from "wrathful graves," one bearing a flaming arrow, another a flaming sling, another a flaming iron hook. They enter each of the three worlds: that of the *klu* (serpent deities) below, that of the *btsan* (warriors) on the earth, and that of the *lha* (gods) above. Finally, the animal effigy turning in the water stops facing the patient, and everyone is greatly relieved. The soul has returned.

But one more test must be performed. The ultimate fate of the soul is decided by a gambling dice contest played by the two forces of good and evil. The white die is rolled by a "white god"—a carefully carved effigy of a male figure with a crown, visualized as living in a kingly palace and identified with the lineage guardian deity of the patient. On the other side is the "black demoness" (*bdud-mo*) represented by a black effigy of a woman dressed in black, carrying a black sling (for tying up the soul) who rolls the black die. She is the demon "born at the time" of the patient, waiting for a chance to take his or her life. The actual dice throwing is

---

7. "Jungpo" is the Tibetan name for wandering ghosts of the dead who have failed to find the path to rebirth.
8. The phrase *bla lug* means "sheep soul," but in actual practice the animal chosen from the twelve-year cycle is the one representing the patient's birth year.

done by a male and female aide, each behind the two figures that face each other.

As the gamblers begin, the demoness may win at first. The lama chants further into the text. It calls on Buddha Tshe-dpag-med (Skt. Amitayus), the Buddha of long life, for life and death are now at issue. He and his Dakini partners are thought to have final authority beyond that of the "white god," who can only gamble for the outcome. By being encompassed by the authority of the Buddha, the outcome is certain. The divination now becomes a parody, as the players merely roll the dice until the white side has the higher number. The demoness is "defeated." The god-player seizes a knife and triumphantly cuts the black die (made of dough) in half. The demoness is hurriedly carried out of the house by the woman-player, who leaves it at the village crossroads along with the ransom (*glud*) exchanged for the soul of the patient.

The soul-recalling rite of the Tibetan lama always ends successfully. The patient puts on the item of clothing, takes back the turquoise, eats the meat of the sheep leg, and the lama puts the small animal effigy on the altar. The rite ends and the audience share the *tshogs* (Skt. *prasad*) that has been offered during the rite.

Unbounded Matrix

The theme of the lure is central for both practitioners. In contrast with the mother who lures the soul of her child from her home, the Paju's bird-goddess dancers and the lama's Dakinis are female enticers in distant realms. The luring mistress or woman from the wild is the more extraordinary technique that achieves the impossible breakthrough.[9] Dakinis are significant as mental-conveyors in Tibetan Buddhism, since at death they can deliver the consciousness to a Buddha field, and are revealers of wisdom in meditational practice.

But the lama's soul-calling rite has no images of an actual journey.[10] The Dakinis are sent out in highly stereotyped mandala patterns, a universal epistemology. The rich, local cosmology and marriage alliance connotations of shamanic luring are absent from the lama's mandala. The Paju shaman suffers the journey's vicissitudes in his mind by engaging in personal struggle with invisible forces. He is a real actor in an unbounded

9. The latter image is a well-developed tradition of the female dancer in "Indra's court" in Indian Tantric legends in Bengal (Dimock 1964) and at Kamakhya in Assam (Maity 1966). Here, the goddess Manasa as an "earth" goddess brings about a fusion with the upper world.

10. The Lamaist soul-calling texts examined by Lessing (1951) and Bawden (1962) also confirm this conclusion. The shamanic journey between worlds is missing in the Tibetan rite.

matrix. When the soul returns there is a "miracle" in the fluttering flower garland, and the audience is reminded that failure is also possible. In contrast, the lama's rite downgrades miracle and surprise, substituting instead a drama of predetermined divinations.

In her study of narrative genres, Susan Suleiman (1983:55) notes how such "redundancies" and dichotomous "exemplary models" are ways of *disambiguation:* they amplify certainty of meaning and final authority. This trend is highly evident in the Tibetan soul-calling text. The dice game of white god versus black demoness presents bounded categories of good and evil, while in the Paju shaman's rite the moral identities of various soul-stealing spirits are highly ambiguous, not easily placed in binary categories. Even gods or ancestors from the upper world may seize human souls, since one is implicated in a vast matrix of alliances and reciprocal exchanges among willing agents.

The lama views his textual rite as authoritative precisely because he is *not* involved in such complexities of social life or in personal struggle, the hierarchical encompassment giving certainty to the ritual outcome. The Gurung Paju's view is the reverse; his own rite is effective because it is contextual and personal, analogically calling to mind collaborations and social entanglements that cannot be transcended, but only balanced out.

The Paju himself is highly critical of the lama's detachment. The Gurung shaman regards his own rite as not only less expensive, but more effective since, as he puts it, "the lama does not even leave the house, while the Paju leaves the house and goes out to search for the soul." When juxtaposed to the Lamaist rite, the Paju shaman's joyous celebration of overlapping boundaries, voices, and images becomes a Rabelaisian challenge to the lama, inviting the latter to "return to the world."

It can be argued, in fact, that shamanic soul calling in Gyasumdo inspires the lamas to elaborate beyond what their texts require. They make their divination drama into what Bakhtin (1984:162–77) calls a carnivalistic parody, temporarily turning the world upside down to create ambivalent combinations that imply there can be no final certainty. While this elaboration does not replicate the Paju shaman's experience of interpenetrating wills, it nevertheless maintains a shamanic underlayer that ultimately resists canonization and keeps alive a dialogic potential that can resurface in other forms.

Chapter Nine

Death Cult of the Ghyabrẽ Shaman

THE OLD GHYABRẼ shaman who taught me his death cult chant lives in Tapje village. He is approximately seventy years old, yet it is he who performs the Gurung deer sacrifice in the sacred grove every spring. In my analysis of that rite and the Ghyabrẽ's personal comment upon it, it is noticeable that this shamanic practitioner is penetrated by the discourse that he hears on the Tibetan side of the river, and troubled by Lamaist arguments. He was, in fact, present among those who gathered in the early 1960s to hear what Lama Chog Lingpa had to say, and heard the searing condemnation of his own tradition.

He cannot give up the deer sacrifice. But he has, since then, dropped the blood offering that used to be performed in the death rite, as will be noted later in the analysis. The Ghyabrẽ has acquired an identity of *becoming*. He has observed the Tibetan Buddhist reforms in Tshap village across the river with great interest, noting that since Lama Chog Lingpa's visit, the Tibetans have avoided ritual collaboration with the Gurung shamans. He wonders whether he might be the last of the great Ghyabrẽs in the region to be able to call the spirits of the ancient ones into his body at will. The younger men in Tapje who are his apprentices lack confidence, or perhaps they are distracted: "The spirits do not seem to come into their bodies."

When the death cults of the Tibetan lama and the Gurung shaman are compared, it is important to note how the destiny of the deceased is defined and how that destiny is interlinked with relations among the living as well as with the natural world. The Gurungs and the Tibetans are acutely aware of the difference between their two models. When Tibetans see their own Wheel of Life painted on the Gompa wall, the six distinct realms of samsaric destiny (*'gro-ba ri-drug*) of the transmigrating consciousness remind them that their dead ancestors are not supposed to remain interlinked with the living; they should not be seen or heard from again.

For the Gurungs, the dead are nearby and recallable. Their presence in the land of the dead at the top of Oblē dome, a day's walk up the trail, is felt psychologically and socially. During the Dasain fall harvest period, the ancestral spirits are called down from Oblē dome, which they call Sa yi Gompa ("earth Gompa"). For the Ghale clan, the name of each spirit is called out from a list. Further, relatives may trek to the base of the Oblē dome to the area called Mi-tshogs (Tibetan for "people gather") and call the deceased kin's spirit into one of the small shrines constructed there. The spirit receives an offering of food and communicates with the living family, who learn of conditions in Sa yi Gompa, and whether or not the spirit has gone higher to Mu gi Gompa ("sky Gompa"), the land of the gods, or whether instead it would like to transmigrate again into the human world.

In contrast to Tibetan destiny in which the karmic past and psychic preparation during life largely determine one's destiny, Gurung destiny is determined by relations of reciprocity among relatives. If the deceased's mother's brother (*asyō*) refuses to provide the white shroud that covers the corpse and also the effigy of the soul, the deceased "will not find the path" and becomes a wandering ghost. For Gurungs the white cloth is the symbol of relational destiny promoted in the shamanic system, in contrast to the psychically bounded, karmic destiny promoted by Lamaism. Tibetan informants most familiar with the Gurung funeral insist that this distinction between the two systems is crucial.

Pignède (1966) and Messerschmidt (1976a, 1976c) have previously described the flow of exchanges between relatives during the funeral among Gurungs living south of Gyasumdo. These earlier studies have very little data on the kind of soul guidance performed by the Ghyabrē shaman that will be given here, and do not mention at all the guidance up the trail to the land of the dead that is so prominent among the northern Gurungs of this study. Only when this technique is understood, may we compare the Gurung shaman's death cult with the famed Tibetan guidance of the consciousness in the Bardo.

The Gurung funeral ensures that the soul will "find the path" to the land of the dead by focusing on the relationship between affines. The white cloth shroud for the corpse and the effigy[1] supplied by the mother's brother represent the wife-giving affines of the deceased. The point, Gurungs argue, is that the deceased cannot find its way without marriage and progeny and the resulting alliance between clans.

---

1. When the white shroud covers the effigy, it covers a bamboo cage, representing the flesh or "body" of the soul inside.

The model of alliance is the cosmological marriage between the Kle (Ghale) clan of the upper world and the Khrõ clan from the underworld. The link between these domains is iconically portrayed by a long pole called the *alã,* described as the "pillar of the world." It is set up alongside the house while the corpse is prepared, then carried straight up in a procession to the cremation ground. *Alã* construction and carrying is the duty of a male of the deceased's own patriline. Strips of cloth of various colors tied to it, along with fruit, cigarettes, etc., are "food for the journey" taken by the soul, which rides on top of the pole. A long white banner, six to seven meters long (*gya kui*) is tied to the *alã* and strung along the procession, carried on the heads of women of the wife-receiving affines (*mo*); men of this kin group carry the corpse wrapped in the white shroud in a sitting position. The long banner "shows the path" to the soul and is white since that is the path that leads to the land of the ancestors and the gods. The other three path choices, red, black, and yellow, represent the directions of *btsan, bdud,* and *klu,* respectively, which would end in confusion and wandering. In the past a goat was sacrificed at this time as the companion of the soul during the journey, but the Ghyabrē of Tapje has dropped this feature.[2]

Male kin of the deceased's family take turns aiming arrows at the corpse to symbolize giving weapons of protection to the deceased to be used on the journey. After the corpse disposal[3] the deceased soul, which begins to wander, must be released from the grasp of demonic agents that have caused the death in the first place. It is here that the Paju shaman's participation is important since there must be an exorcism of the demons still trying to hold on to the soul as it wanders free of the body.

THE PAI RITE: UNDERWORLD EXCHANGE AND SENDING THE BIRD

The entire ritual process that follows, which in some cases may take place months later, is called the *pai* rite. In the Ghyabrē shaman's tradition the rite has two sections: (1) the exchanges that are made between the dead and the living, called the Plenema, and (2) the conclusion in which the Ghyabrē guides the soul to the land of the dead. The Plenema section itself has two parts. In the first, the Ghyabrē must go to the underworld to release the soul from that region. In the second, the soul encounters living kin members after entering the body of an animal.

The Plenema begins when the wife-receiving affines (*mo*) construct the soul effigy: a cone-shaped bamboo cage one meter high. The stick frame

2. The Ghyabrē's reforms and the reason for them will be discussed later.
3. Corpse disposal among Gyasumdo Gurungs usually consists of cutting up the body and throwing it into the Marsyandi river, but burial is also an option.

represents the bones of the deceased, and the white cloth covering it, supplied by the wife-giving affines (*asyō*) is the outer flesh. Nails and bits of hair of the deceased are inserted inside along with some clothing and jewelry.

After the soul is called into the effigy, plates of food, the "provisions for the journey," are offered by women of the *asyō* affines. Some of this food is put into a burnt offering, and as each plate of food is presented, the Ghyabrē calls out the name of the donor household, so the deceased will know which relatives participated in the offering. It is at this time that the shamanic guidance by the Ghyabrē begins.

First the Ghyabrē travels in his mind to the underworld to deliver the food to the wandering soul, an exchange that enables the deceased to relinquish any claims on the wealth of surviving kin. The Ghyabrē goes to Khrō-nasa, delivers the food, and returns with a bird (a pigeon) which the soul of the deceased has entered. The bird then recognizes its patriline members and shakes to indicate that it will depart "without taking the wealth."

Relatives and friends gather on the roof of the house. The pigeon is seen in a cage. The Ghyabrē beats his drum, on which there is a carving of Kle-Nyima, his tutelary bird deity. In front of him stands the *pla* or effigy of the deceased. He begins the chant:

> The bird came down from above and settled in the land, like the blessing of rain, falling from the sky.
> Four birds come, each on one of the four paths. The bird of the *bdud* is black in the path going east, the bird of the *btsan* is red in the path going south, the bird of *klu* and *sa-bdag* is yellow in the path going north, the bird of *lha* is white, in the path going west.
> The white bird shows the path. Its head is gold, its body is turquoise, its waist is silver, its tail is copper, its feet are iron.

These are the same four-directional birds that the Paju shaman sends out to search for the soul in the soul-recalling rite. The Ghyabrē's chant now goes on to provide a legendary model (*pe*) for the loss of wealth that results when the harmony between the living and the dead is broken. The deceased's parents, neglected by their son when they die, curse him into poverty, a replication of the first Paju's curse of humanity from the underworld. The chant tells the story:

> There was a youth named Bar-chog Kle,[4] whose parents died.
> Before they died he took his inheritance and spent his time in the Rodi where he sang and danced. The parents were ill and died from the son's neglect.

4. The term *bar-chog* is Tibetan for "middle direction," meaning the middle human world. *Kle* refers to the Ghale clan.

> The father warned him: If we die and you do not do the rites to
> receive our blessing, you will become poor. You will become small
> as a needle, thin as paper, and weak as water.

The chant continues with the parents' death and their descent into Khrō-
nasa: "They entered Khrō-nasa by opening a golden door on the right and
a silver door on the left. As they went down they met some Khrō-nasa
people going up to visit the world above."

Since the legend takes place during the "first era" there is still access
between the underworld and the human world. The deceased parents make
two requests of the Khrō-nasa people. First, when the latter arrive at the
human world above they are to warn the negligent son of his impending
poverty unless he comes down to the underworld with an offering to receive
their blessing. Second, the Khrō-nasa people are asked to give their
daughter to the Ghale son in marriage. The parents then enter the "four
colored lakes" of the underworld and wait for their son to come, while
the Khrō-nasa people arrive in the human world: "The people from Khrō-
nasa met the son, who was already sick and poor from the parents' curse.
They promised to give him their daughter in marriage, but first he must
go down to Khrō-nasa and receive his parents' blessing." The son, with
the ritual aid of the Ghyabrē shaman who goes with him, now gathers
the food from the relatives and enters the underworld:

> In the manner of a Bompo (nobleman) he gathered meat, rice,
> grains, like a king and offered it to his parents in Khrō-nasa. They
> were satisfied and gave him a gift: a bird of gold, turquoise, silver,
> copper, and iron.
>   The son returned to the human world with the wealth-bearing
> bird. It was the blessing of the inheritance. He married the daughter
> of Khrō-nasa. Rain came down from above. Crops grew up from
> below into the human world. Animals increased. There was great
> wealth. The deceased parents found the path to the land of the
> gods.

This Plenema chant provides a mythical charter for two kinds of relationships. First, it legitimizes marriage exchange between the Kle clan "from
above" and the Khrō clan "from below" as the basis for social reciprocity
in the community. This is linked with the natural harmony in the cosmos
that results in abundance. Second, there is exchange between the living
and the dead as occurs in the ancestor cult. The living receive the deceased's
blessing, ensuring that the remaining wealth will not be seized and taken
to the underworld. Once the exchange between living kin and the deceased
is accomplished, the latter proceed to find the path to the land of the dead.

Both types of exchange are symbolized by the giving of the white cloth to cover the soul effigy (*pla*). The wife-giving affines who give the white cloth are the Khrō-nasa wife givers in the legend. The gift reaffirms the marriage alliance between clans that brings wealth and makes it possible for the deceased to find the path to the ancestors. The legend in the chant provides the model. Social interdependence and personal destiny are inextricably linked. Further, the breach of harmony in the first era is linked with the present sense of guilt for parent neglect, a theme that is prominent in Gurung culture and in the shamanic legends.

As the Ghyabrē proceeds with the chant, he brings a pigeon out of the cage and ties a long string to its neck; the other end is tied to the *pla* effigy so that the soul of the deceased can pass into the bird. Seated in a grand semicircle on the roof are members of the patrilineal clan, each with a plate of food in front. As the Ghyabrē quietly beats his drum, the bird walks from person to person, peering at each. The bird begins to eat from the plates of some, and then "recognizes" the persons it most loves and jumps up on their laps. The audience crowded around watches spellbound. The Ghyabrē chants: "You have died so please do not take the fortune of the family with you. If you are willing to leave the fortune here, please shake your body."

The bird shakes its body.[5] The Ghyabrē picks up the bird and, going around the circle, plucks out small bits of feathers from its body, giving a bit to each person. It is the "distribution" of the bird which would have been given if it had been sacrificed. But it is not, and instead it is released.

The "sending of the bird" in the Plenema rite ensures that the fortune of the patriline will not be taken by the deceased, and it "releases" the soul to proceed to the land of the dead. In the thoughts of the participants, however, the bird is also an index of a recent cultural change. The father and grandfather of this Ghyabrē used to sacrifice a sheep by hurling it from the roof of the house. The meat was cooked and distributed among the wife-receiving affines as a social prestation.

This Ghyabrē, however, had foresaken the death cult sacrifice two decades before, after hearing the Tibetan Lama Chog Lingpa condemn the red offering among Tibetans in Gyasumdo. In the Ghyabrē's view, the deer sacrifice that he still performs each spring is a collective rite that does not affect individual destiny, but he has accepted the lama's view with regard to the death rite. If animal sacrifice is sinful as the lamas say it might jeopardize the deceased's chances of finding the path. Hence he now does only the bird-sending performance.

5. If the bird does not shake, it can be encouraged to do so by pouring water over it, a common practice in Nepal used to gain acceptance from an animal about to be sacrificed.

A prominent shaman, the Ghyabrē has led this shift in the Gurung death cult of the region. He serves the Ghale, who sometimes call first the shaman and later a lama to perform two different death rites; hence it is not surprising that he has to some extent brought his own performance into line with the Lamaist critique. Other reforms in Nepal may also have had influence; for instance, cost-cutting reforms led by Gurungs living in other regions.

The Ghyabrē in Gyasumdo explains his own reform as a personal change of conviction after hearing the lama, a dialogic influence in which, as shall be noted, the folk elements in the lama's death rite are, in turn, influenced by the Ghyabrē's Plenema model of exchange. It should be recognized, however, that while the Ghyabrē says he is listening to the lama, the lama will not say the same regarding the Ghyabrē. The Gurung Pajus, on the other hand, are critical of the Ghyabrē's dropping of the death cult sacrifice. For the old Paju of Rangu village, it is only a further sign of decline in the modern era. Before, there was a real prestation flow cementing the deceased's patriline with their *mo* affines through a feast of the animal's flesh. Now the latter are merely given one rupee each at the end of the rite as a token of symbolic, rather than actual, reciprocity.

GUIDING THE SOUL TO THE LAND OF THE DEAD

There is good reason to regard the Ghyabrē's death cult up to this point as having emerged from the same tradition as the Bon funeral once practiced in Tibet. Marcelle Lalou (1953), in his article *Rituel Bon-po des funérailles royales,* has translated a Bonpo manuscript found in the Cave of the Thousand Buddhas in Touen-Houang in Tibet, now kept in the Paris National Library (Manuscrit Pelliot Tibétain #1042). The manuscript refers to food offerings and services given by relatives, particularly the uncle. There are a "soul canopy" called *thugs-gur* ("soul tent"), "auspicious dances," weapons, food, and utensils "for the journey," which is guided by a "sheep." Numerous animal sacrifices are performed by various Bonpo sacrificers, including those for "the ransoming of the soul" (*thugs-glud*).

In Gyasumdo, however, the Ghyabrē's death rite now arrives at a new stage that is homologous to shamanism of the Siberian type. It is the guiding of the soul up the trail to Oblē dome and the land of the dead. Drum teams arriving from other villages dance, drum, and sing all night the *serga kwe,* the funerary music for which Gurungs are noted. It encourages the soul to find the path. The Ghyabrē calls out the names of the ancestors to come down and help conduct their kin person to the Oblē dome where they live in Sa yi Gompa. Women relatives gather around

Figure 8. The Oblē rock dome in winter, as photographed from the trail

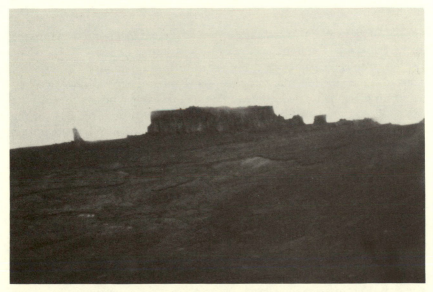

Figure 9. The summit of the Oblē rock dome, the Gurung land of the dead, showing the rock temple of the dead, and to the left of it, the rock column which is the dog hitching post

Figure 10. The *Chu Nag-po,* "Black Water," at the midway point on the trail to the Oblē dome

the *pla* effigy, wailing. Arrows are aimed at the *pla* by male kin to provide weapons against demonic enemies on the trail.

The trail is the same one taken when the Paju shaman recalls the lost soul of a patient. It is the same trail that the ancestor Drong awa first came up when he carried his dead daughter to return her to Tibet in the Ghale legend. The small two-meter-high shrines built at the base of the great Oblē dome are said to number at least ten thousand, most buried under the soil and leaves, indicating the strength of the Oblē dome tradition which in the past, local informants say, used to draw Gurungs from wherever they had settled in Nepal.

As the Ghyabrē begins the journey, he dances slowly around the *pla,* beating his drum and chanting his guiding instructions. He first warns that it must be the "white" trail of the gods they will embark on, not the trails of the *klu, btsan,* or *bdud.* In the chant the soul is first lured away from its former home attachments, exactly reversing the soul-recalling rite. Thus: "Don't stay here! Don't stay in the beer storage room. You no longer have the right to remain at the hearth. Your place is different now. Only alive ones can stay here. You are dead now, go!"

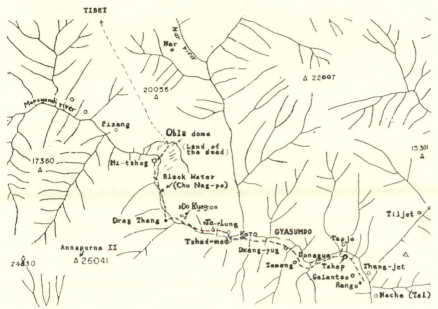

Figure 11. Map of the trail to the Oblē dome, the Gurung land of the dead

This chant is repeated by a chorus of local spirits at each stage of the journey, the first chorus beginning with the spirits of the doorstep, the next with those of the porch, and so on. When the Ghyabrē in his mind guides the soul as far as the trail crossing below Donague village, again there is a chorus of local spirits of stream, soil, and rocks that warn the soul not to remain there, that its home is farther up the trail. The chant continues, naming the local villages of Temang, Dzangyuk, Kato, Tshad-med, rTa-rlung. They arrive at rDo Kyag-sa, a place of huge boulders which young men often try to lift in competitions of strength. Passing the cave of Bare, they come to the midway point, called *Chu Nag-po,* the Tibetan term for "Black Water."[6] It is regarded as one of the doors to the under-world. Here the Ghyabrē must convince the soul to "lie" down on its stomach" and drink the Black Water. It refuses. The Ghyabrē urges again. Finally, it drinks and suddenly realizes fully that it has died and there is no turning back.

The Ghyabrē now offers a libation of grain to "spirits of the four direc-

6. "Black Water" (Chu Nag-po) is a phrase found often in the Tibetan Bon text *The Nine Ways of Bon,* translated by Snellgrove (1980), but it is not given in the context of a death cult.

tions and eight regions," requesting that they "release the way" for the soul of the deceased to proceed: "When he walks, don't hit him on the leg with a stone! When he talks, don't cut off his tongue!" After passing through Drag Thang, a meadow surrounded by huge cliffs and then crossing the Marsyandi River on a bridge, they arrive at the base of the massive Oblē dome, and proceed to the top. They find the first village of the dead, guarded by the same dog that the Paju encounters in the soul-recalling rite. The dog is tied to the rock post, and they proceed.

The top of Oblē is regarded as the entry to Sa yi Gompa, but the chant journeys beyond that point, mentioning in addition rock cliffs and mountains, suggesting that it is Tibet that is actually reached, the Oblē dome in Nepal being the doorway into the other world. Again the Ghyabrē chooses the white path and avoids the red, yellow, and black ones. When they pass a landmark of "108 Mani" (Tibetan prayer wheels), they have arrived at Sa yi Gompa. The ancestors greet the deceased, who distributes the food brought from relatives.

Before the Ghyabrē returns, he has two kinds of instructions to offer the deceased. The first kind gives advice regarding further destiny; the second urges the deceased to remain, and not wander back to the living world. For the first, the chant emphasizes a choice: the deceased can either remain in Sa yi Gompa or take another human rebirth, according to preference: "Your place is now in Sa yi Gompa, but you can take another birth if you choose. If you do take rebirth, you should choose to be an important, wealthy, skillful, or religious person. But you do not have to return, you can stay here and remain with your ancestors."

Here, there is an optional rebirth eschatology, with no mention of retribution or a weighing on karmic scales to determine destiny as found in the Tibetan system. Rebirth, suffering, and death are no longer necessary once Sa yi Gompa is entered, although the Ghyabrē mentions in his commentary that a select few may arrive at the higher Mu gi Gompa, the land of the gods above, without offering criteria for this higher access.

The second kind of instruction warns against premature return to the world of the living, for a human soul can be stolen by spirits from the upper realms: "Don't put your mind on your property or your relatives. They will die later and come here to meet you. Don't return home to see a show in your village. You are dead and must remain here. I am alive so I must return to the land of the living."

Now the Ghyabrē adroitly avoids being followed back down the trail. He tricks the soul that he has delivered with a distraction. Pointing to a show going on in Sa yi Gompa, he says, "Look there at how those cats and snakes are playing together!"[7] While the deceased turns to watch, the Ghyabrē magically transforms himself into a vulture and flies down Oblē dome, returning to the Gurung village in Gyasumdo. Then he and the community pick up the *pla* effigy and carry it out of the village, where it is thrown into the river.

CONTENDING MODELS OF DESTINY

The Gurung death cult of the Ghyabrē shaman is in the process of change, involved in dialogue with both the Paju shaman within the same tradition and the lama who argues from a Buddhist perspective. Below, I will introduce both debates, keeping in mind the issue raised by Weber (1963) and more recently by Haimendorf (1967) and Obeyesekere (1980), regarding how an older, nonretributional destiny is transformed through "ethicization" toward a karmic eschatology, analogous to Bakhtin's "sealed-off individual sequence."

The Gurung underworld Khrō-nasa appears to represent what Eliade has called a "paradisal image" at a fundamental level of Gurung mythical consciousness. It has the character of both a womb in the earth, in which occupants become tiny infantlike beings, and a source of fertility and abundance: crops grow to gigantic size and animals are enormous. The image is not unlike the land of Mayal in Sikkim (Gorer 1967).

In contrast to this underworld image, the Ghyabrē's death cult focuses attention on an ancestral land "above" as the proper destiny, reached through the local Oblē dome and beyond. This emphasis differs from that of the Paju shamans, who may be called underworld specialists. The Pajus argue that Sa yi Gompa "above" and Khrō-nasa "below" are *both* ancestral regions that are equally valid afterlife destinies. Both, for instance, are visited by the Paju. The Ghyabrē's soul guidance death rite, however, begins with a rescue operation from Khrō-nasa wandering, giving the underworld a negative connotation.

Since the Ghyabrē is the sacerdotal legitimizer of the Ghale nobles, he is expected to promote the "sky" (*mu*) ancestral origin as superior. The Pajus are not death rite specialists in Gyasumdo, hence their Khrō-nasa view is not promoted in the death cult. In Pignède's (1966) study of southwestern Gurungs in the Pokhara region, however, there is no mention

---

7. The show trick appears as a reversal of the "dance" that the Paju uses to lure the soul back home in the soul-recalling rite. In each case a show is conjured up either to attract or distract.

of conducting the soul to an upper world or to Oblē dome. Instead, the dead are said to join their ancestors in the underworld, rebirth in the human world being a vague option. The picture presented by Pignède is that of a closed cycle: death arrives at the point of origin in the womb of the earth, a region of fertility and first-age ancestors.

For northern Gurungs in Gyasumdo, there appears to have been greater influence from the Bon model of Tibetan kingship. The Ghyabrē repeatedly tells the legend of the sky or *mu* origin of the Ghale nobility, the land of the gods from which the earliest kings descended; the story is similar to Bon legends of descent down the Tibetan *dmu* rope or ladder (Stein 1972:48–9). While the Paju's legends emphasize the initial harmonious reciprocity between upper world and underworld origins, the Ghyabrē's legends reflect the hegemony of the Ghale nobility in Gyasumdo, the image of equal exchange having been incorporated into a hierarchical scheme. Hence the preferred destiny gains a vertical dimension. It is a path "up" the trail.

The Ghyabrē death cult is criticized by the Tibetan lamas, however, from the same ethical standpoint as that of the Buddhist critics of the Bonpo in Tibet. For the Ghyabrē, afterlife destiny is not a merited fate. There are no ethical criteria for the selection of those who deserve reward or punishment. For the Tibetan lama this view is outrageous. Most Tibetan lay persons are quick to point out that the Gurung death rite "makes no distinction between sin [*sdig-pa*] and virtue [*dge-ba*]." Gurung destiny does not promote merit making among the laity and does not inspire a renunciatory religious calling.

The Ghyabrē is highly aware of the Tibetan critique, which he calls the *yala-mala* ("up-down") point of view (a model of vertical "reward or punishment"). We have seen that the Ghyabrē's death rite is undergoing a process of transformation through its dialogic encounter with the Lamaist perspective. The Ghyabrē related to me the excruciating experience of two decades previously, when he heard the condemnation of animal sacrifice in the oratory of Lama Chog Lingpa. He dropped the sacrifice from the death cult with the approval of the Ghale lords, only to find that other Gurungs interpreted this as a betrayal of his own father's tradition.

By substituting the bird for the sheep, the Ghyabrē appears to accept the lama's retributional logic, but has not incorporated the full implications of the Buddhist merit system. The sacrifice has been the model for reciprocal prestations. By admitting that the red offering might jeopardize the deceased's "search for the path," the Ghyabrē begins to shift the emphasis of the rite: concern for an individual destiny that is sealed off, extricated from participation in the human community. Traditionally, if the affinal relatives gave the white cloth shroud, arrival at the ancestral land on Oblē dome was guaranteed. But what if the lamas are right?

The Ghyabrē's ambivalence on the matter is revealed in an alternative story about afterlife destiny which he tells to critical Tibetans. I had an opportunity to hear this story during the time that the Ghyabrē was recording his conventional death rite chant in my room. My Tibetan landlady entered the room. Seeing what the Ghyabrē was doing, she offered the remark: "The difference between your death rite and ours is that you make no distinction between sin and merit." At this the Ghyabrē stopped recording his chant temporarily and told her the following story:

> There was a wicked woman who committed many crimes. She hunted animals for profit and cheated others in business. When she died she could not find that path because of her misdeeds.
>
> Two relatives tried to help her. One was a poor brother who offered the white cloth,[8] but she still could not find the white path because of her crimes. The other was a rich brother who used his wealth to build two huge stupas, one of gold and the other of silver, as well as a large silver prayer wheel. He then called the lama, who instructed the ghost to circumambulate the stupas in the right way, since she had before only known how to go around the wrong way.[9] She did this as the lama read the text, which gave her merit.
>
> Then, using a mirror to see her condition, the lama pulled her up. She went to the land of the gods where she joined her ancestors.

The story appears to be a lamaized version of a Gurung legend in Pignède's study, which explains the origin of the affinal duty to provide the white cloth. But here, "the lama," not a Gurung shaman, pulls her up. While the story could be incorporated into a death rite involving lama-Ghyabrē collaboration, it is clearly not a chant that the Ghyabrē would include in his own funerary performance.

The lama in the story is seemingly promoted. But is he? The lama combines the introduction of the merit factor with a huge expenditure of wealth, which the Ghyabrē portrays as a necessary part of the lama's pulling up technique. Gold and silver stupas are of course beyond the reach of anyone in Gyasumdo and merely provide an image of extravagance, which the legend contrasts with the humble white cloth of the "poor brother" who tries to follow the Gurung tradition. While the story admits

---

8. A brother may represent the affinal group as the wife giver when it is a female that has died.
9. That is, the woman had known only how to go around counterclockwise as is the Bon tradition, rather than clockwise as the lamas teach.

the Lamaist ethical criterion, it reveals why Gurungs are perplexed by what they view as a moral paradox in the lama's argument.

The Ghyabrē shaman's death cult is not definable as a discrete ritual entity. Increasingly, the Tibetan perspective appears around its edges; its meaning is emergent and dialogic. But the same can be said of the Tibetan death rite itself, which cannot be understood apart from the shamanic perspective at its origins and with which it continues to argue and interact. With this in mind, it is the lama's funeral system that we must now examine.

Chapter Ten

Tibetan Death Rite

THE TIBETAN death rite of Tshap village is performed in close proximity to the model of the local shamanic funeral in Gyasumdo that we have examined. Since Gurungs and Tibetans can visit one another's performances, the images of each tradition influence the interpretations of the other in the minds of the participants, even though everyone is aware that each system presents an argument against the other.

Older Tibetans recall various collaborations that used to occur between the two traditions. Decades ago, when the lamas from Nar used to perform alongside the shamans at the village of Tapje, the Ghale lords had forced these lamas to bring a yak, which was sacrificed. Tibetan lamas in Gyasumdo today point out that if such a thing were done the deceased would go straight to hell. Up until the 1960s there had also been a degree of participation by Gurungs in the Tibetan rite. Gurung drummers were invited to Tibetan funerals to perform the famed Gurung drum dance rite, the *serga kwe*. After Lama Chog Lingpa came and condemned Tibetan compromises in the early 1960s, such invitations were dropped. The Tibetan funeral tradition is now felt to epitomize the crucial distinction between the two communities: in contrast to Gurung shamans, the lamas promote merit making and the liberation of consciousness.

This fosters argument between retribution models, as noted in previous chapters. It also raises a question that involves more than one layer in the Tibetan system: Is death an occasion for restoring the circle of prior relationships, or is it an occasion for being extricated from them? The Gurung death cult restores harmony, enacting an offering in each cosmic domain. We should not be surprised to find such themes expressed in the Tibetan death rite as well. The Buddhist system incorporates the pre-Buddhist content. The Tibetan laity are attracted by these older meanings, and are not fully persuaded by everything they hear during the lama's Bardo instruction. They often appear to be emotionally pulled toward the shamanic funeral of the Ghyabrē which they have all seen and regard with great awe, even while thinking it is ethically inferior.

Certain features of the Tibetan funeral have become well known since the *Bar-do thos-grol,* the "liberation through hearing in the intermediate state" (or Tibetan *Book of the Dead*), was translated into English. Besides this, in ethnographic descriptions of the Sherpa funeral (Ortner 1978b, Paul 1982) it has been noted that the Tibetan death rite includes demon exorcism, sacrifice themes, and feasting as merit making. What has been lacking thus far is a thorough integration of textual and ethnographic data. The Gyasumdo study has provided an opportunity to fill this gap. The "textual" component will be a taped oral performance of the Bardo instruction given by Lama Dorje to the wandering consciousness. The ethnographic sequence will be based mainly on the death of one woman in Tshap village, although insights into the event were accumulated through a series of deaths that occurred during the research.

Of particular importance as an original contribution will be the analysis of the use of the horoscope at the time of death, for the horoscope (*rtsis*) has a central role in giving significance to the ritual sequence performed on behalf of the deceased. Because Lama Dorje was particularly adept in the art and extraordinarily cooperative in helping me analyze the taped session of his death horoscope reading, we have this important component in a living context for the first time in a study of Tibetan culture.

Particularly apt for illuminating the lama's Bardo guidance are two themes in Bakhtin's dialogical model. One is the Rabelaisian use of carnival imagery to dissolve the boundaries between opposite terms. The other is Bakhtin's social-psychological insight into how the voice of one person becomes internally persuasive within the internal dialogue of another. This occurs in the Bardo guidance, but in Gyasumdo it becomes further complicated by the simultaneous dialogue going on with the shamanic voice nearby. The following ethnographic analysis will attempt to explore this internal/external dynamic, in a manner that allows all of the voices to be heard.

THE DEATH OF SAMDEN

Samden was the twenty-three-year-old daughter of Pasang, the leader of Tshap village. Her death, which occurred during the period of research, will be our model for examining the Tibetan death rite. She died after returning up the trail from Kathmandu. She had stopped on the trail and received a drink of milk from an old woman. Within an hour Samden was paralyzed below the waist and had to be carried the rest of the way by companions of Tshap village to reach her home.

Her father Pasang called Lama Dorje to perform an exorcism, suspecting witch attack from the old woman. The lama did so, using the exorcism usually reserved to counter sorcery, called "the evil spirit ransom" (*'dre glud*). The chant in the text "calls down weapons like hailstones which will reduce the black sorcerer to dust," and expels the evil by sending out a ransom. The rite failed, and Samden became worse. The government health assistant arrived. Seeing the symptoms of paralysis, heavy breathing, and rejection of water, and hearing she had been bitten by a dog three months earlier, the doctor announced that she was dying of rabies and left.

Villagers gathered in Pasang's house to discuss the two theories and decided to proceed on the theory of sorcery. Suddenly, Samden pointed to lumps of pain near her stomach. Several persons rushed to her, pressing on these points with great force to prevent the demonic spirits from rising to her head, the girl cooperating by saying, "It's here, no, now it's there, press there!"

The father Pasang was desperate. Only one solution remained. He would call the Paju shaman. The lama's exorcism had failed, but by performing it, the lama had legitimated the premise on which the Paju's technique is based, the reality of demonic attack. Now Pasang would stop at nothing. Since local demonic spirits along the Nepal trails may never have been subdued by lamas of the past, they could best be dealt with by the Paju.

When the Paju shaman arrived, he called his tutelary deity into his body and called on the demons within Samden's body to reveal themselves. A high-pitched voice came through Samden's lips, speaking to the Paju: "I'll give you my ring if you cure me," she said. She then confirmed that she had drunk milk on the trail that had been cursed, that three demons had then entered her body. The audience now had all the proof that they needed, and Pasang urged the Paju to proceed.

He took a broom, lit the end to set it on fire, and began to beat Samden over the head repeatedly while blowing mantras into her body. Lama Dorje was present in the house, disapproving, but helpless to stop the shamanic drama. As the Paju whacked the broom over Samden's head, Lama Dorje tried to calm her, and started whispering in her ear the *Zhi-'khro,* instruction given to a dying person.[1]

The broom treatment failed. Now, the Paju concluded, only the red offering of animal sacrifice would satisfy the demons. The lama of course would absent himself during the act. The Paju pointed out that he had left his ritual paraphernalia for doing the red offering in another village

---

1. The *Zhi-'khro* is a section in the *Tibetan Book of the Dead* describing the peaceful and wrathful deities. If it can be heard just before death, the wandering consciousness will better recognize them during the Bardo instruction of the funeral.

and sent a runner to get it. Before the runner returned, it was too late. Samden was dead.

Lama Dorje performed the *'pho-ba,* which means "transference." It attempts to lift the consciousness directly to a Buddha field at the moment of death, a technique of sudden deliverance. He visualized himself lifting her consciousness up through the six body centers, bringing it out of the opening in the head (*che-ba*) so that it might dissolve into the heart of Buddha Amitābha. It is a symbolic effort: the rest of the funeral would proceed on the assumption that the *'pho-ba* had been unsuccessful.

Calculating the Death Horoscope (*gshin-rtsis*)

The death of Samden represented a failure of both the lama's and the Paju's ritual remedies. How were these failures to be explained? Both rejected the rabies theory of the government doctor, for both practitioners had seen visible signs of harming agents in the body. In the Paju's view, the killer demons had triumphed because the animal sacrifice had not been done. The lama of course rejected this view, but how would he explain his own failure? The demonic attack must have been a secondary cause (*rkyen*) of the root cause (*rgyu*) which was Samden's karmic fruition. If this were so, she had died a "timely death" (*dus la shi-ba*).

This judgment would explain the failure of the lama's exorcism, and would also be psychologically appropriate for Samden's family to hear: everyone would be assured that nothing more could have been done. But the assumption of timely death would have to be tested by the horoscope that is read on the following morning on the roof of the house of the deceased.

The death horoscope (*rtsis*) answers a number of questions. First, it tells whether or not the death was timely. Second, it specifies the type and direction of demonic attack, and warns of subsequent attacks that threaten the living. Third, it tells whether the birth horoscopes of members of the community are incompatible with that of the deceased, to indicate who may prepare, carry, or cremate the body. Fourth, it reveals the previous life of the deceased and predicts future possible lives, so that the best among these can be promoted by funerary remedies.

The horoscope system in the rite of death is based on the same correspondences between natural elements and time cycles that appear in the rites of life that we have examined in previous chapters. It reveals the events that are associated with the death event of a person having a particular birth year. Since a different prediction is made for each time cycle, contradictions result, so that the final conclusion depends on the interpretation of the lama.

The death *rtsis* calculated by Lama Dorje is a dramatic event, and numerous laymen crowd around him on the roof as he lays out his pictograph and places white and black pebbles on the various squares, while reading the horoscope text (*gshin-rtsis*). Lama Dorje allowed me to tape-record the reading during the rite of death for Samden, as well as his later commentary on the prognosis. The following analysis is based on those data.

The Timeliness of the Death

Each of five components of personality which wax and wane through predictable cycles are read first. The "soul" (*bla*) and the "life force" (*srog*) of Samden were both black; their blackness signified that they were in a deteriorated condition at the time of death and thus susceptible to spirit attack. This supported the witchcraft cause of death that was suspected.[2]

The weakened soul was confirmed by Samden's experience of the preceding year; her marriage engagement had been broken off and she had suffered depression. In Lama Dorje's view, harmful gossip then resulted in the wandering of her soul. Her failure at that time to come to the lama for a soul-calling rite partly explained the weakness of this component. Further, the black life force (*srog*) indicated that her life was "meant to finish at this time." It was "worn out" (*tshe sas song*) and hence, as Lama Dorje had already suggested, her death had been "timely."[3]

The timeliness of her death was a crucial question. Unfortunately, as Lama Dorje proceeded with other sections of the *rtsis* diagnosis, this first conclusion was contradicted. In the reading for the twelve-year cycle based on her birth year of the boar, her death was defined as "untimely," and six years of her life still remained. Here, the text stated that she had been a nun in her previous life. The nun had had an untimely death, and Samden's recent life had been given so that she could "use up" the unlived years of that nun, which should have taken her life up to age twenty-nine instead of age twenty-three. So her death after all had been "untimely."

Which *rtsis* reading was the correct one, the timely death or the untimely? Lama Dorje went on to examine other time frames. The reading for "weekdays" (*sa*) stated that "there was nothing that could be done," which could only be interpreted as a timely death. The time of day reading

2. Her body (*lus*), destiny power (*dbang-tang*), and luck (*rlung-rta*) were all white and hence not deteriorated, good omens for the surviving family. If her body had been black, she would remain attached to her family and possessions and would try to take them with her. If her luck had been black, the family would be harmed by malicious talk (*mi-kha*) about the circumstances of her death.
3. It would be "untimely" only if a demonic attack ending her life did not correspond with her karmically determined time for death, and in that case an exorcism could have saved her.

stated that "there was no life left." Thus, although the twelve-year cycle usually carries much weight, two out of the three time cycles agreed with the assumption of timely death. This conclusion would be good news for the family's peace of mind, for the *rtsis* had confirmed that nothing more could have been done.

The Immediate Cause of the Death

The immediate cause of the death is typically identified as a "killer demon" (*gshed-ma*). It seizes the life force (*srog*) when the latter is in a "deteriorated" (*nyams*) condition. The "unlucky year" that comes round every twelve years in the twelve-year cycle is the critical time of susceptibility to demonic attack. Samden was twenty-three years old,[4] born in the year of the boar (1959). The year of her death was 1982, the year of the dog, which falls one year before the return of the boar year (1983). This year was also inauspicious, being the "welcoming year" just prior to her unlucky birth year.

The circumstances of the demonic attack are detailed in the reading of the eight trigrams (*spar-kha*), which are equated with relationships between natural elements and the cardinal directions. Her birth trigram was *gin* which is equated with the element "mountain" in the northeastern direction. Since the year of her death was also that same trigram, the text predicts that she would "eat the food of a hermit" which would make her open to demonic attack. Lama Dorje noted that "this rang true with what we knew from her case."

Then what type of demon had killed her? Since the trigram *gin* represents the element mountain in the northeast, the text for that trigram states that a "*btsan* demon of the mountain comes from the east and then heads north," and that it was this harming agent that had "seized the life force." This also rang true. She had indeed taken the old woman's food while walking up the trail from Dumre, coming from the east and heading north. "Here it seems to be exact," added Lama Dorje. The text went on to say that this *gshed-ma* ("demon") would kill again while heading farther north, first harming a black cow and a girl. The house of this next victim "would have a door looking northeast."

But again a contradiction appeared. The text of the time of day cycle, which is based on the hour of her death, states that the killer demon came from the north. "There is another inconsistency here," admitted Lama Dorje, "but since the trigram reading best fits what we already know to be true, we should accept that one."

Handling, Timing, and Direction of Corpse Removal

The preparation, removal, and disposal of the corpse involves numerous stipulations to protect community members whose horoscope readings may be inauspiciously linked to that of the deceased. Since Samden was born in the year of the boar, other boar year persons could not touch or carry the corpse, for persons having similar birth years drag one another into similar fates.[5] Persons having a seven-year difference in birth year from the deceased (*bdun-zor*) and persons having the same birth trigram may not carry the corpse.

The timing of the removal of the corpse from the house was calculated from the cycles of weekdays and time of day. Samden died on a Saturday night. The *rtsis* text warned that the removal of the body on the same Saturday would bring harm to nine additional persons and ruin the household wealth. Removal on Sunday would dissipate household luck. Tuesday, the most auspicious day suggested, was chosen, but the time of day would also be critical. Her hour of death had been the "time of the ox," and the household wealth would be ruined if the corpse were removed at the same hour. Further, removal could not take place during a time of day that would correspond to the birth year of any household member.[6]

Finally, the direction in which the corpse is carried is determined by the *rtsis* reading. Since Samden's trigram at her year of birth was *gin,* the corpse could not be carried in the direction that comes right after the *gin* trigram (which is *zin*). Hence the corpse could not be carried in the eastern direction. If that were done, it would harm all members of the community that were born in the year of the boar or the year of the rat. That the corpse may be carried in the wrong direction is a great fear. For this reason a banner is carried at the head of the procession, showing a horoscope (*rtsis*) diagram.[7] The banner expels the harm that would come if a wrong direction were taken by mistake.

Prediction of Future Rebirth

The death *rtsis* which predicts the rebirth destiny of the deceased was the climax of the horoscope. It was the news that everyone gathered on the roof was anxious to hear. This prognosis turns up in three time frames: (1) the birth and death year; (2) the nine numerical squares (*sme-ba*); and (3) the time of day of the death. The birth year prognosis was disturbing.

---

4. Lama Dorje gave her age as twenty-four years since Tibetans count a person as already a year old at birth. Hence the first return of the twelve-year cycle falls on what is defined as one's thirteenth year of age, the second return on one's twenty-fifth.

5. The horoscope also warned that persons of serpent, monkey, dog, sheep, and hare birth years could be harmed if they were to touch or carry the corpse.

6. For instance, if a member's birth year is the year of the bird, the corpse should not be removed during the "bird" time of day. The twelve animals of the twelve-year cycle are used as terms to designate as well the twelve two-hour periods of each twenty-four-hour day, which are called the "twelve suns."

7. The *rtsis* banner is called a *srid-pa bap-du* (the "befalling of existences").

It predicted that Samden would be reborn in hell (*dmyal-ba*) for ten days because of great sins accumulated in previous lives that had now come to fruition. "We know this must refer only to her past life," commented Lama Dorje. All on the roof agreed that must be so since her recent life had been exemplary. The *rtsis* text went on to say that if much merit were made during the funeral she could avoid the hell destiny and be reborn a human instead.

The reading from the time-of-day frame, however, gave another destiny. Dying at the ox time of day was a sign that she would be reborn as either a horse or a bird for a hundred days. However, if her family could commission the lama to perform a reading of the appropriate text (the *Nyi-khri*), the animal birth could be avoided and instead she would be reborn in the eastern direction as a male doctor (*am-chi*).

Still another destiny prognosis was given in the reading of the nine numerical squares (*sme-ba*). Here, the text noted that she had died in the year of the square 5-yellow. This *sme-ba* reading promised a rebirth in the southern direction as a male, but only if a certain condition were met: the family would have to commission the making of a Buddha statue (*sku*) or the painting of a Thangka (*thang-ka*).

Unlike the problem of timely and untimely death in which the lama had to choose between alternatives, here he synthesized each rebirth prognosis into a complex scenario. If nothing were done on Samden's behalf by the family, she would, by the fruition of her past deeds, have to spend ten days in hell, after which she would be reborn either a horse or a bird for a hundred days, after which she could be reborn a human. But if the family were to hold a large funeral to gain merit (*dge-ba*), she could avoid hell, and if they were to read the *Nyi-khri* text and also have a Thangka painted, she would avoid all the animal births and become a male doctor, "a human of good circumstances." Within hours this news spread throughout the village. No one doubted that Samden's father Pasang would fulfill the recommendations.

What evaluation can be made of Samden's death horoscope interpretation? It cannot be argued that the lama skipped inconvenient sections. The troublesome and contradictory statements were all read carefully before the audience of laymen and commented upon. Had he manipulated the *rtsis* to promote a hidden agenda? The lama's own theory of horoscope technique, however, allows for choosing among conflicting statements. There are two principles of selection. First, statements that are consistent with others have more weight than isolated, deviant assertions. Second, statements are selected that have the most consistency with known experience. Samden's encounter with the old woman on the trail, her psychological deterioration the previous year, and the suddenness of her passing away all had supported the selection of the timely death prognosis. Room for maneuver is thus built into the text.

The selection principle can be further illustrated by the case of Nyima Drolma's son who had died two years previously. As the boy lay dying, his body full of sores, Lama Dorje had tried but failed to cure him of serpent deity attack. After reading the horoscope, the lama stated that the boy's death had been timely and, further, that his life was supposed to have been shortened so that he could be reborn immediately as a lama. The boy's last moments were a supporting sign: he had seemingly recovered, then suddenly died as if it were predetermined.

The lama admittedly prefers to say that a death is timely. It is psychologically appropriate, it explains the failure of the exorcism, and it teaches the karma doctrine. But do the alternatives of high- and low-rebirth destinies correlate with differentials of wealth or position of the deceased? Other deaths that occurred during the period of research can throw further light on this aspect of horoscope interpretation.

When the small daughter of the local blacksmith died, it was assumed by the Tibetan community that since the family could not afford a Lamaist funeral they could not make any merit on the girl's behalf. The horoscope predicted that she would become a wandering demon, having been seized by the demon The'u-brang. In Lama Dorje's view, "she had no chance to be reborn a human, and after harming others she would descend further into hell, because her family did not have the wealth to pay for a meritorious funeral."

This example illustrates the "downward spiral" (Ortner 1978b) perception of the lowest ranked persons, the horoscope in this case corresponding to the social evaluation.[8] When the poverty-stricken Tibetan called Mingmar died, the horoscope predicted that unless a large merit-making funeral were performed he would be reborn a sheep for a hundred days. Mingmar's wife only provided enough wealth for a meager funeral. The villagers of Tshap commented that she was "stingy" for not paying enough to ensure a human rebirth for her husband. The deaths which followed, however, did not show any correlation of social position in the horoscope reading itself. When the aged wife of the wealthy householder Namgyal died, the prediction was the same as for the poor man Mingmar: she would become a sheep for a hundred days. Namgyal however was able to overturn the prediction to gain the higher, alternative prognosis with a costly funeral. When Tshering Dorje's wife died, the *rtsis* text predicted she would

8. Most Tibetans assume that the blacksmith and butcher in particular are in a downward spiral. Because they have deserved their low births from previous evil deeds, their low birth itself fosters further demerit: the butcher kills and the blacksmith makes steel implements that kill.

suffer a few days in hell, then be reborn a dog that would die quickly so
that she would be reborn an important male in the east. Tshering Dorje
paid for a decent funeral and commissioned a Thangka painting, ensuring immediate rebirth as a human.

It can be seen that wealth can overturn the worst of the prognosis
alternatives, subserving what I have called the social *hierarchy of liberation*.
The horoscope by itself, however, is not an index of this hierarchy, having
no directionality. It presents, rather, an image of circular return. The
horoscope readings give the impression that almost every human deserves
to cycle downward temporarily, dipping into a lower animal rebirth and
again moving upward. This presents no problem for prominent Tibetans
since they accept the indeterminate character of karma fruition theory
(Obeyesekere 1968): an evil deed committed deep in one's past may
suddenly become activated to send downward one who had climbed
upward.

EXORCISING THE DEATH DEMON

The evening after the cremation of the corpse was crucial.[9] The death
demon (*gshed-ma*) still lingered in the home of Samden's family, and would
have to be exorcised to prevent it from seizing others. The exorcism
required was *Za 'dre kha sgyur,* which means "turning away the mouth
of the eating demon." The demon is represented by a torma effigy of a
man riding a tiger and pulled by a rope by a man in front while being
whipped by another from behind. This exorcism need not be described
here since it follows a pattern similar to exorcisms already explicated.

After the lama's exorcism was completed, the Paju shaman quietly went
to Tshap village to meet with Pasang, Samden's father. He warned that
the Tibetan lama's rites would certainly fail to free his daughter from the
killer demon. Only he, the Paju, could identify this particular local demon
who would not be found in the lama's texts. Further, some villagers
suspected that Samden might have been a victim of love magic, called
mohani,[10] which is used in Nepal to seduce lovers, or cause their death
if rejected. She was known to have rejected a lover just prior to her death.
Since the Tibetan lama's rites do not deal with *this* threat, she might still
be under this spell. She would wander in a craze, never to find the path.
The Paju shaman again offered his services.

9. In Gyasumdo Tibetans cannot perform the "sky burial" of leaving the corpse to be eaten
   by vultures, because vultures are not present in the valley. Water burial, in which the
   body is cut up and thrown into the river, is prevalent among the poorest householders.
   Cremation is the most expensive and retains the highest prestige. Data obtained on corpse
   disposal are omitted in order to focus in greater detail on original contributions this
   ethnography makes to Tibetan studies.
10. Mohani is the female apparition of the Hindu god Vishnu.

Pasang was a model Tibetan layman, but the Lamaist voice within him had to contend with the shamanic rejoinder. He would stop at nothing to ensure a good destiny for his daughter. He called the Paju to his home in the middle of the night. The Paju performed the love magic antidote, dropping flowers into a bowl of water one by one, asking his ancestral Paju to remove the curse from the victim's food, ornaments, teeth, etc. He also performed his *Badza tangi* rite to neutralize any The'u-brang demon in the area who may have seized her consciousness. He sent out his own The'u-brang aide, to hunt down the offender in rivers, trees, rocks, and cliffs. Lama Dorje remained in the Gompa, supposedly oblivious of what was happening. After the Paju left, nothing more would be said about the incident, and the funeral would proceed in a standard Tibetan manner.

FEEDING THE DEAD AND THE LIVING: THE SEVERANCE RITE (*GCOD*)

During the forty-nine-day period the funeral rite is performed seven times, once a week. Before dealing with the Bardo—the lama's guidance of the consciousness of the deceased—it is necessary to describe the underlying ritual that provides the context for interpreting the Bardo. We have seen that in the funeral rite of the Ghyabrē shaman, exchanges are made in the underworld, the human world, and the upper world land of the dead. The three levels of the cosmos are reharmonized. In contrast, the Tibetan death rite focuses on *individual* destiny. The background ritual layer, however, is analogous to the Ghyabrē shaman's model.

A burnt offering called a *gsur btang* is repeated each day to feed (through smell) the deceased's spirit. It feeds as well all wandering ghosts (*yi-dwags*), especially those who demand repayment for "debts" (*bu-lon*) that have been owed to them by Samden from her past lives.[11] They are "karmic creditors" (*lan-chags gegs*). While these debts from the past are being paid, a grand distribution of rice cakes (*tshogs*) is carried to all villages in Gyasumdo. Both rites together feed all the living and all the dead without partiality. They pay all debts and accumulate merit on Samden's behalf. Lama Dorje emphasizes that the merit is from feeding universally, which, he adds, is "superior" to the Gurung funeral performed by the Ghyabrē, which "feeds only the relatives" of the deceased.

In Samden's funeral, however, a far grander background ritual was performed as well. It was the "severance" (*gcod*), which I have introduced

---

11. The *yi-dwags* spirits have more than one type. There are the "hungry ghosts" who occupy one of the six realms of existence, but *yi-dwags* are also thought of as a summary term for all spirits of the past who have not "found the path" into another rebirth. They are often thought to live in communities or *yi-dwags* cities.

in chapter seven. It achieves what the lamas call the union of two truth
levels: the severance "cuts away" Samden's ignorance, while at the same
time the "cut pieces" of her corpse are identified with the rice cakes that
are distributed to the other villages in Gyasumdo. What follows is a short
summary and a few quotations from the severance rite text that I recorded on tape, translated by Lama Nyima into the colloquial Tibetan
of Gyasumdo.

As the severance section begins, the goddess Ma-cig lab-dron (*Ma-gcig
slab-sgron*) is transformed into her fierce form rDo-rje Phag-mo (Skt.
Vajravāhārī). She cuts off the top of the skull. Then she peels the skin
down off the body and spreads the skin on the ground. With her sword
she cuts the body into small bits, placing the pieces on the skin in a mandala
pattern of Mount Meru and the four continents: it becomes the total
offering of wealth.

The chopped pieces are gathered up and put into the severed skull cap.
The skull is imagined to be a huge caldron heated over a fire that cooks
the pieces of meat. "Countless Khandromas" (Skt. Dākinī) come to
distribute the food throughout the three worlds of the cosmos, while
chanted mantras multiply the amount of flesh, blood, and bones so that
it "never ends." As the corpse is distributed it takes on a variety of forms
to meet every conceivable need, as well as pay back every debt that Samden
has accumulated from the past. The lama's oral exposition of the text
proceeds as follows:

> Imagine that your corpse has been turned into healing medicines,
> fine clothes, precious jewels, all kinds of grains and domestic
> animals: horses, cattle, elephants. Then it is transformed into
> forests, flowers, and wealth of all kinds. Nothing is lacking. Indeed,
> your corpse has been transformed into the Wish-granting Tree itself,
> along with mansions, gardens, gems, and all desirables to satisfy the
> five senses.

All regions of the cosmos and the beings of each realm are named so
that they may receive their share: *lha* gods of the upper world, *btsan* spirits
of the middle human world, and those of the lower world, described as
the "black land" of *bdud* demons, "blue land" of *klu* serpent deities, the
"green land" of *sa-bdag* territorial owners. This renews the wealth of the
natural world and that of all beings within it. The image then shifts to
the guests both invited and uninvited who come to feed on the flesh that
is visualized as the food of a banquet: Two images are united into one
as the body that is renounced becomes the body that is distributed:

> Since I must die anyway, I give my body to all the guests. All come,
> I'll feed you! Those who like meat, take my flesh. Those who like

blood, take my blood. Those who like bones, take my bones. Those who like skin to wear, take my skin. Take it all, I don't need it!

As the "guests," representing all sentient beings including the worst demons, begin to pour into the scene, the chant continues: "Those guests who have time, cook the meat and eat it. Those without time, eat it raw! Licking chops, slurping lips—hurr! hurr!—as the body is eaten there is a cracking sound—kaa! kaa! Break the bones and suck the marrow. Have enough, be pleased in the night and in the day, sing songs of happiness!"

Exact attention is given to the problem of equal shares. The intestines, the liver, the kidney, the skin, etc., are all designated to different categories of beings. The theme that "no one may be excluded" is the central idea in the rite; no elite is selected to receive a share. This is expressed systematically, using the metaphor of "guests" (*mgron-po*) who are both invited and uninvited to dramatize that even those who are ordinarily excluded in conventional social life must now obtain their share. Among the four kinds of invited guests are all the Buddhas, the Srungma protectors, all beings in the six realms of existence, and also the karmic creditors (*lan-chags gegs*), representing offenses committed against others in the past that must be paid for by the distribution.

Then come the "uninvited guests" (*'bod ma-rung k'i mgron*). Among them are those who are too despicable to invite, "but they come anyway" (*ma-'bod-pa la yong*). These are all demons: rGyal-po, Ma-mo, The'u-brang, etc. Lama Nyima portrays them as scrambling to pick up anything that falls on the floor. They are uncontrollable. They grab whatever they see. They dramatize the principle that no one may be excluded. The total share-out is defined as the compassion of the "Bodhisattva mind." In an ultimate sense, however, the distribution is *deserved* by those who receive it. It is repayment of a debt owed to them:

> I dedicate this offering to all sentient beings because they are my
> mother and father and so I repay them for their kindness: the
> clothes that have been provided for me by my mother, like the first
> fruit that is always given to children. Therefore I offer this to all my
> parents who have been so kind to me. I am in debt [*bu-lon*] to them all.

The reference to the mother is crucial, since she is the model for both parents, to whom one is indebted, and represents every sentient being that has been one's parent at some time during one's transmigrational career. Every relation of obligation created during the whole of the past thus returns as a vision in the consciousness of the deceased. No one may be excluded. Psychic liberation is fused with ethical indebtedness.

The severance rite seeks such a fusion through a more ancient layer of culture in which, as Hertz (1960) has noted, every death was viewed as a sacrifice that renews fertility and abundance in the world of the living. During the cremation phase of the Tibetan funeral, various "wealth" ingredients symbolizing well-being are burned in the fire along with the corpse, meant to benefit the deceased in her future life. In the severance rite, however, the Buddhist Mahāyāna ethic is added, and this benefit is transferred to everyone. It is a return payment that remakes past relationships. Lama Nyima explains that these beneficiaries will become obligated "to pay you back in the future," through a similar sacrifice in *their* death rites.

The severance model, as the underlayer of the Tibetan death rite, can be viewed as a transmutation of an ancient complex, incorporating themes of shamanic initiation (Van Tuyl 1979) and sacrificial exchange. In the Ghyabrē shaman's death rite, we have noted that during the period of wandering by the soul of the deceased, exchanges are made in each realm, benefiting both the living and the dead. The Tibetan severance rite makes sacrificial distributions of the deceased's body in the same three-world cosmos. To this is added an inner psychic Buddhist reflexivity, as the consciousness that is "released" from the body by the goddess watches the entire drama.

The synthesis of psychic liberation on the one hand and interpersonal obligation on the other fuses the domains of death and life. "Inner," mental sacrifice is interwoven with externally shared abundance. It is a fusion, using fantastic, carnivalistic images to merge domains that had been bifurcated (e.g., samsara versus nirvana). For Bakhtin (1984:160), "carnival is past millennia's way of sensing the world as one great communal performance . . . bringing the world maximally close . . . into the zone of free familiar contact. . . ." As do the literary works of Rabelais and Dostoevsky, the Tibetan severance rite transmutes such images. It celebrates the "cheerful death," merging together the funeral and the feast, overturning hierarchy by turning creditors into debtors and debtors into creditors (Bakhtin 1981:176).

> [By] "intermixing carnival hell and carnival paradise, hell and paradise become intertwined. . . . The carnivalized image strives to encompass and unite within itself both poles of becoming: birth-death, youth–old age, . . . affirmation-repudiation, tragic-comic, . . . nobility-degradation . . . opposites come together [and] know and understand one another, . . . everything must be reflected in everything else" (Bakhtin 1984:173–77).

The Tibetan severance rite emerges historically after the karma ethic of "individual life sequences" has thrust subjective identity beyond the ancient (shamanic) matrix. The lama's project of enlightenment brings that ancient layer into a more advanced level, in which all consciousnesses must interact because they are interindebted to one another. It initiates a "third" temporal identity, moving all beings forward into the future together rather than individually. The fusion is dramatized at the end when the evil deeds of all beings are "taken in" to the mind of the lama performer on behalf of the deceased, then "dissipated."

GUIDING THE CONSCIOUSNESS IN THE BARDO

With the severance model in mind we are now ready to interpret the Gyasumdo lama tradition of guiding the consciousness in the Bardo. There are a variety of shorter versions of the famous Tibetan *Book of the Dead* (*Bar-do thos-grol*).[12] Each lama in Gyasumdo uses the one taught by his own teacher from whom he has copied it by hand. The lama reads this text and explicates the meaning for the benefit of the listening consciousness of both the deceased and the audience. In the case of Samden's funeral, the Bardo instruction was performed seven times during the forty-nine-day period, giving me opportunities to tape-record and re-record, as well as to interview the attending lamas during the period. The following is an ethnographic analysis of the Bardo guidance as an oral performance, rather than a study of the written text.

Family members, friends, and relatives gathered in Pasang's home to watch the lama do the Bardo ritual at the beginning of the forty-nine days, but they gathered in the Gompa for its final performance. Lama Dorje called Samden into the paper effigy (*sbyang-bu*) in front of him.[13] As he read from the text, he looked up after each paragraph to paraphrase it in the colloquial Tibetan that the audience could more easily understand. He embellished the text with local imagery, stressing what was psychologically important for Samden's consciousness, as well as for the attending audience.

The first part of the Bardo rite was similar to a Tibetan folk rite that is performed by the laity just before the Bardo begins. Family members communicate with the deceased through food offerings. It is basically a pre-Buddhist tradition that has not been rejected by Lamaism, strikingly similar to the Ghyabrē shaman's Plenema rite when he delivers the family

---

12. Summary texts are shortened versions of the longer Bardo text such as that found in the translation of Evans-Wentz (1960), said to have been composed by Padmasambhava. The summary text used by Lama Dorje in Gyasumdo is called *Gsung gi chos zhal-gdams thos grol bzhugs so* ("Oral teaching of religious guidance for deliverance through hearing").

13. The *sbyang-bu,* a paper effigy, contains a block print of a picture of a woman or a man sitting in an attitude of adoration, and is meant to represent the deceased anticipating entry into a Buddha field.

offerings of food to the deceased. When Tibetan householders in Gyasumdo put on *their* farewell feeding of the departed, they call it *zas-na*. In Samden's funeral, the son-in-law presented the plates of food brought by various members of Tshap village. As he put bits of food into a burnt offering "for her to smell," he chanted:

> Here is food from your relative "x" (or friend "x"). Take this food and depart. Realize you have died! Do you see your shadow in the sun? Do you see your footprint in the sand? Don't be attached to your clothes and jewelry. Don't be attached to your family or you will harm them! Take this food and go. Begone!

During the ceremony relatives wept and some cried out to Samden, feeling her presence in the same manner as Gurung relatives do. The Tibetan *zas-na* is not, however, a direct imitation of the Ghyabrē's rite in Gyasumdo, for as Waddell (1895, reprint 1978:496) pointed out nearly a century ago, feeding the dead by relatives was an ancient Tibetan Bon funerary custom, referred to in the eighth-century writings of Padmasambhava, who found the Buddhist laity unwilling to give it up. Tibetans in Gyasumdo, however, are well aware that their own *zas-na* is equivalent to that of the local Ghyabrē shaman. The shamanic version nearby penetrates the understanding of their own rite as a hidden discourse.

The Bardo instruction of Lama Dorje began in the context of the *zas-na* theme, but he carefully transmuted it to serve a Buddhist end. The strategy takes note of Samden's "natural tendency" to remain attached to her former family, but redefines this tendency as a sign of her past evil deeds (*las ngen*). Once she is made to reflect on this, the Bardo guidance can offer ways out of her karmic dilemma. Each argument becomes convincing only after building on that which precedes it.

Recognition of Signs of Having Died and Signs of Past Deeds

The lama informs Samden's consciousness (T. *rnam-shes*, Skt. *vijñāna*) that she must first realize that she has actually died: "When you were alive there was a sun and moon, but now you can see by the light emanating from your body. Look into the water and see there is no reflection. So that there is no shadow of your body. Place your feet in the sand and see there is no footprint." He moves on to mental evidence of having died, which becomes evidence of her karmic past as well:

> Your mind goes everywhere. When you think of going to the top of a mountain you arrive there; or to the bottom of the sea you arrive there. It is because of the habitual tendencies of your former life. It

is like a person waking up from a dream and continuing to have the thoughts of the dream: walking on a cliff, enjoying wealth and food, whatever. Then later you realize there is nothing there. You have only a body of mental inclinations [*bag-chags yid kyi lus*].

The lama uses the term *bag-chags* (Skt. *vāsanā*), which means psychological propensities inherited from former lives. She must now equate her mental flights with her karmic past: "It is the deeds of your past which hurl you about. Like a frightening wind they carry you to the top of a cliff, back and forth across the river. You must experience these past deeds, not knowing where they will take you."

The "karmic" discourse overlaps with a pre-Buddhist discourse which Tibetans have in common with the Ghyabrē shaman. Included is the fear that Samden will seize the wealth of the family left behind. Lama Dorje now demands that she give up the family wealth in karmic terms, referring to attachments that Samden was known to have:

Samden! You have many clothes in the house. Forsake these. Put them out of your mind! Realize you have died, or you will harm your family and destroy their wealth. These inclinations arise from your former evil deeds that you have not purified. . . . If you harm your family you will not obtain liberation [*thar-pa*].

Lama Dorje has now led her to the point of guilt awareness. Two hindrances had repressed her remembrance of the moral content of her past. First, the illusion of still being alive acted to repress her full memory. Second, the mental influences (*bag-chags*) that she first experienced were fluid, decentered, unbounded. In the Bardo sequence, however, the relevant memories are brought into sharp focus: "Now you will remember all your deeds. You will think, 'I did much *sdig-pa* [sin]. I killed, I chopped, I said bad things, I thought bad things. It seems I must experience it [*nyung*] now!'"

Unlike guilt in the Freudian model, which lacks the transmigrational time depth of Buddhism, the repressed guilt which the lama reveals in Samden's consciousness incorporates all of her former existences. He is able thus to include killing and chopping (the red offering), ultimate crimes assumed to have been committed by Samden in her distant past. These vast mental influences inherited from her past are now bottled up inside a boundary of individual guilt, focusing on virtues and "sins" (*sdig-pa*), as if they were a measurable record of private deeds that can be counted and weighed. Now the scales and the mirror appear, together with the Lord of Death (gShin-rje Chos-rgyal), who has scales for weighing one's past deeds. These metaphors construct a boundary around Samden's subjectivity, molding guilt recognition and fear of karmic retribution. Lama Dorje continues:

> Now you experience regret that you did not practice religion very much while you were alive. Your mental body shakes as you go to gShin-rje Chos-rgyal. You may try to lie, saying, "There is no pile of sin [*sdig-pa*]!" But you are then shown everything in the mirror [*me-long*] of your deeds. . . .
> Now it will appear to your consciousness that gShin-rje Chos-rgyal is coming with a hammer, an axe, a knife in his hands to pound you, to chop you, to tie you up and beat you. . . .

Assistance as Shared Merit

The threatening appearance of the Lord of Death dramatizes what may be in store. But this is not, after all, the moment for counting the past deeds. The lama announces a forty-nine-day period of reprieve before the time of weighing so that merit can be expanded: an accumulation of "virtue" (*dge-ba*) through family "assistance" (*rogs-ram*).

> The Lord of Death says that he grants you leave [*dgong-pa gnang*] of forty-nine days before he will judge you. During that period, go before your father, your mother, brothers and sisters. You didn't do enough virtue during your life so now your family will have to do it for you. Go now to your home for the seven periods [seven weeks to make the forty-nine days]. They will send you the merit they make, saying, "Come, take this *dge-ba!*"
> After that time, return to the Lord of Death. He will ask you, "How much *dge-ba* has your family made? Take it and come! If your virtue wins [on the scales], you will be sent to the highest realm [*mtho-ri gnas*]. If your *sdig-pa* [sin] wins you must experience the worst hell [*gnas song*].

The karmic scales in the Bardo radically individuates moral identity in a manner that would be inconceivable in the Ghyabrē shaman's death cult. But the use that is now made of karma by the lama expands that boundary. It is not, of course, a return to the Gurung model in which one's destiny depends on social alliances between intermarrying families. In the Bardo, once the model of karmic retribution has been dramatized, then a model of shared merit can be introduced. It must, however, remain within a Buddhist framework as an inner process. Lama Dorje asserts that Samden will have to perform the merit-making actions mentally along with her family, and with pure intent: "During that period you must forsake all pride and anger while hearing the *ma-ne* [rosary and prayer wheel mantras] and while the *tshogs* [rice cakes] are distributed and the butter lamps are lit. You must *understand* that it is for you. You yourself must [as a consciousness] circumambulate the Gompa."

But will Samden realize that she needs this merit assistance? The Bardo instruction has just undermined her sense of self-reliance, pointing out her hopeless pile of demerit through the mirror and driving her to her family for aid before it is too late. The guidance now portrays her cry for help to her family for assistance. Lama Dorje has already set up the family for this by telling them that the bad destinies which the horoscope foresaw are in fact *signs* that "Samden is crying for help." To dramatize this, he pulls in a hidden, pre-Buddhist discourse, that of the "last farewell" in the folk layer of the Tibetan death cult, and which we have found in the Ghyabrē shaman's rite when the bird sits on the laps of its loved ones. Lama Dorje continues:

> You will go to your home now and see your family weeping. "Why are you crying, I am here!" you will say, but they cannot hear you. You sit on their laps and hug and kiss them, but they do not see you.
>
> Then you cry out to them, "I have died and have committed much sin [*sdig-pa*]! Please make merit for me so that I won't have to go to hell [*dmyal-ba*]!

Lama Dorje is well aware of the emotional power of the shamanic drama in Gyasumdo. He knows all Tibetans have visited Tapje village and have seen the Ghyabrē "send the bird" into the laps of the Gurung family sitting in a circle. The image is transmuted into the Buddhist model of "sending merit" to the deceased. When Gyasumdo Tibetans compare their death rite to that of the Gurungs, one hears the phrase, "They send the bird, we send merit."

Tibetan household members send merit (*dge-ba btang*) to their deceased,[14] but they also use the term "shared merit" (*dge-ba pi-ma*). Here, they refer to the manner in which household property that is "inherited" by persons who die can be used for merit making on their behalf. Lay persons assert, "Those who share inheritance can share merit." Unlike the vast merit and wealth interdependence that we have seen in the severance rite underlayer, the ritual foreground is merit and wealth that is still bounded up, first, within an individual accumulation, and second, within the household boundary, extending occasionally to the patriline. In the hierarchy of liberation, family wealth can make up for individual merit failures, just as it can overturn the worst prognoses of the horoscope.

---

14. The term *dge-ba* translates as "virtue," but it is used in a generalized sense as "merit" (T. *bsod-nams*, Skt. *punya*).

The Pulling Up Relation ('dren-thabs *and* 'brel-pa)

Merit assistance among relatives is a horizontal relation between persons of equal status. There is another mode of assistance which is vertical. The lama, identified with the Buddha, brings the deceased to a higher destiny through a "pulling up technique" (*'dren thabs*). He will do it only if a "relation" (*'brel-pa*) has been established with the lama before one has died. Lama Dorje thus continues in his Bardo instruction: "What is this assistance like? If you are drowning in a river, a strong person can grab you and pull you out . . . but if you don't ask for help before you die there is no help afterward."

The central metaphor used is the "iron hook" (*chak-gyu*) that catches hold of a "ring" held by the deceased, the ring snapping shut only if a relation of trust has already been established between the two parties. The Tibetan term for "pull up" (*'dren*) is a hybrid construction in Gyasumdo that overlays other discourses. It means to "draw along, conduct along," as in guiding in a journey. Hence the lama's Bardo performance calls to mind the image of the Ghyabrē shaman conducting the Gurung soul up the trail to the land of the dead.

There is another discourse hidden within the Bardo image of pulling up, that of the mother-son relation. Tibetan mothers who give a son to the Gompa for lama training say that their primary motive is the hope that the son will be the performing lama when they die and "pull them up." My landlady Nyima Drolma, who had sent her son to the Gompa, talked often of this expectation. It is a relation of interdependence: the mother "sacrifices her own needs to give her son everything." Then the son becomes a lama and rescues his mother from the fate of a lower existence. In his tape-recorded biography, Lama Dorje himself focused on this image: his own mother had begged him to become a lama so that he could "pull her up."

Yet another discourse can be uncovered. The verb "to pull up" (*'dren*) has the sound of the verb "to recollect" (*dren*). The lama who can remember who a person is can more easily pull her up during the Bardo. When an incarnate lama passes through this district and gives empowerment initiations (*dbang*), lay persons will say, "When I die he will recollect [*dren*] that I received his empowerment and he will pull me up [*'dren*]." Those who go on pilgrimages say they have various sacred lamas with whom this "relation" has been established. When Samden died, her father Pasang sent a runner with a gift (*bul-ba*) to Lama Kongtrul Rinpoche, who was then giving empowerments in Manang village. The messenger showed him a photograph of Samden. The Rinpoche, wherever he might be during Samden's Bardo, was to "recall" her image. This would telepathically aid the pulling up process in Tshap village.

LIBERATION THROUGH AWARENESS

Up to this point the Bardo instruction has been a preliminary to the central theme of liberation through awareness. Now there is a shift from methods of assistance which rescue the deceased from her objective karmic past to methods in which her subjective projections need to be recognized. The complete symbolism of this complex section cannot be elaborated here, and indeed it is not given in complete form in the Bardo performances of the village lamas of Gyasumdo. What does interest us most is the use of local folk imagery that can illuminate contextual use of Bardo symbology.

The consciousness must now examine itself. It can do so, however, only as Lama Dorje's voice becomes persuasive within the internal dialogue of Samden's consciousness. Bakhtin notes that in Dostoevsky's novels, the "confessional" character alternates between denial and confession of guilt. Much of the Bardo guidance provokes such alternation. No one aspect of motivation can be singled out to fully represent the tangled web of relations and memory traces. A personal confession often produces denial of another layer of complicity. A fuller confession must include "sideward glances" at relational layers of awareness. In Gyasumdo this is complicated by the shamanic voice within the dialogue.

The advanced Bardo instruction begins with an opportunity to enter the enlightened state at the level of "truth body" (T. *chos-sku,* Skt. *dharmakāya*), then drops to the penultimate level of a chance to reach a Buddha field (T. *longs-sku,* Skt. *sambhogakāya*), and finally descends to samsaric existence and rebirth, which is the expected destiny for most persons.[15] Each level is represented as experiencing types of "light." One who recognizes a "clear light" (T. *'od-gsal,* Skt. *prabhāsvara*) in the beginning of the guidance enters Buddhahood. If not, a less brilliant, "bright" rainbow of colors appears representing the five Buddha fields of the five wisdom Buddhas (rgyal-ba rigs lnga) in their mild Bodhisattva forms and then later their terrifying forms. Failing at this level, one finally sees six "dull" lights emanating from the six realms of samsaric existence. The lama's role is to urge the consciousness to take hold of the bright lights and shun the dull lights of samsaric rebirth.

The final Bardo instruction of the forty-nine days is given in the Gompa. Behind the performing lamas are painted on the walls the five wisdom Buddhas, iconically represented in their peaceful and wrathful manifestations in the same order that they are introduced in the Bardo

15. Tibetans in general regard birth in a Buddha field as tantamount to achieving ultimate liberation (*thar-pa*) because from there, advancement toward enlightenment is possible without any further suffering or death. Buddha fields are sharply distinguished from the sixth samsaric realm of the gods, which provides only a thousand years of bliss and ends in death and further samsaric suffering.

guidance. The series also represents inner psychological states. If Samden would recognize the primordial consciousness (T. *kun-gzhi rnam-shes*, Skt. *ālayavijñāna*) in her own mind, she would merge with the consciousness of these Buddhas.

Each peaceful Buddha image is united with a consort and surrounded by two Bodhisattvas and two Dakinis. If Samden fails to recognize the blue light of Buddha rNam-par snang mdzad (Skt. Vairocana) in the center, she flees toward the samsaric region of the gods because of her pride (*nga-rgyal*). If she does not recognize the white light of rDo-rje sems-dpa' (Skt. Vajrasattva) in the east, she flees toward the hell realm from anger (*zhe-sdang*). If the yellow light of Rin-chen 'byung-ldan (Skt. Ratnasambhava) in the south is not recognized, her habit of greed ('*dod-chags*) leads toward a human rebirth. If the red light of 'Od-dpag-med (Skt. Amitābha) in the west is not recognized, the inclination of ignorance (*gti-mug*) leads toward the animal realm. If the green light of Las gi rigs (Skt. Amoghasiddhi) in the north is not recognized, the propensity of envy (*phrad-dog*) leads toward the world of demigods.

Failing to recognize these forms, her consciousness moves into awareness of the "wrathful" (*khro-bo*) Buddha images, painted on the Gompa wall as the five Heruka Buddhas. They have three heads, four legs, and six arms; their bodies are covered with serpents; they wear necklaces of human skulls; and each embraces his wrathful consort. Huge Garuda wings protrude from their shoulders, portraying the terrifying bird that destroys the "serpents of delusion." The Herukas are followed by a parade of other wrathful forms: the eight Keurima, the eight Phra-menma, the twenty-eight terrifying animal-headed Dakinis, all holding violent weapons and carrying skull caps filled with blood, human hearts, and corpses.

In Lama Dorje's Bardo instruction he provides some, but not all the details in the latter image sequence, focusing mainly on relating them as a whole to the deceased's experience and using local folk images of Gyasumdo as he engages in dialogue with the deceased's consciousness. The object is to convince Samden that the terrifying images are projections of her own consciousness. There are two illusions to dispose of. The first illusion returns to her experience of karmic "punishment" by demon aides of the Lord of Death (gShin-rje Chos-rgyal). As in the earlier part, she sees them rushing at her. But this time Lama Dorje asks her to view their punishment not primarily as karmically deserved, but rather as self-projections: "These terrifying ones have come from nowhere! They have been produced from your own mental propensities [*bag-chags*]. They will not actually kill you or chop you up. It is your own consciousness that strikes you!"

This perspective diverges sharply from the early portrayal of the Lord of Death weighing her karmic deeds as an objective measurement of retribution. Now there is a shift from "real" guilt to what Freud calls a "sense of guilt." As the consciousness becomes aware of the ultimate emptiness of its mental projections, the accumulation of past karmic deeds lose their objective form. If these punishing images can then be renounced as "false," the fruition of past deeds as "psychic inclinations" (*bag-chags*) can also be dismissed as false.

There is a midway point, however, between what may be called "karmic realism" and psychic awareness of internal states: the wrathful images can also be used to introduce the consciousness to the Buddhas at their penultimate level as Bodhisattvas to be supplicated. It is an alternative to full enlightenment, at the Mahāyāna level of compassion. As Bodhisattvas, the light rays form "hooks" that can draw her up into a Buddha field. Here, rather than declaring the images completely unreal, the lama defines them as something other than what they seem. For this, Lama Dorje draws on local imagery in Gyasumdo:

> Imagine a village down the trail that appears to contain enemies hostile to the people of Tshap village. As you walk toward that village you see people coming toward you and you think, "They are enemies coming to kill me."
>
> But they are not enemies! They are coming to welcome you! You had mistaken welcoming Buddhas for enemies! These terrifying deities are coming to welcome you, there is no need to fear them or to flee.

In Lama Dorje's dialogical method he refers to images of Gyasumdo relationships on a horizontal plane: the villagers down the trail are redefined as Buddhas rather than the demonic beings they were mistaken for. Then he shifts back to vertical images, referring to the grotesque Heruka paintings on the wall behind him:

> Samden, during your life you came often into the Gompa and saw these images on the wall. You learned then that these are not demons, they are really Buddhas. These are the same images that you see now. Try to remember how they looked here, and when you saw them on pilgrimages. It is only those who do not look at them during their life that are afraid and flee.

Iconographic practice by the laity, particularly during pilgrimage, is a lay equivalent of the lifelong image-practice of lamas, monks, and nuns, who are initiated to meditate on the wrathful deities taken as tutelaries (*yi-dam*). Hence, instead of demasking the images as mere projections of the mind, the lama transmutes the deceased's private fantasy of the attacking demonic enemies into the publicly recognized terrifying deities on the Gompa walls. Ultimately, both private and public projections emanate from a primordial consciousness that is both personal and transpersonal (Beyer 1978:81–92). The public iconographic images, however, are "more real" than private fantasies that are still unenlightened. The public images are provisionally apt metaphors for Buddha qualities, understood at the penultimate level in terms of compassion. Hence, instead of saying "they are coming to punish me" the consciousness learns to say "they are coming to liberate me." The demons are Buddhas in disguise.

The Dialogue of Denial and Confession

In the beginning of the Bardo guidance, Lama Dorje forces Samden to admit her karmic record and face retributional justice. Her first "wrathful" projections are denials of her past deeds. The lama unmasks these early projections to lay bare an "objective" record of individual guilt. But once they have taught this lesson, the karmic demons would become a second mode of denial if they were not, in their turn, unmasked. Hence they become redefined as merely the consciousness, punishing itself. Individual guilt is pushed into the background to make way for a more comprehensive awareness.

In this manner, each layer of psychic awareness unmasks the denial of an earlier layer. Bakhtin's (1984) "confessional" model of internal dialogue is a similar process of masking and unmasking. Since varied human voices intersect within the mind, each layer has its own validity as a partial truth in human experience, none being completely falsified. The Tibetan lama's Bardo sequence may be interpreted in a similar manner. Each demonic image represents its own truth, but each must be unmasked, to create a new layer. Lama Dorje leads Samden to recognize both the subjective and the intersubjective aspects of her projections. He calls the wrathful images "appearances" (snang-ba) which arise in the mind, but they are also Buddha manifestations whose reality is only distorted by psychic tendencies. The dialogue is a model of both/and, rather than of either/or.

The lama knows that all images are in a sense "empty" (stong-pa) since none can fully signify ultimate truth (don dam bden-pa). But he also knows that Samden is not advanced enough for that level of awareness. Thus instead of emptying her images he transmutes them. He accepts her images that mask ultimate reality, but uses them to unmask other denials. The inappropriate metaphor of killer demons is transmuted into the more apt image of retributional demons, and from there to the more advanced metaphor of welcoming Buddhas in terrifying forms. Both peaceful Buddha images and the terrifying Heruka Buddhas are ultimately "false," yet "true" as different levels of insight. The identity sequence thus far can be summarized as follows:

1. *The unbounded matrix.* Samden was seized and possessed in a shamanic manner by killer demon spirits (*gshed-ma*). This was the cause of her death. Both Lamaist and shamanic practitioners try to exorcize such demons, which they view as external penetrations. They assume that Samden herself entered their reality in the introductory part of the Bardo instruction, where her consciousness is described as unbounded and hurled about in a whirling matrix of influences.

2. *The bounded self.* Samden is then made to focus on her personal guilt as a sealed-off individual. The demons she has experienced are transmuted into ethically principled agents of hell (*gshin-rje*) who threaten retribution for her karmic accumulations. To confess the karmic layer of individual guilt, she must unmask as unreal the layer of unbounded demons she initially experienced.

3. *Unbounded becoming.* If Samden were to remain stuck at the second layer of private guilt, the demons of hell would become a new mode of denial. The individual merit boundary must now be reinterpreted. Samden is invited to get "help" (*rogs-ram*) from the merit made by her family, from the lamas who pull her up, from the compassionate Buddhas who welcome her. She unmasks the karmic demons and transmutes them into compassionate Buddhas who "appear" as demons. These helping agents all reveal the larger universe of relations to which she is indebted. Subjective guilt shifts toward confession of a much vaster, intersubjective process of becoming.

The final shift requires a severing of the illusion of an "internal" subject sealed off from the "external" world as an objective reality. The demonic images again change their meaning. They no longer teach karmic retribution, nor are they disguised forms of welcoming Buddhas. They are now flesh-eating demons who dismember her mental body: "rShin-rje's servants seize you from the left and the right. Now they have animal heads: tiger, pig, serpents, elephant. They chop your body into pieces."

By radically subjectivizing *both* internal and external reality, these demons shock the consciousness into renouncing attachments to either. Each of the five Herukas is a destroyer of one of the five poisons. They are followed by animal-headed, weapon-bearing furies: each kills or cuts off some aspect of ignorance, anger, and attachment. It is a shift to the subjunctive mood: the images no longer stand for *any* referent. They are treated "as if" they were demonic attackers even after they are understood to be only metaphors, but they are now consciously controlled to teach the lesson of impermanence. They jolt the mind through the vision of cutting, so that Samden can seize on her last chance for liberation. If the

method fails, Lama Dorje warns, "She will flee in horror into the lowest
samsaric realm." He compares the technique to that of "putting a snake
inside a bamboo stick. Either it comes out the top or out the bottom, but
not out the side."[16]

The technique can be interpreted in the context of the corpse imagery
that Lama Dorje employs to evoke disgust with samsaric rebirth. His Bardo
guidance continues:

> If you were to collect all the corpses of those who have ever died
> from the beginning up to now, they would make a pile higher than
> the highest mountain, and if all the pus and blood from these
> corpses were to be gathered, there would be an ocean greater than
> any in the world. Thus there is no escape from this suffering if you
> continue to take birth in samsara without becoming a Buddha.

Image strategies of corpse dismemberment and disgust are further
joined with other modes of appeal having the same end. Lama Dorje draws
on the biographical data of each deceased person he instructs in the Bardo
to evoke disgust with rebirth. In the instruction given to Mingmar after
he died, the lama asserted: "Mingmar! Don't try to be reborn in Tshap
village again in order to return to your family and possessions. Your wife
and your brother Pasang are old and about to die. Your daughter is
mentally retarded. You can never regain these possessions of yours
anyway."

Such appeals to "renounce" (spang, 'dor) samsaric birth are climaxed
in the classic Bardo formula: each of the six realms is equated with one
of the possible kinds of suffering of sentient beings. Lama Dorje goes
through the whole list as follows:

Realm	Corresponding Inclination	Type of Suffering
Hell	Anger (zhe-sdang)	Severe heat and cold
Hungry ghosts	Avarice (ser-sna)	Hunger and thirst
Animals	Mental torpor (gti-mug)	Burden bearing, stupidity
Humans	Passion ('dod-chags)	Birth-illness-aging-death
Demigods	Jealousy (phrag-dog)	Never-ending strife
Gods	Pride (nga-rgyal)	Death awareness

As the lama names each realm, the "rebirth gate" (skye-sgo) in each
is ritually closed to prevent rebirth, and at the same time the deceased
is shown small initiation cards of the six Buddha incarnations of the

16. Lama Dorje identifies this as the use of gsang sngags, which Tucci translates as "Tantric
    formulae" (Tucci 1980:269).

Bodhisattva Avalokiteśvara (Chenresig, T. *spyan-ras-gzigs*) who enters each realm to liberate its occupants. In some forms of the Bardo guidance in Gyasumdo, the performing lama draws the six realms across the floor, and the paper effigy is moved from one to the next as each rebirth gate is closed. It is the last chance for the consciousness to renounce the six inclinations that lead to birth in each realm.

As the Bardo reaches its climax a dialectic emerges between two perspectives. The model of karma as psychological traces of past deeds within the psyche (*bag-chags*) alternates with the model of karma as a relation *between* the deceased and her past retributional creditors who demand payment (*lan-chags*). The difference can be seen in the term used to resolve the karmic problem for each. To liquidate psychological inclinations, the technique is to "forsake, abandon" (*spang*). To clear away retributional debt, the method is "cleanse, purge, dissolve" (*sbyang* or *sbyong*).

In the death rite of the Gyasumdo lamas, it appears that while a psychic transformation of consciousness is progressively fine tuned in the Bardo, the relational model of interindebtedness returns again and again in the background rituals of the forty-nine-day period. In one of these rites, Lama Dorje dissolved (*sbyang*) Samden's past deeds by pouring water over his mirror (*me-long*). He then burned away her karmic past by inhaling her evil deeds into his nostrils, blowing them out onto a small dish on which seeds were drawn in the image of a scorpion (*sdig-pa ra-dza*). He burned the seeds.

The lama commented on these ritual acts: "It is not just the deceased's evil deeds, but all evil deeds ever committed by sentient beings from the beginning up to now" that are purged in the fire. He thus expressed a concept of shared destiny between the lama, the deceased, and all other beings whose karmic debt is collectively burned, irrespective of their mental progress at that moment. Here, there was no appeal to renounce, no faith qualifier. It was simply *bu-lon sbyang,* debt cleared.

THE IRONY OF ENLIGHTENMENT

As we have seen, much of Bardo instruction is a "confessional," Samden being required to admit the full record of her evil deeds, the lama unmasking her denials. Halfway through, however, an extraordinary dialogue erupted in Lama Dorje's oral performance. He portrayed Samden as trying to project the blame back onto himself. Lama Dorje countered her denial with his own denial: "You will become angry when you find

that the lama cannot purify all of your past sin (*sdig-pa*) if your evil deeds
have been too great. You will say, 'The lama does not want to gain my
liberation, but only to gain my wealth!' This contrary attitude of yours
itself comes from evil karmic tendencies emanating from your mind."

It is the lama's own rejoinder to an anticipated accusation, reflecting a
suspicion among Tibetan householders who have paid for costly funerals.
The suspicion is also expressed in the Gurung shaman's rejoinders to the
lama's critique of the shamanic death rite. Each denial is interlinked with the
others. Bakhtin analyzes this complexity, noting that

> characters are paired in Dostoevsky so that each of them is
> intimately linked with the internal voice of the other [so that] the
> rejoinders of the one touch and even partially coincide with the
> rejoinders of the other's interior dialogue . . . [in] a deep essential
> bond or partial coincidence between the borrowed words of one
> hero and the internal and secret discourse of another hero (Bakhtin
> 1984:254).

The manner in which Lama Dorje counters Samden's denials with his
own rejoinders exposes a mutual confession of complicity, a dialogical
realization that consciousness is unbounded. Such awareness is embraced
toward the end of Dorje's Bardo performance in a manner that is not
evident in literary translations of the Bardo. Enlightenment arrives at a
point of ironic dialogue, between subjective and intersubjective awareness.
It centers on the Bodhisattva figure Amitābha (T. 'Od-dpag-med), whose
Buddha field is said to lie in the west. Amitābha's compassion is
the last chance of deliverance from samsaric rebirth after everything else
in the Bardo guidance has failed. The lama's explication makes reference
to the three prostrations that are to be done by a male relative on behalf
of the deceased before Amitābha's image on the altar, the paper effigy of
the deceased's consciousness being tied to the back of his head.

Access to this Buddha field appears to depend on what is called "one-
pointed faith" (*dad-pa tse gcig*), but the argument which Amitābha himself makes is a refusal to remove his individual psyche from the relational
field to which it is indebted. The dialogue is presented as a debate between
the previously enlightened Buddhas, who have already left the world, and
Amitābha, who as a Bodhisattva has gained the capacity to become a
Buddha.

Lama Dorje presents his oral version of the narrative toward the end
of the Bardo. He dramatizes how "all the Buddhas" invite the Bodhisattva
to "come to a Buddha field." They proclaim the orthodox view: "Each
one, alone, must renounce his [her] karmic deeds! Since you have no further
deeds to renounce, you are ready."

The Buddhas employ the term *spang* ("renounce") as an inner psychic process. But Lama Dorje portrays the Bodhisattva as refusing to be liberated. He replies: "All sentient beings of the six realms are my mother and my father. If I were to be liberated by myself it would be unpleasant as long as they are suffering. If they are not ready to be born in a Buddha field, then how can I be ready?"

On the one hand, the Bodhisattva is "qualified" for extrication from the relational field, but on the other hand, he cannot forsake the relational field. Buddhist liberation is reformulated into an ironic paradox: the psyche that is ready for enlightenment knows that it cannot be liberated as long as there is suffering anywhere, for a wound would remain within the psyche.

The Bodhisattva's refusal is a highly reflexive confession of intersubjective complicity, appearing on the other side of inner awareness. In short, he cannot "forget" his mother and father. The definition of enlightenment itself is involved in this dialogue. Unlike the unenlightened who remember only the parents of their last birth and must be urged to renounce them during the Bardo, the Bodhisattva recollects the entire sequence of all mother-child links through time. It is a temporal enlightenment that does not empty out the history of sentient beings, but rather incorporates historical links into an ironic awareness from which there is no escape.[17]

The Tibetan death rite ends when the paper effigy into which the deceased's consciousness has entered is burned. As the other lamas, monks, and nuns playing the ritual instruments bring the sound and rhythm to a crescendo, Lama Dorje gradually lowers the effigy into a burning flame. The community packed into the Gompa watch intently as the paper catches fire. The consciousness is now released to find the path to a new existence.

In the Gurung shaman's death rite, the focus was on restoring harmony through reciprocal exchanges made in all three levels of the cosmos. The deceased receives offerings in the underworld, then makes exchanges with kin relations in the human world, and is finally guided by the shaman up the trail to the ancestral land where offerings are again distributed. In the Lamaist death rite this concern to restore harmony still appears as a shamanic layer within the Tibetan system. The imagery in the severance rite not only replicates an ancient model of shamanic initiation, it also pictures a grand offering of the severed corpse to this ancient three-world cosmos.

17. The provisional resolution that is offered is well known: Amitābha agrees to set up a Buddha field where those with sufficient "one-pointed faith" may go. It is not, however, psychologically real for most Tibetan lay persons in Gyasumdo, who have more confidence in the prognoses of the death horoscope, the best prognosis being a good human rebirth.

Although the Bardo instruction is a Buddhist transmutation, it is a soul guidance technique that is animated by the older shamanic layer. The paths, however, are quite different: the trail to the land of the dead in the Ghyabrē shaman's rite is locally spatialized in the everyday lives of the Gurung community. They know the villages that are passed through, and they see the landmarks named in the chant, such as Black Water and Oblē dome with its outjutting rock where the dog is tied. In contrast, the Tibetans do not see a path when guided by their lama; they see only the six realms of existence painted on the Gompa wall. This abstract diagram reflects the universal Buddhist ethic and individuated destiny, a personal time sequence no longer embedded in the time and space of the shamanic matrix.

The Tibetan funeral thus presents a bifurcation between the samsaric world and a quest for liberation (*thar-pa*). It initially draws a boundary around each merit-making and enlightenment career. Social-economic positions become visible signs of the degree of extrication from the world. Wealth is assumed to count for a better destiny since it overrides the worst prognoses of the horoscope. Religious individuation is still signified by a visible hierarchy of liberation.

In the Tibetan death rite performance of Gyasumdo, however, there is an alternative discourse, hidden within the official one. It draws on the older, shamanic layer which reemerges in a postdoctrinal, dialogical form, expressed through layered uses of demonic imagery and spontaneous Bardo discourse. In the distribution of rice cakes (*tshogs*), the Tibetan carriers tour the other villages of Gyasumdo, handing them out "without discrimination," even searching for the most needy of each village. It replicates in social practice the extraordinary, carnivalistic food distribution during the severance rite that destroys symbolic bifurcations. The visible hierarchy is undermined by the invisible, uninvited demons who crash the party.

Such imagery is far more than a parcelling out of a disposable body, for it is interpreted in light of the Bodhisattva's confession of universal kinship. The despicable beings who rush in from the village periphery also come unbidden from past layers of memory, half-forgotten, historic relationships returning to interrogate present awareness. They demand confession of the debt owed to them which, through denials, one had tried to forget. The result is a new layer of temporal identity: an interior, intersubjective form of historical consciousness.

Part IV

Historical Consciousness

Chapter Eleven

Dialogue of Good and Evil Eras

A THREE-PERIOD MODEL of history has been explicated in the Tibetan ritual sequence. The first period of harmony with the natural world and the second period of the human kingdom may be defined as positive. The third period, one of deterioration, ritually addressed in demon exorcism and the death rite, is a negation of the first two. The former, positive images are not forgotten, however. Each layer continues to interpenetrate with the others. The image of decline at the end is therefore difficult to interpret. It may be a transition toward a new era, a turning point. Further, since cultural narratives are becoming increasingly interwoven, the story of a people cannot be fully told, it remains unfinished.

Because of the historicity of all discourse, Tibetan images of good and evil eras combine into a variety of hybrid constructions (Bakhtin 1981: 358–62). In certain moments of crisis, their meanings may take particular direction, but this cannot be predetermined, as analysis in previous chapters has shown. In this chapter I will examine the argument between the three periods or eras, which are Tibetan ideal images of temporality: (1) the hidden land of the first era, called Beyul, (2) the Wheel-turning Kingship of historic, Buddhist civilization, and (3) the evil era, called *dus ngen-pa,* referring to the decay of nature, society, and the dharma.[1]

The model of three eras is prevalent in Gyasumdo and its adjacent regions. In Snellgrove's (1979) translation of a Tibetan pilgrimage text in Muktinath the three historical periods are explicitly called a "first world age," an "intermediate world age," and "the evil age." In Tibetan ethnic consciousness, however, the historical rise of the Buddhist dharma occurs after the establishment of Buddhist kingship in eighth-century Tibet. Tibetans in Gyasumdo thus tend to view the first era as primal and magical, the second as the rise of Buddhist textual orthodoxy, and the third as the latter's decline.

1. A four-period model of historical decline can also be found in certain Tibetan texts (Templeman 1981:48). Keith Dowman (1973:9–10), translator of the famed *Legend of the Great Stupa,* concerning Bodhanath in Kathmandu Valley, also notes three eras in Tibetan thought.

The manner in which these temporal images interact provides insight into Tibetan historical consciousness. Such images are penetrated by local history as well as by the shamanic influence in the region. In Gyasumdo, when village informants refer to the "good age" (*bskal-pa bzang-po*), they often combine the first-age harmony with a second-period triumph of Buddhism in Tibet before they migrated into Nepal, including the era of the flying lama Duwang Tendzin in nineteenth-century Gyasumdo. After that, the recent generations and the future come under the evil era of deterioration (*dus ngen-pa*), illustrated with a variety of local examples. Each passing decade adds new events to the "signs" (*rtags*) of decay.

References to the signs of historical decline were heard repeatedly in lectures given by the Lama Dorje to the laity. Since Tibetan Buddhists are "inside ones" (*nang-pa*), the narrative of decline moves from Buddhist internalism toward the modern "externalism" of Nepal's development program and the technologically advanced nations. In 1981–83 this once remote region of the Himalayas was beginning to be penetrated by government development workers, and the Tibetans of Gyasumdo were taking advantage of these programs. But development as "progress" (N. *bikas*) had no narrative significance for them. It was not a positive Buddhist narrative of moving from "external to internal" (chapter two), in which Tibetans still would be the main characters of a story unfolding on the world stage.

Lama Dorje's sermons were full of references to superficial "appearances." Buddhism, after all, had been a movement to get beyond the world of appearances. The government schools, for instance, "were for job training, centers of externalization" rather than internal wisdom. Further, the new medicines coming into Gyasumdo would cure only secondary causes, not the internal root causes. As for the new bridge being built across the Marsyandi river, it too was external. Had not Lama Duwang Tendzin ridden across the river on a goat skin? The same applied to modern airplanes seen flying overhead. Flying with the aid of "external" metal containers could not compare with the internal flying of lamas in Tibet's good age.

As a concept, *dus ngen-pa,* the "evil era," has an orthodox frame of meaning that is generally agreed on. Among Tibetans in Kathmandu as well as in Gyasumdo, the gradual decline of the Buddhist dharma along with the physical condition of the world and of human beings is assumed. The classic image is the eventual shortening of the life-span to only ten years and the disappearance of the dharma. The process is inevitable, but it can be delayed. The "renewing of the stupa" at Bodhinath in Kathmandu valley has become the organizing symbol of delaying the predicted deterioration, just as in Tibetan villages of Gyasumdo local stupas (*mchod-rten*) are reconsecrated each spring.

Beyond this base model, local images elaborate the evil age conception. The lamas and the laity have their lists of signs (*rtags*) of evil age deterioration which include decay in nature, society, and religious capacity. Decay in nature is evident in the declining fertility of the soil, inspiring predictions of future famines (*mu-ge*). In Tshap village, with regard to social decay, there is a list of five signs, called *nyigs-ma lnga* (the "five deteriorations"). In the most orthodox texts the emphasis is on deteriorations of religious and ethical capacities,[2] but in a village folk tradition, more pragmatic criteria such as the rise of market values are placed in the foreground.

The following is a brief summary of Lama Dorje's own list of the five deteriorations which I recorded on tape: (1) the deterioration of food from the expansion of marketed tastes, (2) the deterioration of clothing as marketed fashions replace village-made garments, (3) the deterioration of cooking vessels from gold to silver to copper to iron and finally today's aluminum, (4) the deterioration of wealth as family treasures are sold off and replaced by silver coins, and finally by mere paper money, and (5) the deterioration of the times shown for example by the nomadic wandering of peoples who had previously remained in local communities.

I played this tape to a group of lay persons to see if they would agree. They did, and defended each item even over my objections. "But isn't it good to have aluminum vessels that are lightweight for carrying on the mountain trails?" I asked. It was a ridiculous suggestion, met by immediate scorn. The significance of these Tibetan reactions, however, is not settled. A highly dialogized background of two good era images is hidden within these negative images: the communal harmony of the first era and the later aristocratic hierarchy of historical Tibet.

There is a more fundamental image of evil era decline, however, one that is stressed by the lamas and accepted by most of the laity. We may define the conception as the decline of the liberation hierarchy. In the first chapter I examined how lamaization has transformed the older clan-substance hierarchy into a code of degrees of liberation, shifting the meaning of social hierarchy from a past origin to a future destiny. The evil era can be characterized not merely as the decline of religion but as the loss of visible indices of destiny selection that were once assumed to be reflected

2. The five corruptions (*snyigs-ma lnga*) often listed pertain to (1) life span (*tshe*), (2) conflicting emotions (*snyon-mongs*), (3) character of sentient beings (*sems-can*), (4) time (*dus*), and (5) views (*lta-ba*).

in social inequalities. One can no longer be sure to what extent external differences of social privilege represent inner differences of merit fruition.

Since the apex of the liberation hierarchy has been the lamas, monks, or nuns, it is not surprising to find that the evil era is epitomized by the fading of dharmic commitment among these *chos-pa* ("religious ones"). The texts foretell this, predicting the coming time when nuns will concern themselves with their appearance, "looking in the mirror." Lama Dorje had much to say on this, noting that as time goes on, the *chos-pa* will only be persons wearing robes. They will be "*chos-pa* in name only."

THE HIDDEN LAND

The tradition of the Tibetan hidden land, called "Beyul" (*sbas-yul*) is highly developed in Nepal, since it is the region where a number of hidden lands are said to be located. Among the best known are Serang Beyul in Kutang District northeast of Gyasumdo, described by Aries (1975), and farther east the famed Khembulung Beyul, east of Mount Everest, studied by Bernbaum (1981).

According to Gyasumdo tradition, behind the great wall of rock on the west side of the valley rising in front of Mount Manasalu, there is a hidden land. It is not well known by the outside world, and extremely difficult to reach. Hunters or pilgrims, both Gurung and Tibetan, have visited the region and speak of "evidence" of the Beyul, its door being hidden in a high cliff overlooking a lake. Some report seeing old boots thrown down into the lake by the Beyul people. Elders tell of a legend concerning a hunter, the only local person to find the door, enter, and return:

> The hunter followed a deer up the cliff and saw a crevice leading into a valley. He chased the deer into the valley and found a village with people in it. They said, "How did you get in here? You should not have come here!" They allowed him to stay one night. He hung his bow on the wall inside a house and slept. In the morning the people said he would have to go, for they had already become polluted and sick by his presence. "You are like a *bdud, btsan,* or *klu* to us, just as we are to you."
>
> They decided to trick the hunter into leaving. They called their lama to do a rite of exorcism and built a huge effigy of a horse, which would serve as the ransom (*glud*). They put the hunter on the horse and he rode out of the village. He had been expelled. Suddenly he found himself outside the cliff door where he had first entered. He had forgotten to bring his bow, but when he looked back he saw the bow hanging on the cliff.

Features of this legend are immediately recognizable. The hunter chases the deer into a hidden land, just as the Gurung hunter had chased a deer into the Khrõ-nasa underworld to learn the lesson of reciprocity, and another hunter had chased a deer into the cave of the Tibetan saint Milarepa, his bow also remaining on the cliff. Hence the hidden land motif participates in these other underworld traditions. It is a Tibetan Buddhist image, yet it contains the abundance and mode of immortality of the shamanic underworld.

The eldest among my Tibetan informants offered additional images. Beyul does exist, but the door must be found by a lama who knows its secret. In one view, the door would open and close as rapidly as clashing boulders, so that only one with perfect faith could slip through without being crushed. Once inside, one would never again experience the suffering of death since the inhabitants begin each day as an infant, grow old in one day, and die in their sleep at night, waking up again as a reborn infant "just as the sun grows old and expires at night, then is reborn each morning."

It is a cyclical immortality which contrasts with the lama's descriptions of a distant Buddha field, irreversibly deathless, where consciousness expands toward enlightenment. Further, while a Buddha field can be reached only after death, the hidden land may be discovered in the world by persons still alive. The images focus on this-life concerns: in Beyul there is no poverty, since crops grow without need of human labor. All share the wealth, all are equally provided for, and all are even "equally beautiful." Most important, all have *sems-pa bzangpo,* a "good mind."

There is not complete agreement on how to think of the present status of the hidden land. Are there inhabitants in Beyul even now? "Yes," said one informant, "because I saw their boots, thrown by them into the lake." But another Tibetan in the gathering said he had reached that lake and had seen nothing. One lay woman had seen a vision that was "like Beyul" inside a lake north of Gyaru. In the water she had seen a Tibetan Buddhist Gompa surrounded by soldiers who were guarding it. Later, the others that were in her pilgrim party were interviewed separately. They all told the same story.

While the present reality of the hidden land is regarded as debatable, there is more agreement on its temporal significance in the Tibetan folk tradition. It is like a womb from which the first people emerge to begin the world again after all others have been destroyed by a holocaust at the end of the age. They are called "seed people" because they repopulate the earth. As the last days of this degenerate age approach, lamas that have foreknowledge (*ngo she khyen*) locate the doors of various hidden lands, joined by a select group of faithful Tibetans. In Beyul they will preserve the dharma until the "doors reopen" to begin the next era.

The Tibetan Beyul has a striking resemblance to Taoist imagery in China, which utilizes the same notion of a seed people who live an Eden-like existence between world catastrophes. Needham (1965:29) states:

> As the sins of mankind's evil generation increase to a climax, world catastrophes, flood and pestilence sweep all away—or nearly all, for a "holy remnant," a "seed people" (*chung min*), saved by their Taoism, win through to find a new heaven and a new earth of great peace and equality. . . . Then everything slowly worsens again until another salvation is necessary.

The temporal consciousness promoted by such hidden land imagery is that of historical recurrence, an outcome at the end of history being identical to the beginning. Between the two ends the historical sequence moves from "good age" (*bskal-pa bzang-po*) to "evil age" (*dus ngen-pa*).

MANDALA OF THE WHEEL-TURNING KING

In contrast to the communal hidden land utopia, a civilizational utopia is presented through the image of the Universal Monarch, known as the Chakravārtin in India, and called the Wheel-turning King (*stong 'khor-lo bsgyur-ba'i rgyal-po*) in the Tibetan Buddhist tradition. The symbols of the universal king are strikingly evident in the iconography of the Gompa at Tshap village. Below the main Buddha icons on the altar, the front wooden panels are filled with paintings of the king's "seven precious items," and they again appear in panel paintings in the lama's own private chapel. These images are also found on tiny cards stuck in the pyramid offering of grain, called the mandala offering,[3] which stands for the totality of all wealth, which the world king offers to the Buddha.

The lama of Tshap village explicates his historical consciousness through these images. The first era was natural, magical, and harmonious. It declined when greed took the form of property divisions, resulting in inequalities, envy, and fighting. Kingship then intervened to bring a new order. This civilization, however, was still sufficiently close to the first era to qualify as the universal monarchy portrayed in the kingship mandala. Each of a series of universal monarchs was, for Lama Dorje, "the Buddha in former Bodhisattva incarnations."

The birth of Gautama Buddha (fifth century B.C.) signified the beginning of decline into the evil era. The theme of renunciation of samsara now becomes prominent. On the other hand, in the manner of the Sin-

---

3. The Tibetan term used here is the Sanskrit word *mandala*. In this usage it refers to the symbolic offering of the whole universe, and should be distinguished from the other type of Tibetan "mandala" called *dkyil-'khor,* referring to a "circle of divinities."

halese kings portrayed in the *Mahāvāmsa* chronicle, the Buddhist kings in Tibet, who appear much later, aspire to construct a dharmic order which emulates that of the Universal Monarch. Hence the latter image can be applied metaphorically to a second-phase *good era* of Tibetan Buddhist kingship.

The conception of the Wheel-turning King and the associated imagery is understood mainly by the *chos-pa,* the religious ones. In their third initiation they construct and deconstruct the mandala pyramid of grains more than one hundred thousand times on a platter while repeating mantras and visualizing the universal kingdom and its inhabitants in full detail. The basic level of interpretation remains at the Sutra level: the adept offers the wealth of the world to the lama teacher and tutelary deity while meditating on impermanence through the repeated gesture. In later stages of initiation the adept will practice the Tantric "deity yoga" in which one meditates on one's own body as a Buddha form.[4]

Since I was doing an initiation during the time that the lama was preparing the *chos-pa* for the mandala initiation, I was able to tape-record their instructions, a textual reading which included vivid oral commentary by Lama Dorje. The basic set of images are well known by Tibetan scholars and were published by Waddell (1978), Lessing (1942), Haarh (1959), and Wayman (1973). These purely textual descriptions, however, do not capture the emphasis and elaborations given by the Gyasumdo village lama's oral commentary.

The primary foundation of the diagram consists of Mount Meru (*ri-rab*) in the center surrounded by seven rings of iron mountains which are separated by seven oceans. At the outer rim of these circles are four continents lying in the four directions, each with two minor satellites. Each continent is pictured as having a magical source of abundance. For instance, the Wish-granting Tree goes with the southern continent, Dzambuling (*'dzam-bu gling*), designated as the human world and generally referring to the Indian subcontinent.

The initiate is then required to visualize the "seven precious items" (*rin-chen bdun*) that go with the Wheel-turning King: the wheel, the jewel, the queen, the elephant, the horse, the chief minister, the general. The remainder of the text details items such as eight sacrificial goddesses, the sun, moon, honorific umbrella, and victorious banner, thirty-seven items in all, each of which is offered by the adept while putting the grains on the platter.

The oral commentary surprised me. I had expected a more esoteric

4. For a discussion of the distinction between Sutra and Tantra vehicles and the ideal of fusing them, see Hopkin's (1985) introduction to the Kalachakra Tantra.

emphasis, but instead the lama enthusiastically elaborated the same kinds of this-world utopian images that are found in hidden land discourse. After showing how the foundation of Mount Meru, the four continents, and the elements of nature work together in cycles of harmony, he spent a great deal of time on the Wish-granting Tree, which produces from its branches jewels, beautiful clothes, ornaments, and healing medicines. Likewise, the "cow of plenty" has jeweled horns and produces whatever one wishes while being milked. The "harvest without ploughing" provides an image of food without work: "No one has to plough, and if I harvest today, the crops grow again tomorrow."

From this base of plenty, the universal king's seven items were all interpreted to show how citizens living in his realm would benefit from the perfect sovereign. When the king turns his golden wheel (*gser k'yi khor-lo*), golden light from it strikes the citizens so that they become immortal. The king's precious jewel (*nor-bu rin-po-che*) guarantees abundance and health, since it can be transformed into food, drink, and magical medicines. The precious queen (*tsu-mu rin-po-che*) "is so beautiful that one cannot take one's eyes off of her," and everyone becomes beautiful like her "with no need to apply beauty cream: it is automatically applied." The queen is also a model woman of the feudal court: "she obeys the king, is never envious, and never talks 'idle nonsense,' " speaking harmoniously and openly "so that no secrets are kept: everyone can intuit the thoughts of others, without talk."

The king's precious horse (*rta-chog rin-po-che*) carries the monarch around the entire realm in a day without fatigue, while intuitively understanding the king's mind so that it needs no guidance. The precious elephant (*glang-po rin-po-che*) is the king's power, which can defeat any enemies that may invade the kingdom. Yet while doing so, "it keeps the dharma, for it does not step on a single insect under its feet." The king's chief minister (*lon-po rin-po-che*) intuitively knows the thoughts of the king and carries out the king's plans "without despising the people or oppressing them." The king's general (*dmak-pon rin-po-che*) subdues any enemies of the kingdom single-handedly without any need to recruit an army from among the citizens. By not causing suffering, "the general acts in accord with the dharma."

The hidden land and the mandala of the Wheel-turning King are both good era images, the former representing an ideal harmony within nature, the latter representing the Buddhist civilizational ideal. The former, which has no hierarchy, has been incorporated into the latter, and this helps to legitimate the hierarchical rule of the world kingdom. But this hierarchy is different from the "liberation hierarchy" of unequal degrees of karmic advance that characterizes present social systems. By incorporating the magical qualities of the primal harmony, the signs of merit difference have been removed. Further, by defining the system as fully encompassed by Buddhist law, the administrative hierarchy by definition cannot be oppressive. The ideal model transcends any actual historical order achieved.

The hidden land image has affinity with the rites of exchange with the underworld which seek harmony with the natural order, while the mandala of kingship underlies rituals of Buddhist royalty such as those of the guardian deities. Both images are affirmative. The final image, that of the evil era, is negative. It is the reverse of the first two, and becomes the focus of demon exorcism.

THE ARGUMENT BETWEEN IMAGES

The three images epitomize periods of history conceived as ideal models. They are not logical oppositions as a structural approach would define them. The first two ideals together form an argument against the third era's decline. This includes a critique of the contemporary hierarchy of liberation. Hence, the kingship mandala that is used for meditation and which has legitimated Buddhist kingship throughout Asia (McKinley 1979) can also become a moral argument struggling to construct its ideal in an emerging historical process.

Obeyesekere (1984:325) has shown how a Sinhalese mythic model of Buddhist kingship has served to express moral criticism of royalty that makes oppressive demands for corvée labor. A similar use of the model can be observed in Gyasumdo, where the Ghale nobility have come to represent pre-Buddhist kingship in opposition to the Lamaist project. Lama Dorje openly criticizes the present Ghale leaders in terms of his model of Buddhist kingship: "The Ghale claim to be descendants of Tibetan kings. So, they should be dharmic kings [*chos kyi rgyal-po*]. But in fact they are not dharmic kings at all! They hunt and kill and eat the meat right after the kill, and sponsor animal sacrifices."

For Tibetans in Gyasumdo the magical capacities in the kingship mandala are still operating in diminished form. They are residues of the first era, which in theory might still be returned in the future. They retain this magical model, but they can also use it as a metaphoric model for social criticism. Both uses of temporal imagery are available, since the transformation of a transcendent model into a historical realization is a possibility, even if not a certainty.[5]

5. It is like asking whether or not the lama "really" transforms himself into a Buddha during ritual performance. As one nun put it, "He does become a Buddha, but on the other hand he is 'like' a Buddha. Perhaps it depends on how great a lama he is." It is a potential, not a certainty.

The same ideal image can serve either as ideology that justifies a social order or as utopia that challenges it. Leach (1965) in his highland Burma analysis assumed that such alternatives are held by opposed social groups. The Buddhist kingship mandala suggests, in agreement with Jameson (1981), that within ideological symbolism, utopian alternatives are already present as traces. At certain historic moments such traces may be carried to center stage by persons of diverse social origins.

The Tibetan Shambhala image, for instance, boldly fuses primal harmony with the civilizational ideal: a universal monarch rides out of a hidden underworld kingdom to conquer the world and set up an ideal reign before the evil era ends. At the time of the research, such anticipation was vague and uncertain among Tibetans in Gyasumdo. Yet, a variety of folk images expressed a Shambhala anticipation in other forms, as a possibility that the good era might soon return in Tibet. "The good age may return as soon as Kar-ma-pa's next incarnation appears," said one lama, referring to the famed reincarnate lama who had recently died. "When the Chinese see the child, they will be amazed and withdraw. Then the Dalai Lama will return."

The Dalai Lama's announcement of his hope to return to Tibet was kindling such anticipation, particularly among Drogpa nomads in Gyasumdo who were receiving word from relatives in Tibet that the situation was ripe for going back. Some of these Drogpas still sing the Tibetan epic of Gesar of Ling, in which Gesar says he will "return" like the king in the Shambhala story. The Drogpas were not confident that he would actually return as predicted. These were matters for speculation, not matters of belief.

"When will the good age return? Not during this life, but probably in my next life," a nun, Ani Drolma, remarked after a moment of thought. She had recently completed a month's retreat meditating on the mandala of the Wheel-turning King. In hoping for a return of the good age in Tibet, Ani Drolma does not mean a return to the feudal model's liberation hierarchy of privilege. "Put it this way," she continues. "When a man dies in Tshap village today, if he comes from a wealthy family much wealth is spent on sending merit to him. He gets a better rebirth than a person from a poor family. But in a new Tibet, since property would be shared, everyone would contribute to the merit of everyone else."

The dialogue still emerging thus includes various combinations of good era images caught up in arguments regarding their historical implications. As was noted in the first chapter, the Gurung shamans of Gyasumdo draw on the magical capacities of the first era. They highlight the visual magic of their own rituals and their memorized knowledge, in contrast to the Lamaist texts. The Gyasumdo lamas counter this argument by recounting legends about the historic period's "bringing of the texts" from India to Tibet. While the Gurung shamans view the present degeneration as the decay of first-era magical capacities, the lamas describe it as the decline of the second era's religious doctrines.

By arguing for Buddhist canonicity the lamas promote their philosophy of history against that of the Gurung shamans. In making their appeal to the Tibetan laity, however, they find themselves drawing on first-era images, such as Lama Duwang Tendzin, who brought down the landslide. Lama Dorje privately questions the laity's need for "such magic" (*mig-'phrul*). Yet to buttress his own authority, he himself narrates the legends of the extraordinary "first lamas [*lama dang-po*] of the good age." It is a discourse that remains hidden within the texts and within Lama Dorje's own identity.

A Biography of the Evil Era

Lama Dorje's biography is an illustration of his own discourse on temporal ages: the magical beginning, the rise of Buddhism in the middle, and the decline at the end. He grew up in Gyasumdo in the 1940s, when Nepal was still closed off from the world. It was a period when some of the magical capacities of the first era were still present in the lamas. They could not fly as did Lama Duwang Tendzin five generations ago, but they could control rain, "and stop a thief on the trail by reciting mantras." It was also the period of a compromised dharma, the lamas looking the other way as the laity obeyed the Ghale Lord's injunction to perform the red offering.

When he was in his twenties as a young Nyingma lama, he saw dramatic progress of the Buddhist dharma. When Lama Chog Lingpa arrived from Tibet and condemned the red offering, Lama Dorje consolidated local Tibetan identity. Gyasumdo Tibetans came to view themselves as the "people of the Bodhisattva mind" with a historic mission. The Tibetan repudiation of animal sacrifice had a great impact on the young lama, and because he was celibate and intelligent, he zealously promoted the message of the Buddhist moral conscience in Gyasumdo after Lama Chog Lingpa had left.

Every Gurung village came to know that their shaman's sacrifices were abominable in the eyes of this lama, and because his articulate speech and flawless performances were convincing, he gained clients among established Gurung sponsors. At the same time, he was reforming the Tibetans, removing them further from the influence of the shamans. He became the most adept lama in the Tibetan horoscope (*rtsis*) calculation and divination (*mo rgyab*), arguing that the Lamaist rites give not only this-life benefits as do rites in the shamanic system, but next-life benefits as well. There had long developed a lama-shaman competition in Gyasumdo history, but this lama had brought the rivalry into a new level of ideological self-consciousness. The result was a renaissance of Tibetan Buddhism. The Tshap village Gompa began to attract young monks and nuns from the established families into a celibate *chos-pa* order, a visible sign of Buddhist advance that was contradicting the expected decay of the evil era.

Then suddenly, the lama fell. It was during my second year of research in Tshap village. One morning the village woke up to find that Lama Dorje and one of the nuns were missing from the Gompa. A message had been left behind: they were hiding in the forest. The nun was pregnant, and the lama was admitting his guilt. If the village decided to reject them, he would flee with the nun and never return. Shock waves ran through every household. The other nuns were weeping bitterly in the Gompa compound. The guilty nun was the daughter of the village leader, Pasang. He proclaimed that he was rejecting his daughter and would never again enter the Gompa. In a day, all that had been built up through the years was about to crumble.[6]

Representatives from each household gathered in the home of the village leader Pasang, whose family had inherited control of the village for generations. If he were to reject the lama and his daughter and withhold support from the Gompa, all would be lost. One by one the villagers argued to allow them to return. One of the nuns threw herself at the feet of the leader Pasang, weeping and begging on behalf of her lama. Pasang continued to refuse: "They have cut my nose!" (destroyed my honor). Several men brought a cup of chang and placed it before Pasang, and bowed before him several times. If he would drink it, it would mean that he was giving his daughter to Lama Dorje, who would return to the Gompa and resume his position, but as a married lama.

I had thought the request a reasonable one, but was told that in traditional Tibet, the offenders would have been automatically exiled. A celibate lama who falls with his own nun-student commits the worst kind of incest, polluting the entire village. It was, in fact, a crisis that forced on them an agonizing choice. To forgive too easily would be to take lightly the Buddhist precepts this lama had taught them. Yet everyone in the room hoped that the leader Pasang would drink the chang.

First, a fundamental question had to be answered. Who, in fact, was to blame? Had the nun seduced the lama? If so, perhaps Lama Dorje had been a victim of a moment of demon-inspired passion. For it was this nun who had been born on the day of "*sme-ba* 2-black" in the Tibetan horoscope, revealing that in her previous birth she had been a demon. But there

---

6. The events described here are public and well known in this region of Nepal.

was another possibility: Could it be that this lama never had been the saint they had imagined, but had strategized to deceive the people all this time? To deal with the question of the fallen lama's intentionality, Lama Dawa, the oldest celibate lama of Gyasumdo who lived across the valley, entered the gathering.

Lama Dawa gave a long speech. He argued that in no sense should Lama Dorje's fall be regarded as a deliberate act of will. It had happened after a lifetime of keeping his celibate vow and an extraordinary advance in knowledge. Such a sudden fall can have two sources. First, in a distant past life he may have committed a grave sin (*sdig-pa*), and only at this point in time did this evil deed reach fruition and cause the tragedy. The second theory excused the lama in terms of the present historical context of the evil era. Seeing the lama's great advance had stirred up "envious talk" (*mi-kha*). This became manifest as demonic "hindrances" (*bar-cad*) that had struck him down at the height of his achievement.

The two theories taken together formed a denial of evil intent. The denial in this case is the reverse of that which we have analyzed in the Bardo instruction in the death cult. In the Bardo the deceased is led into a confession of karmic guilt. Then for the sake of advancing personal destiny, guilt is redefined as a psychic disposition (*bar-chags*) which disappears through a change of mind. In the case of the fallen lama, however, continued social relations were at risk, and present ill intent had to be denied in order to reharmonize the community, as would be the emphasis in Gurung shamanism.

We may define this as guilt denial serving relational ends. The harm of external envy is blamed, but since the ethical seriousness of the transgression must also be recognized, the concept of ill intent *is* admitted as a distant, invisible karmic past, to restore the subject's relationships in the present. For Tibetans in Gyasumdo, the denial of present ill intent employs a double reference: the source of evil is pushed far back into the karmic past, and is also dispersed into the collective ill will of the present era of decline.

Pasang, the village leader, drank the chang put before him. By drinking, he showed his acceptance of the "marriage" between Lama Dorje and the nun, who could now return from the forest to the Gompa. But the analysis would be misleading if it were to imply that the above arguments were fully convincing. Debate continued around hearths in lay households. While some defended the lama, others ridiculed him. My landlady said, "He had warned us about going to hell, now he himself will have to go." Others predicted that now his "knowledge" (*yon-dan*) would decline. Many asserted openly that the lama had now become "just like the rest of us," entangled in domestic life. The Gurungs and their shamans were saying,

"He condemned our animal sacrifices, now look what he does." Many of his Gurung clients would now revert back to the services of the shaman.

The Gompa itself became viewed as leveled down to the lay condition. Before, informants would invariably assert that the *chos-pa* in the Gompa were not implicated in the contextual sins of the laity. Now another view could be heard. On one occasion a joking debate burst out in the Gompa compound between a nun and a prominent layman. He joked that the *chos-pa* "do nothing" in an easy, secluded life. She countered that at least *chos-pa* were not engaged in the laity's "sinful" activities. The layman quickly retorted, "If it were not for our laboring activities the *chos-pa* would have no food to eat." On the surface the exchange was lighthearted, but underneath a different perspective was coming to the fore.

We may define this as ironic, evil-age discourse. Such consciousness is itself predicted by the Tibetan theory of history. *Mi-kha,* "envious talk," is defined in the exorcism texts as one of the most prominent signs of the evil age. Lay sponsorship of the grand rites increasingly become external spectacles, the audience taking note of the status strategy of the sponsor more than the symbolic meaning. It is not that strategy motives were absent before. What is new is that they become foregrounded, as discourse becomes preoccupied with a hermeneutic of suspicion. Lama Dorje himself views the evil era as accelerating in such a manner: "It is the era of *ngen kha che* ["triumph of the evil mouth"]. No one wants to hear a good report, instead taking delight in hearing the bad, wanting to believe it, and suspecting the worst."

In this atmosphere of suspicion the hierarchy of liberation appears to become leveled. The leveling is expressed by lamas in Gyasumdo as well as by the laity. The oral Bardo instruction of Lama Dorje includes a section that lays bare a lay question: "Is the lama promoting the rite for personal gain?" Gyasumdo lamas pessimistically predict the coming of *tags tshen dzen-pa' i bden-pa,* "the truth of those who only hold a name." "It is like the knowledge they teach in the government schools: *jagir gyi yon-dan,* 'learning for careers.'" The displacement of wisdom by job training will gradually come to characterize even lamas toward the end of the age. It is an ironic consciousness of incongruity between a vertical hierarchy of liberation that is still visible and suspicion that those at its peak are implicated in the motivations and actions of those at the bottom. The evil age expectation provides the interpretive context in which the fall of Lama Dorje is understood: "He has become just like the rest of us."

Within a month criticism ceased. Another tragedy had occurred. Lama Tashi of Tilje village, returning from a pilgrimage, was suddenly killed in a bus that plummeted over a cliff. The Tibetans of Tshap, again shaken, felt they were fortunate to have a lama at all. Perhaps Lama Dorje's sudden fall and Lama Tashi's sudden death had both been signs of evil era acceleration.

IRONY AND HISTORICAL BECOMING

In his discussion of how historical periods can be characterized by tropes, Vico (1968:131) pointed out that "irony," which comes after a sequence of ages of gods, heroes, and men, "could not have begun until [after] the period of reflection" upon the gap between a truth that has been proclaimed, and a perception of its failure. Such ironic consciousness arises after an ideal has already been put forward. But all ironies cannot be lumped together, since irony is a negative metacommentary on a particular cultural sequence. It may be summarized by the theme of "puzzled defeat" and the "story of a fall" (White 1978).

The point can be illustrated by comparing Lamaist and shamanic evil age discourse in Gyasumdo. The shamans also express a kind of irony when they talk of the present decline, but it is not the same discourse as that of the Tibetan lamas. The Gurung shamans point out that their powers and knowledge are declining with each generation, for as knowledge is passed on, some of it is held back or forgotten. They note with irony that their present rituals fail to demonstrate many of the extraordinary features seen only a generation back. Beyond this, the shamans take note of an additional decline: the Ghale nobles can no longer be considered the gods their ancestors were; now they can only be called "father" as the most powerful landlords of the region. Even the Ghale lords joke about the hypocrisies of the "so-called kings" of recent generations.

This irony expresses the "story of a fall," but it is a different fall from the fall in the Tibetan image in which "nuns look in the mirror." The Ghale-shaman fall is a decline of inborn magical or divine powers inherited from the past. But to take note of the fall of a commitment to personal liberation in the future is an irony of a different mode of reflexivity, well expressed by Kierkegaard in his work *The Concept of Irony*. This heroism "falls back" into the historical arena from which it was to have been extricated through correct "belief" (*dad-pa*) and pure intent. When this imaginary boundary is breached and decentered, one is forced to "return to the world," but it is a different world from the former one that had once been repudiated.

As Bakhtin (1981) observes, after individual life sequences have become sealed off from the social history of the world in order to gain an "interior perspective," the plunge back into that world brings with it an intersubjective understanding of history, as personal destiny becomes fused with the "historical becoming" of the whole. The Tibetan image of the evil era is an ironic recognition in negative form that individual consciousness will be recontextualized into a historical becoming from which there will be no escape.

Such historical consciousness appears at first as a negative evaluation of events. But it is precisely because it still has a story with a plot unfolding in history that a culture is kept alive (Kermode 1967). If it looks for "signs" of its plot, even that of its own decline, it can hope that another version of its first vision may reverse the negation: in Vico's terms, a "return of its pristine force, but not in the pristine form." In this sense, evil age discourse is *double voiced* and also double layered. The irony admits hypocrisy and levels all participants into a common humanity. But the deconstruction may signify a turning, a coming reconstruction.

After the fall of the lama, I asked some informants to evaluate the future. Mingmar, a poor Tibetan of low birth, described the leveling that was expected in the evil age, but he did so in a manner that was double voiced (Bakhtin 1981:361). "Perhaps," he concluded with a twinkle in his eye, "when there are no more high and low lineages, all will have to share the same wealth, right?" He pointed to my camera and tape recorder as an illustration.

The village leader Pasang saw the meaning of decline in terms of the rise of the new ideology of "development," called *bikas* by the Nepali government. "Perhaps it is as they say," he told me, "that we are all equal. If we cut ourselves with a knife, don't we find that the blood and bone underneath are all the same?" The statement ran counter to the traditional Tibetan view that inheritance of bone (*rus*) from the father and blood (*khrag*) from the mother is the basis of clan hierarchy.

The fallen Lama Dorje on the other hand was highly suspicious of *bikas,* particularly the "external" knowledge taught in the village school, a "job training" which he could only view as a further sign of the evil era. Could then, "internal" knowledge ever be restored? Perhaps in the future he would try again to carry out the vision he had once had. At present he would go into a three-year retreat as a penance and would not leave Tshap village during the period.

Each of these persons reveals a desire to see a "possibility" in the negation, as if folk alternatives underlying the orthodox prediction of decay are available to call upon the moment that decay is felt most deeply. O'Flaherty (1971), in her analysis of legends of the Hindu *kali yuga,* likewise finds a background message of reversal: the leveling of caste hierarchy is seen as an opportunity to introduce an alternative means to raise up those who had been previously excluded. The thirteenth-century Japanese Buddhist monk Nichiren likewise interpreted the age of decay as a new opportunity (Dollarhide 1982, Hardacre 1984).

The Tibetan feudal model of inequality, interpreted through Buddhist ideology as a hierarchy of liberation, assumed that individuated time sequences had separated persons into different destinies. The erosion of the hierarchy in modern times is viewed negatively as the decline of inner purity: all become implicated in historical decline. Nevertheless, in Gyasumdo two alternative temporal models contradict both the hierarchy of liberation and its modern decay: Beyul, the hidden land as the first-era communal harmony and the civilizational image of the Wheel-turning King. Together they form a time consciousness of remembrance and anticipation, contending with the present condition and making positive reconstruction conceivable.

The Dalai Lama, as the leader of all Tibetans and one of the most dialogical personalities of our time, has invited scholars to debate the question of the form Buddhist society might take if he were ever to return to Tibet. He argues that it is time to visualize a new order. Could a comprehensive image of human enlightenment determine the shape of the social-economic structure? As this historical dialogue continues, Tibetan Buddhist identity will become further layered and unbounded.

Conclusion

The internally persuasive word is half-ours and half-someone else's
. . . a variety of alien voices enter into the struggle for influence
within an individual's consciousness, just as they struggle with one
another in surrounding social reality (Bakhtin 1981:245–48).

To articulate the past historically does not mean to recognize it "the
way it really was." It means to seize hold of a memory as it flashes
up at a moment of danger (Benjamin 1969:255).

IN THIS WORK I have examined the rituals of village lamas in a
Tibetan community in Nepal, in dialogue with a shamanic tradition. In
Gyasumdo, villages on opposite sides of the Marsyandi river represent rival
traditions that are nevertheless interwoven; the local images are unbounded, evolving historically between the two communities. The coming
of Lama Chog Lingpa in the early 1960s instigated a dramatic break. The
lama seized hold of a memory which, in Benjamin's terms, "flashed up"
to remind the Tibetans of their historic purpose. The ritual sequences we
have examined reveal an intensified process of debate and self-consciousness that was triggered by that critical moment.

The shamanic nostalgia for an older form of mutual collaboration has
been repudiated by the Tibetans for the sake of a Buddhist liberation
(*thar-pa*). Both ritual traditions continue to interpenetrate, however, the
discourse of each being found in that of the other. The shaman and the
lama can be viewed as two historical layers of tradition that have become
opposed as rival models of hierarchy and retribution. A third layer is that
which is emerging between them. In the conclusion I will attempt to draw
out the implications of this interpenetration, in terms of Tibetan Lamaism
as an enlightenment project involving reflexive dialogue with the shamanic
layer.

The recognition that cultures are inherently unbounded and implicated
in a larger historical process of meaning formation is dawning in anthro-

pological analysis as well as in the minds of the people we study. As a world process, it is acutely felt by those who find that the authentic way back to tradition is not through patriotic closure within memberships as formerly conceived but rather through dialogue with all traditions. As Bakhtin (1981) notes, history is moving us into a period of reciprocal illumination. When cultural identities become decentered by the perspectives of others, the way is forward, plunging ever more deeply into the interpenetration. It is a remedy that is partly shamanic but can be highly reflexive, as it is in the severance rite (*gcod*) of the Tibetan lamas.

In Gyasumdo the shamans do not regard such a trend with dismay, for they do not draw a boundary around their identity of mutual collaboration. They embrace the interpenetration of different wills, allowing spirits from the periphery and from previous eras to enter their own being. They enter alien realms on behalf of the community. They admit their complicity in the transgression of their sacrifice, which expresses indebtedness to all realms. Because of this self-image the Paju and Ghyabrē are able to view their own motives and images as unbounded, incomplete, and historically changing. Their legends refer to influences from other traditions, including that of the lamas. They view their own truths as partial and in need of further elaboration from other sources.

In contrast, the starting model of the Tibetan lamas builds a defense against unbounded influences. The Tibetan Nyungne fast as a lay mode of merit accumulation draws a boundary against mental interpenetration by defining a Buddhist community in contrast with those of "opposed view" (*log-lta*). In this manner the lamas of Gyasumdo attempt to extricate Tibetans from their earlier shamanic collaborations. As a researcher I too was warned of the risk of incorporating both Lamaist and shamanic traditions, my project appearing as a sign of the evil age.

A doctrinal or ideological boundary that has initiated a project will later come to prevent its maturation, since it was only meant to be a provisional metaphor. We find in Tibetan Buddhism, however, that a Mahāyāna-Tantric synthesis can move toward a higher, unbounded mode of reflexivity. In Gyasumdo this process may be viewed in part as a reincorporation of the shamanic matrix of interindebtedness, which is now experienced in a dialogical manner. It is expressed in Atiśa's (1983) formula of a third level of realization in which the sufferings of all others somehow come to "belong to one's own consciousness stream." Less heroically, we are dragged into it by intersubjective experiences that erode closure and plunge us into the historical consciousness stream.

This third model develops historically in Gyasumdo through interaction between ritual regimes. In the Tibetan folk rites, there is an ancient layer that is somewhat equivalent to the shamanic matrix of harmony. It appears in the horoscope images that are inserted at the base of each Tibetan ritual that we have examined. This ancient matrix, as an ambivalent whole, keeps returning in more ethically reflexive forms by means of the lama's transmutations. The sequence of ritual types express these in different layers of meaning, recapitulating from past to present a series of turning points in Tibetan historical consciousness. Each ritual type, rites of the underworld, guardian deity protection, demon exorcism, and finally the death rite, marks a new context for recapitulating the previous layers and then making further commentary.

The lama of Tshap village first captures over to the Tibetan side of the river the hegemony of the Ghale-shamanic regime. In doing so, he injects a deliberate reflexivity into each ritual type, changing its significance. This brings Tibetan rites into contention with the pre-Buddhist ideal of reciprocal exchange. When the Tibetan community enacts its version of the spring rite, part of the meaning is that it is no longer the red offering given by the shamans across the river. This triggers in turn an uncontrolled reflexive process, since the shamans argue back, even with ethical counterarguments. The lamas are themselves forced to reflect on the different layers in their own system. Alternative meanings contend in the minds of the audience during each performance. Like Bakhtin's "hybrid constructions," two discourses are illuminating one another, further eroding the boundaries of both cultures.

ALTERNATIVE NARRATIVES AND THE THIRD MODEL

The Tibetan ritual sequence communicates transformation stages in both inner self and outer world, revealing a philosophy of the history as well as a philosophy of the mind. But the ritual meanings evoke contending background narratives. The Gyasumdo lamas share a fundamental narrative of history with the local shamans, and then "reemplot" (White 1978) the critical turning points to form a Buddhist narrative. Both traditions communicate three periods: (1) a first-era harmony between humans and the natural world is broken; (2) a partial restoration is achieved through the construction of kingship and social hierarchy; (3) a historical decline occurs as this hierarchy decays.

The lamas rework the narrative at each historical crisis point, providing an alternative plot structure to that of the Gurung shamans. For the period of the primal era, both traditions recall a break from an original idyllic condition. The shamans attribute this first crisis to the failure of humans to make proper exchanges with the underworld, which they seek to correct through yearly sacrifices. The lamas redefine the cause of the break as human destructions of the serpent deity underworld. They succeed in removing the shamanic sacrifice, but only by introducing an alternative narrative that "rebuilds" the polluted underworld kingdom with the Buddhist texts.

In the second period, that of historic kingship, the shaman narrates the origin of the hierarchy of divine kingship that protects the social order. The lama reemplots this period, substituting a dharmic kingship that acquires a religious mission. Social hierarchy is redefined as representing degrees of merit leading to liberation. In the third period, the hierarchy of clan nobility decays, but the merit hierarchy also becomes confused. In the shamanic story the third period brings decay of magical and divine qualities of past eras. The lamas reemplot the crisis as an evil era decline of the Buddhist world project.

The Tibetan sequence of ritual stages thus recapitulates from past to present a series of turning points, but the shamanic definition of these critical points is still visibly present as an alternative. Many Tibetans are still not sure, for instance, whether the decline of magical powers or the decline of the dharma is of greater historical significance. The opposed narratives contend within their minds.

The moments that are recalled are shared critical events (Clifford 1982), including events that have occurred in recent times. The power of the local Ghale lords was undermined when the Rana regime fell in Kathmandu in 1951. In the early sixties Tibetan refugees came through Gyasumdo telling of the fall of Tibet. Then the powerful incarnational lama arrived from Tibet and condemned compromises with the shamanic regime. In 1968 a landslide swept down the mountain and buried half the village. During the period of research the fall of the main lama in Tshap village triggered yet another crisis.

Such events become memory traces. They are interwoven into ritual narratives that are already filled with recollections of past events such as the landslide curse of Lama Duwang Tendzin. The significance of these events cannot be predicted or controlled. An event makes either narrative more persuasive or may redefine the crisis points of the entire series. The lamas have seized on these crises, hoping to transmute them into the Tibetan memory stream, but they are dialogized by alternative, shamanic memories. Neither side can dominate the process emerging between rival traditions. Personal recollections are decentered with interpenetrating memory sources. The result is a third narrative: the story of *betweenness*.

The contending narratives have portrayed opposed models of retribution. The shamanic system is a cosmic hierarchy in which the Gurung shamans restore harmony in terms of reciprocal retribution. It is challenged by a second retribution model based on karma that establishes the Tibetan hierarchy of merit, with inequalities of social position as degrees of liberation (*thar-pa*) from samsaric suffering. Such a hierarchy remains culturally plausible only as long as the claim of individual merit is still interwoven with aristocratic clan substances, still drawing on traces of the older cosmic hierarchy.

As individual merit totalizes the ethic of "inner intent," personal identity becomes increasingly freed from its former aristocratic entanglement. The notion of a bounded "private" intentionality was a provisional metaphor for launching the Buddhist ethic. But subjectivity does not exist by itself. Eventually we arrive at an ironic intersubjectivity, becoming aware that we are contaminated by other wills. Identity then appears to be pulled into a decaying historical context. The lamas of Gyasumdo come to be viewed as implicated in the compromises of the world of the laity. As the liberation hierarchy declines, the motives of wealthy sponsors also become suspect, and the plausibility of a hierarchy of merit is undermined.

Such an evil age (*dus ngen-pa*) expresses implicitly a third model of retribution. The Tibetan term most often heard is *rnam-rtog,* meaning "scruples," or "doubt" arising in the divided mind penetrated by other wills. Demonic afflictions of "envious talk" (*mi-kha*) are thought to accelerate because of this intersecting of inner and outer. The demons of envy become increasingly difficult to exorcise beyond the village boundary. While the lamas emphasize the eroding of the focused mind, the Tibetan laity predict catastrophes of family conflict, wars, landslides, famine and disease, the selling of sacred things in the market, the coming of alien outsiders. Such events are occurring in Gyasumdo, a once isolated valley now decentered and drawn into a larger world of interdependence.

As the intertextuality of the world invades self-awareness, karma, the cause of meritorious actions, comes to be viewed as intercausal. This relational understanding of karma has already developed explicitly in Hua-yen Buddhism in China (Chang 1971, Cook 1977), but it is also implicit in the formula repeated often by the lamas of Gyasumdo: "All beings have been my mother at some time in the past." In such a formula of remembrance, one becomes implicated in an ethical network of interindebtedness. It is a recognition that reverses the evil age negation into a positive anticipation. In the ironic words of Lama Nyima, perhaps there will be a "return of the mother goddess" at the end of the age.

DENIAL AND RECOGNITION

We have noted how the Tibetan community retreats into a period of fasting during the Dasain festival when the shamans lead the Gurungs into massive animal sacrifices. On the following day the Tibetans come and buy the sacrificed meat for food. Since the market is defined as morally neutral, they are not implicated in the "evil deed" of the sacrifice. The Gurung shamans reject the logic of such a view, arguing that we are all interwoven in a world of mutual complicity. Their red offerings are a way of admitting this and making return payments. They cannot see how merit or demerit can accumulate as a mental process.

Bourdieu (1977:133) has noted that whole societies often play a "game of two fold truth." One truth is produced, but it then operates "to deny a truth otherwise understood by all . . . everyone agrees to be deceived." As cultures become mutually entangled in a larger global field, an imaginary boundary is still retained to deny recognition of it. The lamas deny worldly complicity as the shamans define it, by replacing external animal sacrifice with an "internal" sacrificial process. More fundamentally, there is denial of the participatory personage that is basic to the Gurung shaman's sacrificial identity.

But in Tibetan village Lamaism there is recognition of a more comprehensive participation that returns at other levels of Buddhist realization. In a temporal interplay between denial and recognition, that which is denied at one level is readmitted through ritual expression, returning to consciousness in other forms, and spilling over into other domains of life. In the Bardo instruction, consciously crafted levels of demonic imagery create a dialogue between denial and recognition, as an act of "sequential unmasking." The demons are presented as metaphors of mental projections, then as destroyers of those projections, and they themselves are finally unmasked so that one's psychic inclinations can be "renounced" (spang). Here, past transgressions are defined as a privately owned subjectivity (bag-chags) for the sake of provoking inner examination. But the intersubjective mode of karmic retribution is not forgotten. It reappears in the ritual background of the death rite in which creditor demons of retribution (lan-chags) rush in to be fed. They are memory traces of reciprocal indebtedness, recognized as the reality of one's past and present. This too is the enlightenment process.

Just as in the historical narrative, earlier stages must be learned before their truths can be unmasked and reinterpreted, so also for personal consciousness. Without experiencing half-truths, more ultimate awareness does not emerge. The Bardo death guidance together with its severance rite provokes an interplay which formulates for the dead that which is emerging historically among the living: a sequence of denial and recognition leading in the direction of unmasking and reflexive awareness.

The historical sequence evolves through encounters in the world. The process is recognized in Tibetan evil age discourse, which must admit that our words and intentions are becoming "half-ours and half-someone else's."

The Tibetan view of historical decline is in part an emerging dialogical awareness expressed as ironic negation. It is when alien penetrations come to be embraced willingly, however, that irony itself may be transmuted. According to the lamas of Gyasumdo it is during the final period of decline that techniques emerge for "uniting samsara and nirvana."

This fusion is initiated through a model of alternation. The repudiation of relationships of the world can, as noted above, be used as a "provisional" boundary drawing, a denial which instigates another kind of realization at a future time. Two themes of renunciation clearly express this alternation in Tibetan Lamaism in Gyasumdo: (1) renunciation of kin ties and (2) renunciation of the wealth of the world. In each case a larger return is anticipated.

In the Ghyabrē shaman's Gurung death cult, the linkage with deceased family members continues. One is rejoined with one's own ancestors. The Tibetan lamas clearly forbid such a notion. Renunciation (*spang*) of partiality toward one's own kin is explicit; the lamas promote a "forgetting" of kin boundaries. This produces an absence that is refilled with a more profound recognition of "universal" ancestry.

In the initiation which I myself underwent I was instructed to dedicate myself repeatedly to the "enlightenment of all sentient beings who are my mother and father." The disappearance of one's own kin instigates the reappearance of "all" kin. As in Lacan's (1968) view the initial relation between child and parent is renounced, but as a displacement, the family relation returns as a grander intersubjective dialogue within the self. The dialogue incorporates all layers of the past in order to transform the future, conceived as a history in which all beings move forward together.

In the case of renunciation of the wealth of the world, the return is explicitly linked to the paradigm of the gift that is magnified through the lama's visualizations. The immediate return found in the exchanges of the Gurung shamans is displaced by Tibetan Buddhism into a symbolic substitute: a visualized, "total" offering is imagined to return after a long temporal delay. The model is explicit in the ritual use of the mandala of the Wheel-turning Kingship.

During the Nyungne fast when the laity come to the Gompa for temporary renunciation, the Wheel-turning King's images of sovereignty are displayed below the altar, stuck into the tiers of grain representing Mount Meru and the four continents. It is the wealth of the entire world. The laity gathered on the Gompa floor are given grain, and wait for the right moment during the ritual. Suddenly each person holds up two hands and crosses the fourth fingers together as an image of Mount Meru. The other fingers cross to become the four continents. Then everyone throws their grain toward the altar.

It is done on behalf of the Wheel-turning King: they give the entire world kingdom to the Buddha, then wait for a future return. It is a paradigm of exchange found in the temporary forest renunciation practiced by ancient kingship in India (O'Flaherty 1984). In the Jataka legends, "the king laid his kingdom at the Bodhisattva's feet, but the Bodhisattva returned it to the king."

TRANSMUTATION OF THE WORLD

Bakhtin's insight regarding the dialogic nature of meaning has emerged during a historical decline of bounded cultures and epistemologies of "one truth." Noting the emerging "heteroglossia," he celebrates the return of the ancient matrix into a modern form of participatory identity on the world stage. The self discovers its destiny not through drawing a boundary that extricates it from the surrounding world but through incorporating its full multiplicity. This celebration is postdoctrinal, after religious creeds and ideologies have arrived at a crisis point. The "reality" to which one returns is not one of scientific neutrality, but rather a world of interpenetrating voices undergoing both personal and historical becoming.

In Tibetan Buddhism, images that combine the Sutras and the Tantras present a samsara-nirvana union. The Gyasumdo lamas explicate this union through spontaneous oral interpretations that are not obvious in their texts. Two such visualizations have been analyzed in previous chapters. The first is the *gcod* (severance) rite, the second is the mandala of the Wheel-turning King. In village Lamaism, they become deconstructive uses of imagery.

The visualizations are rehearsed by the lamas during periodic retreats, after which they reemerge with deeper perception of social reality. Ordinary discourse comes to be understood differently, each meaning gaining more "profound" (*gting ring-po*) significance than before. In so far as the lamas' argument for these inner substitutions becomes persuasive, lexical terms such as *exchange, sacrifice,* and *kinship* also become redefined again and again as the lamas' definitions contend with those of the laity.

Inner visualization defamiliarizes conventional meanings for the sake of changing the destiny of all beings. It is a deconstructive practice which falls short of the ultimate insight of emptiness (*stong-pa nyid*), but which can have historical consequences. Unlike the language of philosophical abstraction, the profound visualizations of Gyasumdo lamas deliberately employ the most base images to evoke emotions that shatter conventional expectations.

The *gcod* (severance) rite can be interpreted as a fusion that employs Bakhtin's carnival sense of the world with Rabelaisian style. As happens in Walter Benjamin's method of seizing on images of suffering and hope in the popular imagination, the lamas wrench fragments out of their conventional contexts and reconstruct them "in the extreme" to invoke their hidden implications. When one offers one's body to all beings, that which is identified with the domain of death is associated with life, the great feast. All past and present beings of the world come, both invited and uninvited guests, to feed on the corpse of the performer. Renunciation and compassion are joined together. In oral interpretations of the severance rite, the Gyasumdo lama stresses the rite's distributional imagery. It implies an alternative model: if both the invited and uninvited partake in the distribution of food and merit, then there is no selection of those who receive a greater share or a better destiny. Full explication of this imagery to the laity is forbidden, and the lamas do not agree on what it means. The implications are still emerging.

In the mandala of the Wheel-turning King there is also a nirvana-samsara fusion. A kingdom is visualized in which the conventional merit hierarchy is strikingly absent. No one suffers, no one is burdened with labor. For these village lamas of Gyasumdo the oral instruction of this mandala to initiates is filled with the enjoyment of juxtaposing earthy, utopian images. Such oral performance is not displayed in the texts. In village Lamaism these visualizations can spill over into further modes of practice, since the culture is still in transition.

Hence in the oral tradition, Tibetan ritual practice is dialogical rather than canonical. Economic, social, and religious arguments are intertwined and not separable into different domains. The lama's interpretations are capable of incorporating other voices, including the shamanic one. For their part, the shamans expose the hidden connections between all persons and domains. Having maintained the ideal of the ancient matrix, they are in a position to comment with irony on the emergence of an interdependent world that decenters all inner intentions. This underworld view does not remain silent. It argues back, particularly through the voices of those not selected, who may be equated with the metaphor of the uninvited guests. The shamans represent one of those voices, but not the only one.

The Tibetan philosophy of history has celebrated the importance of the quality of inner subjectivity. The final plot, however, portrays a crisis at the end of the age when external appearances will be foregrounded. But the Tibetan oral tradition is capable of revealing more than one possibility. As subjectivities become increasingly interwoven, the focus of meaning shifts to a dialogue about the future of the world rather than escape from it. It is a return to historical becoming that appears to be transforming great traditions in all parts of the globe.

For the Tibetan lamas of Gyasumdo, their master images of visualization are still available for further transmutations. Having promoted the inner life, they can now draw the larger world into the basic aspiration of their unfinished project: the construction of a cultural order responsible for the destiny of humanity and organized for the enlightenment of all beings.

Local Text Written by Lama Chog Lingpa

Tshap kyi yul bdud btsan klu gsum gsol mchod
("Petition offerings for the three area gods of Tshap village: *bdud, btsan,* and *klu*"; translated from the Tibetan)

By the elixir of life that removes human sorrows and bestows blessings, I bow to the incomparable Lama [Padmasambhava] of sentient beings. This is written in order to benefit the ignorant beings of existence, since they and various demons and all those who perform the red offering [*dmar-mchod*] will go to the Hell Realm [*ngen 'gro*]; with good intention of helping others and in compliance with the Buddhist scriptures, I have developed this short burnt offering rite [*gsur-btang*] easy to perform for the three area gods: *klu, btsan,* and *bdud,* as well as for any other demonic beings of the region.

To perform the petition offering for these three, put a torma [effigy] of each on a clean container, dress them in good clothes, and offer them all kinds of food and grain. To the *bdud* and *btsan,* you must give meat-decorations, and to the *klu* with clothes, the first fruit of chang [beer], and any other things you can collect, including the three white and three sweet offerings, the provisions of the burnt offering mixed with herbal medicines.

I prostrate before the Buddha, dharma, and sangha, and to all sentient beings of the six realms who are my parents and whom I would lift up to the Buddha field, wishing them to be possessed of the four unmeasurables.

In the midst of the sphere of emptiness is spread the highest intelligence. I myself am Pema Chungne [Padmasambhava], who has traversed the nine levels, holding a dorje in the right hand and looming over the sky of all envisioned existence. Everything that is visible in the existing world is subdued by his glorious power. In the left hand he holds a flask of elixir, his three-pointed trident decorated with colorful cloths, binding the three regions with the letters of his dorje, sitting on a lotus flower of sun and moon, and at his heart there is a moon surrounded by a white letter *Sri*. It is surrounded on the right side by a radiating, circumambulating Tantric rosary.

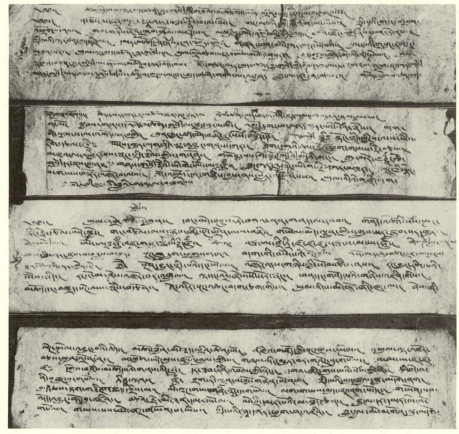

Figure 12. Photographs of the petition offerings for the three area gods of Tshap village as handwritten by Lama Chog Lingpa

Area gods and demons of the land, you are gathered together without power since you have been subdued, so yield now to these orders. Give up your harming thoughts and develop compassion. Fulfill without deviation the duties which have been entrusted to you.

In the beginning there was only self-originating transcendent wisdom. Then there arose thought of "samsara and nirvana," and you became "gods and demons" devoted to benefit and harm. We, the Tantric masters and the people of this land, give as religious alms the property and fields and houses of this land. Like large clouds the sky is filled with mantras.

I invite the area god and his retinue, [since] their minds can travel anywhere through their powers of emanation. Come over to this place as soon as possible. The altar we have set at this place with pure heart, the cloth, precious things over the seat: come and sit on the soft seat we have prepared for you. Be happy with respectful mind, be seated.

From a high cliff comes the demon king [*bdud rgyal-po*]. He is colored black with tiger and leopard skins tied below the waist and human skin wrapped above. In his right hand is a demon's sling, and in the left is a jewel of demon origin. The effigy [*gtor-ma*] of the *bdud* is black, and the tip is decorated with a Garuda bird.

The *btsan* chief is red with a red shawl wrapped around his body. In his right hand is a fire sling; in his left, the power of deluding [*shed-gar*]. The effigy of the *btsan* is red and triangular, and the tip is decorated with a snow lion.

The king of *klu* is white, wearing a white cloth. His two hands hold a wish-fulfilling gem. Surrounding him are countless spirits of the eight regions. The effigy of *klu* is white, and the tip is decorated with a blue turquoise dragon.

We offer you our homes, clothes, farms, belongings, our animals both domestic and wild such as yak, sheep, horse: all these including all the wealth that you can see in the existing world without ending. This offering given to you has the quality of bringing about all that you desire without ending. We make no mistake in offering them to you, for by your accepting them, both of our hopes can be fulfilled. Anything we have done against your wishes, such as killing wild animals, or polluting by digging the earth, breaking stones, and stirring up waters—for all such actions we beg forgiveness.

By entrusting you with responsibilities [we hope this:] May the truth of the dharma spread. May those who uphold it have long life, and may all lands, particularly this land, have timely rains pour down, that we may have good harvest and increase of grains, and may all sentient beings practice religion. May happiness and prosperity expand. For us sponsors in particular, may our transgressions and causes of disharmony be dispelled. May all wishes be fulfilled. May we have a feeling of auspiciousness and well-being day and night. May disharmonies that cause sudden death to animals, devastation of crops by insects or hailstones and landslides, be removed.

Throw the tormas to a clean area. The burnt offering should be sprinkled with clean water and then burned in a fire; with great unmeasurable compassion, recite the mantra "Om mane padme hum," filling the sky with mantra blessings while uttering the names of the enlightened ones.

From the beginningless beginning, you have been wandering through samsara in ignorance as intermediate beings [bar-do sems-can] without bodily form. You are space-wandering ghosts [yi-dwags] with mind forms only [yid kyi lus] so that your mental inclinations [bag-chags] become your imagined enemies and you feel pain from your own thoughts. Hence you become divided into good and evil spirits by your inclinations and arrogance. You wait around for offerings and for chances to seize the souls, the lives, and the life essences of humans.

Without neglecting anything, listen to my words of truth and ponder their meaning: the result always follows the cause [rgyu-'bras] without fail. This religious aim of the burnt offering includes the special quality that all you desire will be realized without ending. Accept these offerings without fear, with intent to benefit us, and our possessions and our subjects. Now return to the regions where you are happy, ridding yourselves of sin and seeking to be enlightened.

This text is written by Ter-chen Chog Lingpa in the locality of Tshap in the land ruled by the Gorkha king in order that the people of Tshap may renounce their earlier practice of the red offering and correctly follow Buddhist teaching. With this in mind it has been written. So by virtue of writing this, may [we receive] benefit on the present day and permanently in the future.

Local Text of
Srungma rDo-rje Shugs-ldan

Rdo-rje Shugs-ldan mchod-thabs gsol-kha
("Method of offering-petitioning rDo-rje Shugs-ldan"; translated
from a photographed copy of a householder's Srungma text in Tshap
village)

In accord with the sacred action of the victorious one using magical powers [*mthu*]
to protect the dharma: when you have the need to make offerings to rGyal-chen
[rGyal-po Shugs-ldan], face your preferred direction at the altar of your lama and
tutelary and guardian deities, both general and particular, all before your eyes.
In a jeweled container, set the chief torma, surrounded by four small tormas.

The chief torma should be decorated with colorful butter decorations. Visualize
an ocean of blood in which there is a human skull and human heart. Decorate
the torma further with flames of fire, visualizing boiling blood. If possible put up
a red umbrella-cloth over it. To the right side, place a medicinal first fruit offering.
Put the ingredients of oath binding to the left, adding raw meat to the blood (or
beer). In front of this, set up a triangular torma and set up the offering bowls.
Then set up the ritual paraphernalia such as the dorje and thigh bone trumpet.
Before you begin the rite, sprinkle water and beer, as a preparation for the practice of generating the god as yourself [*bdag-bskyed*], and generating the god before
you [*mdun bskyed*].

From the midst of emptiness [*stong-pa nang ne*] inside the skull container is
a pleasant-appearing torma, scented, tasty, of good quality. It is formed out of
the flesh and blood of the enemy harmer [*dgra-bgegs*]. May this turn into an ocean
of nectar.

From the midst of emptiness a black wind arises in the shape of a dome, in
the middle of which is the syllable *Thi*. From this syllable arises rDo-rje Shugs-
ldan, the great king and protector of the dharma. The color of his face is dark
red, he has two hands, the right raised to the sky, the left holding a skull containing blood and a human heart. This he holds as his [own] heart. He rides a black
horse. The emanations surrounding him are unimaginable.

From your heart [the performer's] you radiate light rays as you welcome rDo-rje Shugs-ldan. Please come from your great house of god, with your retinue, to fulfill the requests of the performer and protect the truth of the Buddha. rDo-rje Shugs-ldan, protector of the region, I offer to you and to your warring retinue the entire envisioned world. Please accept this and protect the Buddha dharma.

To increase the prestige of the Buddha, dharma, and sangha, and protect the religious will of the sangha, be our protector and that of our surrounding people. From this moment, until I am enlightened, the obstructions that hinder attainment of the Bodhisattva mind — bodily and mental sickness and misery — may all be dissipated. May you have human wealth, food, life, and good fortune.

Hear this and meditate on it, realize it within yourself. Follow this sacred work. May you be to us as guru to disciple, and may your retinue subdue the enemy harmers. May all your thoughts be compatible so that your religious practices may be fulfilled.

Praise to you the fearsome, quick fulfiller of desires, you great king. Through your emanation power you can travel in one second through the three worlds of emptiness (*stong-gsum*) to fulfill whatever you have been entrusted with without hesitation.

Hail to the great king and his retinue. Anything you remember in your mind, whatever you think of even without asking, he provides it. Religion protector and wish-fulfilling gem, please fulfill all my desires, without leaving out anything. Particularly in this life, bless me with long life, no disease, with a downpour of nine desires, may my treasure house be filled. May you subdue the people of Tibet and India and then multiply their prosperity. May the three worlds [*sa gsum*] tremble, may I obtain all my wishes.

From the midst of emptiness, from a perfectly wrathful house, the external, internal, and secret modes of hindrance [sickness, mental suffering, meditation hindrances] may they be put into the torma as the flesh and blood of the enemy harmers. May this be transformed through visualization into an ocean of nectar, consisting of all the perfections, encompassing all qualities in order to please the great king; the offerings becoming heaps of clouds that fill up the sky.

From the palace, in an ocean of blood of fire, wind, and commotion, I welcome rDo-rje Shugs-ldan and his followers, the great protector of the region, who protects the dharma and prevents its destruction. Please fulfill the sacred work in order to repel external and internal enemies of the ten regions. Please come immediately from the four directions to fulfill your orders, with the force of your army: the emanations of Za [Rahula], *bdud,* the eight brothers, butchers and blood drinkers.

Your palace walls are built with wrathful, arrogant, and frightening human skulls, and from human intestines, lungs, hearts. The bone marrow is burned as a burnt offering, with Shugs-ldan and his retinue sitting in the midst of the smoke of this offering. You, the dharma protector of the victorious one, remember your oath of initiation given by Khro-ba rGyal-po [lama of the Sakyapa sect] before whom you made your promise, agreeing to take responsibility not to transgress your promise. May the life of the dharma beholder be long. May the practitioner of religion, his group, and his wealth be protected.

You, dharma protector of the victorious one, before your eyes, the external, internal, and secret offerings are made to you. The external offering is black yak, sheep, bird, red dog. The internal offering is red horse, monkey. The secret offering is the Wheel of Life, the offerings on the altar representing body, speech, and mind. By offering these, the dharma protector's desires are fulfilled. May his order fulfillers, Za, *bdud,* and butcher, also be filled, and may their deteriorations be restored.

The very red greasy blood, like the ocean and the five senses, the flame, piled up like the mountain [Mount Meru], the meat and marrow in the burning smoke, fills up space like clouds. Butter lamps shine like the sun and moon. These wrathful offerings are set up either in reality or they are imagined. May your minds be filled.

In the spacious light derived from the syllable *Ra* arises a special container with the flesh and blood of the enemy that is repelled from the ten regions. From this meat and blood is built a red torma, big as the hill and the ocean, obtained in actuality or in the imagination. I offer this, having blessed it with a mantra. I pray that your mind may be filled, charmed by the beautiful sounds of the blowing of the trumpets.

The eight auspicious signs and the eight ingredients and the five qualities of your desires, the totally victorious Great House, with gardens and ponds, with fruits growing without cultivation, where there [also] exists the Wish-fulfilling Tree on Mount Meru, surrounded by the four continents and their seven jeweled subsidiary continents, with all the available wealth of India and Tibet: gold, silver, clothes, jewels, the snow lion, tigers, leopards, bears, apes, owls, wild birds that cry when frightened, birds that move in the night, and countless animals that can talk like humans. With all this may your mind be filled.

There is a horse with telepathic knowledge, the color of the jungle and of the rays of the sun. The saddle of the horse is beautified with the five kinds of jewels. There is also a red male yak, like the color of a cloud, agitated like fire and wind; when its tail waves the three worlds tremble. There is the ferocious cry of a dragon, decorated with soft, beautiful cloth, and there is a golden-eyed elephant, and snow lion: all are dharma protectors.

Other offerings consist of sword, gun, armor, bow and arrow, iron hook, sling, bell, all sorts of offerings needed in this cyclical existence of wealth. Whether the sponsor owns these weapons or not, I offer them to you. Thus bestow on us all kinds of luck, bestow on us the Tree of Life, and unending wealth. May we be possessed of faith, studious, and compassionate. All those capable of preserving the dharma, may they be vessels for continuing the tradition like the summer ocean that overflows. May we overpower the kings of India, Tibet, Mongolia, and their kingdoms, ministers, subjects, and wealth as well as their Srungmas. By doing so, may we spread the dharma to people with inferior faith and intelligence too inferior for meritorious acts, and with no opportunity to practice the dharma. May all their minds be directed to the dharma.

The enemy harmers and those who conspire against us, whose oaths of allegiance have deteriorated, you, the powerful one, repel them in the name of religion, without delaying a single month in the year, and put them under my control. Fulfill whatever I wish as my friend, spreading the dharma without deterioration.

May persons like us have long life in all lands of the world, and in this land in particular. Don't afflict them with diseases, don't send harms to domestic animals, don't send hail storms or drought for our crops. May we as wisdom holders have long life and have our wishes fulfilled.

rDo-rje Shugs-ldan, the time has come to display your power and talent. The force of your *btsan* army and four garrisons: command them to be harsh! Gather more force, don't hesitate. Don't be impartial. Repel the hated enemy and harming agents by the spirit of religion. Resort to wrathful acts! Blow fire of red and black. Don't belittle your own power and capacity. Subdue the enemy force. Join forces with the gods, the *btsan,* and others; make as much wrathful noise as possible! Set out in your unending wrathful war against those who destroy the Buddha dharma, those who drag down the prestige of the Buddha, dharma, and sangha, those who harm the body of the lama, the vajra holder.

Whatever schemes they do, wherever they live, whether above ground or underground, with great power and force, destroy them completely! Repel bad dreams and evil thoughts in the subjects. May you repel rGyal-gong, *'dre,* and *btsan:* may their magical weapons [Zor] be repelled. Their evil thoughts, like poison that is softly and sweetly spoken but has evil designs, may they be repelled. Repel also the curses of women and the 420 types of sicknesses.

From the midst of a boiling ocean of blood, may the great king take ferocious form, repelling all enemies and harmers. Destroy the enemy completely. Kill them immediately. Send the butcher killers and blood drinkers to the land of the enemy and kill them right off. Reduce them to dust! Fulfill my requests. Whatever you speak, like the roar of a thousand dragons, may the hearing of it destroy all the enemy harmers of the ten regions. Even if their life force is made of diamonds, may they be reduced to dust.

Protect the dharma in general, and in particular the Sakyapas. I praise you, who have agreed to be the Srungma of the Sakyapas.

Bibliography

Ahern, Emily. 1981. *Chinese Ritual and Politics*. Cambridge: Cambridge University Press.

Alekseev, N. 1984. Helping Spirits of the Siberian Turks. In *Shamanism in Eurasia*, part I, ed. M. Hoppal. Göttingen, Germany: Herdot.

Anderson, Benedict. 1983. *Imagined Communities: Reflections on the Origin and Spread of Nationalism*. London: Verso Editions/NLB.

Anisimov, A. F. 1963. Cosmological Concepts of the Peoples of the North. In *Studies in Siberian Shamanism*, ed. Henry N. Michael. Toronto: University of Toronto Press.

Aries, Michael. 1975. Report on the University of California Expedition to Kutang and Nupri in Northern Nepal in Autumn 1973. *Contributions to Nepalese Studies* 2, no. 2:45–87.

Asboe, W. 1936. Sacrifices in Western Tibet. *Man* 36:75–6.

Atiśa. 1983. *A Lamp for the Path and Commentary of Atiśa*. Trans. Richard Sherburne. Winchester: Allen and Unwin.

Aziz, Barbara. 1978. *Tibetan Frontier Families*. Durham, N.C.: Carolina Academic Press.

Aziz, Barbara. 1979. Indian Philosopher as Tibetan Folk Hero. Legend of Langkor: A New Source Material on Phadampa Sangye. *Central Asiatic Journal* 23, nos. 1–2 (1979):19–37.

Babcock, Barbara. 1980. Reflexivity: Definitions and Discriminations. *Semiotica* 30, nos. 1–2:1–14.

Bakhtin, Mikhail. 1968. *Rabelais and His World*. Trans. Helene Iswolsky. Cambridge, Mass.: M.I.T. Press.

Bakhtin, Mikhail. 1981. *The Dialogic Imagination*. Trans. C. Emerson and M. Holquist. Austin: University of Texas Press.

Bakhtin, Mikhail. 1984. *Problems of Dostoevsky's Poetics*. Ed. and trans. Caryl Emerson. Minneapolis: University of Minnesota Press.

Bakhtin, Mikhail. 1986. *Speech Genres and Other Late Essays*. Ed. Caryl Emerson and Michael Holquist, trans. V. W. McGee. Austin: University of Texas Press.

Barthes, Roland. 1975. *The Pleasure of the Text*. Trans. R. Miller. New York: Hill and Wang.

Basso, Keith. 1984. "Stalking with Stories": Names, Places, and Moral Narrative among the Western Apache. In *Text, Play, and Story: The Construction and Reconstruction of Self and Society,* ed. E. Bruner. Washington, D.C.: American Ethnological Society.

Bawden, C. R. 1962. Calling the Soul: A Mongolian Litany. *Bulletin of the School of Oriental and African Studies* 25:81–103.

Benjamin, Walter. 1969. *Illuminations.* New York: Shocken Books.

Bergson, Henri. 1910. *Time and Free Will.* London: Allen and Unwin.

Bernbaum, Edwin. 1981. *The Way to Shambhala.* New York: Anchor Books.

Beyer, Stephan. 1978. *The Cult of Tara.* Berkeley: University of California Press.

Bloss, L. W. 1973. The Buddha and the Naga: A Study in Buddhist Folk Religiosity. *History of Religions* 13, no. 1:36–53.

Bogoras, G. 1928. The Shamanistic Call and the Period of Initiation in Northern Asia and Northern America. New York: *Proceedings of the 23rd International Congress of Americanists.* Nendeln/Liechtenstein; Kraus-Thomson: 441–44.

Bourdieu, Pierre. 1977. *Outline of a Theory of Practice.* Cambridge: Cambridge University Press.

Brauen, Martin. 1980. The Pha-spun of Ladakh. In *Tibetan Studies,* ed. M. Aries. Delhi: Vikas Publishing House.

Bruner, Edward, and Phyllis Gorfain. 1984. Dialogic Narration and the Paradoxes of Masada. In *Text, Play, and Story: The Construction and Reconstruction of Self and Society,* ed. E. Bruner. Washington, D.C.: American Ethnological Society.

Burkert, Walter. 1983. *Homo Necans: The Anthropology of Ancient Greek Sacrificial Ritual and Myth.* Berkeley: University of California Press.

Bushell, S. W. 1880. The Early History of Tibet from Chinese Sources. *Journal of the Royal Asiatic Society* 12:435–537.

Chang, Garma C. C. 1962. *The Hundred Thousand Songs of Milarepa.* Vols. 1 and 2. New York: University Books.

Chang, Garma C. C. 1971. *The Buddhist Teaching of Totality: The Philosophy of Hua-yen Buddhism.* University Park and London: Pennsylvania State University Press.

Clifford, James. 1982. *Person and Myth: Maurice Leenhardt in the Melanesian World.* Berkeley: University of California Press.

Collins, Steven. 1982. *Selfless Persons.* Cambridge: Cambridge University Press.

Cook, Francis. 1977. *Hua-yen Buddhism: The Jewel Net of Indra.* University Park and London: Pennsylvania State University Press.

Cook, Francis. 1979. Causation in the Chinese Hua-yen Tradition. *Journal of Chinese Philosophy* 6:367–85.

Crapanzano, Vincent. 1980. *Tuhami: Portrait of a Moroccan.* Chicago: University of Chicago Press.

David-Neel, Alexandra (with Lama Yongden). 1959. *The Superhuman Life of Gesar of Ling.* London: Rider.

Davis, Robert Con. 1983. Lacan, Poe, and Narrative Repression. In *Lacan and Narration*, ed. Robert Con Davis. Baltimore: Johns Hopkins University Press.

de Heusch, Luc. 1984. *Sacrifice in Africa*. Bloomington: Indiana University Press.

Dimock, Edward, and A. K. Ramanujan. 1964. The Goddess of Snakes in Medieval Bengali Literature, part II. *History of Religions* 3, no. 2:300–22.

Dollarhide, Kenneth. 1982. History and Time in Nichiren's Senji-sho. *Religion* 12:233–45.

Dowman, Keith. 1973. *The Legend of the Great Stupa and the Life Story of the Lotus Born Guru*. Berkeley: Dharma Publishing.

Dowman, Keith. 1984. *Sky Dancer: The Secret Life and Songs of the Lady Yeshe Tsogyel*. London: Routledge and Kegan Paul.

Dumont, L. 1972. *Homo Hierarchicus*. London: Paladin.

Dwyer, Kevin. 1982. *Moroccan Dialogues*. Baltimore: Johns Hopkins University Press.

Ekvall, Robert. 1964. *Religious Observances in Tibet: Patterns and Function*. Chicago: University of Chicago Press.

Eliade, Mircea. 1964. *Shamanism: Archaic Techniques of Ecstasy*. New York: Bollingen Foundation Series 76, distributed by Pantheon Books.

Emerson, Caryl. 1986. The Outer World and Inner Speech: Bakhtin, Vygotsky, and the Internalization of Language. In *Bakhtin: Essays and Dialogues on His Work*, ed. Gary Morson. Chicago: University of Chicago Press.

Epstein, Lawrence. 1977. Causation in Tibetan Religion: Duality and Its Transformation. Ph.D. dissertation, University of Washington.

Evans-Pritchard, E. E. 1956. *Nuer Religion*. New York: Oxford University Press.

Evans-Wentz, Walter Y. 1960. *The Tibetan Book of the Dead*. New York: Galaxy.

Fernandez, James. 1986. The Argument of Images and the Experience of Returning to the Whole. In *The Anthropology of Experience*, eds. Victor Turner and Edward Bruner. Urbana: University of Illinois Press.

Fischer, Michael M. 1986. Ethnicity and the Post-Modern Arts of Memory. In *Writing Culture*, ed. James Clifford and George Marcus. Berkeley: University of California Press.

Foucault, Michel. 1975. Film and Popular Memory: An Interview with Michel Foucault. Trans. Martin Jordin. *Radical Philosophy* 11 (Summer 1975).

Fürer-Haimendorf, C. von. 1967. *Morals and Merit*. Chicago: University of Chicago Press.

Geertz, Clifford. 1973. *The Interpretation of Cultures: Selected Essays by Clifford Geertz*. New York: Basic Books.

Gilberg, R. 1984. How To Recognize a Shaman among Other Religious Specialists? In *Shamanism in Eurasia*, part I, ed. M. Hoppal. Göttingen, Germany: Herdot.

Goldstein, Melvyn. 1975. Preliminary Notes on Marriage and Kinship. *Contributions to Nepalese Studies* 2, no. 1:57–69.

Gorer, Geoffrey. 1967. *Himalayan Village: The Lepchas of Sikkim.* New York: Basic Books.

Govinda, Lama Anagarika. 1969. *Foundations of Tibetan Mysticism.* London: Rider and Co.

Granet, Marcel. 1977. *The Religion of the Chinese People.* New York: Harper Torchbooks.

Gurung, Nareshwar Jang. 1976. An Introduction to the Socio-Economic Structure of Manang District. *Kailash* 4, no. 3:295–96.

Haarh, Erik. 1959. Contributions to the Study of Mandala and Mudra. *Acta Orientalia* 1959:57–91.

Haarh, Erik. 1969. *The Yarlung Dynasty.* Copenhagen: G.E.C. God's forlag.

Halifax, Joan. 1979. *Shamanic Voices.* New York: E. P. Dutton.

Handler, Richard. 1988. *Nationalism and the Politics of Culture in Quebec.* Madison: University of Wisconsin Press.

Handwerk, Gary. 1985. *Irony and Ethics in Narrative: From Schlegel to Lacan.* New Haven: Yale University Press.

Hardacre, Helen. 1984. *Lay Buddhism in Contemporary Japan: Reiyukai Kyodan.* Princeton: Princeton University Press.

Hart, George. 1975. *The Poems of Ancient Tamil.* Berkeley: University of California Press.

Heesterman, J. C. 1985. *The Inner Conflict of Tradition: Essays in Indian Ritual, Kingship, and Society.* Chicago: University of Chicago Press.

Heissig, Walter. 1953. A Mongolian Source to the Lamaist Suppression of Shamanism in the 17th Century. *Anthropos* 48:493–533.

Heissig, Walter. 1980. *The Religion of Mongolia.* Trans. G. Samuel. London: Routledge.

Herrenschmidt, Olivier. 1982. Sacrifice: Symbolic or Effective? In *Between Belief and Transgression,* eds. M. Izard and P. Smith. Chicago: University of Chicago Press.

Hertz, R. 1960. *Death and the Right Hand.* New York: Free Press.

Hitchcock, John. 1976. Introduction to *Spirit Possession in the Nepal Himalayas,* ed. John T. Hitchcock and Rex Jones. New Delhi: Vikas Publishing House.

Hoffman, Helmut. 1961. *The Religions of Tibet.* London: George Allen and Unwin.

Hoffman, Helmut. 1979. *Tibet: A Handbook.* Bloomington: Research Center for the Language Sciences, Indiana University.

Holmberg, David. 1980. Lama, Shaman, and Lambu in Tamang Religious Practice. Ph.D. dissertation, Cornell University.

Holmberg, David. 1984. Ritual Paradoxes in Nepal: Comparative Perspective on Tamang Religion. *Journal of Asian Studies* 43, no. 4:697–722.

Holquist, Michael, and Katerina Clark. 1984. *Mikhail Bakhtin.* Cambridge: Harvard University Press.

Hopkins, Jeffrey. 1977. *Tantra in Tibet.* London: George Allen and Unwin.

Hopkins, Jeffrey. 1984. *The Tantric Distinction.* London: Wisdom Publications.

Hopkins, Jeffrey. 1985. *The Kalachakra Tantra.* London: Wisdom Publications.

Jameson, Fredric. 1981. *The Political Unconscious.* Ithaca, N.Y.: Cornell University Press.

Jankovics, M. 1984. Cosmic Models and Siberian Shaman Drums. In *Shamanism in Eurasia,* part I, ed. M. Hoppal. Göttingen, Germany: Herdot.

Jäschke, H. A. 1977. *A Tibetan-English Dictionary.* London: Routledge.

Jochelson, Waldemar. 1926. The Yukaghir and the Yukaghirized Tungus. In The Jesup North Pacific Expedition. *Memoir of the American Museum of Natural History* IX. New York.

Johnson, Barbara. 1980. *The Critical Difference.* Baltimore: Johns Hopkins University Press.

Kapferer, Bruce. 1983. *A Celebration of Demons: Exorcism and the Aesthetic of Healing in Sri Lanka.* Bloomington: Indiana University Press.

Karmay, Samten G. 1972. *The Treasury of Good Sayings: A Tibetan History of Bon.* London: Oxford University Press..

Kawakita, J. 1957. Ethnographical Observations of the Nepal Himalaya. In *People of Nepal Himalaya.* Vol. 3, ed. H. Kihara. Kyoto: Kyoto University.

Kermode, Frank. 1967. *The Sense of an Ending.* New York: Oxford University Press.

King, Winston. 1979. Hua-yen Mutually Interpenetrative Identity and White-headean Organic Relation. *Journal of Chinese Philosophy* 6:387–410.

Kirkland, J. Russell. 1982. The Spirit of the Mountain: Myth and State in Pre-Buddhist Tibet. *History of Religions* 20, no. 3:257–71.

Lacan, Jacques. 1968. *The Language of the Self.* Trans. Anthony Wilden. New York: Dell.

Lalou, Marcelle. 1953. *Rituel Bon-po des funérailles royales.* Paris: Journal Asiatique.

Lasch, Christopher. 1984. *The Minimal Self: Psychic Survival in Troubled Times.* New York: W. W. Norton.

Leach, Edmund. 1965. *Political Systems of Highland Burma.* Boston: Beacon Press.

Lee, Orlan. 1967. From Acts-to Non-Action-to Acts: The Dialectical Basis for Social Withdrawal or Commitment to This World in the Buddhist Reformation. *History of Religions* 6, no. 4:273–302.

Leenhardt, Maurice. 1979. *Do Kamo.* Chicago: University of Chicago Press.

Lessing, Ferdinand D. 1942. *Yung-Ho-Kung: An Iconography of the Lamaist Cathedral in Peking.* Reports from the Scientific Expedition to the North-Western Provinces of China under the Leadership of Dr. Sven Hedin, vol. 8. Stockholm, 1942.

Lessing, Ferdinand D. 1951. Calling the Soul: A Lamaist Ritual. *Semitic and Oriental Studies. University of California Publications in Semitic Philology* 11:263–84.

Lévi-Strauss, Claude. 1966. *The Savage Mind.* Chicago: University of Chicago Press.

Loewe, Michael. 1982. *Chinese Ideas of Life and Death: Faith, Myth and Reason in the Han Period (202 B.C.–A.D. 220).* London: George Allen and Unwin.

Lyotard, Jean François. 1979. *The Postmodern Condition: A Report on Knowledge.* Minneapolis: University of Minnesota Press.

MacDonald, Alexander. 1975. *Essays on the Ethnology of Nepal and South Asia.* Kathmandu: Ratna Pustak Bhandar.

McHugh, Ernestine. 1986. Self, Other, and the World of Fanciful Beings. Manu-

script read at the 85th Annual Meeting of the American Anthropology Association, Philadelphia.

McKinley, Robert. 1979. Zaman dan Masa, Eras and Periods: Religious Evolution
and the Permanence of Epistemological Ages in Malay Culture. In *The Imagination of Reality: Essays in Southeast Asian Coherence Systems.* Norwood,
N.J.: ABLEX Publishing.

Maity, P. K. 1966. *Historical Studies in the Cult of the Goddess Manasa.* Calcutta:
Panthi Pustak.

Mauss, Marcel. 1954. *The Gift.* London: Cohen and West.

Messerschmidt, Donald. 1976a. *The Gurungs of Nepal.* Warminster, England: Aris
and Phillips.

Messerschmidt, Donald. 1976b. Ecological Change and Adaptation among the
Gurungs of the Nepal Himalaya. *Human Ecology* 4 (April 1976):167–85.

Messerschmidt, Donald. 1976c. Ethnographic Observations of Gurung Shamanism
in Lamjung District. In *Spirit Possession in the Nepal Himalaya,* ed. J. Hitchcock and R. Jones. Warminster, England: Aris and Phillips.

Mumford, Stan Royal. 1986. The Temporal Hermeneutic after Geertz. *Anthropology and Humanism Quarterly* 11, no. 3:62–68.

Nebesky-Wojkowitz, R. M. 1956. *Oracles and Demons of Tibet.* The Hague:
Mouton.

Needham, Joseph. 1956. *Science and Civilisation in China,* vol. 2. Cambridge: Cambridge University Press.

Needham, Joseph. 1965. Time and Eastern Man. *Royal Anthropological Institute
Occasional Paper* no. 21:1–9. Glasgow: University Press.

Norbu, T., and C. Turnbull. 1972. *Tibet.* Middlesex, England: Penguin Books.

Nowak, Margaret, trans. 1977. *The Tale of the Nishan Shamaness: A Manchu
Folk Epic.* Seattle: University of Washington Press.

Obeyesekere, Gananath. 1968. Theodicy, Sin, and Salvation. In *Dialectic in Prac-
tical Religion,* ed. E. Leach. Papers in Social Anthropology No. 5. Cambridge:
Cambridge University Press.

Obeyesekere, Gananath. 1980. The Rebirth Eschatology and Its Transformations:
A Contribution to the Sociology of Early Buddhism. In *Karma and Rebirth
in Classical Indian Traditions,* ed. W. O'Flaherty. Berkeley: University of California Press.

Obeyesekere, Gananath. 1981. *Medusa's Hair.* Chicago: University of Chicago
Press.

Obeyesekere, Gananath. 1984. *The Cult of the Goddess Pattini.* Chicago: University
of Chicago Press.

O'Flaherty, Wendy. 1971. The Origin of Heresy in Hindu Mythology. *History of
Religions* 10, no. 4:271–333.

O'Flaherty, Wendy. 1984. *Dreams, Illusion, and Other Realities.* Chicago: University of Chicago Press.

Oppitz, M. 1968. *Geschichte und Sozialordnung der Sherpa.* Innsbruck and
Munich: Universitäts Verlag Wagner.

Ortner, Sherry. 1978a. The Decline of Sherpa Shamanism: On the Role of Meaning in History. Manuscript. Department of Anthropology, University of Michigan.

Ortner, Sherry. 1978b. *Sherpas through Their Rituals*. Cambridge: Cambridge University Press.

Paul, Robert. 1970. Sherpas and Their Religion. Ph.D. dissertation, University of Chicago.

Paul, Robert. 1976. Some Observations on Sherpa Shamanism. In *Spirit Possession in the Nepal Himalaya,* ed. J. Hitchcock and R. Jones. Warminster, England: Aris and Phillips.

Paul, Robert. 1982. *The Tibetan Symbolic World*. Chicago: University of Chicago Press.

Pignède, Bernard. 1966. *Les Gurungs*. Paris: Mouton.

Prince Peter of Greece and Denmark. 1963. *A Study of Polyandry*. The Hague: Mouton.

Rabinow, Paul. 1977. *Reflections on Fieldwork in Morocco*. Berkeley: University of California Press.

Rabinow, Paul. 1986. Representations are Social Facts: Modernity and Post-Modernity in Anthropology. In *Writing Culture: The Poetics and Politics of Ethnography,* ed. James Clifford and George Marcus. Berkeley: University of California Press.

Ragsdale, Tod Anthony. 1979. *Ethnicity and Educational Change: The Gurungs of Nepal and the New Educational Plan*. Ph.D. dissertation, Duke University.

Ricoeur, Paul. 1970. *Freud and Philosophy: An Essay on Interpretation*. New Haven: Yale University Press.

Ricoeur, Paul. 1971. The Model of the Text: Meaningful Action Considered as a Text. *Social Research* 38:529–62.

Rieff, Philip. 1966. *The Triumph of the Therapeutic*. New York: Harper and Row.

Rock, J. F. 1959. Contributions to the Shamanism of the Tibetan Chinese Borderland. *Anthropos* 54:798–818.

Rorty, Richard. 1979. *Philosophy and the Mirror of Nature*. Princeton: Princeton University Press.

Samuel, Geoffrey. 1985. Early Buddhism in Tibet: Some Anthropological Perspectives. In *Soundings in Tibetan Civilization,* ed. B. Aziz and M. Kapstein. New Delhi: Manohar Publications.

Saso, Michael R. 1972. *Taoism and the Rite of Cosmic Renewal*. Seattle: Washington State University Press.

Schlagintweit, Emil. 1863. *Buddhism in Tibet*. London: Trubner and Co.

Sharma, Prayag Raj. 1977. Caste, Social Mobility, and Sanskritization: A Study of Nepal's Old Legal Code. *Kailash* 5, no. 4:277–99.

Sharma, Prayag Raj. 1978. Nepal: Hindu-Tribal Interface. *Contributions to Nepalese Studies* 8, no. 1:1–14.

Siikala, A. L. 1984. Finnish Rock Art, Animal Ceremonialism and Shamanic Worldview. In *Shamanism in Eurasia,* part I, ed. M. Hoppal. Göttingen, Germany: Herdot.

Snellgrove, David. 1979. A Description of Muktinath, the Place of Promenade,

Ku-tsab-ter-nga, Mount Mu-li, the Guru's Hidden Cave and the Sna-ri Lord (text translation). *Kailash* 7:106–28.

Snellgrove, David. 1980. *The Nine Ways of Bon: Excerpts from the gZi-brjid.* Boulder: Prajña Press.

Snellgrove, David. 1981. *Himalayan Pilgrimage.* Boulder: Prajña Press.

Snellgrove, David, and H. Richardson. 1968. *A Cultural History of Tibet.* New York: Praeger.

Stein, R. A. 1972. *Tibetan Civilization.* London: Faber and Faber.

Suleiman, Susan. 1983. *Authoritarian Fictions: The Ideological Novel as a Literary Genre.* New York: Columbia University Press.

Tambiah, Stanley. 1970. *Buddhism and the Spirit Cults in Northeast Thailand.* Cambridge: Cambridge University Press.

Tambiah, Stanley. 1976. *World Conqueror and World Renouncer.* Cambridge: Cambridge University Press.

Taranatha, Jo-Nan. 1981. *The Origin of the Tara Tantra,* ed. and trans. D. Templeman. Dharamsala: Library of Tibetan Works and Archives.

Taussig, Michael. 1987. *Shamanism, Colonialism, and the Wild Man.* Chicago: University of Chicago Press.

Tedlock, Dennis. 1983. *The Spoken Word and the Work of Interpretation.* Philadelphia: University of Pennsylvania Press.

Trungpa, Chögyam. 1978. Some Aspects of Pön. In *Himalayan Anthropology: The Indo-Tibetan Interface,* ed. James Fisher. The Hague: Mouton.

Tucci, Giuseppe. 1949. *Tibetan Painted Scrolls.* 3 vols. Rome: La Libreria dello Stato.

Tucci, Giuseppe. 1955. The Sacral Character of the Kings of Ancient Tibet. *East and West* 6:197–205.

Tucci, Giuseppe. 1966. *Tibetan Folk Songs from Gyantse and Western Tibet.* Ascona, Switzerland: Artibus Asiae Publishers.

Tucci, Giuseppe. 1980. *The Religions of Tibet.* London: Routledge and Kegan Paul.

Turner, Victor. 1974. *Dramas, Fields and Metaphors.* Ithaca, N.Y.: Cornell University Press.

Vaihinger, H. 1924. *The Philosophy of "As If."* London: Routledge.

Valeri, Valerio. 1985. *Kingship and Sacrifice: Ritual and Society in Ancient Hawaii.* Trans. P. Wissing. Chicago: University of Chicago Press.

Van Tuyl, Charles. 1979. Mi-la Ras-pa and the gCod Ritual. *Tibet Society Bulletin* 4, no. 1:34–40.

Vico, Giambattista. 1968. *The New Science of Giambattista Vico.* Trans. T. G. Bergin and M. H. Fisch. Ithaca, N.Y.: Cornell University Press.

Vinding, Michael, and S. Gauchan. 1977. The History of the Thakali According to the Thakali Tradition. *Kailash* 5, no. 2:97–184.

Vygotsky, L. S. 1962. *Thought and Language.* Ed. and trans. Eugenia Hanfmann and G. Vakar. Cambridge, Mass.: MIT Press.

Waddell, Austine. 1978. *Buddhism and Lamaism of Tibet.* New Delhi: Asian Publishers.

Watters, David E. 1975. Siberian Shamanistic Traditions among the Kham-Magars of Nepal. *Contributions to Nepalese Studies* 2, no. 1:123–68.

Wayman, Alex. 1973. *The Buddhist Tantras.* New York: Samuel Weiser.

Weber, Max. 1963. *Sociology of Religion.* Boston: Beacon Press.

White, Hayden. 1978. *Tropics of Discourse.* Baltimore: Johns Hopkins University Press.

TIBETAN TEXTS QUOTED

Indigenous texts (written locally or family owned)

Lha bdud btsan klu gsum gsol mchod kyi Tshap kyi yul (Petition offerings for the three area gods of Tshap village: *klu, btsan,* and *bdud*).

Rdo-rje Shugs-ldan mchod-thabs gsol-kha (Method of offering-petitioning rDo-rje Shugs-ldan).

Horoscope (rtsis) *texts*

Gshin-rtsis (Death calculation).

Lha-mo brgyad rtsis gza' 'bras dang bcas-pa (Calculations of the eight planetary goddesses with results of their influences).

Nag-rtsis kyi sdon 'gro'i' lag-len (Introduction to the practice of Chinese calculation).

Serpent Deity (klu) *and* sa-bdag *rites*

Gnam chas sa snying sgrub thabs kyi mdun bskyed las sa-bdag 'khrug bcos bsdus pa bzhugs so (Remedying the agitation of *sa-bdag*).

Klu 'bum dkar-po, klu 'bum nag-po, klu 'bum khra-po (The 100,000 white, black, and mixed serpent deities).

Sa-bdag sgo dbye gser-skyems zhis bya-ba bzhugs so (Libation for opening the *sa-bdag* doors).

Exorcisms

Brgya-bzhi'i cho-ga'i 'dod don lhun grub rtsis bya-ba bzhugs so mi-kha'i lto bsgyur bzhugs so (Rite for obtaining the mass of 400 desirable things).

Gto nag mgo gsum kyi cho-ga bzhugs so (Rite of expelling the three-headed black one).

Leu bcu dgu za-'dre kha bsgyur stag bzhon shin tu zab-pa bzhugs so (Turning away the mouth of the nineteen eating demons).

Soul recalling

O-rgyan padmas mdzad-pa'i 'chi rtag bla bslu zhis bya ba bzhugs so (The work of luring and calming the soul showing foretokens of death as composed by Padmasambhava).

Death rite texts

Gcod kyi tshogs las kyi cho-ga (Rite of merit gathering through severance).
Gsung gi chos zhal-gdams thos grol bzhugs so (Oral teaching of religious guidance for liberation through hearing).

Index

Ahern, Emily, 110
Akyenedong (community god), 81, 87, 118, 123
Alā (G. world pillar), 182
Ālayavijñāna (Skt., T. *kun-gzhi rnam-shes,* storehouse of consciousness), 19, 216
Am-chi (doctor), 202
Amitābha (Skt., T. 'Od-dpag-med, Bodhisattva/wisdom Buddha), 198, 216, 222–23
Anātman (Skt. no-self doctrine), 19
Asyō (G. wife-giving affines), 181, 183
Atiśa, 27, 34, 246
Avalokiteśvara. See Chenresig
A-zhang (maternal uncle), 39
Aziz, Barbara, 48, 162

Babcock, Barbara, 28
Bag-chags (Skt. *vāsanā,* mental inclinations), 47, 90, 211, 216–17, 221, 239, 250, 260
Bakhtin, Michail, on dialogue:
—Dialogic (or dialogical) imagination: 12–13, 22; decentered meaning, 13–15, 17, 167, 194, 246, 249, 253–54; intersubjectivity, co-consciousness, 13–15, 19–23, 28, 138, 164, 167, 211, 219, 222, 245–46, 254; internal dialogue, rejoinders, 14–15, 17, 22, 25, 35, 63, 78, 135, 138, 148, 196, 205, 215, 218, 222
—Discourse: internally persuasive discourse, 14–15, 138, 196, 215; monologic (authoritative) discourse, 14–19, 25, 41, 45, 112, 246; double voiced/ironic discourse, 18, 22, 26,

28, 53, 114, 116, 222–23, 240–42; threshold discourse, 22, 25–26; alien discourse, 22, 141, 245; confessional discourse, 22–23, 153, 215, 218, 221–24; hidden discourse, 36, 96, 114, 139, 210–14, 224, 237
—Heteroglossia: 13, 252; interillumination, 5, 13, 17, 23, 114, 158, 196, 246–47; interpenetrating truths/voices, 11, 13–14, 17, 114, 153, 179, 218, 252; dialogized background, 14, 23, 114, 229
—Hybrid constructions: 29, 34, 48, 51, 56, 58, 77, 126, 128, 138, 214, 247; as layered interpretations, 11–12, 28, 34–35, 46, 164, 224, 245–49, 251; as traces, 12–13, 35, 97, 114–16, 136–39, 141, 223–24, 236, 248; of historical images, 227, 235–37, 241–43
—Narrative: 35, 41, 91–92, 137–39, 253–54; time-distanced epic hero, 17, 45, 51; turning points, 41, 137–39, 245, 247–48; dialogue between, 40–46, 49–59, 228, 235–37, 247–48
—Rabelaisian: demasking, 15, 17, 21, 29, 114, 158, 167, 218, 250; *ambivalent whole,* 18, 21, 29–30, 179, 246; restoring of ancient matrix, 21–23, 115, 158, 167, 179, 208, 253; carnival sense of the world, 21, 29–30, 115, 158, 167, 179, 196, 208, 224, 253
—Temporal identities (three): 16, 23, 26–27, 92, 164, 167, 219, 227–28, 247; ancient matrix, 16–17, 21, 23–26, 29–30, 77, 93, 96, 115, 158, 167–68, 178–79, 208, 219, 224, 246,

New Directions in
Anthropological Writing
History, Poetics, Cultural Criticism

George E. Marcus, Rice University
James Clifford, University of California, Santa Cruz
Editors

Nationalism and the Politics of Culture in Quebec
Richard Handler

Belonging in America: Reading Between the Lines
Constance Perin

The Pastoral Son and the Spirit of Patriarchy:
Religion, Society, and Person among East
African Stock Keepers
Michael Meeker

Himalayan Dialogue:
Tibetan Lamas and Gurung Shamans in Nepal
Stan Royal Mumford

People as Subject, People as Object:
Selfhood and Peoplehood in Contemporary Israel
Virginia R. Domínguez

Wombs and Alien Spirits:
Women, Men, and the Zār Cult in Northern Sudan
Janice Boddy